Sacred Natural Sites

Sacred Natural Sites
Conserving Nature and Culture

Edited by Bas Verschuuren, Robert Wild, Jeffrey McNeely and Gonzalo Oviedo

publishing for a sustainable future
London • Washington, DC

First published in 2010 by Earthscan

Copyright © International Union for Conservation of Nature and Natural Resources 2010

Published in association with: IUCN (International Union for Conservation of Nature), Rue Mauverney 28, 1196 Gland, Switzerland

Earthscan Ltd, Dunstan House, 14a St Cross Street, London EC1N 8XA, UK
Earthscan LLC, 1616 P Street, NW, Washington, DC 20036, USA
Earthscan publishes in association with the International Institute for Environment and Development

For more information on Earthscan publications, see www.earthscan.co.uk or write to earthinfo@earthscan.co.uk

ISBN: 978-1-84971-166-1 hardback
ISBN: 978-1-84971-167-8 paperback

Typeset by Composition and Design Services
Cover design by Andrew Corbett
Cover photos by Bas Verschuuren. Top image: Dressed Shinto statue and Buddha statue in the Sensoji (Buddhist) temple forest garden in Asakusa, Tokyo. In Tokyo, temple forest gardens still exist despite the increasing market value of the land. The Ginkgo Biloba tree (here shown in the background) is classified on IUCN's Red List of Threatened Species as 'endangered'. Ginkgo has been reintroduced into the wild from monastery gardens and some populations survived that were tended by Chinese and Japanese monks.

Bottom image: Santa María Volcano (3772m), named Gagxanul in the local K'iche' language, is an active volcano in the Western Highlands of Guatemala, close to the city of Quetzaltenango. A large area of the mountain has been declared a protected area, which has helped to secure the cultural and spiritual use of this sacred natural site. Traditional Mayan ceremonies are carried out on the mountain as well as many Catholic rituals that fuse with traditional Mayan spirituality. The lead up to these ceremonies is a pilgrimage from the surrounding villages onto the mountain's summit.

A catalogue record for this book is available from the British Library

Library of Congress Cataloging-in-Publication Data

Sacred natural sites : conserving nature and culture/edited by Bas Verschuuren...[et al.].
      p. cm.
   Includes bibliographical references and index.
   ISBN 978-1-84971-166-1 (hardback) – ISBN 978-1-84971-167-8 (pbk.) 1. Natural areas. 2. Protected areas. 3. Sacred space. I. Verschuuren, Bas.
   QH75.S234 2010
   333.95'16–dc22   2010015465

At Earthscan we strive to minimize our environmental impacts and carbon footprint through reducing waste, recycling and offsetting our CO_2 emissions, including those created through publication of this book. For more details of our environmental policy, see www.earthscan.co.uk.

Printed and bound in the UK by MPG Books, an ISO 14001 accredited company.
The paper used is FSC certified.

CONTENTS

List of Figures and Tables   ix

About the Authors   xiii

Foreword by Julia Marton-Lefèvre,
IUCN Director General   xix

Preface   xxi

List of Acronyms and Abbreviations   xxiii

Glossary   xxv

Chapter 1
Introduction: Sacred Natural Sites
the Foundations of Conservation   1
Bas Verschuuren, Robert Wild,
Jeffrey McNeely and Gonzalo Oviedo

SECTION ONE
Towards the Science and Spirituality
of Sacred Natural Sites   15

Chapter 2
Conservation of Biodiversity in Sacred
Natural Sites in Asia and Africa:
A Review of the Scientific Literature   19
Nigel Dudley, Shonil Bhagwat,
Liza Higgins-Zogib, Barbara Lassen,
Bas Verschuuren and Robert Wild

Chapter 3
Sacred Mountains and Global Changes:
Impacts and Responses   33
Edwin Bernbaum

Chapter 4
Falling between the 'Cracks' of
Conservation and Religion: The Role
of Stewardship for Sacred Trees
and Groves   42
Edmund G.C. Barrow

Chapter 5
The Enchanted Earth: Numinous
Sacred Sites   53
Denis Byrne

Chapter 6
Arguments for Developing Biocultural
Conservation Approaches for Sacred
Natural Sites   62
Bas Verschuuren

SECTION TWO
Sacred Natural Sites:
Mutual Learning, Analysis,
Planning and Management   73

Chapter 7
Nature Saint and Holy Island,
Ancient Values in a Modern Economy:
The Enduring Influence of St Cuthbert
and Lindisfarne, United Kingdom   77
Robert Wild

Chapter 8
Tourism Meets the Sacred:
Khumbu Sherpa Place-based
Spiritual Values in Sagarmatha
(Mount Everest) National Park
and Buffer Zone, Nepal   87
Jeremy Spoon

Chapter 9
The Road to the Future? The
Biocultural Values of the Holy
Hill Forests of Yunnan Province,
China   98
Pei Shengji

Chapter 10
Uncovering the Intangible Values
of Earth Care: Using Cognition to
Reveal the Eco-spiritual Domains
and Sacred Values of the Peoples
of Eastern Kham   107
John Studley

Chapter 11
Ancestral Beliefs and Conservation:
The Case of Sacred Sites in Bandjoun,
West Cameroon   119
Sébastien Luc Kamga-Kamdem

Chapter 12
The Crocodile is our Brother: Sacred
Lakes of the Niger Delta, Implications
for Conservation Management   129
*E.D. Anwana, R.A. Cheke, A.M. Martin,
L. Obireke, M. Asei, P. Otufu and
D. Otobotekere*

Chapter 13
How African-based Winti Belief Helps
to Protect Forests in Suriname   139
Tinde van Andel

Chapter 14
Seeking and Securing Sacred
Natural Sites among Jamaica's
Windward Maroons   146
*Kimberly John, Collin L.G. Harris and
Susan Otuokon*

SECTION THREE
Sacred Natural Sites: International
Recognition, Global Governance
and Field Action   157

Chapter 15
Sacred Natural Sites, Cultural
Landscapes and UNESCO's Action   161
Thomas Schaaf and Mechtild Rossler

Chapter 16
Synergies and Challenges for Legal
Protection of Sacred Natural Sites
in the South Pacific   170
Erika J. Techera

Chapter 17
Wetland Cultural and Spiritual Values,
and the Ramsar Convention   180
Thymio Papayannis and Dave Pritchard

Chapter 18
Sacred Natural Sites, Biodiversity and
Well-being: The Role of Sacred Sites
in Endogenous Development in the
COMPAS Network   188
*Freddy Delgado, Cesar Escobar,
Bas Verschuuren and Wim Hiemstra*

Chapter 19
Sacred Natural Sites in Technologically
Developed Countries: Reflections from
the Experience of the Delos Initiative 198
*Josep-Maria Mallarach and Thymio
Papayannis*

Chapter 20
Developing a Methodology and Tools
for Inventorying Sacred Natural Sites
of Indigenous Peoples in Mexico   209
*Mercedes Otegui-Acha, Gonzalo Oviedo,
Guillermo Barroso, Martín Gutiérrez,
Jaime Santiago, Bas Verschuuren*

Chapter 21
Culture-based Conservation of Sacred
Groves: Experiences from the North
Western Ghats, India   219
*Archana Godbole, Jayant Sarnaik and
Sameer Punde*

SECTION FOUR
In Our Own Hands: Living Culture and
Equity at Sacred Natural Sites   229

Chapter 22
Community-based Ecotourism at
Tafi Atome Monkey Sanctuary,
a Sacred Natural Site in Ghana   233
Alison Ormsby and Craig Edelman

Chapter 23
Sacred Valley, Conservation Management
and Indigenous Survival: Uch Enmek
Indigenous Nature Park, Altai Republic,
Russia   244
Joanna Dobson and Danil Mamyev

Chapter 24
Towards a Sustainable Management
and Enhanced Protection of Sacred
Marine Areas at Palawan's Coron
Island Ancestral Domain, Philippines   254
Arlene G. Sampang

Chapter 25
Culture, Conservation and Co-management:
Strengthening Soliga Stake in Biodiversity
Conservation in Biligiri Rangaswamy
Temple Wildlife Sanctuary, India   263
*Sushmita Mandal, Nitin D. Rai and
C. Madegowda*

Chapter 26
The Devi as Ecofeminist Warrior:
Reclaiming the Role of Sacred Natural
Sites in East-Central India   272
Radhika Borde and Alana Jules Jackman

Chapter 27
Conclusions: Sustaining Sacred Natural
Sites to Conserve Nature and Culture   280
*Robert Wild, Bas Verschuuren and
Jeffrey McNeely*

Annex 1
A Statement of Custodians of Sacred
Natural Sites and Territories   292

Annex 2
A Preliminary Strategy and Action Plan
for the Conservation of Sacred
Natural Sites   297
*WCPA Specialist Group on the Cultural
and Spiritual Values of Protected Areas*

Index   *300*

List of Figures, Tables and Boxes

Figures

0.1 Indigenous Ranger Marlangaj Yunupingu presents Julia Marton-Lefèvre with a Yidaki at the launch of the Sacred Natural Sites Guidelines at the IUCN World Conservation Congress, Barcelona 2008   xx

1.1 Karamat of Shaykh Hohamed Hassen Ghaibie Shah al-Qadiri at Lion's Head, Signal Hill within Table Mountain National Park (Cape Town is ringed by a Holy Circle of Islamic Shrines)   3

1.2 The goddess Jomo Miyo Lang Samba from Pangbuche Monastery who lives on Mount Everest   4

1.3 The 'Tagyl' is a stone ritual altar used for group prayer meetings held twice a year at the beginning of the summer 'green leaves' and in the autumn, 'yellow leaves'   6

1.4 Framework for the conservation of sacred natural sites   8

1.5 World map and legend linking the approximate location of sacred natural sites to the chapters in this book   10

I.1 Mt Kailas in the Himalayas is sacred to millions of Buddhists, Hindus and Bonn shamans   17

2.1 The Chewa Graveyard Forests of Malawi are often the only remaining woody vegetation in an otherwise cleared landscape   20

2.2 Elders of Kaya Kinondo (one of 11 biodiverse sacred forests recognized as outstanding universal value as the Sacred Mijikenda Kaya Forests World Heritage Site)   24

3.1 Pilgrimage to Ausangate Glacier   36

3.2 St. Catherine's Monastery at foot of Mount Sinai   39

4.1 The Fever Tree   44

4.2 Tree planting ceremony near Badrinath, India   48

5.1 Pre-Christen sacred 'well' and pilgrimage destination in Westerhoven, Southern Netherlands   54

5.2 A spirit (phi) shrine at Chiang Saen, northern Thailand   56

6.1 The ruins of Tikal are situated in the World Heritage Site and national park 'Peten' in Guatemala   64

6.2 Galapagos, Stained glass window celebrating Galapaganian diversity from the Church of St Francis, Puerto Ayora, Galapagos World Heritage Site   66

II.1 The mountain (5761m) is home to the protector deity Khumbu-Yul-Lha and is flanked by Tengbuche Monastery in Nepal   75

7.1 Lindisfarne National Nature Reserve with Holy Island at centre   79

7.2 Political divisions of northern Britain indicative of St Cuthbert's era   80

7.3 St Mary's Church on the site of St. Aidan's Church next to the ruins of the abbey also showing the edge of the village   82

7.4 Pilgrims crossing the sandflats of the Pilgrims Way   84

8.1 Map of Sagarmatha (Mount Everest) National Park and Buffer Zone (Khumbu and Pharak)   88

8.2   View from Gokyo Ri (5357m) across
       Sagarmatha National Park and
       Buffer Zone at sunset   89
8.3   Flags placed on the slopes of the
       sacred mountain for the protector
       deity Khumbu Yul-Lha during the
       annual Dumji ceremony   92
8.4   Results of multiple regression analysis
       for Khumbu Sherpa place-based
       spiritual value knowledge   95
9.1   Location of Yunnan Province
       and of Xishuangbanna Autonomous
       Prefecture   99
9.2   Map of Xishuangbanna
       in Yunnan   100
9.3   Xishuangbanna landscape of
       settlement, paddy, agricultural land
       and natural forest on Holy Hills   101
9.4   Votive offerings made within
       a Holy Hill forest   104
10.1   Map of the Kham region   109
10.2   A Mosuo shaman   110
10.3   Lartse (la btsas)   111
10.4   Cognitive map of forest concepts
       or values in Eastern Kham   112
10.5   Distribution of mean forest concepts
       or values across Eastern Kham   113
10.6   Overlap analysis of forest concepts/
       values and dialects in Eastern
       Kham   114
10.7   Bearing analysis of forest
       concept/value data among
       Khamba speakers   114
11.1   Traditional subdivision of Bandjoun
       with Western Cameroon inset   120
11.2   Participatory maps of sacred
       sites in Hiala   121
11.3   Coronation ceremony of a queen
       at Simdzedze place   123
11.4   Tchuép-Poumougne sacred site   124
12.1   Sacred Lakes Adigbe and Esiribi
       in the Niger Delta in Nigeria   131
12.2   Priest and assistant in front of shrine
       erected for sacrifices to the lake
       god at Lake Esiribi (Biseni)   133
12.3   Fishing activities on Lake
       Adigbe (Osiama)   134
13.1   A ritual herbal bath for happiness
       and good luck, Paramaribo   141

13.2   *Ceiba pentandra* tree spared from felling
       along a public road in Paramaribo,
       Suriname   142
14.1   Nanny Falls with the present
       Colonel of the More Town
       Maroons, Wallace Sterling,
       in the foreground   148
14.2   Location map of the Park   149
14.3   River View in Rio Grande valley
       looking west at the Maroon
       sacred natural sites of Pumpkin
       Hill (highest peak) in the Blue
       Mountains   151
III.1 Local women meeting with the
       Applied Environmental Research
       Foundation in the temple at Janvale
       to discuss management strategies and
       governance for their local sacred
       groves in the Western Ghats,
       Maharastra, India   159
15.1   The Sacred Suleiman Mountain
       (Kyrgyzstan) inscribed on the
       UNESCO World Heritage list
       in 2009   163
15.2   Kaya Rabai Elders in procession
       (Sacred Mijikenda Kaya Forests
       World Heritage property, Kenya)   164
16.1   Chief Roi Mata's Domain World
       Heritage Area, Efate, Vanuatu   171
16.2   Eretoka Island, Chief Roi Mata's
       Domain World Heritage Area,
       Vanuatu   174
17.1   Fishing communities on Lake George,
       a Ramsar site in Uganda, have a
       strong fishing culture and live
       closely with wildlife   181
17.2   Patriarch Bartholomew visits an
       indigenous village, Santarem,
       Amazon, Brazil   184
18.1   Sacred natural sites, biodiversity
       and human well-being   191
18.2   Santa Vera Cruz festival, Bolivia   192
18.3   Endogenous development indicators
       for biodiversity management at
       sacred natural sites   194
18.4   Indicators and quantitative progress
       for material, social and spiritual
       well-being comparing 2006
       and 2009   195

18.5   Community members and university staff join in a ritual to ask for protection from the ancestors at Incaracay, an Inca fort which now represents the ancestors, therefore a socially constructed sacred natural site, Bolivia   195

19.1   Orthodox monastery of Rila, spiritual and cultural heart of Bulgaria, nested in the middle of a natural park managed as a nature reserve created by the Orthodox Church of Bulgaria   202

19.2   Fire-lighting ceremony in a temple of the Kii Mountain Range, a Buddhist-Shinto pilgrimage complex protected by several national parks, south of Kyoto, Japan   205

20.1   A proposed framework for developing an inventory of sacred natural sites   211

20.2   Seri Indian 'Comcaac' singing and praying in ceremony with Tiburon Island in the background   213

20.3   Signing a free, prior and informed consent agreement with the Mayo Community in Mexico   216

21.1   Map of Maharashtra State in India with Ratnagiri District   221

21.2   Sacred grove of Sayale village and renovated temple   221

21.3   Gods and goddesses are placed in Palkhi during the Holi festival   224

IV.1   Soliga and Ashoka Trust for Research in Ecology and the Environment are mapping sacred sites using a handheld GPS in the Biligiri Rangaswamy Temple Wildlife Sanctuary, India   231

22.1   Location of Tafi Atome Monkey Sanctuary within Ghana   235

22.2   Map of Tafi Atome Monkey Sanctuary, a sacred forest   236

22.3   Main road through Tafi Atome village with sacred grove on the left   237

22.4   True mona monkey   239

23.1   Location of Altai Republic and Uch Enmek Indigenous Nature Park   245

23.2   Map of the Karakol valley indicating magnetic magnetite outcrops and approximate locations of Kurgans   246

23.3   Mount Uch Enmek in the background and Bronze Age Stellae amongst horses   248

23.4   Magnetic field of the Archaeological site 'Neijhnee Soru' at the Karakol Valley   249

23.5   Excavated kurgan   252

24.1   Map of the ancestral domain of the Calamian Tagbanwa in Coron Island, Palawan, Philippines   257

24.2   Entrance to Kayangan Lake, sacred to the Calamian Tagbanwa   258

24.3   General assembly in Cabugao village discussing the details of the research project   259

25.1   A Soliga paying his obeisance at a Devaru site in BRTWS   266

25.2   Locating yelles on the map   267

26.1   A sacred-grove worship ceremony in Arsande village, Jharkhand   273

27.1   Rock art in the Karakol valley in the Altai Republic, Russian Federation   281

27.2   Rogelio Mejia: Colombia and José de los Santos are Tayrona from the Sierra Nevada de Santa Martha in Colombia   283

27.3   Ceremony at Bogd Khan Mountain, Mongolia   288

A1.1   Gathering of sacred natural sites custodians, supporters and conservation biologists during a dialogue at the IUCN World Conservation Congress, Barcelona October 2008   292

A2.1   Custodians Chagat Almashev of Altai Republic and Kadyrbek Dzhakypov of Kyrgyzstan presenting their group's recommendations for action, Custodians Dialogue, Barcelona 2008   298

Tables

4.1 Some examples of sacred groves 45

11.1 Different criteria for considering sacred areas in Bandjoun 122

19.1 Case studies of The Delos Initiative 203

20.1 Step 2: Analysis of potential distribution of sacred natural sites 212

20.2 Sacred natural sites proposed registration template 215

21.1 Criteria used for the Forest Intactness Rating (FIR) 222

22.1 Distribution of tourism revenue at Tafi Atome Monkey Sanctuary 239

Boxes

11.1 Factors threatening sacred areas 125

12.1 Biseni and Osiama as exemplars of Community Conserved Areas 135

20.1 Free, Prior and Informed Consents (FPIC) 216

About the Authors

Editors

Bas Verschuuren is a scientist and facilitator with EarthCollective, project coordinator with Comparing and Supporting Endogenous Development (COMPAS) and serves as Co-chair with the International Union for Conservation of Nature's (IUCN) Specialist Group on Cultural and Spiritual Values of Protected Areas. Bas has over 10 years of international experience integrating cultural and spiritual values in conservation management and policy, and does applied research on the links between cultural and biological systems.

Robert Wild is an ecologist and social scientist with 25 years' practical experience of working with communities at protected areas in East Africa, Caribbean, Indian Ocean and Europe. He is chair of the IUCN Specialist Group on Cultural and Spiritual Values of Protected Areas.

Jeffrey A. McNeely is Senior Science Advisor at IUCN. He has worked in international conservation for over 40 years and has written or edited dozens of books on a wide range of topics that include cultural values of nature.

Gonzalo Oviedo is an anthropologist and environmentalist and works as Senior Adviser for Social Policy at IUCN, facilitating the integration of social issues in conservation work worldwide. Gonzalo focuses on livelihood security, culture, rights and governance.

Other contributors

Eno Abasi D. Anwana has over eight years' experience working with different indigenous people groups in Nigeria on various aspects of biodiversity management and conservation. Her research interests are in indigenous knowledge systems, adaptive management and coastal zone management. Eno has a PhD in Natural Resource Management from the Natural Resources Institute, University of Greenwich at Medway, United Kingdom.

Meschach Asei played a pivotal role in the Osiama community and he is a knowledge custodian of the customs and indigenous beliefs of the Osiama people.

Guillermo Barroso is the President of the Pronatura Federation, Mexico's largest and most influential conservation organization. Guillermo played a key role in the formation of Pronatura's Biocultural Unit and has promoted the validity of biocultural conservation with, amongst others, key governmental representatives in Mexico. Guillermo graduated with an Engineering Degree from the Anáhuac University.

Edmund G.C. Barrow has been working in over 20 countries in Africa for nearly 35 years on community conservation, natural resource management and agroforestry. He currently works with IUCN as the Africa Regional Forest Advisor.

Edwin Bernbaum, PhD, is a Senior Fellow at The Mountain Institute and author of the award-winning book *Sacred Mountains of the World* (1997, University of California Press, Berkeley). He has done research on the meanings of mountains around the world and has worked with parks and protected areas on developing interpretive materials based on the cultural and spiritual significance of features of mountain environments and ecosystems.

Shonil Bhagwat is Senior Research Fellow at the School of Geography and the Environment, and Director of the MSc programme in biodiversity, conservation and management at the University of Oxford. Shonil has over 10 years' research experience on sacred groves in the Western Ghats, India. Shonil works closely withthe Alliance on Religion and Conservation (ARC), is a member of the Steering Committee of the IUCN Specialist Group on Cultural and Spiritual Values of Protected Areas; and President ofthe Society for Conservation Biology's (SCB) Working Group on Religion and Conservation Biology.

Radhika Borde is a researcher and social entrepreneur with an academic background in literature and religious studies. She has worked in the fields of education, children's book publishing and activist media. She is currently in the process of initiating the revival of an ancient tribal craft and is also providing consultancy to grassroots-level NGOs in India.

Denis Byrne, PhD, leads the research programme in culture and heritage at the Department of Environment, Climate Change and Water in Australia (NSW). He is adjunct professor at the TransForming Cultures Centre, University of Technology Sydney. Denis's research interests and publications focus on the social and intangible value of heritage sites and landscapes and the interface between popular religion and the heritage discourse.

Robert A. Cheke is professor of Tropical Zoology, a pest and vector control entomologist and ornithologist. He is Principal Scientist, Natural Resources Institute, University of Greenwich at Medway, United Kingdom. Robert has country experience in east, west and southern Africa. His research interests are in applied ecology, conservation and parasitology.

Freddy Delgado is Director of Agro-Ecology of University of Cochabamba (AGRUCO) of the Universidad Major San Simon (UMSS), Bolivia; see www.agruco.org.

Joanna Dobson has an MA from Cambridge University in Modern and Medieval languages and is fluent in Russian. She has been working and living with the indigenous Altai population in the 'Uch Enmek' Indigenous Nature Reserve since 2002. Her research work particularly focuses on the study of ancient petroglyphs.

Nigel Dudley is an ecologist and consultant. His work focuses particularly on broad scale approaches to conservation, the planning and management of protected areas, the wider values of natural ecosystems and measurement of ecological integrity. He works mainly with non-governmental organizations and UN agencies and is a member of the IUCN World Commission on Protected Areas.

Craig Edelman is the ExecutiveVice President of Africa Aid, a non-profit development organization operating in west and east Africa. He is completing a Masters degree in International Development at Harvard University and holds a BSc in Environmental Systems and Earth Science from the University of California. Craig's focus area is the intersection of environmental protection and economic development in low-income nations.

Cesar Escobar is a staff member of AGRUCO and regional coordinator for COMPAS Latin America.

Archana Godbole is Founder Director of AERF, a conservation practitioner from India, engaged in protection and management of sacred groves with community's partnerships in north Western Ghats of India. A trained taxonomist and recipient of the Whitley Associate Award in 2007, he has been responsible for developing and implementing the long-term conservation strategy of AERF for the conservation of valuable biodiversity of north Western Ghats.

Martin Gutiérrez is the General Director of Pronatura Mexico. He holds a degree in

Evironmental Law from the Iberoamericana University (Mexico DF) and is leading work on legal innovative tools to encourage the protection of Mexico's natural resources. Martin has been a driving force behind the development of the methodology and tools.

Collin L. G. Harris is a retired Colonel from Moore Town Maroons, Jamaica. Harris is a Maroon educator who was principal of Moore Town's main school from 1954 to 1980 and Colonel of the Moore Town maroons from 1964 to 1995. He has written several books and papers and was awarded an honorary doctorate from the University of the West Indies in 2006.

Wim Hiemstra is coordinator of the international COMPAS programme facilitated by ETC Netherlands. COMPAS focuses on conserving biocultural diversity and endogenous development through partner organisations in Latin America, Africa and Asia; see www.compasnet.org.

Liza Higgins-Zogib is Manager, People and Conservation, at WWF International where she currently coordinates the development and implementation of WWF's social policies. She is finalising her PhD thesis in Yoga Philosophy and Meditation and has worked and published extensively on sacred natural sites.

Alana Jules Jackman has a background in palliative care working closely with the terminally ill. She has filmed two TV pilot shows and spoken on BBC Radio on the importance of clinical ecology in battling life threatening illness. Alana Jules has an MA in Religious Studies and is currently undertaking research for a PhD in Social and Political Theory.

Kimberly John is the Sustainable Waters Manager of the Southeast Caribbean Programme of The Nature Conservancy. She has a BSc and MSc in Geography and Zoology from the University of the West Indies. She has over 10 years of conservation and research experience in freshwater and traditional knowledge which earned her a fellowship at IUCN from the Alcoa Foundation and a Sustainable Watershed Management Award from Swiss Re.

Sébastien Luc Kamga Kamdem holds a BSc, an MSc and a PhD in forestry from Georg-August University in Germany. Sebastian worked with Cameroon's Ministry of Forest and Wildlife and is a founding member of the African Centre of Applied Forestry Research and Development. He has consulted on landscape management and forestry with organizations such as IUCN and WWF.

Barbara Lassen works for Deutsche Gesellschaft für Technische Zusammenarbeit (GTZ) in their Programme Implementing the Biodiversity Convention, and is a member of the IUCN Commission on Environmental, Economic and Social Policy (CEESP). She holds a degree in Landscape Ecology and an MA in International Environmental Policy. Currently her work focuses on biodiversity governance by indigenous peoples and local communities, and on access to genetic resources and benefit sharing.

Chikkananjegowda Madegowda is a Senior Research Associate at ATREE, Bangalore, India. His interests include understanding and implementing sustainable harvesting of non-timber forest produces, environmental education and indigenous knowledge on forest conservation. He actively advocates for the rights of Soligas under the Forest Rights Act 2006 and represents them on the district level committee for implementing the Act.

Josep-Maria Mallarach is a geologist and environmental consultant with 30 years experience in planning, management and evaluation of protected areas on which he has written and edited 15 books and numerous articles. He is a member of the IUCN World Commissions of Protected Areas, the Commission on Environmental Economic and Social Policy, the Co-coordinator of The Delos Initiative and Steering Committee member of the Specialist Group on Cultural and Spiritual Values of Protected Areas.

Danil Mamyev is Altaian, from Uch Enmek, and holds degrees in Geography and Geology from Tashkent University, Uzbekistan. Danil is founder of the 'Tengri – Soul Ecology School' and 'Uch Enmek' Indigenous Nature Park where he currently holds the position of Park Director. He also established the government land relations office for the Ongudai region and directs the region's Special Protected Nature Territories Association.

Sushmita Mandal is a development professional from Tata Institute of Social Sciences, Mumbai, India. She is responsible for strengthening interdisciplinary research components within the Conservation and Livelihoods Programme at Ashoka Trust for Research in Ecology and the Environment (ATREE). An active community worker, she explores anthropological and cultural issues of Soligas and analyses policy spaces available for them to advocate for protected area co-management and decentralized natural resource governance mechanisms.

Adrienne M. Martin is a social and institutional development specialist and the leader of Livelihoods and Institutions Group, Natural Resources Institute, University of Greenwich at Medway, United Kingdom. Adrienne has long term experience in Sudan and Syria. Her research interests include community-based natural resource management (NRM), social capital and NR policy formulation.

Luckson Obireke is Chief and clan head of the Biseni community. He played an important role in knowledge mobilization activities in Biseni and was key informant on the traditions and culture of the Biseni people.

Alison Ormsby is Associate Professor of Environmental Studies at Eckerd College, USA. She has a PhD in Environmental Studies from Antioch University New England, an MSc in Environmental Studies from the Yale University School of Forestry and Environmental Studies, and a BSc in Environmental Science from the College of William and Mary. She has conducted research at sacred forests in Ghana and India.

Mercedes Otegui-Acha is the Director of the Biocultural Conservation Unit of Pronatura, Mexico. Mercedes holds a BSc in Biology from Lawrence University (WI) and an MSc in Environmental Management from Duke University (NC). Mercedes worked with WWF for 10 years in Washington DC and Mexico City. She has worked with WWF, IUCN, UNESCO and Pronatura Mexico to advance and promote biocultural conservation approaches.

Dimie Otobotekere has skills in the behavioural patterns of freshwater fisheries, primates and avian species. He currently works in the Institute of Pollution Studies and Environmental Management of the River State University of Science and Technology, Port Harcourt, Nigeria.

Pasiya Otufu is a fisheries expert from the Biseni community. He currently works as a wildlife assistant in the Biological Science department, Faculty of Science, University of Port Harcourt, Nigeria.

Susan Otuokon is the Executive Director of the Jamaica Conservation and Development Trust since 2002. She has an MSc in Aquatic Resources Management from Kings College, University of London and is currently defending her doctoral thesis on 'Ecotourism as a Tool for Protected Area Management in the Caribbean' at the University of the West Indies.

Thymio Papayannis is an architect, planner and environmentalist and Director of the Mediterranean Institute for Nature and Anthropos (Med-INA) and Co-coordinator of the Delos Initiative with the specialist group on Cultural and Spiritual Values of Protected Areas (CSVPA) at IUCN's World Commission of Protected Areas (WCPA). Since 2000 he has been responsible for the incorporation of cultural values in the work of the Ramsar Convention and coordinates its Culture Working Group.

Dave Pritchard is a conservationist and environmental arts specialist who has worked with the Ramsar Convention in a variety of capacities for over two decades, including leading BirdLife International's involvement in the Convention. Now a consultant to the Ramsar Secretariat, he also sits on the Convention's Scientific and Technical Review Panel and its Culture Working Group.

Sameer Punde is an AERF core team member, trained conservation botanist and young Conservation Leadership Award winner of 2007 and 2009. He has been working on the forest health of sacred groves and their role in conservation of rare and endangered tree species for the last five years.

Nitin D. Rai is a Fellow at the Ashoka Trust for Research in Ecology and the Environment (ATREE), Bangalore, India. He received a PhD from Pennsylvania State University. His current research incorporates ecological science, history of landscape transformation, cultural ecology and local knowledge in association with the indigenous Soliga community in Biligiri Rangaswamy Temple Wildlife Sanctuary, India.

Mechtild Rossler has a PhD from the faculty of earth sciences from the University of Hamburg. She worked as Visiting Professor at the University of Berkeley (USA) and the National Centre For Scientific Research (CNRS) (France). She joined UNESCO's Man and the Biosphere Programme in 1991 and in 1992 the UNESCO World Heritage Centre. She is currently Chief of Europe and North America at the World Heritage Centre.

Arlene G. Sampang is Senior Research Assistant at the WorldFish Center's FishBase project. Her work with the Calamian Tagbanwa started in 2002 as a Master Thesis in Environmental Science major in Community-based Coastal Resource Management at the University of the Philippines Los Baños. Her research interest is on traditional fisheries management and local ecological knowledge.

Jaime Santiago is a biologist educated at the Mexican National Autonomous University (UNAM) and has ten years of community conservation experience working with indigenous peoples in Mexico. An indigenous Mixtec from Oaxaca, Jaime is currently coordinating the inventory of sacred natural sites in the field in Mexico.

Jayant Sarnaik is an AERF founder member, passionate community conservation worker and expert in communication and networking. He is a mathematician by training with over 13 years of experience in biodiversity conservation in the field.

Thomas Schaaf has a PhD in geography. After several years serving as an Assistant Professor for geography at the University of Freiburg (Germany), he joined UNESCO's Man and the Biosphere Programme in 1987. He is currently the Chief of UNESCO's Section for Ecological Sciences and Biodiversity.

Pei Shengji is a professor at Kunming Institute of Botany (KIB), Chinese Academy of Sciences (CAS) and President of Center for Biodiversity and Culture Conservation, Yunnan, China. Born in 1938, engaged in ethnobotany, economic botany and biodiversity conservation, he was Director of Xishuangbanna Tropical Botanical Garden, CAS, Deputy Director of KIB and Diversion Head of Mountain Environment/Natural Resources of ICIMOD, published 22 scientific books and 120 papers.

Jeremy Spoon, PhD, is an Assistant Professor of Anthropology at Portland State University and a Research Associate at The Mountain Institute. He has conducted research on indigenous ecological knowledge in and around mountainous protected areas in the Nepalese Himalaya, Great Basin, Hawaiian Islands and Rift Valley. Dr Spoon's experience includes 13 years collaborating on protected area resource management and interpretation.

John Studley is an ethnoforestry consultant, a Fellow of the Royal Geographical Society and a Chartered Geographer. He has a PhD in ethnoforestry, an MA in Rural Social Development and Diplomas in Forestry, Cross-cultural Studies and Theology. He has spent most of his life in High Asia working for the state, the voluntary sector and since 2001 as a consultant.

Erika J. Techera, PhD, is a Senior Lecturer in the Macquarie University School of Law. Her research interests include marine environmental law, community-based natural resource management and cultural heritage law. Erika is a member of the IUCN Commission on Environmental Law and World Commission on Protected Areas. Prior to joining Macquarie University she practised as a barrister in Sydney.

Tinde van Andel holds a PhD and is an ethnobotanist specializing in Amerindian, Creole and Maroon plant use in Suriname and Guyana. Tinde works at the National Herbarium of the Netherlands, Leiden University. Her research focuses on similarities between west African and Afro-Caribbean ethnobotany, especially plants used in African rituals and for women's and children's health.

Foreword

Our species evolved within nature, with our ancestors fitting in as a part of the many ecosystems which they shared with the rest of the plants, animals and micro-organisms that made every locality unique. By perhaps 200,000 years ago, they already were using fire and tools which gave them a dominant position in their ecosystems. Much evidence collected by paleontologists indicates that, even in the early stages, human cultures recognized that some parts of their territory had characteristics that required special treatment, and that some of the species that contributed to their welfare needed powerful management (such as by taboos) if they were to survive. Some places were therefore designated as special breeding grounds which needed protection against over-exploitation, if the species was going to continue to provide meat, eggs, furs, feathers and other comforts for our ancestors. Other places were sources of springs that provided pure water in critical times of the year, or trees that attracted a multitude of creatures that people found useful, or just attractive. Other places were sites where the elders, and sometimes unfortunate younger people, were buried.

One result of these intimate relationships between ecosystems and the people who depended on them was the treating of some places as sacred, providing a foundation of human spirituality and the religions that appear to have ancient origins. Thus the sacred natural sites discussed in this book may be considered to be an important part of the development of spirituality and religion as well as the earliest form of protected areas. Both religions and protected areas have become much more complex, though perhaps not as diverse, and this book offers rich material to support active debates on such ideas.

For IUCN, with over 1000 member organizations and over 10,000 members of six Commissions, sacred natural sites play a particularly important role, demonstrating that nature and people have a special relationship, and that this relationship survives in many different ways in the four corners of the Earth. By helping to promote the recognition of sacred natural sites, we are seeking to maintain and strengthen the relationship between people and nature. As more of us move to cities, this relationship sometimes seems to be weakening, leading to what some have called 'nature deficit disorder'. Modern technology has certainly given us access to more information than ever before, but too much of this information separates us from nature rather than helping us understand better how much we depend on the goods and services provided by the ecosystems that make our planet productive.

This book is being published in the International Year of Biodiversity, which gives it special importance as an expression of the special relationship between people and the rest of nature. It offers us an opportunity to remind ourselves of the deep and meaningful relationships that many religions and faith communities have with nature, demonstrated by their devotion to sacred natural sites such as those described in these pages. The nurturing of these special sites, in diverse settings – both cultural and natural – helps give meaning to our lives. At the same time, we need to reflect on how we are treating such areas. Why are many of them being abandoned, degraded or lost completely? How can we decide what kinds of land use and resource management practices are most appropriate for which areas? IUCN is

Figure 0.1 Indigenous Ranger Marlangaj Yunupingu presents Julia Marton-Lefèvre with a Yidaki at the launch of the Sacred Natural Sites Guidelines at the IUCN World Conservation Congress, Barcelona 2008

working with local communities, faith groups, scientists and resources managers (including from the private sector) in all parts of the world to answer such questions.

IUCN will continue to strongly support sacred natural sites and contribute to these discussions by facilitating dialogues and partnerships, and drawing the attention of our members, decision-makers and the general public to the many values of these

sacred sites that give nature its special meaning for human well-being.

Julia Marton-Lefèvre
Director General, the International Union for
Conservation of Nature
Gland, Switzerland
15 February 2010

Preface

This book was motivated by a deep concern over continuing species extinctions, environmental degradation and loss of culture on our planet, often the result of what may at first sight appear to be 'progress'. The ecosystems that enable life to flourish in all of its variety often seem to be treated by development as if they exist merely to provide commodities for humans to consume. The result is heedless over-exploitation of forests, fields and waters, and accelerating loss of biodiversity. The efforts of the conservation movement have been admirable and have even led to some successes, however fleeting they may be. But ways of living sustainably must be found, and we have been inspired by the great variety of cultures that understand nature as sacred, worthy of our highest respect. A call for many of us to return to a deep respect of nature is made in the eloquent poetry that Altan Erdeni, a shaman of the Buryat people, created for the IUCN World Conservation Congress in Barcelona in 2008. As a guardian of important sacred natural sites she wrote the following poem about Alkhanai Mountain, one of the most important sacred natural sites of the Buryat People:

Though you have no faith in God,
Treasure what God has given!
You long to have it all at once:
Redemption for sins, a cure for illness…

You glance at the holy water, sacred and ancient,
As if it were some magic marvel.
You scoop it up greedily
To brew medicinal tea.

It doesn't occur to you
That faith's power lies in the soul.
What are you tourists doing, so-called pilgrims?
This sacred place reels, drunk, from you.

Liquor wafts like a poison.
The air smells only of intoxication.
All around, cigarette smoke fills the nose.
Children misbehave just like the adults.

This place of prayerful worship is littered with butts.
Instead of sweets and white milk,
You offer whatever filth is at hand
And receive in return what your actions deserve.

What are we hoping for,
Setting this example for our children?
Over how many centuries, how many ages
Do we want to destroy nature's wonder?

How long will the patience
Of Alkhanai's spirits endure?
If only you could hear
The messages they send us…

As one voice, they say:

"The Earth moans at people's ignorance.
They don't perceive us as protectors!
For ages, our names have been forgotten.
    They all beg, 'Come and help us!'
        Whether they believe or not, they come in droves.
        Our souls are exhausted.
Those of you who are spiritual, be reasonable,
Teach the correct path,
Not a drunken example.
    The gods' wrath knows no mercy!
    The gods' patience has an end!"

They will depart for the place
Where the mountain streams' might is worshiped.
With our help, the power of the Protectors will fade,
And those who come after us will answer for it.

So think and ponder:
This treasure lies in our own home.
A prophet dwells on the Alkhanai.

The spirit who guards the power of the caves,
The spirit, the protector of mountain streams,
The lord of the deer, Alkhanai's protectors:
These are our eternal guardians.

Altan Erdeni
(translation by Tristra Newyear)

We have been heartened by the increasing number of voices from indigenous and local communities, and mainstream world religions, seeking to build a new relationship between people and the rest of nature. Therefore this book in part carries their message and is a call for further engagement with the conservation movement to find sustainable ways of living and open dialogue with other sectors of society and industry alike.

This book is drawn largely from the work of the Specialist Group on Cultural and Spiritual Values of Protected Areas (CSVPA) of IUCN's World Commission on Protected Areas, supported by numerous collaborating organizations and individuals both within and outside IUCN. Central to this effort has been the holding of a series of workshops organized by the United Nations Educational, Scientific and Cultural Organization (UNESCO), IUCN or collaborating institutions. These meetings have been held in India (1998), China and South Africa (2003), Mexico and Japan (2005), Spain (2006), Mongolia, Greece and the UK (2007). These workshops have developed a significant body of information regarding sacred natural sites and inspired workshops held at IUCN's World Conservation Congress (WCC4) in Barcelona, Spain, in October 2008, where early versions of many of the papers contained in this book were first presented. We have also sought additional contributions to fill gaps and help present a comprehensive and coherent view of sacred natural sites as of the end of 2009.

The content of this book and its chapters, as well as the way in which this is expressed, is the responsibility of the individual chapter authors of this book and does not reflect or abide by any institutional policy. All chapters have been peer-reviewed with a view towards scientific rigour and verification of the information presented. In addition all information has been presented with

free and prior informed consent of the original knowledge holders, be it indigenous, cultural or scientific. A debt of gratitude is acknowledged to all those individuals and institutions, custodians and guardians at all the sacred natural sites described here who freely gave of their time and energy to develop the case study chapters.

The collaboration between IUCN and the Alcoa Foundation Conservation and Sustainability Fellowship Programme has been essential to this book, with five of the 'Fellows' contributing chapters and one of the editors also being a Fellow. The Alcoa Foundation also generously contributed core funding for this volume and a series of four workshops on sacred natural sites at the WCC4.

We are pleased to acknowledge the long-term and generous assistance of The Christensen Fund for their support with producing, translating and testing the 'Best Practice Guidelines 16, Sacred Natural Sites: Guidelines for Protected Area Managers', and for the participation of many of the custodians who took part in the dialogue between custodians of sacred natural sites at the 4th World Conservation Congress in Barcelona 2008 (WCC4).

The editors are also indebted to their institutions (IUCN and EarthCollective), and our long-suffering families for making them available to work on this book. We are especially indebted to the chapter authors, who have patiently responded to queries and comments from peer reviewers and the editors. We are also grateful to the many colleagues that provided the peer reviews for specific chapters, ensuring the quality of all contributions, and guided the development of the book. A special thanks to Wendy Price who has performed above and beyond the call of duty offering support throughout the production of the book.

We hope that this book will contribute to a better understanding of sacred natural sites, provide food for thought on the deep connectivity of nature and humanity and stimulate considered respectful and effective action.

Bas Verschuuren
Robert Wild
Jeffrey McNeely
Gonzalo Oviedo

List of Acronyms and Abbreviations

ACCU	Asia/Pacific Cultural Centre
ADB	Association pour l'appui au Développement de Bandjoun
AERF	Applied Environmental Research Foundation
AGRUCO	Agroecologia Universidad Cochabamba
ATREE	Ashoka Trust for Research in Ecology and the Environment
BRTWS	Biligiri Ranganswamy Temple Wildlife Sanctuary
BZMC	Buffer Zone Management Committee
BZUC	Buffer Zone User Committees
CADC	Certificate of Ancestral Domain Claim
CARFAD	Centre Africain de Recherches Forestières Appliquées et de Développement
CBD	Convention on Biological Diversity
CCA	Community Conserved Areas
CCFU	Cross Cultural Foundation Uganda
CEPF	Critical Ecosystem Partnership Fund
CEPROSI	El Centro de Promoción de las Sabidurías Interculturales
CFSA	Community Forest Stewardship Agreement
CI	Census of India
CIKOD	Centre for Indigenous Knowledge and Organisational Development
CIPCRE	Centre International pour la Promotion de la Création
CIPSEG	Cooperative Integrated Project on Savannah Ecosystems in Ghana
CNRS	National Centre For Scientific Research
CNUED	Conférence des Nations Unies sur l'Environnement et le Développement
COAMA	Consolidation of the Colombian Amazon Programme
COE	Centro Orientamento Educativo
COMPAS	Comparing and Supporting Endogenous Development
CONABIO	Commission for the Knowledge of Biodiversity
CSICH	Convention on the Safeguarding of Intangible Cultural Heritage
CSVPA	Specialist Group on Cultural and Spiritual Values of Protected Areas
DENR	Department of Environment and Natural Resources
DNPWC	Department of National Parks and Wildlife Conservation
EAC	European Archaeological Council
EEA	European Environmental Agency
FAO	Food and Agriculture Organization
FFPRI	Forests and Forest Products Research Institute in Japan
FIR	Forest Intactness Rating
FISH	Fisheries Improved for Sustainable Harvest
FME	Federal Ministry of Environment
FPIC	Free and Prior Informed Consent
GEF	Global Environment Facility
GIS	Geographic Information System
GPS	Global Positioning System
GTZ	Deutsche Gesellschaft für Technische Zusammenarbeit
HCVF	High Conservation Value Forest
ICC	Indigenous Cultural Communities
ICCA	Indigenous and Community Conserved Areas

ICOMOS	International Council on Monuments and Sites
ICCROM	International Centre for the Study of the Preservation and Restoration of Cultural Heritage
INSA	Indian Natural Science Academy
IP	Indigenous Peoples
IPA	Important Plant Area
IPRA	Indigenous Peoples Rights Act – Philippines
ITTO	International Tropical Timber Organization
IUCN	International Union for Conservation of Nature
IUCN CEESP	IUCN Commission on Environmental, Economic and Social Policy
JCDT	Jamaica Conservation and Development Trust
JNHT	Jamaica National Heritage Trust
LMMA	Locally Managed Marine Area
MA	Millennium Ecosystem Assessment
MAB	Man and Biosphere
Med-INA	Mediterranean Institute for Nature and Anthropos
MedWet	Mediterranean Wetlands Initiative
NARESCON	Natural Resources Conservation Council
NCRC	Nature Conservation Research Centre
NE	Natural England
NEST	Nigeria Environmental Study/Action Team
NIPAP	National Integrated Protected Areas Programme
NIPAS	National Integrated Protected Areas System
NNR	National Nature Reserve
NRM	Natural Resource Management
NTFP	Non-Timber Forest Products
PA	Protected Area
PAFID	Philippine Association for Intercultural Development
PIFS	Pacific Islands Forum Secretariat
PRI	Panchayati Raj Institutions
RFRA	Recognition of Forest Rights Act
RNSCC	Regional Network for the Synergy between the Convention on Biology Diversity and the Convention to Combat Desertification in West and Central Africa
SAEDP	Southern African Endogenous Development Programme
SAIIC	South and Meso American Indian Rights Center
SCB	Society for Conservation Biology
SFM	Status of Tropical Forest Management
SIDS	Small Island Developing States
SNPBZ	Sagarmatha National Park and Buffer Zone
SNS	Sacred Natural Site
TFCI	Tagbanwa Foundation of Coron Island
TMC	Tourism Management Committee
TTCIA	Tagbanwa Tribe of Coron Island Association
UNAM	Mexican National Autonomous University
UNDRIP	United Declaration on the Rights of Indigenous Peoples
UNESCO	United Nations Educational, Scientific and Cultural Organization
UNPFII	United Nations Permanent Forum on Indigenous Issues
UNU	United Nations University
VDC	Village Development Committee
WCED	World Commission on Environment and Development
WCMC	World Conservation Monitoring Centre
WCPA	World Commission on Protected Areas
WDPA	World Database of Protected Areas
WHC	World Heritage Convention
WTO	World Trade Organization
WWF	World Wildlife Fund

Glossary

Acculturation is the process by which visitors acquire the knowledge, skills, attitudes, values and behaviours that enable them to become functioning participants of a new sub/culture through the process of adaptation.

Adivasis are Indian populations that are culturally distinct from the Indian mainstream and considered to be indigenous to the sub-continent.

Buddhization is the cultural assimilation of animistic peoples into Buddhism and the cultural transformation of the meaning of their environments and deities.

Cognition is the mental process of knowing, including aspects such as awareness, perception, reasoning and judgement.

Dharma in the context of Buddhism is most commonly used for the body of the teachings of the Sakyamuni Buddha (in other words, the historical Buddha, Gautama).

Eco-Spirituality is a spiritual view of, and context for, human relationships with the Universe and the Earth. It has the potential to transcend boundaries between spiritual traditions and also between science and spirituality.

Endogenous means proceeding from within and is used to describe a process emanating from within a culture.

Folk religion is used to indicate ethnic, local or regional religious customs under the umbrella of one or more organized religions, sometimes outside the official doctrine and practices.

Indigenous is used in the sense of being native or belonging to a place. The more restricted meaning of Indigenous People is adopted as determined in Convention 169 of the International Labour Organization (ILO), but it is recognized that many local communities are in fact indigenous to their areas despite not being considered Indigenous People under the ILO definition.

Mainstream religions are institutionalized religions practised by large sectors of humankind, each one including different branches and views of nature. In many countries a particular mainstream faith may be followed by a minority of people. These are, in alphabetical order; Baha'i, Buddhism, Christianity, Daoism, Hinduism, Jainism, Judaism, Islam, Shinto, Sikhism and Zoroastrianism.

Modernity means a series of developments in which, beginning in 17th-century Europe, scientific discoveries provide a platform for an industrial revolution that rapidly increased the economic base of the west and allowed it to extend its influence globally.

Numina are spirits, deities or a divinity inhabiting sacred sites which have certain powers that are commonly described as supernatural or magical.

Scientism is the view that empirical natural science has authority over all other interpretation of reality and life, such as religious, spiritual, philosophical, mythical or humanistic explanations.

Sanskritization is the cultural assimilation of animistic peoples into Hinduism and the cultural transformation of the meaning of their environments and deities. Sacred Natural Sites are areas of high natural value and biodiversity, recognized by some form of protection status, which simultaneously are considered to have significant spiritual value by a society or social group.

Spiritscape is used to indicate that sacred natural sites are frequently networked across a physical and a mental landscape which are linked by creation mythologies, or by the genealogical relationships of ancestral beings.

Technologically developed countries are defined by the Delos Initiative as countries with a high level of technical expertise and production, which may or may not be related to high cultural and/or spiritual development.

1

Introduction: Sacred Natural Sites the Foundations of Conservation

Bas Verschuuren, Robert Wild, Jeffrey McNeely and Gonzalo Oviedo

Uluru (Ayers Rock), Mato Tipila (Devil's Tower), Mt Kilimanjaro, Mt Kailash, Sagarmatha/Chomolongma (Mt Everest), Lake Titicaca, Lake Baikal, the Ganges and Brahmaputra rivers are but a few of the sacred natural sites that include some of the most iconic places on the planet. Among such sacred natural sites are thousands more that remain little known and unsung, such as the Dai Holy Hills, the Holy Island of Lindisfarne, the Golden Mountains of Altai, the sacred groves of the Western Ghats, the sacred lakes of the Niger delta and the numerous sacred islands, groves, and springs found throughout the world. The list is very long, uncounted and in a sense uncountable.

In these places nature and humanity meet, and people's deeper motives and aspirations are expressed through what is called 'the sacred'. Many of these places are virtually ignored, some receive pilgrims by the million, and yet others are the closely guarded secrets of their custodians. People of faith or religion, or of no particular faith, find inspiration in these places, and they resonate across a wide spectrum of humanity.

With habitats and ecosystems degrading and the extinction of animal and plant species increasing, sacred natural sites have drawn attention from the conservation movement as reservoirs of biodiversity. It is being proposed that the effective

conservation of sacred natural sites will help to protect diverse human cultures and a substantial portion of increasingly vulnerable nature. Sacred natural sites, therefore, concern the well-being of both nature and humans and encompass the complex intangible and spiritual relationships between people and our originating web of life. This book speaks, then, of places that matter at the depths of human emotions.

Sacred natural sites: An overview

For the purpose of this book, sacred natural sites are 'areas of land or water having special spiritual significance to peoples and communities' (Oviedo and Jeanrenaud, 2007). This working definition is deliberately broad and open and recognizes the limitations of each of the words 'sacred', 'natural' and 'site'. Other terms are used in this book in recognition of this openness and it is important that the concept remains open to further articulation.

Each term 'sacred', 'natural' and 'site' has its limitations. 'Sacred' has different meanings to different communities. At the basic level it denotes deep respect and 'set aside' for purposes of the spiritual or religious. The original term had an aspect of 'fear' that is now less current. The word 'natural' is used in this context to contrast areas with little or no nature (e.g. mosques, churches or temples), this being the common understanding of sacred site in much of the developed world. Thus natural denotes that a site contains 'nature' of some kind that is often valuable. What exactly 'natural' means or should mean has long been debated within the conservation world. In the context of sacred natural sites, it does not mean an absence of human connection, influence or interaction. In the context of sacred natural sites, the term 'site' is a broad concept which includes areas and places of all kinds and encompasses complete territories, extensive landscapes and can also be as small as a single rock or tree. The term sacred natural sites therefore needs to remain an open concept with an evolving articulation.

Sacred natural sites are part of a broader set of cultural values that different social groups, traditions, beliefs or value systems attach to places and which 'fulfil humankind's need to understand, and connect in meaningful ways, to the environment of its origin and to nature' (Putney, 2005, p132).

Sacred natural sites consist of all types of natural features including mountains, hills, forests, groves, rivers, lakes, lagoons, caves, islands and springs. They can vary in size from the very small: an individual tree, small spring or a single rock formation, to whole landscapes and mountain ranges. They consist of geological formations, distinct landforms, specific ecosystems and natural habitats. They are predominantly terrestrial but are also found in inshore marine areas, islands and archipelagos. They may also be the location of temples, shrines, mosques and churches, and they can incorporate other features such as pilgrimage trails. In some sites nature is itself sacred, while in others sanctity is conferred by connections with spiritual heroes, religious structures or sacred histories.

The interest in sacred natural sites from the perspective of nature conservation lies in the components of biological diversity that they harbour, such as the species of animals and plants, the habitats and ecosystems, as well the ecological dynamics and functions that support life within and outside the places. Linked to such biological diversity is the array of distinct human cultures that care for them and hold them sacred. Many sacred sites are primarily built places, such as temples, and while being supportive of their conservation, such archaeological or architectural elements are not specifically addressed in this book.

Sacred natural sites and religion

The term 'sacred natural sites' implies that these areas are in some way holy, venerated or consecrated and so connected with religion or belief systems, or set aside for a spiritual purpose. The word 'spiritual', which relates to the human spirit, as opposed to material or physical things, does not imply a religious institution and many people who experience spiritual emotions about nature (including secular scientists) do not belong to a formal religion. But sacred sites associated with living cultures always have institutions and rules associated with them. These institutions are usually religious or spiritual in nature and may be distinct from other parts of society, while in some communities of indigenous and traditional peoples, sacred site institutions are closely integrated within society with little distinction between the sacred and the secular, the religious and the civil.

The vast majority of sacred natural sites were arguably founded by indigenous or folk religions and spiritualities, but many were subsequently adopted or co-opted by mainstream religions. There is consequently a considerable 'layering' and mixing of religious and other spiritual or belief systems. Within the larger mainstream religions there are many if not more autonomous or semi-autonomous sub-groups. While 50 per cent of the world's population profess to belong to either Christianity or Islam (see Figure 1.1), and many others are Hindus or Buddhists, 80 per cent of all people ascribe to a mainstream religion, a large part of which continue to adhere to at least some traditional or folk religion (O'Brien and Palmer, 1997). Sacred natural sites are thus connected to a wide range of socio-cultural systems and institutions, some more complex than others, and to different dynamics of change and cultural interaction.

Sacred natural sites are just one of many domains where religions or belief systems interact with nature. Most if not all religions have mythology, cosmology, theology or ethics related to earth, nature and land. Contemporarily, such connections are being revived or rearticulated through ethical positions expressed for example in statements that many of the mainstream faiths have produced, setting out their relationship to the

Figure 1.1 Karamat of Shaykh Hohamed Hassen Ghaibie Shah al-Qadiri at Lion's Head, Signal Hill within Table Mountain National Park (Cape Town is ringed by a Holy Circle of Islamic Shrines)

Source: Robert Wild

natural world and their responsibility towards the planet (O'Brien and Palmer, 1997).

Establishing a duality between 'indigenous', in the sense of being native or belonging to a place, and 'mainstream', while pragmatic for discussion, does present some problems. Several mainstream faiths can be considered indigenous in much of their range, e.g. Daoism, Shinto, Hinduism and Jainism, while Zoroastrianism now has very few followers and is essentially no longer 'mainstream'. More problematic is that this duality renders invisible the many merged or syncretic faiths and folk variants of mainstream religions where elements of the preceding indigenous beliefs are still practiced. These folk religions can have much stronger nature ethics than the more symbolic orthodox form (see Figure 1.2 and Byrne, Chapter 5; Studley, Chapter 10). Within human history, religion has been used (or abused) as a tool of domination. These issues, although much reduced, have not gone away and some faiths still seek

converts from other faiths. The destruction of sacred sites has been part of that domination and still continues today.

Conversely, most faiths over long periods of time have peaceably co-existed and shared sacred sites. Mutual respect and accommodation have often been reached. Further, compassion and peace-building lie at the heart of many religious traditions and belief systems.

There are important elements to take into account regarding indigenous or traditional spirituality. The growing recognition of the political status of indigenous peoples provided in 2007 by the United Declaration on the Rights of Indigenous Peoples (UNDRIP, 2007) has significantly increased awareness of the deeper dimensions of oppression and also of resilience. Centuries of religious colonialism in various degrees extirpated traditional spiritual beliefs and practices. The many different situations and histories gave rise to a large diversity of

Figure 1.2 The goddess Jomo Miyo Lang Samba from Pangbuche Monastery who lives on Mount Everest

She provides 'norbu' (wealth) for the Sherpa people. In the past, norbu included food and other necessities and now also encompasses tourism. Mountain climbers and their family members worship the mountain deities to produce safe passage on ascents and descents.

Source: Jeremy Spoon

spiritualities amongst indigenous peoples which is largely made up of a body of beliefs, values and practices intimately connected to nature.

Some scholars would associate sacred sites of indigenous peoples with animism, understood in anthropology as the belief in the existence of 'spiritual beings' embodied in natural elements – plants, animals, or inanimate constituents of nature, as classically described by Taylor in 1871, or more contemporarily as 'a relational ontology in which the world is found to be, and treated as, a community of persons not all of whom are human' (Bird, 2002). In 'animist' spirituality there is an intrinsic sacramental dimension in natural sites themselves.

For most mainstream religions, primarily in monotheist traditions, a fundamental feature of belief is the purely non-material nature of divinity; de-sacralization of nature has been the norm for them rather than the exception. In the case of Christianity, this was closely connected with the Platonic doctrine about the soul as an entity essentially separated from nature, a doctrine that would become the foundation of many philosophical and theological formulations, including rationalism, centred on the separation between soul and body and between spirit and nature. Although some trends in theological thinking promote new embodiment of beliefs in nature, the distance between animism-based spirituality and mainstream faiths remains wide and probably inevitably at the roots of theology.

Sacred natural sites are, with the exception of Antarctica, found on every continent and probably in every country. Some of them are surely among the oldest venerated places on Earth and at the same time new sacred natural sites are still being established, in some cases by migrants to new countries (Dudley et al, 2005; Verschuuren, Chapter 6). Paleo-anthropological evidence indicates that earlier humans such as Neanderthals practised the cult of ancestors in burial sites over 60,000 years ago, which is arguably one of the origins of sacred sites. Ancestor worship and veneration of burial grounds seem to be a common trait of every culture of modern humans, as well as the adoration of natural features of great significance such as high mountains or large rivers. Australian sacred sites may go back at least 50,000 years; rock art considered of a sacred nature dates to 20,000 years ago and some of the Neolithic henges date from 5000 years ago.

At a landscape level, anthropologists have long recognized the sacred status that cultures have given to nature not only in specific sacred sites (e.g. Frazer, 1890) but also in larger areas of cultural significance and entire landscapes. Interest on the importance of sacred sites for living cultures has seen an upsurge since the mid 1990s, which has contributed to the exploration of new paradigms and multidisciplinary views to the advantage of both the understanding and the conservation of sacred sites (Berkes, 2008; Carmichael et al, 1994; Posey, 1999).

Because of their diversity, origins, and different and varying degrees of sacrality of their elements, it is not really possible to have full knowledge about the number of sacred sites existing in the world today. Registering and recording sacred natural sites has be initiated at the request, and with FPIC, of custodian communities. However, estimates have been made for some countries, notably India, where at least 13,720 sacred groves have been reported and experts estimate that the total number for the country may be in the range of 100,000 to 150,000 (Malhotra et al, 2001). India may be exceptional because of its size, cultural diversity and widespread practices about sacred groves, but it would not be unrealistic to estimate that sacred natural sites must exist in the hundreds of thousands.

Why are they important for the conservation of nature and culture?

Many sacred natural sites have been well protected over long time periods and have seen low levels of disturbance. Many are demonstrably high in biodiversity and represent a strong biodiversity conservation opportunity (see Chapter 2). Sacred natural sites also represent ancient and profound cultural values. The roles of sacred sites' custodians from indigenous, local community and mainstream religions are expressions of dedicated efforts that cultures that have specifically, if not always consciously, cared for nature in various ways.

While sacred natural sites are connected to the human spirit and intangible heritage they also have strong material components. In addition to being places where animals and plant species survive, they provide resources such as water and medicines and other ecosystem services, they are the location of events and ceremonies, and traditionally are sites of education. They link to livelihoods in many ways and the concepts of cultural services and human well-being are associated with them (Millennium Ecosystem Assessment, 2005). They support pilgrimages and tourism, both of which have large associated service sectors and generate significant economic activity.

Despite their many values and functions, sacred natural sites were not on the agenda of nature conservation worldwide until recently. Apart from some pioneering work of documenting sacred groves for example in India, the literature that highlights the conservation value of sacred sites only started to emerge in the late 1990s. Scholars interested in specific ecosystems such as mountains, forests or rivers, or in the new trends of disciplines like ethnobiology and ecological anthropology, had for some time been actively promoting the integration of cultural concerns in ecology and conservation; but sacred sites as such became a subject of consideration in conservation circles only about a dozen years ago. Following a series of seminal workshops organized by UNESCO in 1998 (Lee and Schaaf, 2003; Schaaf and Lee, 2006), international conservation organizations like WWF and IUCN, working with indigenous groups and networks such as the Rigoberta Menchú Tum Foundation, started to explore ways to integrate sacred natural sites in their conservation work. A number of international events and processes followed, and case studies and scientific and practitioner articles started to appear in books and journals. These events marked the urgency for protection of sacred natural sites and for bridging the knowledge gap that persists with many conservation managers and agencies. The 2003 Fifth World Parks Congress, held in Durban, South Africa, was the first global venue where sacred natural sites entered the formal protected areas agenda of the world. It was also a turning point in the work of IUCN on the non-material values of protected areas (Harmon and Putney, 2003).

After the 2003 Congress, IUCN's Specialist Group on the Cultural and Spiritual Values of Protected Areas (CSVPA) that had formed in 1998 continued the work on guidelines for the management of sacred natural sites (Wild and McLeod, 2008). CSVPA has since advanced a significant amount of work on sacred natural sites and speices including this volume, Mallarach and Papayannis, 2007; Papayannis and Mallarach, 2009 and Pungetti et al in press.

International importance of sacred natural sites

The urge for the protection of sacred natural sites have also been recognized by the Convention on Biological Diversity (CBD) and the UN Permanent Forum on Indigenous Issues. The CBD in 2004 developed the Akwe Kon voluntary guidelines for the conduct of cultural, environmental and

Figure 1.3 The 'Tagyl' is a stone ritual altar used for group prayer meetings held twice a year at the beginning of the summer 'green leaves' and in the autumn, 'yellow leaves'

Source: Daniel Mamyev

social impact assessments regarding proposed developments that may affect sacred sites and on lands and waters traditionally occupied or used by indigenous and local communities (Secretariat of the Convention on Biological Diversity, 2004).

At the political level, as described before, the adoption of the United Nations Declaration on the Rights of Indigenous Peoples (UNDRIP) is an important benchmark. Article 12 in particular provides significant political leverage for developing appropriate policies for the protection and recognition of sacred natural sites at the national level. It states:

> *Indigenous peoples have the right to manifest, practice, develop and teach their spiritual and religious traditions, customs and ceremonies; the right to maintain, protect, and have access in privacy to their religious and cultural sites; the right to the use and control of their ceremonial objects; and the right to the repatriation of their human remains.* (UNDRIP, 2008)

Among international conservation NGOs, The Nature Conservancy has developed a planning tool for the conservation of sacred sites and cultural heritage in protected areas and tested it across countries in Central America such as Honduras, El Salvador, Mexico and Guatemala (Secaira and Molina, 2005). The WWF, in Dudley et al (2005), studied sacred sites in 100 protected areas. The Millennium Ecosystem Assessment (MA) adopted the concept of cultural services (including spiritual) as one of the four kinds of ecosystem services (the others being protecting, provisioning, and regulating). In the 'Conditions and Trends Assessment' (deGroot et al, 2005) and 'Policy responses' (Ghosh et al, 2005) developed under the Millennium Ecosystem Assessment sacred sites are recognized as areas of key interest for the conservation of biodiversity and culture but it is also concluded that more research is needed to understand how they further contribute to human well-being.

The aim of this book

This book underscores humanity's deepest response to the biosphere – the sacred values of nature as exemplified by sacred natural sites. By applying a multidisciplinary socio-ecological approach and including ways of knowing from many different worldviews and sciences, this book examines where this approach may help and where it is falling short. In remaining true to traditional knowledge holders, the book also employs perspectives that reflect custodian interpretations and realities that manifest in these special places and, this way, the book also aims to carry their voice.

Building on over a decade of work by nature conservationists and increasing engagement with their custodians over sacred natural sites the aims of the book are to:

- bring to the attention of a wider audience an improved understanding of natural sites that are held to be sacred to different societies;
- make the case that sacred natural sites support high biodiversity values;
- document the losses of sacred natural sites and draw attention the threats and pressures that many still face;
- highlight the multi-faceted and often complex cultural dimensions of sacred natural sites
- present case studies exemplifying both the differences and the commonalities of sacred sites;
- exemplify how sacred site custodians, ecologists, anthropologists, archaeologists, social scientists and others are collaborating on understanding and protecting these special places;
- make recommendations to decision makers at local, national and international levels in support of conserving sacred sites.

A conceptual framework for the analysis of sacred natural sites

This book brings together critical analysis and experience of sacred natural sites in different ecological, cultural and economic contexts. It relates these disciplines to the loss of biological and cultural diversity and the issue of equity in natural resource management. It adopts complex multidisciplinary perspectives across various geographical scales and governance levels (see Figure 1.4), without assuming that any particular perspective is necessarily valid in all settings. The book presents a wide diversity of opinions. But these diverse views are united by their respect for the sacred in nature and by adopting a framework for conceptualizing its interdisciplinary, multi-level and multi-scale approach (see Figure 1.4).

Sacred natural sites are central to this book and under the framework presented in Figure 1.4 they are placed central to localized cultural, spiritual and socio-economic values in order to elicit their importance to human well-being. Essentially humanity is a part of nature and clearly these human value domains also need to be viewed as a part of nature. The framework does not want to suggest that sacred values are exclusively found where the cultural, spiritual and socio-economic value domains intersect but instead seeks to clarify the contribution of sacred natural sites to human well-being and are so depicted centrally. It is recognized that sacred sites exist which share only one or two of these value domains and in some cases sacred natural sites have existed without proximate or contemporary communities attributing sacredness to them for periods of time because they were used for seasonal celebrations or because their custodians had disappeared. In such cases they have usually retained a cultural element.

Description of the components of the framework for conservation of sacred natural sites

Value domains central to human well-being

The conceptual framework (see Figure 1.4) differentiates three human value domains that constitute human well-being as a part of nature:

1 cultural values;
2 spiritual values;
3 socio-economic values.

For example, cultural values typically include inspirational value, and sense of place all of which

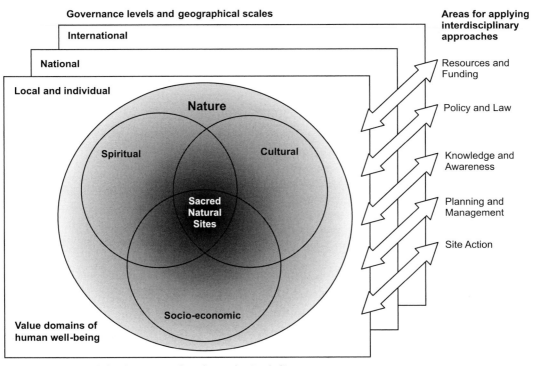

Figure 1.4 Framework for the conservation of sacred natural sites

may be central to sacred natural sites. Spirituality is a unique value domain attached to sacred natural sites – irrespective of the actual belief system. Spirituality for much of mainstream religion has itself become isolated or abstracted from nature but in animistic traditions and folk religions spirituality is typically invoked by and experienced in relationship with nature. Spirituality is also experienced in nature and at sacred natural sites by people from modern societies without any specific religious background. Similarly, the socio-economic values domain is based on the (material) ecosystem services derived from sacred natural sites. This underlines human spiritual dependence on nature and at its simplest refers to meeting basic human needs and lifeways. As such socio-economic values are linked to a) lifeways which refer to indigenous ways of life, b) livelihoods which refer to different occupations in a more differentiated community and c) economy which links to indigenous, local and global economies. The three cultural, spiritual and socio-economic value domains depicted in this model are of course interdependent and play a crucial role to people's

well-being and the relationships they develop with nature.

Geographical scales and governance levels

The conceptual framework identifies three mains scales of operation: 1) individual and local ways, 2) national and 3) international, while recognizing there are finer gradations between them; subnational, continental and so on.

Many individuals recognize a 'spiritual' dimension to their lives, and this book focuses especially on those spiritual values in relation to nature and sacred natural sites. For many however, these are expressed in a local community either with a religious grouping or an indigenous community, these may or may not have collectively identified sacred natural sites.

The framework suggests that sacred natural sites are local phenomena that can also be viewed as an international network, the conservation of which requires action at various geographical scales. Conserving local sites requires different actions and from different actors than supporting actions that help conserve single sites or a regional or national network of such sites. Recognizing sacred natural sites as a network derives as much from the indigenous custodians who strongly recognize this (Dobson and Mamyev, Chapter 23) as from conservation biology and ecological connectivity theory. Because sacred natural sites require working with multi stakeholder networks these networks ideally interact across various geographical scales and intersect with respective levels of governance. For example, the international level is inhabited with various institutions, agreements, conventions and processes where sacred natural sites are gaining increasing recognition. This way specific tools and guidance developed at this level, such as the IUCN-UNESCO and the CBD Guidelines, can be applied at other levels with respect to national and traditional governance structures. At the national level this is critical because this is where national policies are set as well as laws and state actions and it is at this level that sacred natural sites are the least recognized.

Applying interdisciplinary approaches to key areas of work

As the cultural, spiritual and socio-economic domains are increasingly understood as interrelated and mutually dependent aspects of human well-being, interdisciplinary approaches need to be developed across all governance levels and geographical scales. Interdisciplinary approaches should therefore also be inclusive and give equal weight to different ways of knowing, wisdom and sciences across different cultural worldviews. Because of the complexity of this, it is indicated that these integrated approaches should be applied to key areas for working with sacred natural sites:

- resources and funding: the conservation of sacred natural sites needs funding from a wide range of sources;
- policy and law: policies and legal frameworks are essential for the protection of sacred natural sites;
- knowledge and awareness: increased knowledge of all kinds is necessary for the proper management of sacred natural sites and in

addition there needs to be broad public awareness to garner support for their conservation;
- planning and management: appropriate inclusion of and tools for taking into account sacred natural sites in management and planning processes are of critical importance to business, industry, government and nongovernmental organizations;
- site action: effective conservation of sacred sites essentially happens in the field where sacred sites need to be safeguarded and their existence secured.

Taking into account that multidisciplinary approaches need not only be applied across these key areas but also across the cultural worldview, the contours of the effort for conserving sacred natural sites begin to draw out more clearly.

Whom is the book meant for?

The book is aimed at a wide audience including decision and policy-makers, protected area planners and managers, faith groups, local communities, scholars, students and those working in the private sectors who wish to learn about how their interests may intersect with sacred natural sites. The book may also be valuable as a comprehensive introduction to a general audience interested in learning more about the subject. More generally, the book aims to encourage and inspire people to support the communities that are custodians of these sites to continue to defend them, often in the face of considerable challenges.

Structure and scope of the book

The chapters of the book are structured into four parts:

- Section 1: Towards the science and spirituality of sacred natural sites.
- Section 2: Sacred natural sites: mutual learning, analysis, planning and management.
- Section 3: Sacred natural sites: international recognition, global governance and field action.
- Section 4: In our own hands: living culture and equity at sacred natural sites.

Each separate part of the book starts with a short introduction describing the main content of the

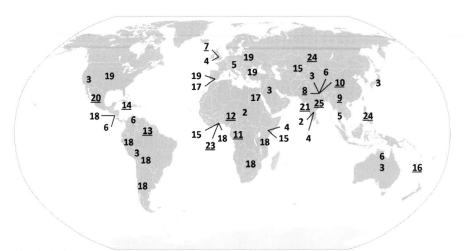

** Underlined chapter numbers indicate that this chapter solely focuses on this location.

2. Asia and Africa - A review of over 100 scientific articles.
3. Ecuador (Mt. Cotocachi), Nepal, Tibet (Mt. Kailas), American Southwest (San Francisco Peaks) and Egypt (Mt. Sinai) - Impacts and responses to global change on mountains.
4. United Kingdom (dressed trees and church gardens), Kenya (Kayas) and India (sacred groves) and many more - Stewardship for sacred trees and groves.
5. Europe (Syncretism of sacred sites and Christianity) and Thailand (Buddhist temple forests and ecological management).
6. Himalaya (Mt. Kailash), Australia (Uluru and Kakadu) and Guatemala (Tikal) - Biocultural conservation approaches for sacred natural sites.
7. United Kingdom (Lindisfarne Holy Island) - Ancient values in a modern economy.
8. Nepal (Jomolangma/Sagarmatha/Mount Everest) - Place-based spiritual values.
9. China (Yunnan Province, Holy Hills) - Bio-cultural values of forests.
10. Tibet & China (Eastern Kham) - Intangible values of earth care.
11. Cameroon (Bandjoun) - Sacred areas.
12. Nigeria (Niger Delta) - Conservation management of sacred lakes.
13. Suriname - Winti belief helps to protect forests.
14. Jamaica (Rio Grande) - Sacred natural sites among the Windward Maroons.
15. Ghana (Northern), Kenya (Kayas) and Kirgizstan (Mt. Suleiman) - UNESCO's action on sacred natural sites.

16. South Pacific; Vanuatu, (Efate, Eretoka Island), Samoa (Fagaloa Bay, Ti'avea) - Legal Protection of Sacred Natural Sites.
17. Egypt (The Nile) and Spain (Doñana National Park & El Rocío Pilgrimage) - The Ramsar convention and sacred natural sites in wetlands.
18. Guatemala (Ruins of Petén), Bolivia (Incaraqay Ruins at Santa Vera Cruz), Chile (Guillatun ritual), Peru (Tata Auzangati mountain), Zimbabwe (Marange sacred grove) and Uganda, Ghana (Tanchara wetland) - Sacred sites in endogenous development.
19. Estonia (national inventory of 2500 sacred natural sites), Spain (El Rocío Pilgrimage), Northern America (sacred mountains) and Romania (monastic lands) - Sacred natural sites in technologically developed countries.
20. Mexico, Isla Tiburon (Seri), San Louis Potosi (Wirikuta Huichols) - A methodology for the inventory of sacred natural sites.
21. India (North Western Ghats, Maharastra) - Recovery of sacred groves.
22. Ghana, (Tafi Atome, Sacred Monkey Sanctuary) – Community based ecotourism.
23. Altai Republic (Russia) - Uch Enmek Indigenous Nature Park.
24. Philippines (Palawan's Coron Island Ancestral Domain) - Sacred Marine Areas.
25. India (Biligiri Rangaswamy Temple Wildlife Sanctuary) - Mapping Soliga Sacred Natural Sites.
26. India (East-Central) - Reclaiming the Role of Sacred Natural Sites.

Figure 1.5 World map and legend linking the approximate location of sacred natural sites to the chapters in this book

Source: Bas Verschuuren

chapters and how they relate to each other. A concluding chapter wraps up the discussion and sets out general recommendations that are then elaborated in Annex 2 as a preliminary action plan for further conservation work on sacred natural sites. The sacred natural sites that are subject to the separate chapters can be viewed on a world map (see Figure 1.5) where they have been linked to the chapters that discuss them. The map can therefore be used as an index to finding the chapters in the book that discuss particular sacred natural sites that may be selected on basis of their geographical position.

The scope of the book is primarily that of sacred natural sites, the communities associated with them and their natural values. Within that scope the book portrays a broad coverage of many different contexts. The book has a broad geographical scope and includes examples of many types of religion faith and spirituality. It does not, unfortunately, have chapters focusing on Islam or Shinto, although these do form part of the body of experience from which the case studies learn (see Figure 1.1). Although the book refers to the private sector, it does not include chapters that discuss sacred natural sites in relation to the mining, forestry and transportation sectors or producers of commodities. While it does recognize that 50 per cent of humanity live in urban and suburban environments, urban sacred natural sites do exist but are not specifically covered here.

Cross cutting themes related to sacred natural sites

The conservation of sacred natural sites presents challenges and opportunities that set the stage for the individual chapters. Some cross cutting themes emerge from this that are introduced here.

Values, threats and urgency

Two of the key lessons of nearly two decades of work is that sacred natural sites have high biodiversity and cultural values and that many have already been destroyed while the remainder are under severe threat. Despite having survived hundreds and in some cases thousands of years, human-induced global change is fast diminishing them. Sacred natural sites provide a unique conservation opportunity but demand an urgency of action.

Towards understanding faith and science

Social and cultural values are explained by Jepson and Canney (2003) to be 'sets of ideals and beliefs to which people individually and collectively aspire and to which they desire to uphold. They structure the traditions, institutions and laws that underpin society.' This suggests that people believe certain things, not because they are necessarily logically evident, but because they live in a group where these ideas are supported and confirmed (Stark, 1996). The recent financial history indicates that this is evident as much in the beliefs about the behaviours of economic markets as it is in the realm of religion (Akerlof and Shiller, 2009). Reductionist science is being re-considered, leading to an increasing movement toward holism in science, not only understanding the individual parts but also how the whole functions. Blind faith in reductionist science and technology (scientism) is also being challenged (Harding, 2009). This does not mean a rejection of rationality or scientific method but a greater openness to different ways of knowing (Goodwin, 2007; see also Chapters 5 and 6). At the same time some indigenous groups are willing to put their 'indigenous sciences' under the spotlight of contemporary scientific enquiry (see for example Chapter 23). For many scientists all phenomena must come within the natural laws of the universe, whereas for many religionists certain action is attributable to supernatural forces, and this presents a fundamental difference in views. Commonality is reached, however, over a shared concern for conserving nature and culture at sacred natural sites, and shared inspiration by these biocultural icons.

Sacred natural sites and the ethics of research and inventory

It is particularly important to raise the concept of free prior, informed consent (FPIC), which has emerged as a standard for engaging with indigenous people and local communities. This is particularly important with regard to sacred natural sites. For many custodians of sacred natural sites secrecy is of the utmost importance and needs serious consideration and respect (Wild and McLeod, 2008). At the same time it needs to be recognized that research and inventory can be powerful tools for the communication and conservation of sacred natural sites.

Sacred natural sites and global change

Within the chapters of the book significant global changes have been identified, many of which affect sacred natural sites and their custodian communities. These include:

- global human population increase;
- modernity and erosion of traditional culture;
- biodiversity loss, habitat and species decline, species extinction and ecosystem damage;
- industrialization of agriculture, forestry, fisheries or other types of land and sea use;
- extractive and energy industries;
- growth of cities, urbanization and transport networks;
- increased conflict over resources;
- weakened livelihood systems and poverty;
- social and political changes and conflicts in the geopolitical realm;
- globalization of the dominant economic model based on continual growth, detached from ecological realities;
- decline in spiritual values;
- climate change.

Many of the drivers of these global changes are mutually reinforcing and affect cultural and biological diversity and the many services that sacred natural sites provide to human well-being.

Generating a greater recognition of the sacred dimensions of nature focused on sacred natural sites is expected to be an important means of building public support for the policies that conserve biodiversity, ecosystem services and the diversity of human adaptations to a changing environment. It is hoped that within its pages this book can serve as a stimulus toward that end.

References

Akerlof, G.A. and Shiller, R.J. (2009) *Animal Spirits: How Human Psychology Drives the Economy and Why it Matters for Global Capitalism*, Princeton University Press, Princeton, NJ

Berkes, F. (2008) *Sacred Ecology, Traditional Ecological Knowledge and Resource Management*, Routledge, New York and London, p314

Bird, D.N. (2002) 'Animism revisited', in Harvey, G. (ed) *Readings in Indigenous Religions*, Continuum, London, pp73–105

Carmichael, D.L., Hubert, J., Reeves, B. and Schanche, A. (1994) *Sacred Sites, Sacred Places*, Routledge, Oxford

Dudley, N., Higgins-Zogib, L. and Mansourian, S. (2005) *Beyond Belief, Linking Faiths and Protected Areas to Support Biodiversity Conservation*, WWF, Equilibrium and The Alliance of Religions and Conservation (ARC)

Frazer, J.G. (1890) *The Golden Bough*, Macmillan, London

Ghosh, A., Traverse, M., Bhattacharya, D.K., Brondizio, E.S., Spierenburg, M., deCastro, F., Morsello, C. and deSiqueira, A. (2005) 'Cultural services, policy responses', in *Volume 3: Global & Multiscale Assessment Report*, as part of the Millennium Ecosystem Assessment, Island Press, Washington, DC

Goodwin, B. (2007) *Nature's Due: Healing our Fragmented Culture*, Floris Books, Edinburgh

Graham, H. (2006) 'Animals, animists, and academics', *Zygon*, vol 41, pp9–20

Groot, R.S. de, Ramakrishnan, P.S., Berg, A.E. van den, Kulenthran, T., Muller, S., Pitt, D., Wascher, D.M., Wijesuriya, G. (2005) 'Cultural and amenity services', in *Ecosystems and Human Well-being; Volume 1 Current State and Trends*, Millennium Ecosystem Assessment Series, Island Press, Washington, DC

Harding, S. (2009) *Animate Earth: Science, Intuition and Gaia*, 2nd Edition, Green Books, Totnes, UK

Harmon, D. and Putney, A.D. (2003) 'The full value of parks: From economics to the intangible', Rowman and Littlefield A. Lanham

Jepson, P. and Canney, S. (2003) 'Values-led conservation', *Global Ecology and Biogeography*, vol 12, pp271–274

Lee, C. and Schaaf, T. (2003) 'The importance of sacred natural sites for biodiversity conservation', Proceedings of the International Workshop held in Kunming and Xishuangbanna Biosphere Reserve, People's Republic of China, 17–20 February 2003, UNESCO, Paris

Malhotra, K.C., Ghokhale, Y., Chatterjee, S. and Srivastava, S. (2001) *Cultural and Ecological Dimensions of Sacred Groves in India*, Indian National Science Academy, New Delhi

Mallarach, J.-M. and Papayannis, T. (eds) (2007) *Protected Areas and Spirituality*, IUCN and Publicacions de l'Abadia de Montserrat, Gland, Switzerland

O'Brien, J. and Palmer, M. (1997) *The Atlas of Religion*, University of California Press, Berkeley, CA

Oviedo, G. and Jeanrenaud, S. (2007) 'Protecting sacred natural sites of indigenous and traditional peoples', in Mallarach, J.M. and Papayannis, T. (eds) (2007) *Protected Areas and Spirituality*, IUCN and Publicacions de l'Abadia de Montserrat, Gland, Switzerland

Papayannis, T. and Mallarach, J.-M. (eds) (2009) 'The sacred dimension of protected areas', Proceedings of the Second Workshop of the Delos Initiative, Ouranoupolis 2007, Gland, Switzerland, IUCN and Athens; Greece: Med-INA

Posey, D. (ed) (1999) 'Cultural and spiritual values of biodiversity', a comprehensive contribution to the UNEP Global Biodiversity Assessment, Intermediate Technology Publications, London

Pungetti, G., Hooke, D. and Oviedo, G. (in press) *Sacred Species and Sites: Advances in Biocultural Conservation*, Cambridge University Press, Cambridge

Putney, A. (2005) 'Building cultural support for protected areas through sacred natural sites', in McNeely, J. (2005) *Friends for Life*, IUCN, Gland, Switzerland and Cambridge

Schaaf, T. and Lee, C. (2006) 'Conserving cultural and biological diversity: The role of sacred natural sites and cultural landscapes', Proceedings of UNESCO-IUCN International Conference, Tokyo, Japan, UNESCO, Paris

Secaira, E. and Molina, M.E, (2005) 'Planning for the conservation of sacred sites in the context of protected areas', an adaptation of a methodology and lessons from its application in the Highlands of Western Guatemala, The Nature Conservancy, UNESCO

Secretariat of the Convention on Biological Diversity (2004) 'Akwé: Kon voluntary guidelines for the conduct of cultural, environmental and social impact assessment regarding developments proposed to take place on, or which are likely to impact on, sacred sites and on lands and waters traditionally occupied or used by indigenous and local communities', CBD Guidelines Series, Montreal, p25

Stark, R. (1996) 'Why religious movements succeed or fail. A revised general model', *Journal of Contemporary Religion*, vol 11, pp133–146

UNDRIP (2007) 'Declaration on the rights of indigenous peoples, United Nations', General Assembly, 61st session, agenda item 68, Report of the Human Rights Council

Wild, R. and McLeod, C. (2008) 'Sacred natural sites. Guidelines for protected area managers', Best Practice Protected Area Guidelines Series No 16, IUCN, Gland

Section One

Towards the Science and Spirituality of Sacred Natural Sites

This section highlights scientific insights on the importance of sacred natural sites to biodiversity conservation in one of the first comprehensive reviews of biodiversity studies carried out on sacred natural sites. The human and cultural dimensions of sacred sites are also explored, based on ideas about how humans relate to two culturally significant biomes, mountains and forests. These chapters underscore the deep-rooted way that the human species has interacted with these key elements of its habitat as expressed through myth, legend and religious practice (see Figure I.1). These chapters also provide reflections of the contemporary consequences of these relationships. The phenomenon of cultural or folk religion and its implications for nature conservation is also evaluated. The section examines the rift that emerged between nature and humanity following the European Reformation and the challenges re-engagement with religion presents to the part of the scientific biodiversity community that remains rooted in reductionist science. Finally ideas are presented for bridging the divide between nature and humanity through the developing theory and practice of 'biocultural' conservation strategies with a focus on the role of sacred natural sites.

Sacred natural sites are known to have specific values for biodiversity conservation as they occur in many different ecosystems and often appear to be spared from conversion into other forms of land use. In addition to their spiritual value to one or more faith groups, sacred natural sites often harbour rare and endemic species as well as high levels of species richness in comparison to the surrounding lands. Combining 100 scientific studies Dudley et al analyse the biodiversity conservation values primarily of sacred groves in Asia and Africa. The studies cover a variety of biological and ecological research on birds, butterflies, reptiles, mammals, plant diversity, forest structure and eco-regions. They conclude that the biodiversity value of sacred natural sites is of global importance. Despite being deeply rooted in local communities many sacred groves have been destroyed or damaged, succumbing to the ecologically degrading power of the global human economy. This undermines the efficacy of sacred natural sites for biodiversity conservation and argues for their inclusion in national conservation strategies in ways supportive of their custodian communities.

Figure I.1 Mt Kailas in the Himalayas is sacred to millions of Buddhists, Hindus and Bonn shamans

See also Chapters 3 and 6.

Source: Edwin Bernbaum

Mountains represent one of humanity's strongest spiritual symbols. Religious values have contributed to the conservation of mountains and mountain biomes (see Chapter 3). These are now under threat from global changes, especially climate change which is pushing species into higher elevations and ultimately to extinction. In Chapter 3 Bernbaum analyses the cultural responses to the threats this poses to humans living in mountainous areas. As threats such as water shortages, floods and landslides become more severe, sacred natural sites may play a role in formulating responses to climate change, through local community action in collaboration with both scientists and the global popular movement countering climate change.

Forests and trees provide another universal archetype expressed within human culture. Barrow (Chapter 4) provides an overview of the sacred dimensions of trees through different religions, spiritual traditions and cultures of the world. Drawing on examples from Hinduism, Islam, Judaism, Buddhism, Animism and various indigenous cultures, Barrow describes how the practices and ritual celebrations of people's spiritual relationships with trees have contributed to the conservation of the natural world. Some of these basic religious tenets have been forgotten and leaders of indigenous religions and particularly of mainstream faiths are called to take a more conscious role of stewards of the planet's trees and forests.

Describing the spiritual qualities almost universally attributed to features of the landscape by human societies, Byrne (Chapter 5) explains the functions that 'numina' – spirits, deities or a holy presence – play in terms of agents affecting the human lives, exploring in particular the folk variants of mainstream faiths derived from their animist or other antecedents. Despite the challenges that religions present to rational reductionist conservation biologists, it is argued that a dialogue is not only necessary, but in the case of folk religionists also productive in achieving the shared goal of nature conservation. The tension, however, is not only with science but also the orthodoxies of mainstream faiths and he records the bravery of Buddhist monks drawing on folk religious elements in the front line protection of forests in the face of commercial pressures and opposition from their religious hierarchy. With the urgent need to conserve and restore nature it behoves all mainstream faiths to develop a sympathetic relationship with their folk variants which often show a deeper concern of nature and implement practical action towards nature conservation.

Verschuuren (Chapter 6) investigates how sacred natural sites have become sacred to mainstream faiths and traditional spiritualities and how sacredness is attributed to nature by contemporary means. People are also shown to place special importance on the existence and conservation of protected areas and World Heritage Sites which in some cases have grown beyond the iconic to what some might term sacred. These sacred dimensions are further explored in the context of the biological and cultural diversity that is often found at sacred natural sites all across planet earth. Biocultural conservation strategies are a suggested solution for bridging the gap between nature and culture and examples are given of how sacred natural sites play a key role in this. The chapter concludes with recommendations for sensitizing people to the spiritual dimensions of sacred natural sites.

2

Conservation of Biodiversity in Sacred Natural Sites in Asia and Africa: A Review of the Scientific Literature

Nigel Dudley, Shonil Bhagwat, Liza Higgins-Zogib, Barbara Lassen, Bas Verschuuren and Robert Wild

Summary

Sacred natural sites are frequently better protected than many officially protected areas, but an overall understanding of their role in conservation strategies is lacking. Over the last few years, scientists have assembled quantitative data from sacred natural sites, comparing their biodiversity values with those of the surrounding officially protected areas and other management approaches such as forest reserves. This chapter draws on information from over a hundred studies throughout Africa and Asia, which provides concrete evidence that many sacred natural sites have great importance to biodiversity conservation, in addition to their spiritual value to one or more faith groups. Sacred natural sites appear to be extremely common in some countries, although much remains to be learned about their global extent, as research reported in the scientific literature tends to be focused on a few countries. Sacred natural sites are often the only remaining patches of natural or semi-natural habitat in cultural landscapes (see Figure 2.1) and can contain rich biodiversity, sometimes exceeding nearby protected areas and forest reserves. Sacred natural sites are sometimes heavily modified or even planted; a proportion of these may nonetheless retain a rich complement of biodiversity at local level. Sacred natural sites are often recognized and used by local communities for their secular values, including medicinal plants, non timber forest products and other ecosystem services such as tourism or watershed protection. However, a number of problems have been identified threatening the role of sacred natural sites in long term conservation strategies. They are often too small to support a full complement of expected species and many sites are suffering from increased anthropogenic pressure, in some cases exceeding the capacity of the ecosystem to maintain its integrity. Unfortunately, many sacred natural sites are now degrading or have already disappeared in recent years. The pattern of loss has not been quantified but it is recognized to be increasing. Integration of sacred natural sites into conservation strategies can be complicated but provides an important way of preserving these unique places and the biological and cultural values they represent. Where appropriate from social and conservation perspectives, the conservation of sacred natural sites should be included in national conservation plans.

Figure 2.1 The Chewa Graveyard Forests of Malawi are often the only remaining woody vegetation in an otherwise cleared landscape

Source: Robert Wild

Rationale

Because of the long term protection they have received, many sacred natural sites support high levels of biodiversity. As a result there is increasing interest in their role in national and regional conservation strategies, either by being incorporated within protected area networks or as components of landscape approaches (Dudley et al, 2009).

In theory, such an approach, when carried out sensitively, can help support both local communities and conservation aims, by increasing levels of security for both the sacred site and its biodiversity. But mixing faith and conservation can be complicated. Some groups are concerned about loss of control over their site and risks of increased visitation. Some conservation scientists doubt the ecological value of sacred natural sites. Many questions remain about if, when and how sacred natural sites should be recognized as protected areas.

The research summarized here seeks to answer one of these questions: whether sacred natural sites have value as reserves for biodiversity. This information has been compiled from studies that sought to measure the biodiversity values of sacred groves, waters and mountains. Although English, French and Spanish literature was searched, the papers that were found and reviewed here are mainly in English. Because the question has been asked primarily by conservation scientists the survey was confined to peer-reviewed journal articles and conference papers. This is by no means to undervalue other sources of information and expertise; the current compilation should be viewed as a subset of a wider survey.

Results

Although this chapter found studies from all over the world, research tends to have been concentrated in a few places, particularly south Asia (India and Nepal), China, Ghana, Benin and Tanzania. Although the value of sacred landscapes is recognized in Latin America (e.g. Castro and Aldunate, 2003; Garcia-Frapolli et al, 2007), the Middle East (Dafni, 2006), Europe and Russia (e.g. Klubnikin et al, 2000; Mallarach and Papayannis, 2007) and Australia (Rose et al, 2003), there has been less explicit research into conservation values of sacred lands in these regions. The following results are grouped under major findings.

Geographical spread of studies on sacred natural sites

Sacred natural sites are common in many parts of Asia and Africa but broader geographic survey work is currently incomplete. However, where studies have occurred they often show a high density of sacred natural sites. India is perhaps the best surveyed country and sacred groves exist in 19 out of 28 states; it is estimated that there are between 100,000 and 150,000 such sites in the country. In addition, there are many sacred rivers, waterfalls, meadows and even individual trees (Subash Chandran and Hughes 2000; Bhagwat and Rutte 2006). For example, 240 groves were inventoried in western Kerala and a similar number in the Maharashtra region of the Western Ghats (Ramakrishnan, 1996). Kodagu district in the Western Ghats of India has over 1200 sacred groves, with one grove every 300 ha of land (Bhagwat and Rutte, 2006; see also Chapter 21). Gadgil and Vartak (1975) mention sacred groves throughout the Western Ghats, in Rajasthan, northeastern India and Madhya Pradesh. Sacred groves were found in 77 per cent of 220 villages surveyed in Orissa (Malhotra, 1998). Holy hills, among other sacred natural sites, are also common in Xishuangbanna, South Yunnan, China and detailed surveys have been undertaken (Pei and Luo 2000; see also Chapter 9).

Comparable densities of sacred natural sites are found in the few African countries where detailed surveys have taken place. In Tanzania a total of 920 traditionally protected forests have been found in sample areas in the Handeni district and Mwanga district, covering about 6000km^2 (Mwihomeke et al, 1998). In addition, the well-studied northern Ethiopian church forests contain the last fragments

of original Afromontane forests (Wassie et al, 2009).

Nature under the protection of sacred natural sites

Most of the studies described here focus on sacred groves and forest remnants; the few studies of sacred waters and other sacred features suggest that these are also a valuable source for research on sacred natural sites (for example, for sacred natural sites in wetlands see Chapters 12 and 17).

Sacred natural sites often represent the only remaining natural or semi-natural places within cultural landscapes. In the highly modified landscapes of much of Asia, sacred forests often contain the only remnants of original ecosystems, albeit frequently modified themselves. Ecological studies in northwest Yunnan, China demonstrated that sacred forests preserve old growth trees and forest structure (Salick et al, 2005; 2007). Similarly, the forest cover of Xishuangbanna, China, is decreasing and fragmenting, and some vegetation types, such as montane rainforest, can now only be found on the holy hills (Huijun et al, 2002; see also Chapter 9). The Feng Shui woods in Hong Kong are the only forests older than 60 years occurring below 500m and contain a rich tree flora including some species not found elsewhere (Zhuang and Corlett, 1997). These woodlands form the only reference point for understanding the biogeography of the original ecosystems (Marafa, 2003) and preserving the species endemic to the island.

The sacred groves of the Western Ghats in India appear to be remnants of the original forest cover, supporting rich climax vegetation including many rare plants; they are also often a last refuge for arboreal birds and mammals (Vartak and Gadgil, 1981; Gadgil and Vartak, 1981; Gadgil, 1987; see also Chapter 21). Two relatively undisturbed sacred groves in Kerala were found to be similar to other forests of the area when measures such as stem density, basal area and species diversity were compared (Chandrashekara and Sankar, 1998a). In Coromandel-Cicar, southern India, the only remaining tropical dry evergreen forests occur in the sacred groves and temple forests (Parthasarathy and Karthikeyan, 1997) and support a rich liana diversity (Sridhar Reddy and Parthasarathy, 2003).

Similar ecological characteristics of sacred groves are seen in the north (Alemmeren Jamir and Pandey, 2003). Research in Pondicherry found sacred sites protecting remnants of tropical dry evergreen forest (Ramanujam and Kadamban, 2001). Sacred trees and forests are also an integral part of the landscape of Khumbu in Nepal, where the potential role of sacred natural sites in protecting natural vegetation is recognized more generally (Bhattarai and Baral, 2008; Spoon and Sherpa, 2008). They often include substantial areas where trees are strictly protected from cutting (Sherpa, 1999; Stevens, 1999).

In Japan, the grounds of Shinto temples provide virtually the only sites of ancient lowland forests, sometimes deliberately preserved to provide building material for temples. Sacredness also protects important mountain forests. Mount Tatera, for example, is regarded as holy and the hundred hectare Tatera Forest Preserve has been strictly conserved since ancient times (Manabe et al, 2000; Miura et al, 2001). In Indonesia, the 'secret sites' of the Dani in Irian Jaya have a floristic composition that is almost identical to that of primary forest (Purwanto, 1998).

Similar patterns emerge throughout Africa. The sacred forests of Burkina Faso are remnants of formerly widespread deciduous dry forests (Guinko, 1985). In the highlands of northern Ethiopia, remnants of the original Afromontane forest vegetation are largely restricted to churchyards and other sacred groves in a matrix of cropland and semiarid degraded savannah (Aerts et al, 2006). The kaya forests of coastal Kenya are the remnants of a tropical forest ecosystem rich in rare hardwood trees and shrubs (Nyamweru, 1998). Sacred sites are the only places where some tree species are found in Serengeti, Tanzania (Kidegheso, 2008). In northern Morocco sacred forests, protected as holy burial places, have a distinct stand structure and species composition, and are considered as remnants of the original forests of the region, for example supporting large Algerian oak (*Quercus canariensis*) trees (Ajbilou et al, 2006).

Sacred sites conserving species and biodiversity

Sacred natural sites are often rich in species, being sometimes more diverse than even protected areas or forest reserves. Their remnant nature and high level of protection means that areas protected as sacred natural sites often have a particularly rich biodiversity, a phenomenon recorded continually in Africa and Asia. Local people frequently protected sacred sites more carefully than official protected areas.

For example, detailed surveys in the Jaintia Hills of northeast India found a sacred grove containing 82 tree species in 0.5ha (Upadhaya et al, 2003) and higher than average levels of vascular plant diversity in three sacred groves, including 54 endemic species (Jamir and Pandey, 2003). High diversity was also found near Pondicherry, with sacred groves containing tree species not found elsewhere in the region (Ramanujam et al, 2003) and in Sikkim (Avasthe et al, 2004). In 1995, 79 sacred groves were recorded in Meghalaya state (Tiwari et al, 1998b). One survey found 133 plant species, 4 per cent of the total species in the state, restricted to sacred forests. Of these 133 species, 96 are endemic to the state – representing 7.7 per cent of the total endemic species in Meghalaya (Latif Khan, 1997). Other surveys found over 500 rare and endangered species confined only to sacred groves in Meghalaya (Haridasan and Rao, 1985, cited in Tiwari et al, 1998b); birds, butterflies and bats, primates and small mammals all successfully conserved (Chandran et al, 1998) and high levels of biodiversity in sacred groves in Uttarkhand Himalaya (Bisht and Ghildiyal, 2007). Surveys of sacred Tibetan sites in Yunnan, China, also found high levels of species richness (Anderson et al, 2005). Similarly, a study of 10 sacred sites in Oelolok, West Timor, Indonesia, found 189 plant species. Inventories outside the sacred sites recorded only 46 species, with only 15 species found in both sacred and non-sacred sites (Soedjito and Purwanto, 2003).

In some cases sacred sites are already recognized as a critical factor in species conservation. For example, the only surviving population of *Trionyx nigricans*, the freshwater turtle, is found in Bangladesh in a sacred pond dedicated to a

Muslim saint (Gadgil, 1985, cited in Kothari and Das, 1999).

Comparing biodiversity in and outside sacred natural sites

Some surveys have compared sacred natural sites with surrounding areas, including other protected forests. An inventory of 25 sacred groves in Kodagu district suggested that they are as rich or richer in species of trees, birds and macrofungi in comparison with the government forest reserves (Bhagwat et al, 2005a). Comparison of sacred groves with government forest reserves in the Western Ghats of India found that density of fungi tended to be higher in sacred groves; despite the latter being long isolated from continuous forests they had the highest sporocarp abundance of all forest types studied (Brown et al, 2006). The biodiversity of sacred groves in Kerela was found to be very good when compared to well-protected evergreen forests. For example, the 90km² Silent Valley National Park has 960 species of angiosperms compared to 722 species in a 1.4km² area occupied by sacred groves (Rajendraprasad, 1995, Balasubramanian and Induchoodan, 1996, cited in Pushpangadan et al, 1998). Threatened trees in sacred groves in Kodagu were more abundant than in a nearby forest reserve (Bhagwat et al, 2005b). Davidar et al (2007) also found three times the plant species density in sacred sites compared with other natural forests in the Puducherry region. In general, species diversity in the sacred groves in northeastern India is much greater than in other forests (Rao et al, 1990, cited in Tiwari et al, 1998b). A survey in west Midnapore, Orissa compared bird diversity in sacred groves and surrounding sal forests; four species were recorded only from the sacred groves (Deb et al, 1997).

A survey of sacred groves of the Yi people in Yunnan, China compared plant species diversity and found that the total species and endemic species in the sacred grove were higher than those in a nature reserve and the common forest (Liu et al, 2000). A study of 28 holy hill forests of the Dai people in rare dry evergreen seasonal rainforest and semi-evergreen seasonal rainforests found 268 plant species, 15 of which are recognized by IUCN as Red List species of conservation concern. The index of plant species diversity was very near that in a comparable nature reserve (Liu et al, 2002).

Similarly, in Africa high diversity has been recorded in sacred natural sites including sacred Kaya coastal forests in Kenya (Githitho, 2003, Figure 2.2); Tanzania (Mgumia and Oba, 2003); sacred groves around graves in Morocco (Deil et al, 2005); Nigeria (Ladipo, 1998); Cote d'Ivoire (Ibo, 2005); Ghana (Telly, 2005; O'Neal-Campbell 2005); Mozambique (Virtanen, 2002); Benin (Lachat et al, 2006); and Togo, where a survey of sacred forests found 15 species new to science (Kokou et al, 2005; 2007). Decher (1997) found evidence for the ecological value of sacred groves based on a study of small mammal communities on the Accra Plains of Ghana.

Sacred natural sites, fragmentation and disturbance

The small size of many sacred sites often limits biodiversity as compared with larger areas of natural habitat, both in overall abundance and in the range of species supported. For example, studies in Ghana found that sacred groves held higher plant diversity than surrounding forest reserves (O'Neal-Campbell 2004; 2005) but less diversity of mammals (Decher and Bahian, 1999) and fruit-eating butterflies (Bossart et al, 2006). A study of 13 sacred forests in the Mpigi District of central Uganda found that these were very small and therefore contained a limited number of species (Gombya-Sembajjwe, 1998). In India, a study in Kerala found that sacred groves were too small to preserve whole ecosystems and concluded that the areas contained widely-distributed species to the disadvantage of endemic and regionally characteristic species; however, some coastal species have only survived due to the existence of sacred groves (Pascal and Induchoodan, 1998). A study in Kodagu district in the Western Ghats of India compared biodiversity of 25 sacred groves and the surrounding landscape and concluded that tree-covered landscape surrounding sacred groves is essential for maintaining biodiveristy within these forest fragments (Bhagwat et al, 2005a).

Furthermore, while some sacred groves appear to have preserved original vegetation, others have been substantially modified, reduced to areas so

Figure 2.2 Elders of Kaya Kinondo (one of 11 biodiverse sacred forests recognized as outstanding universal value as the Sacred Mijikenda Kaya Forests World Heritage Site)

Source: Robert Wild

small that they are no longer ecologically viable, or even planted. A comparison between sacred forests and a continuous forest stand in Kodagu, Western Ghats shows that human pressure in the groves has created habitat fragmentation, causing half the endemic species to disappear, being replaced by more ubiquitous species (Garcia et al, 2006). Studies of seedling mortality in some sacred groves in India suggest that they may be too small to support tree cover in the long term (Tambat et al, 2005). While mild disturbance can increase species richness, increased disturbance can sometimes lead to losses (Mishra et al, 2004) and can hamper the success of regeneration in sacred groves (Barik et al, 1996, Rao et al, 1997, cited in Tiwari et al, 1998b; Laloo et al, 2006). In other cases, increased diversity may conversely represent further changes from natural conditions. A study of Hariyali Sacred Forest in Garhwal Himalaya, which covers 5.5km², found diversity is slightly lower than in a non-sacred forest, which may be due to human induced disturbances in the latter leading to invasion by early successional species like pine (Sinha and Maikhuri, 1998).

In Indonesia, the tembawang (sacred forests) in settled parts of west Kalimantan are the only semi-natural habitat visible in many lowland areas. In fact they are planted, serving as both sacred burial sites and fruit gardens. Over time they have developed many of the characteristics of mature forests in terms of species structure and diversity (Marjokorpi and Ruokolainen, 2003).

Similarly, studies in Togo, West Africa found that while species diversity is high in sacred forest fragments, the original species composition is often altered, both through exchanges with surrounding vegetation and deliberate additions through human activities (Juhé-Beaulaton and Roussel, 2002). Chouin (2002) also challenged whether the sacred groves in Ghana are remnants of original vegetation. The northern Ethiopian Church forests have been identified as the last remnants of original afromontane forests, but are in many cases severely degraded due to anthropocentric pressures such as fire wood consumption and grazing, which have already impacted on the broader landscape outside the church forests (Bingelli et al, 2003; Aerts et al, 2006). Although anthropogenic influences are undeniable, the shrinking remnants in Ethiopia are the last remaining places where indigenous tree species regenerate naturally (Wassie et al, 2009).

Sacred natural sites and ecosystem services

Many sacred natural sites function partly as sources for valuable plants, particularly medicinal plants, and other ecosystem services; they may be managed to enhance survival of desired species. The medical uses of sacred groves has been recorded on many occasions in India (Bharuch, 1999; Boraiah et al, 2003; Devi Khumbongmayum et al, 2005; 2006), in China (Pei and Luo, 2000) and in Africa including Sierra Leone (Lebbie and Guries, 1995) and the western Usumbara Mountains of Tanzania (Msuya and Kideghesho, 2009). Sacred groves protect several crop wild relatives in Tamil Nadu, India including varieties of mango, jamun, fig and rare rattan species (Swamy et al, 2003). Sacred groves also provide people with other ecosystem services such as acting as windbreaks in parts of Rajasthan (Mitra and Pahl, 1994, cited in Kothari and Das, 1999) and provision of water sources to local villages in Maharashtra, India during the summer months (Bharuch, 1999). A study of sacred forests and hunting among the Iban people of western Kalimantan, Indonesia, found that sacred sites played an important role in peoples' livelihoods (Wadley and Colfer, 2004). Another study noted that in northern India sacred groves contain certain species that perform key functions in nutrient conservation and could play an important role in the rehabilitation of the surrounding degraded landscapes (Ramakrishnan, 1996). The role of remnant sacred forests in forest rehabilitation has also been recognized in Tibet (Miehe et al, 2003).

Challenges and threats

In general, evidence suggests that sacred natural sites have been well protected in the past. This is illustrated by aerial photographs of the Zambezi Valley of northern Zimbabwe spanning over three decades showing that loss of trees is dramatically less in forests that are considered sacred (Byers et al, 2001). The potential of sacred sites in conservation of species and ecosystem services has been reiterated in many of the papers cited earlier. However, increased pressures on resources and changing social norms and belief systems are undermining many sacred sites that have survived for hundreds of years. In 1984, for example, around 400 holy hills were identified in Xishuangbanna, China, whereas in 2005 only 250 of these were reported, of which 10–15 per cent were in a pristine state (Huabin, 2003). A surveyed forest on a holy hill revealed that 21 tree and shrub species were lost over three decades (Huijun et al, 2002). In south India 59 per cent of the area of sacred groves has been lost during the 1990s, and others may have been reduced to below their ecologically viable size (Chandrakant et al, 2004; 2006). Similarly, in Bihar, northern India, many of the ancient sacred groves established around 2400 BC have recently been degraded (Ramakrishnan, 1996). Among 166 inventoried sacred groves around Manipur only a few (11 per cent) are well preserved, while most are threatened (Devi Khumbongmayum et al, 2004; 2006). Losses are also occurring in Garhwal Himalaya (Anthwal et al, 2006). A similar pattern of loss of sacred sites is emerging in Africa, recorded in for instance Kenya (Bagine, 1998) and Zanzibar Island in Tanzania (Madewaya et al, 2004). In Australia, loss of culturally significant species such as turtle and dugong in a marine sacred site has been observed over a period of 30 years, due to the practice of unsustainable fishing methods and increasing tourism (Verschuuren et al, 2009).

Management and policy responses

Despite the effectiveness of many community-managed sacred natural sites, their values have until recently largely been ignored by conservation practitioners. Many sacred natural sites have been incorporated into government protected areas, suggesting implicit recognition of their conservation values but often without also recognizing their traditional custodians. Lack of recognition of sacred natural sites is partly due to a lack of understanding amongst conservationists, and in some cases due to traditional custodians maintaining secrecy as a form of protection or even a tenet of their faith, hence rendering the sites invisible to the eyes of outsiders. Fortunately,

this oversight is now being reversed and the potential conservation role of sacred natural sites is increasingly acknowledged. However because of the increasing pressure on natural resources, often including within sacred natural sites, it is a race against time to secure them before they disappear.

Many authors are consciously drawing links between sacred sites and conservation (e.g. Rabetaliana et al, 1999; Devi Khumbongmayum et al, 2004; Xu et al, 2006), practical management strategies are being discussed (e.g. Chandrashekara and Sankar, 1998b; Verschuuren, 2010) and conservation organisations are starting to investigate how they can be incorporated into broad conservation policies (Dudley et al, 2009; Wild and McLeod, 2008; Mallarach and Papayannis, 2007; Verschuuren, 2007). Faith groups are often supportive, because protection strengthens security of the site and usually fits into the philosophy of the faith.

Although research and guidance has been undertaken to support the integration of sacred natural sites in conservation planning and management (Verschuuren, 2007, Verschuuren et al, 2009; Wild and McLeod, 2008) further research is needed in a number of areas. These include:

* to expand the geographical range of studies;
* to increase the types of habitats and ecosystems covered;
* to generate specific management advice for custodians regarding management and regeneration of sacred natural sites.

In the light of climate change, research is also needed to assess:

* the impact of climate changes on sacred natural sites;
* their ecological and social resilience;
* options for planning adaptive measures.

Despite the increase in recent studies, the implementation of such approaches is still in its infancy and practitioners must recognize that the questions raised need to be addressed in a cross disciplinary manner (Sheridan, 2009). However, although we recognize the need for further studies, evidence for the conservation value of sacred natural sites is already clear enough to justify their incorporation within conservation strategies. It is therefore recommended that national conservation priorities urgently include the safeguarding of sacred natural sites for both their social and biological importance.

References

Aerts, R., Van Overtveld, K., Haile, M., Hermy, M., Deckers, J. and Muys, B. (2006) 'Species composition and diversity of small Afromontane forest fragments in northern Ethiopia', *Plant Ecology*, vol 187, pp127–142

Alemmeren Jamir, S. and Pandey, H.N. (2003) 'Vascular plant diversity in the sacred groves of Jaintia Hills in northeast India', *Biodiversity and Conservation*, vol 12, pp1497–1510

Ajbilou, R., Marañón, T. and Arroyo, J. (2006) 'Ecological and biogeographical analyses of Mediterranean forests of northern Morocco', *Acta Oecologica*, vol 29, pp104–113

Anderson, D.M., Salick, J., Moseley, R.K. and Xiaokun, O. (2005) 'Conserving the sacred medicine mountains: A vegetation analysis of Tibetan sacred sites in Northwest Yunnan', *Biodiversity and Conservation*, vol 14, pp3065–3091

Anthwal, A., Sharma, R.C. and Sharma, A. (2006) 'Sacred groves: Traditional way of conserving plant diversity in Garwhal Himalaya, Uttaranchal', *Journal of American Science*, vol 2, no 2, pp35–38

Avasthe, R.K., Rai, P.C. and Rai, L. K. (2004) 'Sacred groves as repositories of genetic diversity: A case study from Kabi-Longchuk, North Sikkim', *ENVIS Bulletin: Himalayan Ecology*, vol 12, no 1, pp25–29

Bagine, R.K.N. (1998) 'Biodiversity in Ramogi Hill, Kenya, and its evolutionary significance', *African Journal of Ecology*, vol 36, pp251–263

Balasubramanian, K. and Induchoodan, N.C. (1996) 'Plant diversity in sacred groves of Kerala', *Evergreen*, vol 36, pp3–4

Barik, S.K., Tripathi, R.S., Pandley, H.N. and Rao, P. (1996) 'Tree regeneration in a subtropical humid forest: Effect of cultural disturbance on seed production, dispersal and germination', *Journal of Applied Ecology*, vol 33, pp1551–1560

Bhagwat, S.A., Kushalappa, C.G., Williams, P.H. and Brown, N.D. (2005a) 'The role of informal protected areas in maintaining biodiversity in the Western Ghats of India', *Ecology and Society*, vol 10, no 1, p8

Bhagwat, S.A., Kushalappa, C.G., Williams, P.H. and Brown, N.D. (2005b) 'A landscape approach to biodiversity conservation of sacred groves in the Western Ghats of India', *Conservation Biology*, vol 19, pp1853–1862

Bhagwat, S.A. and Rutte, C. (2006) 'Sacred groves: Potential for biodiversity management', *Frontiers of Ecology and the Environment*, vol 4, no 10, pp519–524

Bharuch, E. (1999) 'Cultural and spiritual values related to the conservation of biodiversity in the sacred groves of the Western Ghats in Maharashtra', in Posey, D.A. (ed) *Cultural and Spiritual Values of Biodiversity: A Complementary Contribution to the Global Biodiversity Assessment*, United Nations Environmental Programme, Nairobi, Kenya

Bhattari, K. and Baral, S.R. (2008) 'Potential role of sacred grove of Lumbini in biodiversity conservation in Nepal', *Banko Janakari*, vol 18, pp25–31

Bingelli, P., Desissa, D., Healey, J., Painton, M., Smith, J. and Teklehaimanot, Z. (2003) 'Conservation of Ethiopian sacred groves', *European Tropical Forest Research Network Newsletter*, vol 38, pp37–38

Bisht, S. and Ghildiyal, J.C. (2007) 'Sacred groves for biodiversity conservation in Uttarkha Himalaya', *Current Science*, vol 92, pp711–712

Boraiah, K.T., Vasudeva, R., Bhagwat, S.A. and Kushalappa, C.G. (2003) 'Do informally managed sacred groves have higher richness and regeneration of medicinal plants than state-managed reserve forests?', *Current Science*, vol 84, pp804–808

Bossart, J., Opuni-Frimpong, E., Kuudaar, S. and Nkrumah, E. (2006) 'Complementarity of fruit-feeding butterfly species in relict sacred forests and forest reserves of Ghana', *Biodiversity and Conservation*, vol 15, pp333–359

Brown, N., Bhagwat, S. and Watkinson, S. (2006) 'Macrofungal diversity in fragmented and disturbed forests of the Western Ghats of India', *Journal of Applied Ecology*, vol 43, pp11–17

Byers, B.A., Cunliffe, R. and Hudak, A.T. (2001) 'Linking the conservation of culture and nature: A case study of sacred forests in Zimbabwe', *Human Ecology*, vol 29, no 2, pp187–218

Castro, V. and Aldunate, C. (2003) 'Sacred mountains of the highlands of the south-central Andes', *Mountain Research and Development*, vol 23, pp73–79

Chandrakant, M., Bhat, M.G., and Accavva, M.S. (2004) 'Socio-economic changes and sacred groves in south India: Protecting a community-based resource management institution', *Natural Resources Forum*, vol 28, pp102–111

Chandrakant, K.W., Tetali, P., Gunale, V.R., Antia, N.H. and Birdi, T.J. (2006) 'Sacred groves of Parinche Valley of Pune District of Maharashtra, India and their importance', *Journal Anthropology and Medicine*, vol 13, no 1, pp55–76

Chandran, M.D.S., Gadgil, M. and Hugues, J.D. (1998) 'Sacred groves of the Western Ghats of India', in Ramakrishnan, P.S., Saxena, K.G. and Chandrashekara, U.M. (eds) *Conserving the Sacred for Biodiversity Management*, Science Publishers, New Hamphire, USA

Chandrashekara, U.M. and Sankar, S. (1998a) 'Structure and functions of sacred groves: Case studies in Kerala', in Ramakrishnan, P.S., Saxena, K.G. and Chandrashekara, U.M. (eds) *Conserving the Sacred for Biodiversity Management*, Science Publishers, New Hamphire, USA

Chandrashekara, U.M. and Sankar, S. (1998b) 'Ecology and management of sacred groves in Kerala, India', *Forest Ecology and Management*, vol 112, pp165–177

Chouin, G. (2002) 'Sacred groves in history: Pathways to the social shaping of forest landscapes in coastal ghana', *IDS Bulletin*, vol 33, pp39–46

Dafni, A. (2006) 'On the typology and the worship status of sacred trees with a special reference to the Middle East', *Journal of Ethnobiology and Ethnomedicine*, vol 2, p26, doi:10.1186/1746-4269-2-26

Davidar, P., Nayak, K.G. and Dharmalingham, M. (2007) 'Effect of adult density on regeneration success of woody plants in natural and restored tropical dry evergreen forest fragments in Puducherry region, India', *Current Science*, vol 92, pp805–811

Deb, D., Deuti, K. and Malhotra, K.C. (1997) 'Sacred grove relics as bird refugia', *Current Science*, vol 73, no 10, pp815–817

Decher, J. (1997), 'Conservation, small mammals and the future of sacred groves in West Africa', *Biodiversity and Conservation*, vol 6, pp1007–1026

Decher, J. and Bahian, L.K. (1999) 'Diversity and structure of terrestrial small mammal communities in different vegetation types on the Accra Plains of Ghana', *Journal of Zoology*, vol 247, pp395–408

Deil, U., Culmsee, H. and Berriane, M. (2005) 'Sacred groves in Morocco: A society's conservation of nature for spiritual reasons', *Silva Carelica*, vol 49, pp185–201

Devi Khumbongmayum, A.D., Khan, M.L. and Tripathi, R.S. (2004) 'Sacred groves of Manipur: Ideal centres for biodiversity conservation', *Current Science*, vol 87, no 4, pp430–433

Devi Khumbongmayum, A., Ashalata, M.L. and Tripathi, R. (2005) 'Sacred groves of Manipur, northeast India: Biodiversity value, status and strategies for their conservation', *Biodiversity and Conservation*, vol 14, pp1541–1582

Devi Khumbongmayum, A.D., Khan, M.L. and Tripathi, R.S. (2006) 'Biodiversity conservation in sacred groves of Manipur, northeast India: Population structure and regeneration status of woody species', *Biodiversity and Conservation*, vol 15, pp2439–2456

Dudley, N., Higgins-Zogib, L. and Mansourian, S. (2009) 'The links between protected areas, faiths, and sacred natural sites', *Conservation Biology*, vol 23, pp568–577

Gadgil, M. (1985) 'Cultural evolution of ecological prudence', *Landscape Planning*, vol 2, pp285–300

Gadgil, M. (1987) 'Diversity: Cultural and biological', *TREE*, vol 2, no 12, pp369–373

Gadgil, M. and Vartak, V.D. (1975) 'Sacred groves of India: A plea for continued conservation', *Journal of the Bombay Natural History Society*, vol 73, pp314–320

Gadgil, M. and Vartak, V.D. (1981) 'Sacred groves of Maharashtra: An inventory', in Jain, S.K. (ed) *Glimpses of Indian Etnobotany*, Oxford and IBH Publishing Co, New Delhi, pp279–294

Garcia, C., Pascal, J.P. and Kushalappa, C.G. (2006) 'Les forêts sacrées du Kodagu en Inde: Ecologie et religion', *Bois et Forêts des Tropiques*, vol 288, pp5–14

Garcia-Frapolli, E., Ayala-Orozco, B., Bonilla-Moheno, M., Espadas-Manrique, C. and Ramos-Fernandez, G. (2007) 'Biodiversity conservation, traditional agriculture and ecotourism: Land cover/land use change projections for a natural protected area in the northeastern Yucatan Peninsula, Mexico', *Land Use and Urban Planning*, vol 83, pp137–153

Githitho, A.N. (2003) 'The sacred Mijikenda Kaya Forests of Coastal Kenya and biodiversity conservation', in 'The importance of sacred natural sites for biodiversity conservation', Proceedings of the International Workshop held in Kumming and Xishuangbanna Biosphere Reserve, People's Republic of China, 17–20 February 2003, UNESCO, Paris, France

Gombya-Sembajjwe, W.S. (1998) 'Sacred forests: An alternative way of conserving for cultural and biological diversity', in 'Natural sacred sites, cultural diversity and biological diversity', International Symposium UNESCO-CNRS-MNHN, Paris, 22–25 September 1998

Guinko S. (1985) 'Contribution à l'étude de la végétation et de la flore du Burkina Faso: Les reliques boisées ou bois sacrés', *Bois et forêts des Tropiques*, vol 208, pp29–36

Haridasan, K. and Rao, R. (1985) *Forest Flora of Meghalay*, Bishen Singh, Dehradun, India, vol 1

Huabin, H. (2003) 'Sacred natural sites in Xishuangbanna, in south-western China', in 'The importance of sacred natural sites for biodiversity conservation', Proceedings of the International Workshop held in Kumming and Xishuangbanna Biosphere Reserve, People's Republic of China, 17–20 February 2003, UNESCO, Paris, France

Huijun, G., Padoch, C., Coffey, K., Aiguo, C. and Yongneng, F. (2002) 'Economic development, land use and biodiversity change in the tropical mountains of Xishuangbanna, Yunnan, Southwest China', *Environmental Science and Policy*, vol 5, pp471–479

Ibo, J. (2005) 'Contribution des organisaiton non gouvernmentales ecologistes a l'amenagement des forest sacreses en Cote d'Ivoire: L'experience de la Croix Verte, Vertigo', *La revue en sciences de l'environnement*, vol 6, no 1, pp1–13

Jamir, S.A. and Pandey, H.N. (2003) 'Vascular plant diversity in the sacred groves of Jaintia Hills in northeast India', *Biodiversity and Conservation*, vol 12, pp1497–1512

Juhé-Beaulaton, D. and Roussel, B. (2002) 'Les sites religieux vodun: des patrimoines en permanente evolution', in Cormier-Salem, M.C., Juhé-Beaulaton, D., Boutrais, J. and Roussel, B. (eds) 'Patrimonialiser la nature tropicale. Dynamiques locales, enjeux', *Collection Colloques et Ceminaires*, IRD, Paris

Kidegheso, J. (2008) 'Co-existence between the traditional societies and wildlife in western Serengeti, Tanzania: Its relevancy in contemporary wildlife conservation efforts', *Biodiversity Conservation*, vol 17, pp1861–1881

Klubnikin, K., Annett, C., Cherkasova, M., Shishin, M. and Fotieva, I. (2000) 'The sacred and the scientific: traditional ecological knowledge in Siberian river conservation', *Ecological Applications*, vol 10, pp1296–1306

Kokou, K., Adjossou, K. and Hamberger, K. (2005) 'Les forêts sacrées de l'aire Ouatchi au sud-est du Togo et les contraintes actuelles des modes de gestion locale des ressources forestieres', *Revue electronique Vertigo*, vol 6, no 3

Kokou, K., Adjossou, K. and Kokutse, A.D. (2007) 'Considering sacred and riverside forests in criteria and indicators of forest management in low wood producing countries: The case of Togo', *Ecological Indicators*, vol 8, pp158–169

Kothari, A. and Das, P. (1999) 'Local community knowledge and practices in India', in Posey, D. (ed) *Cultural and Spiritual Values of Biodiversity. A Complementary Contribution to the Global Biodiversity Assessment*, UNEP, London

Lachat, T., Attignon, S., Djego, J., Goergen, G., Nagel, P., Sinsin, B. and Peveling, R. (2006) 'Arthropod diversity in Lama forest reserve (South Benin): A mosaic of natural, degraded and plantation forests', *Biodiversity and Conservation*, vol 15, pp3–23

Ladipo, D.O. (1998) 'Biological diversity in fetish groves: The case of "Igbo Oro" in Ijebu, South West Nigeria', in 'Natural sacred sites, cultural diversity and biological diversity', International Symposium UNESCO-CNRS-MNHN, Paris, 22–25 September 1998

Laloo, R.C., Kharlukhi, L., Jeeva, S. and Mishra, B.P. (2006) 'Status of medicinal plants in the disturbed and the undisturbed sacred forests of Meghalaya, northeast India: Population structure and regeneration efficacy of some important species', *Current Science*, vol 90, no 2, pp225–232

Latif Khan, M. (1997) 'Effectiveness of the protected area network in biodiversity conservation: A case-study of Meghalaya state', *Biodiversity and Conservation*, vol 6, pp853–868

Lebbie, A.R. and Guries, R.P. (1995) 'Ethnobotanical value and conservation of sacred groves of the Kpaa-Mende in Sierra-Leone', *Economic Botany*, vol 49, pp297–308

Liu, A., Pei, S. and Chen, S. (2000) 'Yi nationality's sacred groves and biodiversity conservation in Chuxiong, Yunnan' (in Chinese), *Ying Yong Sheng Tai Xue Bao (Journal of Applied Ecology)*, vol 11, no 4, pp489–492

Liu, H., Xu, Z., Xu, Y. and Wang, J. (2002) 'Practice of conserving plant diversity through traditional beliefs: A case study in Xishuangbanna, Southwest China', *Biodiversity Conservation*, vol 11, no 4, pp705–713

Madewaya, K.H., Oka, H. and Matsumoto, M. (2004) 'Sustainable management of sacred forests and their potential for eco-tourism in Zanzibar', *Bulletin of FFPRI* (Forests and Forest Products Research Institute in Japan), vol 3, pp33–48

Mallarach, J.-M. and Papayannis, T. (eds) (2007) 'Protected areas and spirituality', IUCN and Publicacions de l'Abadia de Montserrat, Gland, Switzerland

Malhotra, K.C. (1998) 'Cultural and ecological value of natural sacred sites in Orissa, India: Threats and opportunities', in 'Natural sacred sites, cultural diversity and biological diversity', International Symposium UNESCO-CNRS-MNHN, Paris, 22–25 September 1998

Manabe, T., Nishimura, N., Miura, M. and Yamamoto, S. (2000) 'Population structure and spatial patterns for trees in a temperate old-growth evergreen broad-leaved forest in Japan', *Plant Ecology*, vol 151, pp181–197

Marafa, L. (2003) 'Integrating natural and cultural heritage: The advantage of feng shui landscape resources', *International Journal of Heritage Studies*, vol 9, pp307–323

Marjokorpi, A. and Ruokolainen, K. (2003) 'The role of traditional forest gardens in the conservation of tree species in West Kalimantan, Indonesia', *Biodiversity and Conservation*, vol 12, pp799–822

Mgumia, F.H. and Oba, G. (2003) 'Potential role of sacred groves in biodiversity conservation in Tanzania', *Environmental Conservation*, vol 30, no 3, pp259–265

Miehe, G., Miehe, S., Koch, K. and Will, M. (2003) 'Sacred forests of Tibet: Using Geographical Information Systems for forest rehabilitation', *Mountain Research and Development*, vol 23, pp324–328

Mishra, B.P., Tripathi, O.P., Tripathi, R.S. and Pandey, H.N. (2004) 'Effects of anthropogenic disturbance on plant diversity and community structure of a sacred grove in Meghalaya, northeast India', *Biodiversity and Conservation*, vol 13, pp421–436

Mitra, A. and Pahl, S. (1994) 'The Spirit of the Sanctuary', *Down to Earth*, vol 2, no 17, pp21–36

Miura, M., Manabe, T., Nishimura, N. and Yamamoto, S. (2001) 'Forest canopy and community dynamics in a temperate old-growth evergreen broad-leaved forest, south-western Japan: A 7-year study of a 4-ha plot', *Journal of Ecology*, vol 89, no 5, pp841–849

Msuya, T.S. and Kideghesho, J.R. (2009) 'The role of traditional management practices in enhancing sustainable use and conservation of medicinal plants in West Usambara Mountains, Tanzania', *Tropical Conservation Science*, vol 2, pp88–105

Mwihomeke, S.T., Msangi, T.H. and Mabula, C.K. (1998) 'Traditionally protected forests and nature conservation in the North Pare mountains and Handeni district, Tanzania', *Journal of East African Natural History*, vol 87, pp279–290

Nyamweru, C. (1998) 'Ecotourism and the conservation of sacred sites: The kaya forests of coastal Kenya', in 'Natural sacred sites, cultural diversity and biological diversity', International Symposium UNESCO-CNRS-MNHN, Paris, 22–25 September 1998

O'Neill-Campbell, M. (2004) 'Traditional forest protection and woodlots in the coastal savannah of Ghana', *Environmental Conservation*, vol 31, no 3, pp225–232

O'Neal-Campbell, M. (2005) 'Sacred groves for forest conservation in Ghana's coastal savannas: Assessing ecological and social dimensions', *Singapore Journal of Tropical Geography*, vol 26, pp151–169

Parthasarathy, N. and Karthikeyan, R. (1997) 'Plant biodiversity inventory and conservation of two tropical dry evergreen forests on the Coromandel coast, south India', *Biodiversity and Conservation*, vol 6, pp1063–1083

Pascal, J.P. and Induchoodan, N.C. (1998) 'Le rôle des bois sacres du Kerala (Inde su Sud) dans la conservation de las biodiversité régionale', in 'Natural sacred sites, cultural diversity and biological diversity', International Symposium UNESCO-CNRS-MNHN, Paris, 22–25 September 1998

Pei, S.J. and Luo, P. (2000) 'Traditional culture and biodiversity conservation in Yunnan', in Xu, J.C. (ed) 'Links between cultures and biodiversity', Proceedings of the Cultures and Biodiversity Congress 2000, 20–30 July, Yunnan, China, Yunnan Sciences and Technology Press, Kunming, China

Purwanto, Y. (1998) 'Tradition sur la conservation de ressources de plantes chez les Dani de la Baliem en Irian Jaya, Indonésie', in 'Natural sacred sites, cultural diversity and biological diversity', International Symposium UNESCO-CNRS-MNHN, Paris, 22–25 September 1998

Pushpangadan, P., Rajendraprasad, M. and Krishnan, P.N. (1998) 'Sacred groves of Kerala: A synthesis on state of art knowledge', in Ramakrishnan, P.S., Saxena, K.G. and Chandrashekara U.M. (eds) *Conserving the Sacred for Biodiversity Management*, Science Publishers, New Hampshire, USA

Rabetaliana, N., Randriambololona, M. and Schachenmann, P. (1999) 'The Andringitra National Park in Madagascar', *Unasylva*, vol 196, pp25–30

Rajendraprasad, M. (1995) 'The floristic, structural, and functional analysis of sacred groves of Kerala', PhD Thesis, University of Kerala

Ramakrishnan, P.S. (1996) 'Conserving the sacred: from species to landscapes', *Nature and Resources*, vol 32, no 1, pp11–19

Ramanujam, M.P. and Kadamban, D. (2001) 'Plant biodiversity of two tropical dry evergreen forests in the Pondicherry region of south India and the role of belief systems in their conservation', *Biodiversity and Conservation*, vol 10, pp1203–1217

Ramanujam, M.P., Praveen, K. and Cyril, K. (2003) 'Woody species diversity of four sacred groves in the Pondicherry region of south India', *Biodiversity and Conservation*, vol 12, pp289–299

Rao, P.B., Barik, S.K., Pandey, H.N. and Tripathi, R.S. (1990) 'Community composition and tree population structure in a sub-tropical broad-leaved forest along a disturbance gradient', *Vegetatio*, vol 88, pp151–162

Rao, P.B., Barik, S.K., Pandey, H.N. and Tripathi, R.S (1997) 'Tree seed germination and seedling establishment in treefall gaps and understorey in a subtropical forest of northeast India', *Australian Journal of Ecology*, vol 22, pp136–145

Rose, D., James, D. and Watson, C. (2003) 'Indigenous kinship with the natural world', *National Parks and Wildlife Service*, NSW, Sydney, available at www.nationalparks.nsw.gov.au/PDFs/Indigenous_Kinship.pdf p66, last accessed 23 May 2010

Salick, J., Yongping, Y. and Amend, A. (2005) 'Tibetan land use and change near Khawa Karpo, Eastern Himalayas', *Economic Botany*, vol 59, pp312–325

Salick, J., Amend, A., Anderson, D., Hoffmeister, K., Gunn, B. and Zhengdong, F. (2007) 'Tibetan sacred sites conserve old growth trees and cover in the eastern Himalayas', *Biodiversity and Conservation*, vol 16, pp693–706

Sheridan, M.J. (2009) 'The environmental and social history of African sacred groves', *African Studies Review*, vol 52, pp73–98

Sherpa, L.N. (1999) 'Human impacts on high-altitude forest structures in the Nangpa and Hinku, Sagarmatha and Makalu Barun National Parks, Nepal', PhD Dissertation, Department of Forestry, University of Washington

Sinha, B. and Maikuri, R.K. (1998) 'Conservation through socio-cultural religious practice in Garhval Himalaya: A case study of Hariyali Sacred Site', in Ramakrishnan, P.S., Saxena, K.G. and Chandrashekara, U.M. (eds) *Conserving the Sacred for Biodiversity Management*, Science Publishers, New Hamphire, USA

Soedjito, H. and Purwanto, Y. (2003) 'Sacred sites of West Timor: Treasuries of biodiversity and cultural heritage', in 'The Importance of Sacred Natural Sites for Biodiversity Conservation', Proceedings of the International Workshop held in Kumming and Xishuangbanna Biosphere Reserve, People's Republic of China, 17–20 February 2003, UNESCO, Paris, France

Spoon, J. and Sherpa, L.N. (2008) 'Beyul Khumbu: The Sherpa and Sagarmatha (Mount Everest) National Park and Buffer Zone, Nepal', in Mallarach J.-M. (ed) *Protected Landscapes and Cultural and Spiritual Values*, Heidelberg, Kasparek Verlag, pp68–79

Sridhar Reddy, M. and Parthasarathy, N. (2003) 'Liana diversity and distribution in four tropical dry evergreen forests on the Coromandel coast of south India', *Biodiversity and Conservation*, vol 12, pp1609–1627

Stevens, S. (1999) 'Sherpa protection of the Mount Everest region of Nepal', in Posey, D. (ed) *Cultural and Spiritual Values of Biodiversity: A Complementary Contribution to the Global Biodiversity Assessment*, UNEP, London, UK

Subash Chandran, M.D. and Hughes, J.D. (2000) 'Sacred groves and conservation: The comparative history of traditional reserves in the Mediterranean area and in south India', *Environment and History*, vol 6, pp169–186

Swamy, P.S., Kumar, M. and Sundarapandian, S.M. (2003) 'Spirituality and ecology of sacred groves in Tamil Nadu', *Unasylva*, vol 54, pp53–58

Tambat, B., Rajanikanth, G., Ravikanthi, G., Uma Shaankeri, R., Ganeshaia, K.N. and Kushalappa, C.G. (2005) 'Seedling mortality in two vulnerable tree species in the sacred groves of Western Ghats, south India', *Current Science*, vol 88, pp350–352

Telly, E. (2005) 'Sacred groves, rituals and sustainable community development in Ghana', in 'Conserving cultural and biological diversity: The role of sacred natural sites and cultural landscapes', International Symposium Tokyo (Japan), 30 May–2 June 2005, UNESCO, Paris, France

Tiwari, B.K., Barik, S.K. and Tripathi, R.S. (1998a) 'Biodiversity value, status and strategies for conservation of sacred groves of Meghalaya, India', *Ecosystem Health*, vol 4, pp28–32

Tiwari, B.K., Barik, S.K. and Tripathi, R.S. (1998b) 'Sacred groves of Meghalaya', in Ramakrishnan, P.S., Saxena, K.G. and Chandrashekara, U.M. (eds) *Conserving the Sacred for Biodiversity Management*, Science Publishers, New Hampshire, USA

Upadhaya K., Pandey, H.N., Law, P.S. and Tripathi, R.S. (2003) 'Tree diversity in sacred groves of the Jaintia hills in Meghalaya, northeast India', *Biodiversity and Conservation*, vol 12, pp583–597

Vartak, V.D. and Gadgil, M. (1981) 'Studies on sacred groves along the Western Ghats from Maharashtra and Goa: Role of beliefs and folklores', in Jain S.K. (ed) *Glimpses of Indian Ethnobotany*, Oxford and IBH Publishing Co., New Delhi

Verschuuren, B. (2007) 'An overview of cultural and spiritual values in ecosystem management and conservation strategies', in Haverkort, B. and Rist, S. (eds) *Endogenous Development and Bio-cultural Diversity, The Interplay of Worldviews, Globalisation and Locality*, Compas/CDE, series on Worldviews and Sciences, No 6, Leusden, The Netherlands

Verschuuren, B, (2010) 'Integrating biocultural values in nature conservation: Perceptions of cultural significant sites and species in adaptive management', in Pungetti, G., Oviedo, G. and Hooke, D. (eds) *Sacred Species and Sites, Guardians of Biocultural Diversity*, Cambridge University Press, Cambridge, UK

Verschuuren, B, Marika, M.I.I. and Wise, P. (2009) 'Power on this land: Sacred sites management at Dhimurru Indigenous Protected Area in Northeast Arnhem Land, Australia', in Papayannis, T. and Mallarach, J.-M. (eds) (2009) *The Sacred Dimension of Protected Areas*, IUCN, Gland, Switzerland and Med-INA, Athens, Greece

Virtanen, P. (2002) 'The role of customary institutions in the conservation of biodiversity: Sacred forests in Mozambique', *Environmental Values*, vol 11, no 2, pp227–241

Wadley, R.L. and Colfer, C.J.P. (2004) 'Sacred forest, hunting and conservation in West Kalimantan, Indonesia', *Human Ecology*, vol 32, pp313–338

Wassie, A., Sterck, F., Teketay, L. and Bongers, F. (2009) 'Effects of livestock exclusion on tree regeneration in church forests of Ethiopia', *Forest Ecology and Management*, vol 257, pp765–772

Wild, R. and McLeod, C. (2008) *Sacred Natural Sites: Guidelines for Protected Area Managers*, IUCN, Gland, Switzerland

Xu, J., Ma, E.T., Tashi, D., Fu, Y., Lu, Z. and Melick, D. (2006) 'Integrating sacred knowledge for conservation value: Cultures and landscapes in southwest China', *Ecology and Society*, vol 10, no 2

Zhuang, X.Y. and Corlett, R. T. (1997) 'Forest and forest succession in Hong Kong, China', *Journal of Tropical Ecology*, vol 13, no 6, pp857–866

3

Sacred Mountains and Global Changes: Impacts and Responses

Edwin Bernbaum

Summary

As the highest features of the landscape, sacred mountains have become associated with the highest values and aspirations of cultures around the world. These associations suggest that sacred mountains have important roles to play in efforts to protect biological and cultural diversity. Mountains function as sacred natural sites in three general ways, ranging from traditional sacred mountains to places of personal inspiration. People around the world experience the sacredness of mountains through their views of them, such as mountain as centre, temple or place of revelation. The relative isolation and multiplicity of microclimates that have made mountains sanctuaries of biological and cultural diversity are now threatened by global changes. Mountains are among the first places to show signs of climate change as species are driven to higher altitude and extinction and snow cover and glaciers that supply water disappear. This chapter presents examples, ranging from Mount Cotocachi in Ecuador to the growth of dangerous glacial lakes in Nepal, of the physical and cultural impacts of glacial retreat on local communities and religious traditions along with their responses. Other kinds of global change, such as modernization and tourism, threaten to overwhelm traditional beliefs and practices that have preserved biological and cultural diversity associated with sacred mountain sites and highlight the need to adapt them to changing conditions. Examples include the re-establishment of a sacred forest in the Indian Himalaya, a foiled attempt to put a casino on top of Mount Sinai and the desecration of the San Francisco Peaks in the American southwest by a ski area development. Local communities have two options in responding to global changes: they can attempt to deal with them directly or they can try to adapt to them and mitigate their impacts. In the case of climate change, the problem is so global that communities mostly have to resort to the second option, although some religious leaders attempt to eliminate the causes of climate change through traditional beliefs and practices. Since the other kinds of changes are more regional, a mix of the two options is possible. For any measures to succeed, stakeholders, both local and non-local, need to be involved as full partners in programmes to preserve biological and cultural diversity in the face of global changes.

Introduction

Because of the way they stand out from the surrounding landscape and soar up toward the sky, mountains have a natural tendency to attract attention and inspire visions of another, higher realm of existence. The clouds that hide their summits, the storms that lash their ridges, the springs that issue from their slopes, the silence that envelopes their isolated cliffs and forests, all combine to suffuse them with an aura of mystery and power. In that aura of mystery and power, people of diverse cultural backgrounds sense the presence of something of ultimate value that gives meaning and vitality to their lives. As a consequence, many cultures and traditions regard mountains as sacred places of special significance imbued with the power to reveal higher and deeper dimensions of reality, whatever their conceptions of that reality.

As the highest, and in many ways the most distinctive, features of the natural landscape, mountains have become associated with the highest and most central values, ideals and aspirations of societies and cultures around the world. Mount Sinai stands out in Jewish tradition as the place where God made the most important covenant with the Jewish people and gave Moses the first five books of the Bible and the Ten Commandments. More than a billion Hindus and Buddhists revere Mount Kailas in Tibet as the centre of the universe and the abode of deities who embody the highest attainments of spiritual liberation. The Hopi of the American southwest regard the San Francisco Peaks – *Nuvatukya'ovi* in the Hopi language – as the dwelling place of the katsinas, ancestral spirits whom they invoke for the rains on which they depend for their existence on the dry reaches of the Colorado Plateau.

The association with the highest and most central values, ideals and aspirations of cultures around the world suggests that sacred mountains have an important role to play in efforts to protect biological and cultural diversity. By visibly linking these key values, ideals and aspirations to prominent features of the natural landscape, mountains highlight the cultural and spiritual importance of nature and provide a powerful means for galvanizing and sustaining efforts to care for the environment. The spiritual and cultural associations of sacred mountains also draw attention to the various ways in which different cultures and societies depend on their relationships with the natural world for their identity and existence.

Mountains function as sacred natural sites in three general ways. Firstly, certain mountains are singled out by religions, cultures and societies as

traditional sacred mountains, their designation clearly indicated by webs of myth, ritual, practice and belief associated with them. Secondly, mountains or mountain ranges that may or may not be revered directly, take on more diffuse auras of sacredness from the smaller sacred sites they contain within them, such as groves, springs, rocks, and places associated with holy personages. Thirdly, in a looser way, mountains may inspire a sense of wonder and awe that makes them appear sacred in the eyes of particular groups or individuals. Many people today go to mountain parks of particular beauty seeking inspiration and spiritual renewal, whether or not they ascribe to religious beliefs or belong to traditional cultures (see Chapter 6).

People experience the sacredness of mountains in different ways, primarily through the views they have of them. At least 10 of these views or themes are widely distributed around the world: the mountain as high place, centre, place of power, deity or dwelling of deities, temple or place of worship, paradise or garden, abode or body of ancestors or the dead, symbol of identity, source of water and other blessings, and place of revelation, inspiration or transformation (Bernbaum, 1997b). Global changes negatively impact not only the physical environments of mountains, but also the ways in which people view them, thereby degrading their experience of the sacred in nature.

The rugged, vertical topography of mountains means that within very small distances and areas they contain a rich diversity of microclimates. Going up only 100m can yield a change in climate equivalent to travelling as much as 100km of longitude at the same altitude. The great diversity of mountain microclimates creates multiple habitats for many different species of flora and fauna, resulting in high levels of biodiversity. The remoteness and difficulty of access of many mountainous regions has helped to preserve this biodiversity, protecting it from the kind of exploitation found in the lowlands. For this reason a large percentage of the world's parks and protected areas with intact environments and ecosystems exist today in mountains, many of which are held sacred. However, modern technology and transportation are making these previously inaccessible strongholds of biodiversity vulnerable to outside exploitation and destruction.

The inaccessibility, remoteness and varied terrain and microclimates of mountains have also made them sanctuaries of cultural diversity. The relative isolation of many mountain regions has enabled people to preserve their cultures and sacred practices and places in the face of forces that have transformed more accessible areas in the lowlands. The advent of modern communications and the growth of tourism, however, have rendered the protective isolation of mountains obsolete. Today, one can find radios, television, VCRs and even cell phones in places as remote as the Sherpa valleys of Khumbu near Mount Everest, exposing individuals and communities to the overwhelming cultural influences of the outside world (see Spoon, Chapter 8).

Sacred mountains and climate change

Among the various kinds of global changes impacting mountains, climate change is the most widespread and potentially devastating. Because of their height and multiplicity of microclimates, mountains are among the first places to show signs of climate change – and among the most vulnerable. Changes in temperature and precipitation caused by global warming are causing drastic loss of snow cover and rapid glacial retreat in mountain ranges around the world. This is a serious problem not only for mountain dwelling communities but also for billions of people living downstream, many of whom get the water they need from rivers flowing from the snow-covered heights of ranges such as the Himalaya, the Andes and the Sierra Nevada of California. The many small microclimates of mountains make them especially sensitive to global warming, as plants and animals are pushed out of narrowly circumscribed habitats and forced to move higher without enough time to adapt to new environments. Those living near the tops of mountains can go no higher and face extinction. Changes in climate also bring diseases that resident species have never encountered: as temperatures rise on sacred Hawaiian volcanoes, for example, native birds at higher elevations are succumbing to avian malaria brought up by mosquitoes from lower altitudes where they had previously been confined (Atkinson and LaPointe, 2009).

Of the many sacred mountains that are facing the effects of climate change, Cotacachi, 4966m high in northern Ecuador, presents a striking example of glacial retreat and its impacts on people and communities that revere the volcanic peak. Due to rising temperatures and decreasing precipitation, its glaciers and permanent snow cover have recently disappeared. The indigenous Quichua people who live around Cotacachi express great concern at the dwindling of springs and streams that depended on runoff from snowmelt. Before the disappearance of the glacier, they used to climb up to get ice blocks to use for healing and other purposes. While the younger people in touch with the outside world blame global climate change, their elders believe that Mama Cotacachi, as they call the sacred peak, is angry at deforestation on the lower flanks of the mountain and has withdrawn glaciers and water as a form of punishment. In response, they have made offerings to Mama Cotacachi and hired shamans to perform rituals to appease her. Local people lament that the mountain is now black, suggesting that it has lost much of its former sanctity symbolized by the white of the snow cover. The shamans feel that the change in the appearance of Cotacachi has diminished their powers as healers (Rhoades et al, 2008).

In the drier parts of the Andes – Peru, Bolivia, Argentina and Chile – where people depend more heavily on water from mountains, glacial retreat caused by global climate change is an even more serious problem. Some researchers estimate that by 2020, 80 per cent of Andean glaciers will have disappeared, leaving many communities without the reservoirs of ice on whose runoff they depend to cultivate their fields (Rhoades et al, 2008). Throughout much of the Andes, indigenous peoples worship mountain deities – known as apus in the Quechua language – invoking them for water and healing. Their shamans derive their powers to diagnose ailments from their relationship to the apu of their particular sacred mountain. Every year up to 50,000 people participate in the pilgrimage festival of Qoyllur Rit'i, which culminates in the ascent of ukukus or bear men to a glacier where they perform a ritual to the apu of Ausangate, a major sacred mountain near the ancient Inca capital of Cusco (see Figure 3.1).

Figure 3.1 Pilgrimage to Ausangate Glacier

Source: Johan Reinhard

Alarmed by the visible retreat of the glacier, which over two decades has melted back 200m, they have ceased their practice of ceremonially taking blocks of ice down for their sacred healing powers. They fear incurring the displeasure of the mountain god and contributing to the fulfilment of a prophecy that the disappearance of snow from the tops of mountains will signal the end of the world (Regalado, 2005). Fundamentalist Catholic priests have reportedly used fears of climate change to stop indigenous people ritually gathering ice as a means of purging Andean Catholicism of pre-Columbian beliefs and practices (J. Reinhard, personal communication, 2007).

In the Himalayas the rapid retreat of the Gangotri Glacier, the sacred source of the Ganges, the most sacred river in the world for Hindus, on whose life-giving waters hundreds of millions of Indians depend for their existence, has provoked great alarm for the future among scientists and meteorologists, as well as religious practitioners. Concerned environmental activists are seeking to use the peril to the glacial source of India's most sacred river to put pressure on the Indian

government to do something about reducing green house gas emissions and reversing climate change (Wax, 2007).

The melting of ice and glacial retreat caused by global warming in mountains ranging from the Andes to the Himalayas has produced a large number of dangerous lakes held back by unstable moraines of loose rocks. One of them in the Mount Everest region of Nepal, Dig Tsho, burst its retaining moraine in a glacial lake outburst flood in 1985 that caused extensive damage, taking out bridges and destroying houses and fields for kilometres downstream. The Sherpa people are especially concerned about a bigger lake, the Imja Tsho, just below Lhotse, the fourth highest mountain in the world, which has grown from a few small ponds in the 1960s to a length of more than 2km in 2006 and an average depth of more than 40m. The massive volume of water contained in Imja Tsho threatens villages, cultivated fields and a tourist trekking route from which local residents derive much of their income. Scientists studying the lake have proposed an early warning system, but the Sherpas want something done to eliminate the threat itself (Bajracharya et al, 2007; Byers, 2007; A. Byers, personal communication, 2008).

The Tengboche Rinpoche, abbot of the principal Tibetan Buddhist monastery on the Nepal side of Mount Everest, regards the valleys of Khumbu where the Sherpas live as a sacred *beyul* or hidden country set aside as a refuge for the practice of Buddhism in times of trouble (see Chapter 8). The abbot has expressed great concern over global warming and attributed the cause to a degeneration of religious observance around the world. In order to counteract this degeneration and reverse climate change, he has embarked on a programme of consecrating sacred vases and planting them in key places in the Himalayan region. In the spring of 2009, he gave one of these vases to the Sherpa who had climbed Mount Everest more times than any other person to take to the summit and leave there. He attributes a recent recession of the size of Imja Tsho glacial lake to the planting of another vase there the previous year (Tengboche Rinpoche, personal interview, 2009).

Sacred mountains and global changes

For much of the past, traditional beliefs and practices have played an important role in preserving the biological and cultural diversity associated with many sacred mountains and mountain sites. The rapid advent of modern transportation and communication, along with other manifestations of global change such as population growth and tourism, however, now threatens to overwhelm traditional controls that have preserved ecosystems and cultures associated with sacred mountains. Local communities and religious traditions need to find ways to adapt their traditional controls to changing circumstances, or the world will lose irreplaceable storehouses of cultural and biological diversity. This section will examine some of the ways in which various kinds of global change are impacting sacred mountains and the responses of the people and cultures affected by them.

The introduction of roads and modern transportation has opened many sacred mountain sites to outside pressures that threaten their natural and cultural integrity. In the early 1960s the Indian government constructed a road to the shrine of Badrinath, the major Hindu pilgrimage place in the Indian Himalaya. Whereas only a small number of pilgrims had previously managed to complete the arduous trek to Badrinath, 400,000 a year were soon coming in trucks and buses during the few months when the high altitude shrine was free of snow. The influx of visitors contributed to the destruction of a forest that included sacred bhojpatra or Himalayan birch (*Betula Utilis*). Attempts by the Indian army and department of forestry to replant trees failed. Concerned about the adverse impacts on the environment, the Rawal or Chief Priest of Badrinath joined forces with Indian scientists to consecrate saplings in a series of ceremonial plantings intended to re-establish the sacred forest. Drawing on Hindu myths and beliefs, the ceremonies generated a great deal of enthusiasm and inspired pilgrims and local villagers to participate in the plantings and to care for the trees afterwards (Purohit and Bernbaum, 1999).

Global change tends to bring with it cultural change, often in the form of westernization and secularization. For most of their history, the Japanese people have revered Mount Fuji, the highest peak in Japan, as a sacred mountain. Historically, the first person to climb the mountain was a Buddhist monk in the 12th century, and the ascent of Fuji thereafter became a religious ritual. As Japan opened to the outside world and the capital moved to modern-day Tokyo, within sight of Fuji, the sacred mountain became a national symbol and people began to climb it for other than religious reasons and by the second half of the 20th century the vast majority of climbers were tourists and recreationists; 400,000 of them in the two months of the climbing season in summer, causing severe environmental problems of litter and waste, so much so that UNESCO discouraged the Japanese government from nominating Fuji as a World Heritage Site (Bernbaum, 1997a; Sacred Land Film Project, 2009).

Increasing global demand for natural resources has put economic pressure on mountainous areas and their sacred sites, to their cultural and biological detriment. In the 1980s tourism developers and factories wanted to build hotels and harvest trees for resin in a sacred oak forest on a mountain ridge adjacent to the shrine of Binsar in the Indian Himalaya. When Mukti Datta, a resident, proposed establishing a sanctuary to protect the area, politicians representing the corporate interests tried to convince local villagers that they should block the proposal because it would restrict their traditional practice of grazing animals and gathering fodder. She, however, argued successfully that water came from the forest and that the deity of the shrine would become angry if the trees were cut down: it was the duty of the people to protect the plants and animals of the sacred site. The proposal gained additional support when the villagers learned that they could continue to graze cattle and collect fodder in the larger protected area surrounding the old growth forest and shrine at its centre. The Binsar Wildlife Sanctuary that was established in 1988 provides a positive model with broad implications for establishing new community led protected areas around previously existing sacred natural sites that would have the leadership, support and understanding of the local populace (M. Datta, personal interview, 1996).

Among the various forms of economic pressure resulting from global change, tourism probably has the greatest and most widespread impact on sacred mountains. The scenic qualities of these dramatic sites and the colourful activities associated with them draw tourists in increasing numbers, putting a strain on their environments and threatening to commercialize their cultural traditions and drain them of spiritual significance. A large number of major UNESCO World Heritage Sites are located on or are themselves sacred mountains and have had to manage the impacts of the large numbers of visitors they attract (Bernbaum, 2008; see also Chapter 15). As the example of Badrinath shows, increases in numbers of pilgrims, often facilitated by improved transportation, can also have adverse effects on the environment, while pilgrimage itself may be in danger of being marketed as a form of tourism, debasing religious beliefs and practices. In addition, because of their topography, many sacred mountains, such as the San Francisco Peaks in the United States and Mount Everest in the Himalaya, have become meccas for recreational forms of tourism such as skiing, trekking and mountaineering, leading to conflicts with traditional stakeholders and their cultural and spiritual values.

In a case that received international publicity, the Egyptian Government announced plans to build a cable car up Mount Sinai and place a casino restaurant on the summit for the benefit of tourists. The proposed development aroused worldwide consternation over the desecration of a sacred place of revelation in Judaism, Christianity and Islam. *Time* magazine published an end-piece titled 'Trashing Mount Sinai' that ended with the caustic remark: 'Perhaps they will make the cable cars in the shape of calves and gild them. The golden calves can slide up and down Mount Sinai and show God who won' (Morrow, 1990, p92). Embarrassed by the negative reaction and fearful of adverse impacts on tourism, the government cancelled the project. The abbot of the Greek Orthodox monastery of St. Catherine's at the foot of the sacred mountain (see Figure 3.2) expressed concern that increasing numbers of tourists were interfering with the practice of monasticism and adversely impacting the fragile desert environment (Archbishop Damiamos, personal interview, 1993; Grainger and Gilbert, 2008).

In the 1970s the US Forest Service and business interests proposed development schemes to expand an existing ski area on the upper slopes of the San Francisco Peaks, sacred to 12 Indian tribes, including the Hopi and Navajo, and to build condominiums on the lower slopes of the mountain. With the aid of newly acquired legal representation, Hopi elders and Navajo medicine men argued that such schemes would infringe on their freedom to practice religion by interfering with their ability to invoke the San Francisco Peaks properly in rituals that linked them to their land, brought rain to their fields and promoted their health and well-being. After winning early cases on technicalities that stopped the condominium development, they lost their legal case against expansion of the ski area in 1978. In 2008 they failed to block the usage of waste water to make snow for skiing, further enabling desecration of the sacred mountain (Bernbaum, 1997a; Sacred Land Film Project, 2009).

An emerging recognition of the cultural and spiritual values of sacred natural sites in general and sacred mountains in particular has helped some traditional stakeholders and local communities to reduce the negative impacts of global change and foster respect for their beliefs and practices.

Figure 3.2 St. Catherine's Monastery at foot of Mount Sinai

Source: Edwin Bernbaum

In 1985, recognizing the importance of Uluru, an imposing rock monolith in Australia sacred to the Anangu people, the Australian Government returned Uluru-Kata Tjuta National Park to them as the traditional owners, and they leased it back to the government as partners in park management. The Anangu role was further strengthened by UNESCO's re-designation of the park in 1994 as a World Heritage cultural landscape. Education programmes and interpretative materials run by the Ananugu asking people not to climb Uluru out of respect for Anangu culture and traditions have succeeded in reducing the percentage of visitors climbing and thereby desecrating the sacred site from 74 per cent in 1990 to 38 per cent in recent years (Uluru-Kata Tjuta National Park, 2009). In 2009 the National Park Management plan proposed a climbing ban on Uluru with expected federal support. Due to strong opposition from the tourism sector and other parties this was not approved, however it was not ruled out in the future (Reuters, 2010).

Conclusions

The examples we have examined suggest that climate change primarily affects sacred mountains as sources of water and life. As glaciers recede and weather patterns change, mountain dwellers and people living downstream from them see decreases in the water supply they need to live and increases in hazards caused by glacial lake outbursts and flooding from intense storms. Traditional cultures view these adverse impacts as more than physical phenomena with purely physical causes: water, especially water that flows from sacred mountains, has a spiritual dimension that sustains a fuller conception of life, making the effects of climate change all the more devastating, a reflection of disharmony in the forces governing the cosmos as well as of human impacts on the environment.

The other kinds of global change we have considered impact a wider range of traditional views of sacred mountains. Population pressure, modernization and economic development can undermine the integrity of sacred mountains and threaten to diminish them as symbols of tribal and national identity. The advent of mass tourism can make it impossible to sustain traditional practices that require solitude and silence. The destructive effects of extractive industries such as logging frequently collide with traditional views of sacred mountains as gardens, temples or abodes of the gods, as well as places of healing and sources of water and life.

Stakeholders and others concerned with sacred mountains can try to deal with the changes directly in the hope of eliminating their causes or they can attempt to adapt to and mitigate their impacts. In the case of climate change, there is little stakeholders can do to reduce green house gas emissions causing global warming. Most of them lack the numbers or influence to do more than mitigate local impacts and adapt to glacial retreat and loss of water at their particular sites. However, a few mountains and mountain sites that command the attention of hundreds of millions of people have the potential to galvanize national and even international support for bringing pressure on governments around the world to curb green house gas emissions. Predictions of the disappearance of the famed snows of Kilimanjaro, an icon of Africa for people around the world, have been used to highlight the need for international action on climate change (Molg et al, 2008). In October 2009, in the lead up to the Copenhagen Climate Change summit, the indigenous Aymara elders, accompanied by scientists and supporters attempted to hold a funeral rite for the Chacaltaya Glacier, Bolivia which had disappeared earlier in the year, as part of global events highlighting the need to keep atmospheric carbon to below 350 ppm. Ironically although the group reached the site of the deceased glacier they could not hold the rite due to a blizzard (350, 2009).

Within the context of traditional views of sacred mountains, some stakeholders are taking ritual measures to reduce what they see as the underlying causes of climate change – the rise of negative influences resulting from the decline of religious knowledge and observance. In Latin America, the Kogi and other indigenous tribes living on the slopes of the Sierra Nevada de Santa Marta in Colombia view their sacred mountain as the heart of the world and believe that what their tribal priests do there through rituals and warnings

can influence people elsewhere, whom they refer to as their 'younger brothers', to take actions to reverse global warming (Ereira, 1992; G. Rodriquez-Navarro, personal communication, 2009).

Many of the other forms of global change are perhaps not as overwhelming as climate change. As a consequence, local communities and other stakeholders associated with sacred mountains have greater opportunities to control and reduce the impacts of population pressure, modernization, economic development and tourism on the biological and cultural integrity of their specific sites. For them to have these opportunities, however, these stakeholders need to be acknowledged and included as full partners in programmes of protected area management that affect sacred mountains. In the case of sites that have significance for large numbers of people and widespread religious traditions, representatives of these non-local stakeholders need to be included as well: in addition to bringing their views and concerns to the table, they are often better positioned to influence the policies and actions of outside interests, such as corporations, government agencies and the general public, responsible for the impacts of global change on the biological and cultural diversity of sacred mountains.

References

350 (2009) 'A day of surprises in the mountains of Bolivia', available at www.350.org/about/blogs/day-surprises-mountains-bolivia (last accessed May 2010)

Atkinson, C.T. and LaPointe, D.A. (2009) 'Introduced avian diseases, climate change, and the future of Hawaiian Honeycreepers', *Journal of Avian Medicine*, vol 23, pp53–63

Bajracharya, B., Shrestha, A.B. and Rajbhandari, L. (2007) 'Glacial lake outburst floods in the Sagarmatha region', Mountain Research and Development, vol 27, no 4, pp336–344

Bernbaum, E. (1997a) *Sacred Mountains of the World*, University of California Press, Berkeley, Los Angeles, London

Bernbaum, E. (1997b) 'The spiritual and cultural significance of mountains', in Ives, J. and Messerli, B. (eds) *Mountains of the World: A Global Priority*, Parthenon, Oxford, pp39–60

Bernbaum, E. (2008) 'Mountains of spiritual world heritage', *World Heritage*, no 51, pp36–45

Byers, A. (2007) 'An assessment of contemporary glacier fluctuations in Nepal's Khumbu Himal using repeat photography', *Himalayan Journal of Sciences*, vol 4, issue 6, pp21–26

Ereira, A. (1992) *The Elder Brothers*, Knopf, New York

Grainger, J. and Gilbert, F. (2008) 'Around the sacred mountain: The Saint Katherine protectorate in South Sinai, Egypt', in Mallarach, J.-M. (ed) *Protected Landscapes and Cultural and Spiritual Values,* GTZ, Heidelberg, Kasparek Verlag, pp21–37

Molg, T., Hardy, D.R., Cullen, N.J. and Kaser, G. (2008) 'Tropical glaciers, climate change, and society: Focus on Kilimanjaro (East Africa)', in Orlove, B., Wiegandt, E. and Luckman, B. (eds) *Darkening Peaks: Glacier Retreat, Science, and Society*, Berkeley, Los Angeles, London, University of California Press, pp168–182

Morrow, L. (1990) 'Trashing Mount Sinai', *Time*, 19 March, p92

Purohit, A.N. and Bernbaum, E. (1999) 'Badrinath: Pilgrimage and conservation in the Himalayas', in Posey, D. (ed) *Cultural and Spiritual Values of Biodiversity*, Nairobi, United Nations Environment Programme, pp336–337

Reuters (2010) 'Ban on tourists climbing Australia's Uluru ruled out – for now', available at www.reuters.com/article/idUSTRE6070UB20100108 (last accessed March 2010)

Regalado, A. (2005) 'The Ukukus wonder why a sacred glacier melts in Peru's Andes: It could portend world's end, so mountain worshipers are stewarding the ice', *Wall Street Journal*, 17 July

Rhoades, R.E., Zapata, X. and Aragundy, J. (2008) 'History, local perceptions, and social impacts of climate change and glacier retreat in the Ecuadorian Andes', in Orlove, B., Wiegandt, E. and Luckman, B. (eds) *Darkening Peaks: Glacier Retreat, Science, and Society*, Berkeley, University of California Press, Los Angeles, London, pp216–225

Sacred Land Film Project (2009) 'Sacred site reports', available at www.sacredland.org (last accessed October 2009)

The Australian (2009) 'Proposal to ban tourists from climbing Uluru "dropped"', *The Australian*, AAP, 20 October

Uluru-Kata Tjuta National Park (2009) 'Nganana Tatintja Wiya – We Never Climb', available at www.environment.gov.au/parks/uluru/ (last accessed October 2009)

Wax, E. (2007) 'A sacred river endangered by global warming', *The Washington Post*, 17 June

4

Falling between the 'Cracks' of Conservation and Religion: The Role of Stewardship for Sacred Trees and Groves

Edmund G.C. Barrow

Summary

Sacred trees, groves and forests exist all over the world, have been important to people for thousands of years, are protected, have strict rules of use and contribute to rural livelihoods. The conservation movement has tended to downplay the importance of sacred trees and groves. Most sacred forests predate government conservation, but due to increasing pressures many groves are under threat. Forest and conservation authorities should increase support for their conservation and management. Likewise most mainstream religions could re-evaluate their relationship to trees and sacred nature because their managing institutions can provide important support for our natural and spiritual heritage. This calls for greater inter- and intra-faith harmony, and reaching out to the environmental movement.

A stewardship ethic can integrate functional and sacred values. Religious and spiritual organizations should re-affirm the importance of the stewardship of nature as a core component of human spirituality out of which emerges practical action consistent with sustainable development and conservation. A mutual concern for trees and sacred groves can engender a greater tolerance for other people's views. This chapter argues for the development of approaches within religious, spiritual and conservation contexts to understand why natural resources are important, how this can improve conservation management and a number of 'easy to implement' actions are suggested.

Introduction

This chapter summarizes key issues relating to trees and spirituality, and comes from a forthcoming book: *Trees and Spirituality: Forest Conservation is More than Mere Use*, by Edmund Barrow (Barrow, forthcoming). Most of the main spiritual beliefs traditionally had strong connections with nature, as they were founded in times dependent on nature. People held nature sacred to varying degrees, especially trees, as the writings of the many religions attest. In our increasingly materially driven world, the separation between religion, spirituality and our environment widens. Now people need to reconnect to the natural world, and what better way to do that than to hold the natural world sacred, and to respect and honour the sacred natural sites of all races, colours and creeds?

Sacred trees and groves are the focus of this chapter, as one example of the central role which nature plays. Even for the secular-minded, woods and forests still provide a special place for finding peace, silence, and beauty – precious values increasingly needed to combat the stresses of daily life. Many trees outlive the short human life by hundreds or thousands of years, and some pre-date formal religions. Religious, spiritual and conservation organizations increasingly acknowledge the importance of the environment to people's spiritual and cultural well-being. The Assisi Declarations (Palmer and Finlay, 2003; Posey, 1999) call on the main world religions to commit to the conservation of the environment. At the same time the Convention on Biological Diversity (CBD) and other multi-lateral environment agreements call for enhanced conservation and community participation (see Chapters 15 and 17).

This chapter uses the terms religion and spirituality to separate formal religious organizations (for instance the world's mainstream religions or faiths) and 'traditional spiritualities' from our spiritual connectivity with God and nature that many people experience. Spirituality focuses on the cause and involves self-reflection and personal experience which is founded on conscious stewardship. The formal religions, on the other hand, are the institutions (with rules and regulations) that serve to organize our inherent spirituality in different ways to suit different needs. In this chapter 'God' is used as a label to represent the deep inner spirituality found in us all. All cultures and religions have their term for 'God', for example 'Universal Awareness, I Consciousness, Ultimate Truth'.

Importance of sacred trees

The ancient forests and trees provided, and continue to provide, people with shelter, food and medicine, but also helped shape their consciousness. Many large and slow growing trees were and are objects of deep respect and reverence. Sacred trees have strong spiritual meanings for people for many reasons. The sheer longevity of trees is a key reason and the ancient yews (*Taxus baccata*) found in many churchyards throughout northern Europe testify to this (Lewington and Parker, 1999), as do Baobab trees (*Adansonia digitata*) in Africa. Homage has been paid to the fig tree in almost every religion and culture. The Bodhi tree (*Ficus religiosa*), under which Buddha attained enlightenment, is

a representation of the axis of the world and the tree of life (Mansberger, 1988; Boachardon, 1998). *Ficus carica* is the first plant mentioned in the Bible where the Prophet Amos was a 'Shepherd and dresser of Sycamores' (Amos, 7:14). For Hindus, the mythic World Tree is represented by a banyan (*Ficus bengalensis*) which sheltered the infant Lord Krishna (Hamilton, 1998). The world tree is associated with the sacred tree of the garden of Eden, or the Tree of Knowledge or Tree of Life (Porteus, 1996). Yigdrasil, the sacred Ash (*Fraxinus excelsior*) was the pillar supporting the different realms of the universe, in Norse, Germanic and early English cosmology. Individual trees were and are revered in many places for many reasons.

Residence of spirits

Bambara villages in Niger usually have a Tamarind tree (*Tamarindus indica*) where the spirits reside, and among the Galla in Kenya a certain tree is consecrated as holy (Porteus, 1996). In Ireland solitary thorn trees (*Crataegus monogyna*) are associated with fairies as a meeting tree. The Waramunga of northern Australia believe that certain trees harbour the spirit of a child. The Baobab has numerous cultural and mythical associations in Africa and Madagascar because of its shape, longevity, multitude of uses and as a residence of spirits (Porteus, 1996; Lewington and Parker, 1999).

Trees and marriage, birth and death

In Kenya, the Mugumu tree (*Ficus thonningii*) was planted to honour deceased clan ancestors, is sacred and to fell one is taboo (Kenya Wildlife Service and Forestry Department, 1994). Trees may be planted at the birth of a new era, as a symbol of marriage or birth. Amongst the Sioux of North America, and the San and Hottentots of South Africa, people are betrothed to a tree before marriage. Among the Dravidian people of southern India it is custom to marry two trees as a mirror of marriage (Boachardon, 1998). In some parts of Nepal tree marriage is practiced, for example to *Ficus religiosa*, or a Neem tree (*Azadirachta indica*) (Ingles, 1995).

Sacred due to tradition

Sacred groves are connected to Buddhism in China and are planted near temples. The Hindu trinity of Brahma, Vishnu and Maheshvara are believed to live among the sacred fig trees. In India, the Tulasi (*Ocimum sanctum*) has a special place among women (Gadgil, 1987; Majupuria, 1988; Ramakrishnan, 1996; Natarajan, 1999).

Trees as national monuments

Certain trees are national monuments and appear on the national flags, for example in Lebanon it is the Cedar of Lebanon (*Cedrus libani*), Canada the Maple (*Acer saccharum*) and for Chile the Monkey Puzzle tree (*Araucaria araucana*). Other species have national symbolism indicating strong cultural links and historic sanctity, e.g. the English Oak (*Quercus robur*).

Monastic and temple trees

In parts of China, holy hill forests in temple gardens were protected, though during the 1960s and 1970s many were destroyed (see Chapter 9). Since the 1980s many have been restored and the number of species is increasing. This recovery of plant diversity helps in the conservation of traditional cultures and benefits the environment (Peng et al, 2003), for example Gingko (*Ginkgo biloba*), which is important economically, survived in such gardens and is used as a basis for restoration (Verschuuren, 2007a).

Trees adorned

Many societies adorn trees with pieces of cloth and other items (Figure 4.1). The Arbor tree (*Populus nigra*) of Aston-on-Clun in England is decorated with multi-coloured flags. North of Inverness in

Figure 4.1 The Fever Tree

This tree has been dressed since pre-Christian times for the purpose of asking for healing. The ruins of the chapel to St. Wallrick stand as a witness to an attempt to assimilate the tree dressing ritual into Christianity. Today the original oak tree (Quercus robur) has been replaced by a juvenile and the site is contained in an area called 'the Holy Corner' which is part of a protected area in Weijchen, The Netherlands.

Source: Verschuuren, 2009

Scotland, a woodland is festooned with thousands of rags above the holy St. Boniface's Well (Morton, 2004). St. Ciaran's bush (Birr in Ireland), is adorned with rags and those who hang rags offer prayers for special intentions (Morton, 2004). Similar adornment is found in Asia and Africa.

Modern tree ordination

New manifestations of the sanctity of trees continue to emerge. In Thailand, Buddhist Monks have been ordaining trees as initiate monks to protect them from illegal logging. Such trees are not cut, as local people feel that this would be tantamount to killing a monk. This has helped villagers to collectively reconstruct their rights as protectors of the forest (Ganjanapan, 2000; see also Chapter 5).

Other reasons for sacredness

In many African societies a special tree is designated as the talking tree or meeting place. Among the Turkana in Kenya, people are named after trees. The Neem tree became sacred in India as a conscious decision by Hindu society (Harmon and Putney, 2003). The Japanese take care of groves that provide wood needed for temple construction (Bernbaum, 2004). Some trees are important for rain-making ceremonies (Campbell et al, 1993; Mwambo, 2000).

Many individual trees all over the world are revered, and the examples cited, though not exhaustive, demonstrate this importance, from the perspective both of conservation (variety, rarity and age) and of religions (spiritual practices, connectedness to nature).

The importance of sacred groves

Sacred groves and forests exist in most parts of the world, have been important to people for thousands of years (Table 4.1) and have been reviewed (Bhagwat and Rutte, 2006). They are protected, usually uninhabited and have strict rules of use. Traditional respect for the environment and access restrictions to sacred sites have led to well-conserved areas with high biodiversity within otherwise degraded environments (Schaaf, 2003). Sacred groves are areas of relatively undisturbed forest with often large and very old trees. While

Table 4.1 Some examples of sacred groves

Type of Site	Examples	Reasons for establishment
Garden of Gethsemane	Israel	Christian Biblical Olive Garden
Cedar groves	Mediterranean, Lebanon	
Yew trees	Europe	Graveyards where yew trees may predate the grave yard
Redwood groves	Pacific coast of N. America	Guardians of spirits of ancestors, burial grounds
Shaman forests	Machiguenga (Matsigenka) in S. Peru	Small clearings related to symbiotic relationship between *Cordia nodosa* and a species of ant – used for protection from evil forces thought to inhabit the cloud forests of the Andean foot hills.
Kaya forests	Kenya – Mjikenda people of the coast of Kenya	91 known covering an area of 10–200ha. each. Over 40 declared as 'National Monuments' and are listed as a World Heritage Site
Sacred groves	Ghana, Zimbabwe, Tanzania, Mongolia, India, Japan	In Japan Shinto and Buddhist sacred groves cover over 110,000 ha (Hamilton, 1998). Ghana has over 2000 sacred groves; China 400; Nepal hundreds; Tanzania (Zigna group) 660. In India 13,720 described but estimates are of over 100,000
Monastic groves	Ethiopia, Eritrea, United Kingdom, Nepal, Thailand	Developed by different religions, often in areas which were or have become sacred. Many of these groves are sources of important relic biodiversity

Sources: Robertson, 1987; Chandrakanth and Romm, 1991; Sayer et al, 1992; Ntiamoa-Baidu, 1995; Negussie, 1997; Jeanrenaud, 2001; Teklehaimanot and Demisse, 2001; Githitho, 2003; Urtnasan, 2003

the size of such sites may not be large, many are rich in biodiversity (Table 4.1).

Sacred groves contribute to rural livelihoods and people may be allowed to collect dry wood, fruit, honey and other products. In some areas grazing is allowed. But the felling of trees typically is not allowed without the expressed permission of the deity. In Nanhini village in Ghana no one is allowed to enter the sacred grove of the Goddess Numafoa or ignore her taboos (Jeanrenaud et al, 2001).

Sacred groves are more associated with India than any other country, where the concept of sacred groves predates the Vedic age, and many of the sacred rights were then integrated into post-Vedic-Hindu ritualism (Ramakrishnan, 1996). Sacred groves are common and locally important in southeast Asia, Africa and South America. Sacred groves are often the last refuge of endemic and endangered plant and animal species; are store-houses of medicinal plants; may contain wild relatives of crop species; may provide for the water needs of nearby communities and may help in soil and water conservation (Malhotra et al, 2001). Though many sacred groves have disappeared, those that remain are islands of biodiversity and a source of genetic material for restoration (Ramakrishnan, 2003). As such, sacred groves are important conservation assets for a number of reasons, including:

- sheer age and number of groves;
- some groves conserve important biodiversity as a by-product of their spiritual and religious values;
- examples of remnant floral communities, and are important historically and ecologically;
- traditional and religious management systems, which manage the sacred sites, are also important from the context of conservation;
- number of sacred groves can create connectivity and could be a future focus for natural forest and landscape restoration, through Indigenous and Community Conserved Areas (ICCAs);
- as a key point of entry for linking rural livelihoods to conservation.

Importance of sacred trees and groves to conservation

Nature conservation has tended to downplay the importance of sacred groves and trees stating that they are: 'too small to be viable, no connectivity in the landscape, and they don't conserve important species'. These arguments are being refuted, as many sacred groves contain endemic species, connectivity exists and can be enhanced and sacred groves offer opportunities for recognition of ICCAs that are community owned and managed (Harmon and Putney, 2003; see also Chapter 2).

Formal conservation approaches are beginning to better recognize the relationship between local environmental knowledge and communities, and between scientific and spiritual perspectives. Recognizing connectivity in the landscape and the importance of negotiated trade-offs to make optimal use of the environmental goods and services may be more sustainable and viable in the long term than the continued separation of people and nature, for example through reserving more national parks to the exclusion of local people.

This argues for decentralizing rights and responsibilities to local levels for sacred groves, and a formal recognition of such rights and responsibilities. Decentralization processes should give customary institutions greater recognition and responsibility for natural resource management. But therein lies a paradox: while such local respect and sanction may have worked in the past and still does in many places, it is increasingly difficult for those responsible for sacred sites at the community level to withstand globalization, and local or external political pressures. Many sacred sites have been included in areas that are gazetted as National Parks, e.g. Shai Hills National Park in Ghana and Mt Kenya National Park in Kenya. Others have been converted by unscrupulous business interests and politicians: where some Kayas along the Kenya coast have been cleared for the development of coastal tourism, others have found protection under the World Heritage Convention (see Chapter 15). Many are vulnerable to people of different religious beliefs and pressures to meet day to day livelihood needs.

Forest and conservation authorities need to move from mechanistic views of forest conservation, and interact more with different religions and rural people with respect to the management of forests, especially sacred ones. Cultural and spiritual values are important driving forces in conservation, but often difficult to represent in decision making (Verschuuren, 2007b). Forest and conservation authorities could engage in a range of activities for the improved management and conservation of such areas including to:

• understand traditional, customary and local institutions responsible for sacred grove management and how these can be strengthened and made more inclusive;
• implement the contents of agreements concerning environment and religion with respect to improved policies, laws and practice e.g. provisions of the CBD and the Assisi Declarations;
• better understand and map biodiversity values of sacred trees and groves;
• assist communities to gain greater statutory recognition of sacred trees and groves;
• redress past inequities, where many sacred groves and sites were reserved as Protected Areas or Forest Reserves;
• acknowledge that the variety of tree species considered sacred is important in itself;
• support diverse management approaches that foster greater connectivity in the landscape;
• engage more responsibly with religious and spiritual organizations for the better conservation management of such sacred sites (Wild and McLeod, 2008; Barrow, forthcoming).

Importance of sacred trees and groves to religions

Now is the time for mainstream religions to re-evaluate their relationship to trees and sacred nature. Many examples in sacred texts attest to the importance of sacred trees and groves. The Date palm is mentioned in the Bible, Qur'an, and Thalmud (Hareuveni, 1980; Waisel and Alon, 1980), while Mohammed once remarked 'Eat the pomegranate, for it purges the systems of every hatred' (Bolton, 1975). One hadith (or saying of

the Prophet Mohammed) states: 'When doomsday comes, if someone has a palm shoot in his hand, he should plant it.' This implies that, even when all hope is lost, such planting is good in itself (Khan, 1999). While many religions have a nature ethic, this ethic is rarely lived out and so it can become 'rhetorical tokenism'.

The Abrahamic religions (Islam, Judaism and Christianity) tend to view nature in anthropocentric terms, whereas eastern religions (Buddhism, Hinduism, Shintoism and Taoism) and the cosmovision of most indigenous and traditional peoples relate to nature in more ecocentric terms (Harmon and Putney, 2003). The religious view of nature requires re-understanding what nature is, and who we are as human beings who act upon nature, because it is impossible to discuss nature without discussing the image that we have of ourselves (Nasr, 1998).

Sacred trees and groves and their supporting institutions are an important natural and spiritual heritage. Given the importance of sacred trees and groves to all the world religions, a revival (or re-emphasis) of their importance should translate into practical action. This requires conserving such trees and groves in the context of spirituality, and calls for greater inter- and intra-faith harmony, as well as reaching out to the environmental movement, including for example to:

• acknowledge and understand the value of sacred trees and groves in terms of the spirituality of local people, irrespective of belief systems;
• implement at national and local levels, the contents of agreements concerning the environment and religion, including the Faith Declarations (Palmer and Finley, 2003), so as to integrate environment issues into pastoral work, for example the work of the Alliance of Religions and Conservation (ARC, 2009);
• appreciate the variety of social institutions and organizations who have responsibility for the management of sacred forests;
• engage with conservation organizations to better manage such sacred sites;
• redefine religious roles and responsibilities with respect to the environment and in particular to forests and trees;

- improve the advocacy role of the mainstream religions on the importance of spiritual values of the environment in wider society (nature is not normally part of religious teachings).

Reconnecting with nature: A stewardship ethic

Stewardship is to hold something in trust for another (Osland, 1999). Stewardship implies present and future responsibility for the environment, and acknowledges the many and varied roles trees and forests play in our lives. Stewardship integrates utilization and sacred values. From the perspective of sacred trees and groves, the principle of 'stewardship' means to improve the management of sacred trees and groves from both conservation and spiritual perspectives. Stewardship springs from impeccable religious and spiritual fundamentals, but is inadequately emphasized. Attitudes of stewardship in religious texts are nurtured by the four virtues of simplicity, moderation, frugality and gratitude, which are not congruent with modern economics.

Stewardship pictures human beings in harmony with nature, and the interdependence of the elements within the natural world (McDonagh, 1986). Indigenous and local peoples have a spiritual relationship with the environment that is often insightful, protective, visionary and reverent, and the language and images they use are often expressed in poetic and visual terms (Kleymeyer, 1994). Amongst Aboriginal groups in Australia it is 'looking after country' (Hill and Press, 1994), while Andean Quechuas speak of caring for 'Mother Earth'. The mainstream faiths also value stewardship. In the Biblical context, stewardship refers to humankind's responsibility for carefully husbanding God's gifts. Stewardship is firmly embedded in Islam, as Allah (God) created human kind and other creatures of the earth for a purpose. God put the human being as God's 'vice-regent' of the planet, meaning that human beings are caretakers of the environment – not the plunderers (Khan, 1999).

Stewardship has many similarities with sustainable development and conservation, where sustainable development is meeting the needs of the present generations without compromising the ability of future generations to meet their own needs (World Commission on Environment and Development, 1987). The parties to the CBD adopted 12 principles of the ecosystem approach (Shepherd, 2004), which recognize the importance of sustainable ecosystem management, and the ecosystem approach has characteristics in common with stewardship.

But there is a two-fold challenge. Religious and spiritual organizations need to acknowledge and re-affirm the importance of the stewardship of nature as a core component of human spirituality; and this needs to be translated into practical action to promote stewardship as part of spiritual work, in a manner that resonates with sustainable development. Recognizing ICCAs is one pragmatic way to steward nature, conserve sacred trees and sacred groves and could be crucial

Figure 4.2 Tree planting ceremony near Badrinath, India

Chief Priest of Badrinath joined forces with Indian scientists to consecrate saplings in a series of ceremonial plantings intended to re-establish the sacred forest.

Source: Edwin Bernbaum

components of conservation policy and practice, as the CBD now recognizes (Kothari and Pathak, 2008). This can be re-enforced by obtaining the ARC Sacred Forest FSC (Forest Stewardship Council) Standard (ARC, 2009).

Conclusion

It is a challenge for religion and conservation to collaborate so that spirituality becomes more meaningful to people and to the environment. This argues for the development of mechanisms within religious, spiritual and conservation contexts to understand why natural resources are important from a spiritual context, and how this can improve conservation management.

Sacred sites can be used as indicators of conservation value and foster the restoration of degraded areas. Scientists and custodians of sacred sites could collaborate to better understand the mechanisms for culture-based environmental conservation and formulate guidelines for decision makers for their enhanced protection (Schaaf, 2003).

In this increasingly deforested and materially driven world, the healing concepts of restoration, repair and rehabilitation have an emotional appeal on which conservationists have not yet capitalized (Hamilton, 1998). While sustainable development, livelihood security and poverty reduction are key goals for the world, we should not forget our cultural and spiritual linkages with nature. Many actions are 'easy to implement' (Brown, 1998; Barrow, forthcoming), including to:

- improve our understanding of people's spiritual and religious views of nature, trees and forests, with regard to what this means for conservation and forest management, for religion and spirituality, and to support a fuller appreciation of nature (see Chapter 6);
- understand that, while biodiversity conservation is not a primary objective, many sacred groves conserve important biodiversity, some of which is representative of relic populations (see Chapter 2);
- take increased responsibility to address the conservation and environmental crisis, in particular with respect to trees and forests,

as religion and conservation are closely intertwined (see Figure 4.2);
- respect the importance of sacred trees and groves, and understand that, while many sacred groves may be small in area, they may be very numerous and there are many more sacred groves and sacred trees than are formally acknowledged;
- develop and implement plans of work to address the integration of religious and spiritual values into forest and nature conservation;
- emphasize in religious teachings and practice the importance of the environment, natural resources and trees;
- reconnect people with place and nature, and build a greater understanding of conservation stewardship and its potential benefits to society;
- strengthen our ability to practice effective conservation stewardship, and encourage new forms of leadership at the community level, which will further partnerships for nature conservation stewardship.

People are the trustees of nature and its trees and sacred groves. To become responsible trustees requires transcending differences, within and between religious groups, and between religion and conservation. As Mahatma Gandhi said: 'There is enough for everyone's need, but not for everyone's greed' (Murphy, 1991). We should show a much greater tolerance for other peoples' views with respect to trees and sacred sites, as sacred trees and sacred groves are universal, and transcend nationality, race and religion. This respect for such sacred trees and forests is not given the importance deserved, either by conservationists or from the major religions. If by working together conservationists and faith groups can embrace their responsibilities as stewards of nature, the future will be brighter for all of creation. A good place to start is with trees.

References

ARC (2009) 'Alliance for Religions and Conservation Project overview', available at www.arcworld.org/projects_overview.asp (last accessed 30 January 2009)

Barrow, E. (forthcoming) *Trees and Spirituality: Forest Conservation is More than Mere Use*

Bernbaum, T. (2004) 'Taking back Tu B'Shevat', available at www.chabad.org (last accessed 30 January 2009)

Bhagwat, S.A. and Rutte, C.A. (2006), 'Sacred groves: Potential for biodiversity management', *Frontiers in Ecological Environmentalism*, vol 4, no 6, pp519–524

Boachardon, P. (1998) *The Healing Energies of Trees*, London, Gaia Books

Bolton, B.L. (1975) *The Secret Life of Plants*, London, Sphere

Brown, J. (1998) 'Stewardship: An international perspective', *Environments: A Journal of Interdisciplinary Studies*, vol 26, no 1, pp3–7

Campbell, B.M., Grundy, I.M. and Matose, F. (1993) 'Tree and woodland resources: The technical practices of small-scale farmers', in Bradley, P.N. and MacNamara, K. (eds) 'Living with trees: Trees for forestry management in Zimbabwe', World Bank, Washington DC, Technical Paper 210, pp29–62

Chandrakanth, M.G. and Romm, J. (1991) 'Sacred forests, secular forest policies and people's actions', *Natural Resources Journal*, vol 31, no 4, pp741–755

Gadgil, M. (1987) 'Diversity: Cultural and biological', *Tree*, vol 2, no 12

Ganjanapan, A. (2000) *Local Control of Land and Forest; Cultural Dimensions of Resource Management in Northern Thailand*, Chiang Mai, Thailand, Regional Center for Social Science and Sustainable Development, Chiang Mai University, Chang Mai

Githitho, A. (2003) 'The sacred Mijikenda Kaya forests of coastal Kenya and biodiversity conservation', in Lee, C. and Schaaf, T. (eds) 'The importance of sacred natural sites for biodiversity conservation', International Workshop on the Importance of Sacred Natural Sites for Biodiversity conservation in Kunming and Xishuangbanna Biosphere Reserve, People's Republic of China, UNESCO, Paris, p19–27

Hamilton, L.S. (1998) 'Forest and tree conservation through metaphysical constraints. Natural sacred sites', in 'Cultural diversity and biological diversity', UNESCO, International Symposium, Paris 1998, p18

Hareuveni, N. (1980) *Nature in our Biblical Heritage*, Kiryatone Israel, Neot Kedumin

Harmon, D. and Putney, A.D. (2003) 'Intangible values and protected areas: Towards a more holistic approach to management', in Harmon, D. and Putney A.D. (eds) *The Full Value of Parks: From Economics to the Intangible*, Rowman and Littlefield, New York, pp311–326

Hill, M.A. and Press A.J. (1994) 'Kakadu National Park: An Australian experience in comanagement', in Western, D., Wright, R.M. and Strum, S.C. (eds) *Natural Connections: Perspectives in Community-based Conservation*, Washington DC, Island Press, pp135–157

Ingles, A.W. (1995) 'Religious beliefs and rituals in Nepal: Their influence on forest conservation', in Halladay, P. and Gilmour, D. (eds) *Conserving Biodiversity Outside Protected Areas: The Role of Traditional Agro-Ecosystems*, Cambridge and IUCN, Gland, pp205–224

Jeanrenaud, S. (2001) 'An international initiative for the protection of Sacred Natural Sites and other places of indigenous and traditional peoples with importance for biodiveristy conservation', a concept paper, WWF International, People and Conservation, Gland, p44

Kenya Wildlife Service, and Forestry Department (1994) *Kakemega Forest: The Official Guide*, Kenya Indigenous Forest Conservation Programme, Nairobi

Khan, K.H. (1999) 'An Islamic perspective on the environment', in Dempsey, C.J. and Butkus, R.A. (eds) *All Creation is Groaning: An Interdisciplinary Vision for Life in a Sacred Universe*, Minnesota, Liturgical Press, pp46–57

Kleymeyer, C.D. (1994) 'Cultural traditions and community-based conservation', in Western, D., Wright, R.M. and Strum, S.C. (eds) *Natural Connections: Perspectives in Community-based Conservation*, Washington DC, Island Press, pp135–157, pp323–346

Kothari, A. and Pathak, N. (2008) 'Defenders of Biodiversity', *Resurgence*, vol 250, pp36–37

Lewington, A. and Parker, E. (1999) *Ancient Trees: Trees that Live for 1000 Years*, Collins and Brown, London

Majupuria, T.C. (1988) 'Religous and useful plants of Nepal and India', Botanical Survey and Herbarium, Katmandu

Malhotra, K.C, Gokhala, Y. and Chatterjee, S. (2001) *Cultural and Ecological Dimensions of Sacred Groves in India*, Indian National Science Academy and New Delhi and Indira Gandhi rashtriya Manav Sangrahalaya, New Delhi and Bhopal

Mansberger, J.R. (1988) 'In search of the tree spirit: Evolution of the sacred tree *Ficus religiosa*', in Daragavel, J., Dixon, K.E. and Semple, N. (eds) *Changing Tropical Forests*, Canberra, CRES, Australian National University, pp399–411

McDonagh, S. (1986) *To Care for the Earth: A Call to a New Theology*, Cassell Publishing, London

Morton, A. (2004) *Tree Heritage of Britain and Ireland: A Guide to the Famous Trees of Britain and Ireland*, Airlife Publishing, Shrewsbury

Murphy, M. (1991) *Why Gandhi is Relevant in Modern India: A Western Gandhian's Personal Discovery*, Ghandi Peace Foundation and Academy of Gandhian Studies, Delhi and Hyderabad

Mwambo, L.R. (2000) *Species Utilisation Preferences and Resource Potential of Miombo Woodlands: A Case of Selected Villages in Tabora, Tanzania*, Stellenbosch, University of Stellenbosch, p99

Nasr, S.H. (1998) *The Spiritual and Religious Dimensions of the Environmental Crisis*, Temenos Academy, London

Natarajan, B. (1999) 'Traditional knowledge, culture and resource rights: The case of Tulasi', in Posey, D. (ed) *Cultural and Spiritual Values of Biodiversity*, UNEP and Intermediate Technology Publications, London, pp268–270

Negussie, G. (1997) 'Use of traditional values in the search for conservation goals: The Kaya forests of the Kenyan coast', African Rainforests and the Conservation of Biodiversity, Proceedings of the Limbe Conference, Limbe

Ntiamoa-Baidu, Y. (1995) *Indigenous vs. Introduced Biodiversity Conservation Strategies: The Case of Protected Area Systems in Ghana*, WWF-Biodiversity Support Program, Washington, DC, p12

Osland, J.O. (1999) 'The stewardship of natural and human resources', in Dempsey C.J. and Butkus, R.A. (eds) *All Creation is Groaning: An Interdisciplinary Vision for Life in a Sacred Universe*, Liturgical Press, Minnesota, pp168–192

Palmer, M. and Finlay, V. (2003) *Faith in Conservation: New Approaches to Religion and Environment*, The World Bank, Washington, DC

Peng, L., Ning, W., Zhaoli, Y. and Shengji, P. (2003) 'Sacred sites in northwest Yunnan, China', in Lee, C. and Schaaf, T. (eds) 'The importance of sacred natural sites for biodiversity conservation', Proceedings of the International Workshop on the Importance of Sacred Natural Sites for Biodiversity conservation in Kunming and Xishuangbanna Biosphere Reserve, People's Republic of China, UNESCO, Paris, pp139–150

Porteus, A. (1996) *The Lore of the Forest: Myths and Legends*, Senate, London

Posey, D.A. (ed) (1999) *Cultural and Spiritual Values of Biodiversity*, UNEP and Intermediate Technology Publication, London

Ramakrishnan, P.S. (1996) 'Conserving the sacred: From species to landscapes', *Nature and Resources*, vol 32, no 1, pp11–19

Ramakrishnan, P.S. (2003) 'Biodiversity conservation: Lessons from the Buddhist "Demajong" landscape in Sikkim, India', in Lee, C. and Schaaf, T. (eds) 'The importance of sacred natural sites for biodiversity conservation', Proceedings of the International Workshop on the Importance of Sacred Natural Sites for Biodiversity conservation in Kunming and Xishuangbanna Biosphere Reserve, People's Republic of China, UNESCO, Paris, pp57–70

Robertson, S.A. (1987) *Preliminary Floristic Survey of Kaya Forests of Coastal Kenya: A Report to the Director of Museums of Kenya*, National Museums of Kenya, Nairobi, p150

Sayer, J.A., Harcourt, C.S. and Collins, N.M. (eds) (1992) *The Conservation Atlas of Tropical Forests: Africa*, IUCN, WCMC, Macmillan and BP, Cambridge

Schaaf, T. (2003) 'UNESCO's experience with the protection of sacred natural sites for biodiversity conservation', in Lee, C. and Schaaf, T. (eds) 'The importance of sacred natural sites for biodiversity conservation', Proceedings of the International Workshop on the Importance of Sacred Natural Sites for Biodiversity conservation in Kunming and Xishuangbanna Biosphere Reserve, People's Republic of China, UNESCO, Paris, pp5–12

Shepherd, G. (2004) *The Ecosystem Approach: Five Steps to Implementation*, Ecosystem Management Series 3, IUCN, Gland, Switzerland, ppvi and 31

Teklehaimanot, Z. and Demisse, A. (2001) *Biodiversity Conservation in Ancient Church and Monastry Yards in Ethiopia: Addis Ababa*, Bangor North Wales, and Addis Ababa Ethiopia, School of Agriculture and Forest Science University of Wales, and the Institute of Biodiversity Conservation and Research Addis Ababa, p25

Urtnasan, N. (2003) 'Mongolian sacred sites and biodiversity conservation', in Lee, C. and Schaaf, T. (eds) 'The importance of sacred natural sites for biodiversity conservation', Proceedings of the International Workshop on the Importance of Sacred Natural Sites for Biodiversity conservation in Kunming and Xishuangbanna Biosphere Reserve, People's Republic of China, UNESCO, Paris, pp83–97

Verschuuren, B. (2007a) *Believing is Seeing: Integrating Cultural and Spiritual Values in Conservation Management*, EarthCollective (FSD) and IUCN, Gland, Switzerland

Verschuuren, B. (2007b) 'An overview of cultural and spiritual values in ecosystem management and conservation strategies', in Haverkort, B. and Rist,

S. (eds) *Endogenous Development and Biocultural Diversity – the Interplay of Worldviews, Globalization and Society*, Compas/CDE Series on Worldviews and Sciences, No 6, Leausden

Waisel, Y. and Alon, A. (1980) *Trees of the Land of Israel*, Division of Ecology, Tel Aviv

Wild, R. and McLeod, C. (eds) (2008) 'Sacred natural sites guidelines for protected area managers', World Commission on Protected Areas, Best Practice Guidelines No. 16, IUCN and UNESCO, Gland

World Commission on Environment and Development (1987) *Our Common Future*, Oxford University Press, Oxford

5

The Enchanted Earth: Numinous Sacred Sites

Denis Byrne

Summary

Attention is drawn to the numinous character – that is having an indwelling spirit – of sacred sites, which are found in the landscapes, or 'spiritscapes' of folk religion. An overview of Southeast Asian folk religions is presented, with particular focus on Thailand, drawing out key characteristics of the relationship between people and numinous sacred sites. Commonalities are identified between Southeast Asian folk religions and the pre-Christian and medieval Christian religious systems of Europe. The radical break triggered in western religious outlook by the Reformation and the scientific revolution killed the idea of a miraculous nature, substituting it with a rationalized 'disenchanted' nature. It is suggested that the recent interest in and appreciation of sacred natural sites by western conservation biologists and others is symptomatic of a dramatic faltering of confidence in the post-Reformation view of nature.

Introduction

Sacred natural sites are mostly places numinous in character (Dudley et al, 2005; UNESCO, 2003). This is to say that those people who hold these places to be sacred believe them to be occupied or constituted by spirits or deities which have certain powers, for instance the miraculous power to cure illness or bring rain. Such powers are commonly described as supernatural or magical but the term

'numinous', indicating the presence of a divinity, seems more appropriate (Levy et al, 2006, p1114). As well as encompassing places such as the sacred mountains of Japan which are believed to be an actual embodiment of kami (Shinto spirits or gods), the category of the numinous also includes many of the Christian pilgrimage sites in Europe. The latter are often places whose sanctification stems from the presence of the bodies or relics of saints, a divine presence which is often manifest in miraculous signs which draw the faithful from afar to pray for spiritual or material benefits.

The numinous character of such sites has had particular implications for their physical integrity, including the preservation of their natural surroundings. The sites possess 'agency' – they are able, miraculously, to act upon people and effect changes in the real world (Gell, 1998). In many cases a fear of this agency, in the form of divine retribution, has been enough to prevent people physically damaging sacred places (e.g. by cutting down trees on a sacred mountain).

Numinous places are particularly associated with folk religions, as distinct from the mainstream faiths or world religions such as Buddhism, Christianity and Islam, etc. Folk religions tend to be geographically localized, are regulated verbally rather than by a written canon, and are characterized by ritual activities carried out by individual believers rather than clergy (although mediums and shamans are often involved). In 'world' religions the sacredness of place is more likely to stem from a belief that nature is the divine work of a creator God or the belief that humans should live in harmony with other life forms. Folk religions historically preceded the arrival of world religions in many parts of the world. In Indonesia and Thailand, for instance, animist religions were in place long before the arrival of Buddhism and Islam. In Europe, animist folk religions that came to be known as 'pagan' preceded Christianity. Rather than a clean break occurring between folk and world religions the tendency has been for elements of the former to continue on in popular practice. In Thailand, for instance, a belief in spirits of place (*phi*) continues to be extremely widespread (Tambiah, 1970) although the *phi* have no place in orthodox, canonical Theravada Buddhism, the state religion.

Numinous sacred sites, however, pose certain difficulties for conservation managers accustomed to basing their work on objectively observable reality. Yet the potential benefits for conservation of engaging with folk religion are immense. Given that a belief in the numinous nature of sacred sites is widespread in most of the countries of Asia, Latin America and Africa, as well as having a significant presence in Europe and the rest of the world (Duldey et al, 2005), it might even be said that we have no option but to engage with it.

Numinous sacred sites in Europe

In its spread across the Mediterranean and continental Europe in the first half of the first millennium AD, Christianity encountered numerous sacred animist sites many of which came to be incorporated into the sacred topography of Christianity (Geary, 1986; Bender, 1993, pp253–255; Meskell, 2004, pp43–44). Wells and springs were named for Christian saints and martyrs and their water became 'holy water' used in Christian rituals (Thomas, 1971, p48; Strang, 2004, p88; see also Figure 5.1). According to folkloric records based on the Celtic times, Britain and Ireland alone had more than 8000 holy wells and many of these were later venerated by Christians (Strang, 2004, pp86–88). Other pagan sites became fused with the Christian concept of the Devil. Ancient ruins, along with certain trees, caves, streams and other natural features were held to be the Devil's haunts (Russel, 1984, p71).

Figure 5.1 Pre-Christen sacred 'well' and pilgrimage destination in Westerhoven, Southern Netherlands

This well, believed to have been sacred in pre-Christian times, has been kept safe from agricultural as well as religious reformation because of its healing properties. Early Christians used the well for baptism and later it was dedicated to St. Valentinus by St. Willebrord (originally from Northumbria, see Chapter 7). Next to it a chapel arose and recently a nature reserve was created on its adjacent agricultural lands.

Source: Bas Verschuuren

The Church deployed its resources against paganism on two fronts: extirpation and assimilation. Nicole Belmont, addressing herself to the situation in Gaul, explains why assimilation was favoured:

> *In 452 the Council of Arles condemns worshippers of rocks; in 538 the Synod of Auxerre stigmatizes those who worship fountains, forests, and rocks. In 567 the Council of Tours recommends that all those who, before rocks, do things unrelated to the ceremonies of the Church be driven from the Church…The continuing struggle was apparently quite ineffective, since the Church was obliged to pursue it until well after the Council of Trent*

[1545–63]. The assimilative method met with much greater success...It consisted in Christianizing practices that were – or were considered to be – of pagan origin. 'It is the same with sacred forests as with Gentiles', declared Saint Augustine; 'one does not exterminate the Gentiles but one converts them, changes them; in the same way one does not cut down sacred groves; it is better to consecrate them to Jesus Christ'. (Belmont, 1992, p245)

In medieval Europe such sites continued to be venerated in landscapes that were increasingly also populated with sacred sites containing saints' relics or tombs. Between the 8th and the 12th centuries relics were 'the primary focus of religious devotion throughout Europe' (Geary, 1986, p169). They consisted of body parts, material associated with a saint's tomb (e.g. oil or dust), or clothing and personal belongings; they were placed in elaborate reliquaries and shrines were built to house them. The primary sacred landscape of Christianity would remain the Holy Land, but relocation of relics from there to Europe and the existence of indigenous European saints and the relics of these saints, together with apparitional sites, enabled a secondary sacred landscape. Europe, too, became a 'holy land', a landscape with its own network of religiously empowered places and objects. It is notable that in Europe – more so in southern Europe – much of the landscape of medieval Christianity remains a living reality for many people today. Thousands, for instance, continue to go on pilgrimage to sacred sites associated with the saints and some of these are now categorized as sacred natural sites (Mallarach and Papayannis, 2007; see also Chapter 17).

Most of what follows will focus on sacred natural sites in Thailand (Byrne, 2009). The purpose of including some initial remarks on numinous sites in Europe has been to guard against any assumption that such places are confined to the non-western world. Rather than being a peculiarity of religion in certain regions, what these places (or what 'the numinous') represents is a characteristic way in which humans everywhere at different times have engaged spiritually with their topographic surroundings.

Sacred natural sites in Southeast Asia

In Thailand, the Buddhist lowland majority of the population as well as 'hill tribe' minority peoples on the country's borders commonly acknowledge and honour spirits of place known as *phi*. These spirits of place are conceptualized anthropomorphically: they have rights, they respond to being treated well, they can be vengeful if harmed. Local people begin learning about such spirits from an early age, acquiring knowledge of a spiritual topography, or 'spiritscape', which coexists with the physical topography of their local landscape. Without this knowledge the landscape would be a veritable minefield of potential danger to them.

Some *phi* are associated with particular trees, fields, forests or swamps, and such striking natural features as mountains, caves, cliffs and waterfalls. These are described as 'nature spirits' by Tambiah (1970, p316). Road intersections, bridges and mountain passes also have resident *phi*. It can be argued that for Thai Buddhists rock outcrops, boulders and caves also have a 'natural sanctity': 'as for rocks, their very nature – essentially miraculous – often turns them into relics and, therefore, into objects of particular devotion' (Munier, 1998, p42). These landscape features are typically venerated via both animist and Buddhist religiosity; as well as having Buddhist shrines or even monasteries erected near them they typically also have spirit (*phi*) shrines.

The *phi* are territorial or 'cadastral' (Mus, 1975; Tannenbaum, 2000) spirits in the sense of being associated with specific points in the landscape and their 'ownership' of these places is acknowledged by the erection of small shrines where propitiatory offerings are made to them. The same has been observed of Laos: 'The *phi* are considered to have property rights that are prior to those of people – human property rights are maintained through the benevolence of the *phi*' (Thierry, 1993, p146). Turton shows how 'non-specific forest spirits' become specific when forest areas are cleared for houses or cultivation (1978, p124).

A researcher's account from southern Thailand illustrates the kind of power typically attributed to *phi*: 'On my most recent visit to Ban Kradangnga in June 1993, I heard the story of a villager, who,

Figure 5.2 A spirit (*phi*) shrine at Chiang Saen, northern Thailand

Source: D.Bryne

seduced by the high price offered for hardwood, cut down and sold a large, old saksit [sacred] dipterocarp tree where villagers customarily made offerings and vows to village spirits. Soon after this transaction, he suffered a fatal motor accident. Villagers were not slow to draw the appropriate moral' (Gesick, 1995, p69).

In Burma animist spirits are known as nats (Spiro, 1967). In Cambodia they are known as *neak-tā*. Some *neak-tā*, according to Thierry (1993, p147), are 'materialized in an object which is somehow permanent – a rock, a statue, or a piece of a statue – while others, more numerous, are content to be present invisibly, "dwelling" in a tree, on a hillock, in a termite hill, in a body of water or a confluence of the waters – marked only by the offerings placed near their supposed habitat'. These remarks could be applied in a generic sense to the rest of Theravada Buddhist Southeast Asia – Burma, Thailand, Laos and Cambodia. In Vietnam (Taylor, 2007), Malaysia and Indonesia, animism also persists in local religious practice, blending and hybridizing respectively with Mahayana Buddhism and Islam.

Assessing the sacred

Ingold urges us to think of human skills 'not as transmitted from generation to generation but [as]... regrown in each' (2000, p139). The spiritual world of folk religion is fluid rather than static; the power of specific spirits is constantly waxing

and waning, meaning that people must constantly 'grow' their knowledge of the world. As Hollan (1996, p233) describes for the Toraja of inland Sulawesi:

> *The Toraja behavioral environment is densely populated with spiritual beings of traditional, Christian and even Islamic origin. For most villagers the question is not: Which of these spiritual beings actually exist and which do not?, but rather, Which of these spiritual beings – at any given moment in one's life – has the power to influence the course of one's faith and fortune, and so should be acknowledged and perhaps propitiated ('behavioral environment' in this context indicates the landscape within which the Toraja live).*

The values assessment processes used in protected area management have been extended in recent years to encompass the spiritual values that local people assign to different areas and sites in their surrounding environment. Verschuuren (2007, p15) notes the difficulty that cultural values can pose for a values assessment process given they are likely to be based on subjective perceptions of the world which are not verifiable using western science. He writes of the propensity of spiritual values to 'get "lost in translation" travelling from experience and perception through assessment and valuation approaches before they reach decision-makers'. Local participants in folk religion are engaged in a more-or-less constant process of auditing their spiritual landscapes in the manner indicated by Hollan (above). This process might be described as a self-assessment of spiritual value.

The driver for these local self-assessment processes is the desire to gain maximum assistance from the spirit world and avoid angering it. Because people seek assistance for things of great importance to them – like ensuring rainfall or the success of an operation on an ill child – they cannot afford to make offerings to gods or spirits which do not deliver. Extensive 'gossip' circulates about miraculous phenomena and people become keen observers of the relative power and influence of different places and their associated spirits. While to outsiders folk religion may seem the ultimate in intangibility, it is actually a realm that calls for acute observation on the part of locals, observation that has similarities to the scientific programme of observation seen in western natural history. Spirits and spirit places might seem, then, to be a counterpart of the animal and plant species that local people depend upon for their livelihood and about which they acquire detailed knowledge. More accurately they might be described as elements of an integrated continuum in which the spirit realm and the natural realm are functionally incorporated into 'a complex network of reciprocal interdependence' (Ingold, 2000, p113). For Southeast Asia, exemplar case studies of cultural groups interacting with local spiritscapes are available for the Meratus Dayaks (Tsing, 1993) and the Bagak Salako (Peluso, 1992) of Kalimantan and the Temiars of Peninsula Malaysia (Roseman, 2003), among others.

Edvard Hviding has observed that folk religion at one level is an effort to manipulate the environment by means of 'magic'. But while the term 'magic' may carry connotations of the highly esoteric, actually: 'These acts appear in everyday life as highly pragmatic, observable "tools" in handling problems posed by the environment' (Hviding, 1996, p173). In the same vein, the anthropologist Raymond Firth (1996, p16) in his classic work on folk religion urges us not to regard religious beliefs as 'passive fixed items of mental furniture' but instead to consider them 'a mode of action'. Where natural environments have been preserved because of their spiritual significance, this is likely to have occurred not because of passive-fixed ideas about their sacredness but because these sites have continued to demonstrate or 'perform' the reality of their sacredness. The preservation of 'natural values' has in this sense been a by-product, rather than the aim, of folk religion.

The emergence of 'ecology monks'

While Buddhism is often seen as embodying a conservation ethic the reality is more complicated. For instance, though Thailand is a predominantly Buddhist society, many Thais conceive of forests as representing darkness and disorder in distinction to the light and civilization of cleared agricultural and urban areas (Stott, 1991). The idea of beauty

has traditionally been associated with human settlements, not with forests (Taylor, 1991). None of this is to say that Buddhism never had a presence in the forests; in fact, in Buddhist Southeast Asia, forests have a deep and profound historical importance as places where monks have sought seclusion to meditate either in forest monasteries or in caves or at other secluded spots in forests (Tambiah, 1984). Rather than repudiating the existence of the forest-dwelling spirits of folk religion, monks tested their own spiritual strength against these spirits and aimed to subdue them with the higher power of the dharma. Prior to the mid 20th century, forest monasteries in Thailand tended to be in areas of extensive forest or woodland but, as the felling of forests for timber and agriculture increased, most of the monasteries came to be situated in often quite small 'islands' of forest situated in a sea of cleared terrain. Many of these forest monasteries served as wildlife refuges, as they had done previously. Tiyavanich (1993) cites the case of a monastery in northern Thailand that was a shelter for monkeys, barking deer, banteng (a species of wild cattle) and crocodiles.

The conception of forests as a zone of darkness sits well with the Thai state's concerted rural development push in the decades following the Second World War when large areas of forest were cleared to support a rapidly growing population (from 15 million in 1938 to 52 million in 1985). It also resonated with an association of forests with the activities of communists in the 1960s and 1970s (reprising that of the Malayan Emergency 1948–60). In the 1970s many of the Buddhist clergy became 'development monks' (Darlington, 1998) who went to work with remote, poor communities, including tribal swidden agriculturalists in the forested highlands of the country's northern periphery, combining a missionary role, an effort to foster grassroots economic development and, against the background of the Indochina wars, an attempt to counter the spread of communism. Tiyavanich (1993) cites the case of a wandering monk who settled in an area near Nongkhai from 1958 to 1962, helping the local villagers to overcome their fear of spirits and clear the forest for rice fields.

All of this serves to highlight the novelty of the approach of the 'ecology monks' (Darlington,

1998) who from the 1980s have worked with rural communities to help them preserve areas of surviving forest. These monks, who comprise an estimated 2 per cent of sangha membership (Darlington, 2003), caution rural people of the dangers that unrestrained profit-seeking poses to their long term viability in local environments where forests are disappearing, over-cropped land is eroding, streams are drying up and rivers are becoming polluted. What is particularly interesting is the way the ecology monks have relied principally on the numinous tenets of Thai folk religion to gain local support for the community conservation areas they promote rather than on Buddhist doctrine itself.

Many prominent ecology monks have modified traditional Buddhist rituals in order to carry out the 'ordination' of particular trees to safeguard them from felling. The ordination of trees, in which saffron 'robes' are tied around them, has the effect of altering their state as physical entities such that it subsequently becomes spiritually hazardous to harm them. Darlington (2003) describes how, in cases she has observed, the guardian *phi* of villages where community forests have been designated have been ritually called upon to give their own protection to the forest. In one tree ordination ceremony, a monk sanctified a bowl of water from which each of the village headmen drank, ritually binding them to protect the forest which was also ritually sanctified during the same ceremony (Darlington, 1998).

In Tannenbaum's (2000) view, tree ordinations also serve to ritually connect the village community to the national community. The King's endorsement of tree ordination in the mid 1990s endowed the activity with a national frame of reference and a new validity.

While it is clearly understood by both the monks and the villagers that an ordained tree is not equivalent to an ordained human, the ordination ritual nevertheless confers anthropomorphic qualities on a tree and on the sanctified forest in which it stands, qualities that contribute to its protection. In a similar innovation, a 'long-life ceremony' that previously was only performed on ill or old people was performed on the Nan River in 1993 by the monk Phrakhru Pitak (Darlington, 2005). This ceremony extended to the river a form of the ritual protection that would normally apply only to humans. Elsewhere in northern Thailand monks have performed the long-life ceremony on community forests (Tannenbaum, 2000). In the interests of conservation, the ecology monks can be seen to be consciously and strategically drawing upon folk religion's idea of numismatic power residing in natural sites and species.

Modernism and religion

If ecology monks have been innovative then they should also be credited as being quite brave. As Darlington (2005) shows, the conservative Buddhist clerical hierarchy has actively opposed and censured ecology monks. The ecology monks have also antagonized commercial interest groups, including the Thai military, large sections of which have been involved in illegal logging and in land development projects, and through their grass-roots activism the monks have exposed themselves to harassment and even personal harm from these powerful interests.

The phenomenon of tree ordination has been addressed at some length here because it would seem to parallel in some ways the international move by conservationists to recognize and support sacred natural sites. Both the ecology monks and those conservationists involved in assessing the cultural and spiritual values of conservation have recognized that folk religion has been instrumental in preserving the natural values of certain areas of landscape. This particular 'turn to the local', however, can be expected to encounter extra-local institutional obstacles. To understand why this is so it is necessary to take an historical view and return to what happened in Europe after medieval times.

At the broadest level, a move to revalidate local sacred sites would seem to work against the current of global modernity. By modernity we mean that series of developments in which, beginning in 17th-century Europe, scientific discoveries provide a platform for an industrial revolution that rapidly increased the economic base of the west and allowed it to extend its influence globally. At the level of religion, the 16th-century Protestant Reformation introduced a relatively narrow view of the ways in which God was manifest. Whereas in Medieval Christianity

God was a living presence in the landscape, manifest in the miraculous efficacy flowing from saintly people, sacred relics and sacred places, in the Protestant view, particularly the Calvinist view, religion was to be a matter between one's soul and a god who dwelt in heaven (Eire, 1986). This effectively removed God from nature as an active, causal force, opening the natural world up to understanding through learned inquiry. It is in this sense that one speaks of the 'disenchantment' of the post-Reformation landscape.

The sociologist Max Weber (1864–1920) wrote: 'The fate of our times is characterized by rationalization and, above all, by the "disenchantment of the world"' (Weber, 1946). He saw this as an inevitable result of a nexus between Protestantism and capitalism, particularly Calvinist capitalism, which sanctified worldly economic effort at the same time as it repudiated belief in the presence of magical and sacramental forces in the landscape.

The Protestant Reformation was partly a reaction against the 'magical' or supernatural element in Catholic popular religion which ascribed miraculous powers to relics and holy places. Counter-Reformation Catholicism, at the Council of Trent (1545–1563), for its part, validated the worship of holy images but warned against regarding them as possessing power in their own right. The revolution in European scientific thought that took place in the 17th century complemented key tenets of the Reformation; in Keith Thomas's (1971, p643) words: 'The notion that the universe was subject to immutable natural laws killed the concept of miracles.' And yet, as noted earlier, the idea among European Christians that certain holy sites have numinous powers has persisted into the present and many of these sites continue to draw pilgrims hoping to benefit from their place-based powers e.g., Santiago de Compostela in Spain, Croagh Patrick in Ireland, Lindisfarne in England (see Chapter 7; Mallarach and Papayannis, 2007).

Modernity came to Asia partly via those colonial governments and education systems installed by western powers in such places as India, Indonesia, the Philippines and Vietnam, partly through indigenous modernizing governments in Japan and Thailand in the second half of the 19th century and partly through the efforts of new generations of the educated elite who saw modernization as the only way to gain an equal footing with the west. Western colonial administrators, Christian missionaries and Asian modernists all identified folk religion as an impediment to modern advancement. Folk beliefs and their associated numinous sacred sites became almost synonymous with the pre-modern state and were given no recognition or role in the institutions of modern education, health care and political administration which were being established as the framework of the new nation state (Anderson, 1991).

Sacred nature in a cosmopolitan world

This chapter has taken as its focus what is perhaps the most 'difficult' issue that sacred natural sites pose for the conservation movement, namely the fact that most modern rationalists do not believe in the reality of the numinous forces that give the majority of these sites their significance to local believers. From its beginnings in 17th-century Europe, modernity has tended to dismiss folk religion as a superseded world view that is now of merely historical interest. Impatient with talk of the non-rational, modernity in its early and middle periods concentrated on technologies of control, including those for the control of nature and the control of colonized people.

Since the second half of the 20th century, however, realization has grown that we are not in control of nature and that nature, in fact, is capable of biting back in unexpected and potentially catastrophic ways. The overweening confidence of high modernism has been badly shaken and destabilized, leading to an increasing openness to cultural differences and alternative view points. The IUCN's embracing of sacred natural sites is an illustration of this: an international community of (predominantly) conservation biologists, practitioners of rigorous science, has willingly stepped outside its 'comfort zone' and engaged with a category of places, the reality of beliefs about which it cannot objectively measure, quantify or verify. This speaks to the cosmopolitan hue of late modernity.

According to the philosopher Kwame Anthony Appiah (2006, p57), while value judgements may differ: 'Cosmopolitans suppose that all cultures have enough overlap in their vocabulary of values to begin a conversation.' Thus conservationists perceive that although belief in the numinous powers of place is strictly non-rational, conservation biology and folk religion have in common the fact that both act to preserve biodiversity.

The modern nation state is capable of accommodating folk religion, despite the impossibility of objective verification of its beliefs. Australia has, since 1976, ceded substantial areas of land to Aboriginal people in a legal process in which the existence of sacred natural sites plays a central role. Following the passage in 1976 of the Aboriginal Land Rights (Northern Territory) Act, Aboriginal people have been able to lodge claims for land for which they can demonstrate traditional ownership. Sacred sites are registered with the Australian Aboriginal Protection Authority, a government department enforcing the Northern Territory Sacred Sites Act of 1984, preventing development from infringing on sacred sites and safeguarding the numinous qualities of sacred sites (Verschuuren et al, 2009). To date, some 560,000 km² of land in the Northern Territory has been successfully claimed, almost 50,000 km² of which is now dedicated in four Indigenous Protected Areas.

Conclusions

A very significant proportion of the world's sacred natural sites have their context in folk religion. An overview of such sites in Southeast Asia shows their numinous character to be of central importance. It is this potential to do good or harm – to bring luck or misfortune – in the everyday lives of believers that fosters an intimate relationship between believers and the physicality of the sites. However, it is important we appreciate that environmental conservation in the modern sense is not a necessary or logical outcome of this relationship. Rather, as in the case of tree ordination in Thailand, folk beliefs can provide a background to successful conservation initiatives. For those of us interested in this potential, it is important we deepen our understanding of the tenets of folk religion.

References

Anderson, B. (1991) *Imagined Communities: Reflections on the Origins and Spread of Nationalism*, Verso, London

Appiah, K.A. (2006) *Cosmopolitanism: Ethics in a World of Strangers*, Norton and Company, New York

Belmont, N. (1992) 'Mythic elements in French folklore', in Bonnefoy, Y. (ed) *Roman and European Mythologies*, University of Chicago Press, Chicago, pp244–248

Bender, B. (1993) 'Stonehenge: Contested landscapes (medieval to present-day)', in Bender, B. (ed) *Landscape: Politics and Perspectives*, Berg, Oxford, pp245–278

Byrne, D. (2009) 'The fortress of rationality: Archaeology and Thai popular religion', in Meskell, L. (ed) *Cosmopolitan Archaeologies*, Duke University Press, Durham NC, pp68–88

Darlington, S.M. (1998) 'Ordination of a tree: The Buddhist ecology movement in Thailand', *Ethnology*, vol 37, no 1, pp1–15

Darlington, S.M. (2003) 'Practical spirituality and community forests', in Greenough, P. and Tsing, A.L. (eds) *Nature in the Global South*, Duke University Press, Durham, NC, pp347–366

Darlington, S.M. (2005) 'Ritual and risk: Environmental Buddhism in practice', Paper to the Buddhism and Ecology Conference, Harvard Divinity School

Dudley, N., Higgins-Zogib, L. and Mansourian, S. (eds) (2005) *Beyond Belief: Living Faiths and Protected Areas to Support Biodiversity Conservation*, Alliance for Religion and Conservation, World Wildlife Fund for Nature, Gland, Switzerland

Eire, C.M. (1986) *War Against the Idols*, Cambridge University Press, Cambridge

Firth, R. (1996) *Religion: A Humanist Interpretation*, Routledge, London

Geary, P. (1986) 'Sacred commodities: The circulation of medieval relics', in Appadurai, A. (ed), *The Social Life of Things*, Cambridge University Press, Cambridge, pp169–191

Gell, A. (1998) *Art and Agency: An Anthropological Theory*, Oxford University Press, Oxford

Gesick, L.M. (1995) *In the Land of Lady White Blood*, Southeast Asia Program, Cornell University, Ithaca, NY

Hollan, D. (1996) 'Cultural and experiential aspects of spirit beliefs among the Toraja', in Mageo, J.M. and Howard, A. (eds) *In Spirits in Culture, History, and Mind*, Routledge, New York, pp213–235

Hviding, E. (1996) 'Nature, culture, magic, science: On meta-languages for comparison in cultural ecology', in Descola, P. and Palsson, G. (eds) *Nature and Society*, Routledge, London, pp165–184

Ingold. T. (2000) *The Perception of the Environment*, Routledge, London

Levy, R.I., Mageo, J. and Howard, A. (2006) 'Gods, spirits, and history', in Mageo, J.M. and Howard, A. (eds) *Spirits in Culture, History, and Mind*, Routledge, New York, pp1–10

Meskell, L. (2004) *Object Worlds in Ancient Egypt*, Berg, Oxford

Mallarach, J.-M. and Papayannis, T. (eds) (2007) *Protected Areas and Spirituality*, IUCN, Gland

Munier, C. (1998) *Sacred Rocks and Buddhist Caves in Thailand*, White Lotus Press, Bangkok

Mus, P. (1975) 'India seen from the east: Indian and indigenous cults', in *Champa, Monash Papers on Southeast Asia*, Vol 3, Centre of Southeast Asian Studies, Monash University, Melbourne

Peluso, N.L. (1992) *Rich Forests, Poor People: Resource control and resistance in Java*, University of California Press, Berkeley

Roseman, M. (2003) 'Singers of the landscape: Song, history, and property rights in the Malaysian rainforest', in Zerner, C. (ed) *Culture and the Question of Rights*, Duke University Press, Durham, pp111–141

Russel, J.B. (1984) *Lucifer*, Cornell University Press, Ithaca

Spiro, M.E. (1967) *Burmese Supernaturalism*, Institute for the Study of Human Issues, Philadelphia

Stott, P. (1991), 'Mu'ang and pa: Elite views of nature in a changing Thailand', in Chitakasem, M. and Turton, A. (eds) *Thai Constructions of Knowledge*, School of Oriental and African Studies, University College of London, London, pp142–154

Strang, V. (2004) *The Meaning of Water*, Berg, Oxford

Tambiah, S.J. (1970) *Buddhism and the Spirit Cults in North-east Thailand*, Cambridge University Press, Cambridge

Tambiah, S.J. (1984) *The Buddhist Saints of the Forest and the Cult of Amulets*, Cambridge University Press, Cambridge

Tannenbaum, N. (2000) 'Protest, tree ordination and the changing context of political ritual', *Ethnology*, vol 39, no 2, pp109–127

Taylor, J.L. (1991) 'Living on the rim: Ecology and the forest monks in Northeast Thailand', *Sojourn*, vol 6, no 1, pp106–125

Taylor, P. (2007) *Modernity and Re-enchantment: Religion in Post-revolutionary Vietnam*, Institute of Southeast Asian Studies, Singapore

Thierry, S. (1993) 'Earth spirits in Southeast Asia', in Bonnefoy, Y. (ed) *Asian Mythology*, University of Chicago Press, Chicago, pp144–150

Thomas, K. (1971) *Religion and the Decline of Magic*, Weidenfeld and Nicholson, London

Tiyavanich, K. (1993) 'The wandering forest monks in Thailand, 1900–1992: Ajan Mun's lineage', PhD dissertation, Cornell University, United States of America

Turton, A. (1978) 'Architectural and political space in Thailand', in Milner, G. (ed) *Natural Symbols South East Asia*, School of Oriental and African Studies, University of London, London, pp113–132

Tsing, A.L. (1993) *In the Realm of the Diamond Queen*, Princeton University Press, Princeton

Verschuuren B. (2007) *Believing is Seeing: Integrating Cultural and Spiritual Values in Conservation Management*, Foundation for Sustainable Development, The Netherlands and IUCN, Gland, Switzerland

Verschuuren, B., Marika, M.I.I. and Wise, P. (2009) 'Power on this land; Sacred sites management at Dhimurru indigenous protected area in northeast Arnhem Land', in Papayannis, T. and Mallarach, J.-M. (eds) (2009) *The Sacred Dimension of Protected Areas*, IUCN, Gland, Switzerland and Med-INA, Athens, Greece

UNESCO (2003) International Workshop on the Importance of Sacred Natural Sites for Biodiversity Conservation, UNESCO, Paris

Weber, M. (1946) 'Science as a vocation', in Gerth, H.H. and Mills, C.W. (eds) *From Max Weber: Essays in Sociology*, Oxford University Press, New York, pp129–157

6

Arguments for Developing Biocultural Conservation Approaches for Sacred Natural Sites

Bas Verschuuren

We understand that what is regarded as sacred is more likely to be treated with care and respect. Our planetary home should be so regarded. Efforts to safeguard and cherish the environment need to be infused with a vision of the sacred.

From 'Preserving and cherishing the earth: An appeal for joint commitment in science and religion' in Knudtson and Suzuki (1992).

Summary

This chapter views sacred natural sites that are part of human worldviews, societies and religions, as well as emerging contemporary phenomena where nature is re-imbued with sacredness. The sacred dimensions of nature are viewed in a historic context where the expansion of mainstream religions, colonialism, scientism, technology and globalization prove to have had a significant negative impact on the survival and conservation of sacred natural sites. Focusing on the modern conservation movement, these negative impacts can be brought down to the development of a divide between culture and nature. Because this divide often impairs the management of biocultural values found at sacred natural sites, the need for a new conservation discourse based on the interaction of cultural and natural values is suggested. In this biocultural conservation discourse the need for multidisciplinarity and for further research on the importance, distribution and integration of sacred natural sites as a conservation network is explained.

Introduction
A short evolution of the sacred in nature

Experiencing the sacred in nature signifies one of the oldest human–nature relationships embedded in the cultural fabric of many societies (Burkert, 1994; Berkes and Folke, 1998). Since the beginning of human history, people have treated nature with awe, leading to fear, veneration and worship at places known as sacred natural sites. From the earliest forms of animism and indigenous spiritualities to present day institutionalized mainstream religions, the reverence of nature reflects the spiritual importance of societies' very life support systems.

The spiritual and cultural ties with nature have contributed to our understanding of sustainable human–nature relationships and are fundamental to the moral and ethical foundations of many of the world's cultures and societies. Scholars and conservation practitioners suggest that the sacred dimensions of nature have helped to constitute the world's first conservation areas which were often sacred natural sites and landscapes (Dudley et al, 2009; Palmer, 2005; Wild and McLeod, 2008).

Despite this, a large part of the human population has lost this sacred relationship to the earth. This may partly be due to a lack of experience and direct interaction with nature and partly because people place less importance on conscious, religious and spiritual connections with nature. The role of sacred natural sites in sustainable human–nature relationships are often rooted deeply into the animistic histories of many cultures. These cultures have often been transformed from being nature based to being fused with the world's cross cultural mainstream religions (Buddhism, Christianity, Hinduism, Islam, Judaism, Sikhism and Taoism) (O'Brien and Palmer, 2007). Byrne (Chapter 5) illustrates how the spread of Christianity has contributed to the loss of many sacred sites such as standing stones, forests, groves, trees, wells and mountains in Europe. In Latin America similar patterns of destruction occur but here there is also evidence of diversification where indigenous peoples blended Christianity with their pre-Columbian spiritual and religious traditions (see Figure 6.2). Today, the mainstream religions increasingly use their teachings for the purpose of conservation as will be elaborated later in this chapter.

The development of science during the age of enlightenment and the technological advances during the industrial revolution have also critically disrupted the worldviews of the people to which sacred natural sites are central. The loss of traditional and indigenous worldviews has been called the 'de-sacralization of the cosmos' by Nasr (1996) and 'disturbing the Sacred Balance' by Posey (1999) and has led to the loss of sacred sites and landscapes. Modernization and development have further accompanied unprecedented resource acquisition and caused the absorption of many great civilizations and cultures through western

colonization. Under such conditions many sacred natural sites have been purposefully or unwittingly destroyed. As a result, they are under threat or go unrecognized and their values unprotected by law.

The importance of sacred natural sites

Sacred natural sites often represent the highest human aspirations and spiritual values of any given culture. In many cases they also have a proven biodiversity conservation effect (Dudley et al, 2009). Mount Kailas in Tibet, for example, is the Axis Mundi, the centre and birth place of the entire world to Buddhists, Hindus and Jains and was also sacred to earlier indigenous spiritualities such as Bon shamanism (Bernbaum, 1997). Because sacred natural sites are central to many local communities' daily practices such as agriculture, health care and education, they form a good starting point for conserving the many ecosystem services that they sustain. Many custodians of sacred natural sites also point to their importance as spiritual healing places. The Kogi, Arhu-aco, Wiwa and Kankuam of the Sierra Nevada of Santa Marta in Colombia call their sacred mountain 'The Hearth of the World' which serves for healing the human relationship to the earth (Rodríguez-Navarro, 2000). Other custodians in the Altai Republic of the Russian federation point out that sacred sites are connected and serve as a worldwide network of places for the healing the energies of the earth (see Chapter 23). Environmental psychologists and other scientists also recognize sacred natural sites as places with special importance for peace keeping, conflict resolution and environmental decision making (Atran and Norenzayan, 2004; Atran et al, 2005; Knudtson and Suzuki, 1992). As such, sacred natural sites support the spiritual well-being that many people find in their relationship with nature.

The veneration of sacred natural sites: Some contemporary examples

Even though the origins of sacredness are often mysterious or unclear – like the essence of the sacred itself – various authors have attempted to explain it based on ancient and contemporary human–nature relationships. In this section examples are used to demonstrate the sacredness and (re)sanctification of sacred natural sites to indigenous peoples, religious groups, tourists and the general public in search of spirituality. Golliher (1999), Harmon (2007), Taylor (2001) and Tiedje (2007) independently suggest that new claims of sacredness can be very strong and may replace earlier claims. An example is the inhabitation of the Isle of Arran in the United Kingdom by Buddhist monks after having been abandoned as a Christian place of contemplation and religious practice and prior to that as a Celtic spiritual site (Soria, 2007). As existing nature can be made sacred or resanctified, new nature can be created in the image of the sacred. The recent planting of sacred Yew trees (*Taxus baccata*) across 700 parishes in England (ARC, 2009) is an example.

Cases are known where a place can become sacred without having been sacred before in a similar way that places that have been desecrated can be made sacred again. An example of resanctification is Nhulun, a sacred hill in northeast Arnhem Land, Australia. Nhulun was desecrated by a bulldozer damaging the mountain for the purpose of road construction in an adjacent mining project. The Yolngu people, the traditional owners and custodians, performed a special ceremony to resanctify the site and assert their rights. By doing so they were at the forefront of the Australian Indigenous Land Rights movement which led to the first Aboriginal Land Rights Act in Australia in 1976 and eventually legal title and empowerment to land and their sacred sites was granted (Verschuuren et al, 2009).

Archaeological monuments are often ancient sacred sites where custodians have disappeared. An example where the spiritual significance of such an archaeological site has been reinstated by their descendants is Tikal in Guatemala (see Figure 6.1). Tikal is a Mayan ceremonial centre, abandoned in approximately 800 AD and rediscovered in the 1960s fully submerged by jungle. After much work by archaeologists, Mayan populations continue the practice of spiritual ceremonies at the site (see also Chapter 18). Claims of sacredness for archaeological sites are also made by seekers of new nature spirituality (Taylor, 2001; Tiedje, 2007). A well-known example is Stonehenge in the UK,

Figure 6.1 The ruins of Tikal are situated in the World Heritage Site and national park 'Peten' in Guatemala

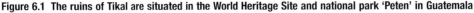

Source: Bas Verschuuren

which for the celebration of the summer solstice in 2009 accommodated roughly 35,000 people. These visitors may be called 'new age spirituality seekers' and 'sacred sites tourists'.

Tourism can aid the conservation of sacred natural sites if it is used as a tool to foster respect for places and people and promote their conservation (see Chapter 22). However it may also have unwanted side effects affecting religious and spiritual practice (Kang, 2009). For example in one single site in Sertsuo (Huanglong, Yellow Dragon) in Tibet (Sichuan, China), tourism is being used by actors from religious, ethnic and government groups, resulting in divergence between the different practices and competition rather than respect for diversification. McLeod (2009) provides the example of the northern Californian Winemem Wintu where in a struggle to protect their holy mountain from the development of a ski resort made public the location of their sacred spring which attracted unwelcome new age spirituality seekers.

Recognition of cultural, spiritual and sacred values in conservation

Bridging the nature culture divide in conservation

The multiple values involved in sacred natural sites management pose challenges for management and policy, especially conservation organizations that are typically used to dealing primarily with biological values. The ideological roots of the western conservation movement – starting some 150 years ago – are embedded in a deep respect and even reverence for nature and creation. However, scientifically expressed natural and biodiversity values have been prioritized over the cultural and spiritual values attached to nature. The 'wilderness' which the new nature conservation movement set out to protect left little space for people. As a consequence people were sometimes removed from their ancestral homes while their lands and sacred natural sites were being incorporated into protected areas (Williams and Hutton, 2007). Many cultural practices and beliefs that related to sacred natural sites went unrecognized and as such

many were lost in the process. This juxtaposition of people and landscapes appeared most dramatically in the context of colonial regimes that subjugated landscapes and people to the will of dominant economic and religious powers.

Fortunately the conservation movement also consolidated respect and dialogue which has led to adopting more comprehensive approaches to conservation based on the understanding that the aesthetic, moral and spiritual values of biodiversity, permeating all cultures and religions, provide a firm imperative for its conservation (Mittermeier et al, 2003). Conservationists have developed more inclusive and participatory forms of management of which Indigenous and Community Conserved Areas (ICCAs) are most notable (Chape et al, 2008). ICCAs include many sacred natural sites that often lack legal protection and recognition of their cultural management. ICCA designation may help change this situation. The guidelines for the management of sacred natural sites developed by Wild and McLeod (2008) are particularly valuable to the management of these places within and outside government designated protected areas. Rather than fencing off the borders of conservation areas, people determine the extent of the conservation areas through practices of sustainable and customary use. Bhagwat and Rutte (2006) have called this the 'the social fence' which depends on shared sacred and spiritual values that form the basis of people's traditional conservation ethics, and sacred natural sites provide an especially good example of this.

Restoring and strengthening the sacred and spiritual dimension of human–nature relationships may help to meet traditional and contemporary spiritual needs and contribute to moral and ethical arguments for nature conservation. In fact, seeing the world's cultural and biological diversity in peril has alarmed people worldwide and appeals to their sense of responsibility for the well-being of humanity and the natural systems on which humanity depends. People's collective awareness of these issues has contributed to the creation of the world's Protected Areas Network and the establishment of World Heritage Sites and Man and Biosphere Reserves, see Figure 6.2. The global recognition of protected areas for their biological and cultural importance has led them to become

Figure 6.2 Galapagos, Stained glass window celebrating Galapaganian diversity from the Church of St Francis, Puerto Ayora, Galapagos World Heritage Site

Source: Robert Wild

icons that have once again taken on a sacred dimension (Engel, 1985; Putney, 2005).

Including cultural and spiritual values in conservation approaches

According to Suzuki and McConnell (1997) and Posey (1999), the equilibrium between nature and culture is mediated through the sacred. This equilibrium is disturbed when the highest form of awareness – spiritual consciousness – is removed from human–nature relationships. Today, the 'Millennium Ecosystem Assessment' (Ghosh et al, 2005) as well as the 'Global Environmental Outlook' (Schomaker et al, 2008) recognize that culture, spirituality and the sacred are dynamic co-creators of biodiversity as well as important drivers of human development processes. It has become clear that failing to recognize cultural

and spiritual values can exacerbate conflicts of interests between local peoples and conservationists and consistently hamper conservation objectives (Verschuuren, in press). Therefore it is important to remember that in its very essence the importance of conserving the diversity of life on earth – for human well-being as well as for intrinsic reasons – is often said to be based on the ethical and moral grounds where life itself is held sacred (Harmon, 2003). Recognizing cultural and spiritual values is essential for respecting the sacredness of life and in doing so the conservation of sacred natural sites has repeatedly shown to yield improved results for conservation of biological and cultural diversity.

Legal recognition of sacred natural sites and their spiritual values has contributed to more effective conservation management in numerous cases worldwide. For example in northern Australia the Jawoyn Traditional Owners claims of cultural and spiritual values attached to Coronation Hill eventually held off uranium mining because they believed damaging the site would bring doom and ill health upon all mankind. Legal recognition of their claims enabled conservation status of the site which is now partly included in Kakadu World Heritage Site and National Park (Ross, 2001). In other cases, such as that of the Windward Maroons in Jamaica, the recognition of sacred natural sites has enhanced development of holistic management of the natural and cultural values of protected areas (see Chapter 14).

Developing biocultural conservation approaches
Exploring biocultural diversity

Because of sacred natural sites' outstanding cultural and biological values, understanding how these values may be linked is crucial to developing appropriate conservation approaches. Posey's statement that biological and cultural diversity are inextricably connected was one of the first articulations of the concept of biocultural diversity (ISE, 2006) and only a few scientists have attempted to define biocultural diversity since. Existing definitions are broad, often based on the overlap of language and the distribution of species in the environment (Harmon and Loh, 2004; Maffi 2001, Stepp et al, 2002), and need to be redefined to a specific local context. The ISE code of ethics (2006) has developed a basic definition suitable for the purpose of conserving sacred natural sites which once adopted does not need to be limited to indigenous peoples, traditional societies and local communities:

> *Biocultural heritage is the cultural heritage (both tangible and intangible, including customary law, spiritual values, knowledge, innovations and practices) and biological heritage (diversity of genes, varieties, species, ecosystems...) of humans, which often are inextricably linked through the interaction between humans and nature over time and shaped by their socio-ecological and economic context.*

Biocultural heritage of sacred natural sites may be passed down from generation to generation,

developed, owned and administered collectively by their custodians and communities. Not surprisingly, significant overlap exists between areas with sacred natural sites that contain high biodiversity and areas with high cultural diversity.

Hotspots of biocultural values?

There is increasing interest to merge biological and cultural diversity into the concept of 'biocultural' diversity to apply it in ecosystem management and nature conservation strategies (Cocks, 2006; Harmon, 2007; Verschuuren, 2007). Several scientific inquiries have been made to map the extent of biocultural diversity (Harmon, 1996; Maffi, 2005; Skutnabb-Kangas et al, 2003; Stepp et al, 2002). For example Loh and Harmon (2005) measure biocultural diversity by parameters for cultural diversity (numbers of languages, ethnicities and religions) and biological diversity (numbers of bird, mammal and plant species) at the national level. While these studies indicate countries where biological and cultural diversity are inextricably linked, they provide only limited guidance for supporting the conservation of sacred natural sites because many sacred natural sites are found outside the high biocultural diversity areas indicated by these studies. Sacred natural sites have been recognized as hotspots of biodiversity (Metcalfe et al, 2009) but also feature outstanding cultural, spiritual and religious values. Therefore the importance of many of these sites may be better reflected when speaking of hotspots of 'biocultural' values.

Including indigenous peoples, mainstream religions and broader society

Indigenous people preserve up to 80 per cent of the world's biodiversity and they speak most of the world's 6000 to 7000 languages commonly accepted as indicators for cultural diversity (Sobrevila, 2008). Many languages are rapidly disappearing, together with the biological and cultural diversity intrinsically connected with indigenous people. Indigenous territories comprise 7 per cent of the world's surface – officially recognized by nation states – and another estimated 13 per cent go unrecognized (Posey and Dutfield, 1997). Examples of these are biodiversity hotspots that cover 2.3 per cent of the earth's surface (Myers et al, 2003), mega diverse wilderness areas cover 44 per cent of the planet (Mittermeier et al, 2003), protected areas 12 per cent and Indigenous and Community Conserved Areas 20 per cent (Chape et al, 2008). Because of the overlap among these landscapes, biocultural approaches to conservation are essential to the success of conservation as a whole.

During the past decade the perception that protection of biological and cultural diversity is often associated with indigenous peoples has been tested and diversified (Cocks, 2006). Certainly in the case of sacred natural sites a wide variety of groups, indigenous, religious, new age and tourists, are taking an interest in the biocultural values of these sites. Religion, for example, is often included in the analysis of biocultural diversity and is a core value to many sacred natural sites. Religious institutions own about 7 per cent of the earth's land surface (Palmer, 2005), oversee a US$7 trillion International Interfaith Investment Group (Bhagwat and Palmer, 2009) and have adherents among 80 per cent of the earth's population (O'Brien and Palmer, 2007). Their involvement in the conservation of biological and cultural diversity is therefore very important and may be combined effectively with concerns over sacred natural sites. Currently the Delos initiative is developing specific guidance for this process (see Chapter 19).

Lessons learned in support of biocultural conservation approaches

The cultural and natural values of sacred natural sites are interrelated so impacts on natural values may also affect the cultural values and vice versa. Because of this interdependence, drivers of change may pose a double impact to the overall values. Strategies for the conservation of natural and cultural values of sacred natural sites should focus on the ways these are both resilient and adaptive to the challenges our society faces today, including the biodiversity crisis, climate change mitigation

and poverty alleviation. Biocultural conservation strategies will therefore need to be supported at various levels of governance and management. Reconciling management strategies and policies for cultural and natural heritage management is key to effective conservation of sacred natural sites. Their conservation can be enhanced through extending protection beyond formally recognized conservation areas into the cultural domain. In order to do this local stakeholders need to be involved in the process and multidisciplinary approaches need to give equal weight to different world views and ways of knowing.

Although lessons are being learned in the course of applying biocultural approaches for the management of sacred natural sites, these are dispersed and often lack an overarching approach. But sacred natural sites could form a global conservation network and be good indicators of biocultural diversity. More information is needed on the levels of biodiversity of sacred natural sites and their capacity for ecological connectivity at a landscape scale. But sacred natural sites are already providing learning opportunities for developing sustainable management strategies based on the fact that the traditional management of these places has already proved resilient and adaptive over the centuries.

Conclusions

The interactions between cultural and biological diversity lead to a state of consciousness that makes us human (Harmon, 2007; Posey, 1999). This chapter therefore suggests that enhanced sensitivity to the interaction between cultural and biological diversity can help societies find new approaches for conservation in general and specifically for the conservation of sacred natural sites.

In order to restore critical spiritual connectivenes that persists in the links between people and nature, besides the commonly recognized pillars of sustainability 'people', 'planet' and 'profit', a fourth pillar – 'spirituality' – may need to be considered. Making people aware of the sacredness of nature requires raising consciousness of spiritual values which are not only found in traditional worldviews but also among the people who dominate today's modern global society. As such, lessons learned from and for sacred natural sites may assist in improving the human–nature relationships of the planet's increasing urban population. Engagement in environmental and sustainable ways of living remains a key issue to the success of conservation and the survival of humanity as a whole. Spirituality is a key value of sacred natural sites and therefore central to the restoration, conservation and protection of the natural and cultural values these places represent.

References

ARC (2009) Available at www.arcworld.org (last accessed June 2009)

Atran, S. and Norenzayan, A. (2004) 'Religion's evolutionary landscape', *Behavioural and Brain Sciences*, vol 27, pp713–770

Atran, S., Medin, D. and Ross, N. (2005) 'The cultural mind: Environmental decision making and cultural modelling within and across populations', *Psychological Review*, vol 112, pp744–776

Berkes, F. and Folke, C. (eds) (1998) 'Linking social and ecological systems for resilience and sustainability', in Berkes, F., Folke, C. and Colding, J. (eds) *Understanding Social and Ecological Systems*, Cambridge University Press, New York

Bernbaum, E. (1997) *Sacred Mountains of the World*, Berkeley University Press, Berkeley CA

Bhagwat, S. and Palmer, M. (2009) 'Conservation: The world's religions can help', *Nature*, vol 461, no 7260, p37

Bhagwat S.A. and Rutte C. (2006) 'Sacred groves: Potential for biodiversity management', *Frontiers in Ecology and the Environment*, vol 4, pp519–524

Burkert, W. (1994) *Creation of the Sacred: Tracks of Biology in Early Religions*, Harvard University Press, Cambridge, MA and London

Chape, S., Spalding, M. and Jenkins, M. (2008) *The World's Protected Areas: Status, Values and Prospects in the 21st Century*, University of California Publishers, Berkeley, CA

Cocks, M.L. (2006) 'Biocultural diversity: Moving beyond the realm of "indigenous" and "local" people', *Human Ecology*, vol 34, no 2, pp185–200

Dudley, N., Higgins-Zogib, L. and Mansourian, S. (2009) 'Links between protected areas, faiths and sacred natural sites', *Conservation Biology*, vol 23, no 3, pp568–577

Engel, J.R. (1985) 'Renewing the bond of mankind and nature: Biosphere reserves as sacred space', *Orion Nature Quarterly*, vol 4, pp52–59

Ghosh, A., Traverse, M., Bhattacharya, D.K., Brondizio, E.S., Spierenburg, M., deCastro, F., Morsello, C. and deSiqueira, A. (2005) 'Cultural services', in Almaco, E. and Bennet, E. *Millennium Ecosystem Assessment* (Volume 3: Global and Multiscale Assessment Report), Island Press, Washington, DC, pp403–419

Golliher, J. (1999) 'Ethical, moral and religious concerns', in Posey, D. (ed) (1999) *Cultural and Spiritual Values of Biodiversity, a Comprehensive Contribution to the UNEP Global Biodiversity Assessment*, Intermediate Technology Publications, London

Harmon, D. (1996) 'Losing species, losing languages: Connections between biological and linguistic diversity', *Southwest Journal of Linguistics*, vol 15, pp89–108

Harmon, D. (2003) 'Biodiversity and the sacred: Some insights for preserving cultural diversity and heritage', *Museum*, vol 55, no 2

Harmon, D. (2007) 'A bridge over the chasm: Finding ways to achieve integrated natural and cultural heritage conservation', *International Journal of Heritage Studies*, vol 13, no 4/5, pp380–392

Harmon, D. and Loh, J. (2004) 'The IBCD: A measure of the world's biocultural diversity', *Policy Matters*, vol 13, pp271–280

ISE International Society of Ethnobiologists (2006) 'Code of ethics', available at www.ethnobiology.net/_common/docs/ISE%20COE_Eng_rev_24Nov08.pdf (Accessed November 2009)

Kang, X. (2009) 'Contesting sacred space on China's ethnic frontier: Two temples, three religions and a tourist attraction', *Sage Publications*, vol 35, no 3, pp227–255

Knudtson, P. and Suzuki, D. (1992) *Wisdom of the Elders; Honouring Sacred Native Visions of Nature*, Stoddart Publishing Co. Limited, Toronto

Loh, J. and Harmon, D. (2005) 'A global index of biocultural diversity', *Ecological Indicators*, vol 5, pp231–241

Maffi, L. (ed) (2001) *On Biocultural Diversity: Linking Language, Knowledge, and the Environment*, Smithsonian Institution Press, Washington DC

Maffi, L. (2005) 'Linguistic, cultural, and biological diversity', *Annual Review of Anthropology*, vol 34, pp599–617

Mallarach, J.-M. (ed) (2008) 'Protected landscapes and cultural and spiritual values', *Values of Protected Landscapes and Seascapes Volume 2*, IUCN, GTZ and Obra Social de Caixa Catalunya, Kasparek Verlag, Heidelberg

Mallarach, J.-M. and Papayannis, T. (eds) (2007) *Protected Areas and Spirituality*, IUCN and Publications de l'Abadia de Montserrat. Gland, Switzerland

McLeod, C. (2009) 'The kiss of death', *Resurgence*, vol 255, pp28–30

McNeely, J.M. and Wachtel, P.S. (1988) *Soul of the Tiger; Searching for Nature's Answers in Exotic Southeast Asia*, Bantam Dell Publishing Group, New York

Metcalfe, K., French-Constant, K. and Gordon, I. (2009) 'Sacred sites as hotspots for biodiversity: The Three Sisters Cave complex in coastal Kenya', *Oryx*, vol 44, no 1, pp118–123

Mittermeier, R.A., Mittermeier, C.G., Brooks, T.M., Pilgrim, J.D., Konstant, W.R., da Fonseca, G.A.B. and Kormos, C. (2003) 'Wilderness and biodiversity conservation', *Proceeding of the National Academy of Sciences*, vol 100, no 18, pp10309–10313

Myers, N. (2003) 'Biodiversity hotspots revisited', *BioScience*, vol 53, pp916–917

Nasr, S.H. (1996) *Religion and the Order Of Nature*, Oxford University Press, Oxford

O'Brien, J. and Palmer, M. (2007) *The Atlas of Religion: Mapping Contemporary Challenges and Beliefs*, Earthscan, London, p128

Palmer, M. (2005) *Faiths and the Environment*, World Bank, Washington, DC, p66

Persic, A. and Martin, G. (eds) (2008) 'Links between biological and cultural diversity-concepts, methods and experiences', Report of an International Workshop, UNESCO, Paris

Posey, D.A. and Dutfield, G. (eds) (1997) *Indigenous Peoples and Sustainability: Cases and Actions*, IUCN Inter-commission Task Force on Indigenous Peoples, International Books, Utrecht, Netherlands

Posey, D. (ed.) (1999) *Cultural and Spiritual Values of Biodiversity, a Comprehensive Contribution to the UNEP Global Biodiversity Assessment*, Intermediate Technology Publications, London

Posey, D. (2000) 'The "balance sheet" and the "sacred balance": Valuing the knowledge of indigenous and traditional peoples', *World Views: Global Religions, Culture, and Ecology*, vol 2, no 2, pp91–106

Putney, A.D. (2005) 'Building cultural support for protected areas through sacred natural sites', in McNeely, J.A. (2005) *Friends for Life*, IUCN, Gland, Chapter 10

Rodríguez-Navarro, G.E. (2000) 'Indigenous knowledge as an innovative contribution to the sustainable development of the Sierra Nevada of Santa Marta, Colombia: The elder brothers, guardians of the "Heart of the World"', *Research for Mountain Area Development: The Americas, Ambio*, vol 29, no 7

Ross, H. (2001) 'Social impact assessment of Coronation Hill', in Baker, R., Davies, J. and SLFP, www.sacredland.org/home/resources/research/reports-guides-and-articles/ethics/

Schomaker, M., Keating, M. and Chenje, M. (2008) *Fourth Global Environment Outlook, GEO 4. Environment for Development*, UNEP, Nairobi, Kenya

Skutnabb-Kangas, L., Maffi, L. and Harmon, D. (2003) *Sharing a World of Difference: The Earth's Linguistic, Cultural and Biological Diversity*, UNESCO, Paris, p56

Sobrevila, C. (2008) *The Role of Indigenous Peoples in Biodiversity Conservation: The Natural but Often Forgotten Partners*, The World Bank, Washington, DC

Soria, S. (2007) 'Holy Island, Isle of Arran: Scotland, United Kingdom', in Mallarach, J.-M. and Papayannis, T. (eds) *Protected Areas and Spirituality*, IUCN and Publications de l'Abadia de Montserrat, Gland, Switzerland

Suzuki, D. (1999) 'Finding a new story', in Posey, D. (ed) (1999) *Cultural and Spiritual Values of Biodiversity, a Comprehensive Contribution to the UNEP Global Biodiversity Assessment*, Intermediate Technology Publications, London

Suzuki, D. and McConnell, A. (1997) *The Sacred Balance: Rediscovering our Place in Nature*, Greystone Books, Vancouver

Stepp, J.R., Wyndham, F.S. and Zarger, R. (eds) (2002) *Ethnobiology and Biocultural Diversity*, University of Georgia Press, Athens

Taylor, B.R. (2001) 'Earth and nature based spirituality (Part II): From earth first! and bioregionalism to scientific paganism and the new age', *Religion*, vol 31, no 3, pp225–245

Tiedje, K. (2007) 'The promise of the discourse of the sacred for conservation (and its limits)', *JSRNC*, vol 1, no 3, pp326–339

Verschuuren, B. (2007) 'An overview of cultural and spiritual values in ecosystem management and conservation strategies', in Haverkort, B. and Rist, S. (eds) *Endogenous Development and Bio-cultural Diversity: The interplay of worldviews, globalisation and locality*, Compas/CDE, series on Worldviews and Sciences, No 6, Leusden, The Netherlands

Verschuuren, B.. Marika, M. II and Wise, P. (2009) 'Power on this land: Sacred Sites management at Dhimurru Indigenous Protected Area in Northeast Arnhemland', paper contributed to the 2nd Delos workshop, Ouranoupolis, Halkidiki, Greece

Verschuuren, B. (in press) 'Integrating biocultural values in nature conservation: Perceptions of cultural significant sites and species in adaptive management', in Pungetti, G., Oviedo, G. and Hooke, D. (eds) *Sacred Species and Sites, Guardians of Biocultural Diversity*, Cambridge University Press

Wild, R. and McLeod, C. (2008) 'Sacred Natural Sites. Guidelines for Protected Area Managers', Best Practice Protected Area Guidelines Series No16, Gland, Switzerland, IUCN

Williams, A. and Hutton J. (2007) 'People, parks and poverty: Political ecology and biodiversity conservation', *Conservation and Society*, vol 5, no 2, pp147–183

Section Two

Sacred Natural Sites: Mutual Learning, Analysis, Planning and Management

A Dai proverb states that: 'Understanding the present is the road to the future'. Based on this, this section contains specific advice drawn from case studies from across the globe. These seven studies explore sacred natural sites in different localities, discuss the threats they and their custodian communities face and report on approaches, activities and methods for work being undertaken in individual or groups of sites. The cases report on an increasing adoption of inclusive management processes and demonstrate their continued values to the people who treat certain areas as sacred (see Figure II.1). They cover a range of ecological contexts from mountains, forests, lakes and islands and a wide range of locations stretching from Europe, Asia, Africa and the wider Caribbean.

The Holy Island of Lindisfarne is one of the earliest Christian holy sites in Britain and one that is not considered to be adopted from earlier religious practice (see Chapter 7). Its association with the lives of the early British 'nature' saints, its long religious history and significant wildlife values are of increasing relevance and resonance to modern Britons. The increased pilgrim, tourist and economic activity has brought its own pressures on both the infrastructure and the long-standing local community. Secular nature conservation bodies, community development and religious institutions have often operated independently of each other but with an increasing recognition that

Figure II.1 The mountain (5761m) is home to the protector deity Khumbu-Yul-Lha and is flanked by Tengbuche Monastery in Nepal

The monastic community protects the forests to the left, right and front of the monastery.

Source: Jeremy Spoon

coordinated and mutually supportive collective action is needed to balance natural, social and spiritual values.

In the Himalayas of Nepal increasing tourism and modernity is also influencing the place-based spirituality of the Sherpa people living on Sagarmatha (Mt Everest National Park). Spoon's study (Chapter 8) shows how this affects, sometimes in subtle ways, the knowledge and attitudes towards Sherpa spiritual values and sacred natural sites. While some of these changes appear positive for the conservation of both nature and culture, others are less so. The chapter examines possible causes for these changes including market driven pressures.

Pei (Chapter 9) describes Yunnan, one of China's most ethnically and biologically diverse areas, but signals an alarming rate of loss of the sacred forests of the Dai Holy Hills. Following over 20 years of study into the ethnobiology and biodiversity of the area, the sacred forests are recognized as having very high conservation values, in both biodiversity and cultural terms. The dramatic loss of 90 per cent of the area of sacred forest is a result of China's rapid economic development. Pei describes the traditional land management systems and argues for its increased recognition in the search for sustainable development and the conservation of those Holy Hills that remain and the restoration of those that can be recovered.

Studley (Chapter 10) also investigates perceptions of earth care and sacredness in the Himalayan region, more specifically in the Eastern Kham area of the Autonomous Region of Tibet, China. Methods for uncovering the intangible values of earth care against the wider context of indigenous forest values are presented. These assist to diversify dominant western research theories regarding the nature of knowledge. Studley recommends that government planning agencies and conservationists develop cross-cultural skills and act as 'knowledge brokers' between indigenous communities and government decision-makers.

Moving to Africa, sacred natural sites in the forests of Cameron are currently under-recognized in national policy and legislation. Kamga Kamden (Chapter 11) provides an assessment of 52 sacred natural sites in the Kingdom of Bandjoun. It is shown that despite the fact that these sites remain deeply embedded in the cultural fabric they are becoming increasingly eroded in the face of livelihood pressures and cultural change. They now represent small fragments of their former extent but retain local cultural and biological value. It is argued that these need to be better understood and communicated and that they need to be supported by appropriate government policy and legislation. Immediate steps will need to be taken to achieve this.

In the lower reaches of the Niger Delta, Nigeria, Anwana et al (Chapter 12) describe how local beliefs, exemplified by two sacred lakes, regulate particular fisheries of the region and protect the endangered dwarf crocodile as well as a rich freshwater biodiversity. These systems have been resilient to change despite 400 years of providing resources to the global economy, including slaves and vegetable and mineral oils. Current ecosystem degradation is putting these systems under severe pressure and action is needed so that they continue to support current cultural and biological values. The geopolitics of the Niger Delta are such that there is significant lack of trust between communities and government. Despite this, it is essential that government supports effective community governance in an effort to slow the rise in poverty and decline in ecosystem function.

In the wider Caribbean area, van Andel (Chapter 13) elaborates the complex relationship between Maroon sacred natural sites, sacred species and traditional medicine. While the extractive use of animals or plants from sacred forests is usually prohibited, the harvesting of medicinal plants, under traditional limits, is a frequent exception in many cultures across the globe. This is similar in Suriname but it now has a thriving trade in medicinal plants, many of which are considered sacred in their own right, having magical properties and treating illnesses of supernatural

nature. Significant urban trade and international export of medicinal plants often leads to a cultural dislocation and the overexploitation of wild medicinal plants. This appears not to be the case in Suriname, as many key plants used are either common in secondary or modified habitats or under local cultivation and some are widespread exotics. Thus the commercial use of medicinal plants may not be of a threat in itself to sacred forests, but breaking the link between the sacred species and the sacred forests may itself create vulnerability. Little is known of the sacred forests located in remote forest areas but their Maroon custodian communities are considered vulnerable to the influence of missionary activity, logging and oil palm development.

Jamaica's Blue and John Crow Mountains are the ancestral domain of a related community, the Windward Maroons. Similar to Suriname the Maroons are the descendants of Amerindians, in this case Tainos, and escaped African slaves. The Windward Maroon sacred sites, as described by John et al (Chapter 14), are closely bound up with their resistance to British colonial rule. Much knowledge about these sites has, however, been lost, and the remaining elders are reluctant to share their knowledge. Originally designated on biodiversity grounds in 1993 the National Park is taking significant steps to include a strong cultural dimension by incorporating Maroon sacred natural sites. Declared by UNESCO as Intangible Cultural Heritage of Humanity, the Maroon culture is facing an uncertain future, while the majority of Jamaicans, having suffered cultural dislocation, do not in general maintain traditional 'bonds of affection' for natural locations. The collaboration between Maroon communities and park authorities might strengthen each other and provide Jamaicans as a whole a greater emotional link to these iconic mountains.

7

Nature Saint and Holy Island, Ancient Values in a Modern Economy: The Enduring Influence of St Cuthbert and Lindisfarne, United Kingdom

Robert Wild

Summary

The Holy Island of Lindisfarne and its surrounding marine wetlands is an important wildlife area for coastal habitats and wintering wildfowl. Most of the area is a National Nature Reserve and a Wetland of International Importance designated under the Ramsar Convention. The island has been a Christian holy site and pilgrimage centre since AD 635, and has played a pivotal role as a 'cradle' of Christianity in northern England and southern Scotland. Nature and spirituality are very much linked here through a line of 'Nature Saints' of which St Cuthbert is best known in the area. He has been considered by some as England's first 'nature conservationist'. The spiritual values of the island are mostly associated with these saints, the places linked with them and the relationship with the island and its wildlife. The island has a small resident community of 150 people and a number of active Christian groups including Anglican, United Reformed Church and Catholic. More

recently it has become a node in the revival of Celtic Christianity, an indigenous, if somewhat contested, type of Christianity where the spiritual values of nature are overtly expressed. The majority of visitors to the island are day trippers, while recent years have seen an increasing number of pilgrimages. Visitors are now estimated in excess of half a million people per year and this number has been increasing over recent years, reflecting trends including an increasing interest in both nature and spirituality.

In addition to natural and spiritual values, the island is important for local community, heritage and also economic values. These values are not necessarily balanced and concerns have been raised especially about the local community values. At one level Lindisfarne is a 'normal' Northumbrian village, with long-term needs such as employment, affordable housing and schools. These needs, to some extent, run counter to a high profile visitor attraction generating high property values. The management of the island itself and surrounding coastal wetlands is distributed among a wide range of entities and institutions, leading to multiple visions for the future of the island. No clear mechanisms have been established to discuss or decide the trade-offs between different visions and development paths.

Holy Island has the potential to bring nature conservation and spiritual values together and infusing the increasingly urgent need for global environmental action with a spiritual dimension. Increasing visitor numbers (and their attendant vehicles) support the local economy but add significant pressures that may compromise the island's overall integrity. A mechanism to generate an overall shared vision among different interests could ensure that all the island's values are in balance and its overall integrity is maintained.

Introduction

> *All places and all people are sacred. We have to recapture that, and respect even the smallest wood as well as the largest rainforest.*
>
> Rev. Canon David Adam, Vicar of Holy Island 1995–2003 (personal communication, 2009)

> *… has shown how much liveliness there is on the island, how much willingness to accommodate new ventures, but also how much determination there is for the future to be shaped by and for the island people. We are not ready to become anyone's theme park, now or ever!*
>
> (Tristram, 2009)

The Holy Island of Lindisfarne is located on the northeast coast of England, on the border with Scotland. It is accessible at low tide, across sand and mud flats, which carry an ancient pilgrim's way and a modern road causeway. It is surrounded by the 3541ha Lindisfarne National Nature Reserve which protects the island's sand dunes and the adjacent intertidal habitats (Natural England, 2005, Figure 7.1). The extensive dunelands, intertidal sand and mud flats, saltmarsh and ancient raised beaches support a wide variety of plant life and attract vast numbers of birds. Almost 300 bird species have been recorded on the Reserve. The total wintering wildfowl population is estimated at 60,000.

Holy Island, Lindisfarne was founded as one of the first Christian monastic communities in England in AD 635, and for 240 years it was a centre of early Christian learning and missionary endeavour. It is one of a number of holy islands off Britain's coast, including Iona and the Holy Island, Arran (now owned by a Buddhist community). It is associated with several saints including St Cuthbert, who lived on the island during the 7th century. Desecrated by the first Viking raid on England in AD 793, the Abbey finally moved St Cuthbert's relics off the island in 875 and Lindisfarne was largely unoccupied until the re-establishment of a Benedictine Priory around 1150. This was destroyed between 1536 and 1541, during the dissolution of the English monasteries by King Henry VIII. This event was part of the founding of the Anglican Church, with the English monarch as its head.

The main settlement on Holy Island is a traditional Northumbrian village reliant on fishing and farming but increasingly engaged in tourism. Many visitors are attracted by the nature and the island's religious and secular history.

The life and legacy of St Cuthbert

Two hagiographies of St Cuthbert exist which are sometimes collectively called the *Lives*. One was written anonymously shortly after his death (c.700), the other by St (the Venerable) Bede AD 716–726 (Bede, 731; Magnusson, 1984; Farmer, 1998). St Cuthbert lived from 634 to 687, in a period when the Britons (ancestors of the Welsh), English, Picts and Dalriada (Irish) were vying for territory and power in northern Britain (see Figure 7.2.). We first hear of him as a 16-year-old youth, upon the Lammermuir Hills of northeast Britain, in what is now southern Scotland. On that night in AD 651 Cuthbert was defending a flock of sheep and during his watch he saw a bright stream of light descending from heaven. This signalled the death and ascension of St Aidan, the remarkable founder of the monastery on Lindisfarne, whose generosity and humility is considered to have established the spiritual pattern of Holy Island. On witnessing this event Cuthbert was moved to become a monk and entered Melrose Abbey, on the River Tweed. Cuthbert excelled as a student and gained a reputation as a preacher and healer. He achieved royal respect and on his death the Lindisfarne Gospels, one of Europe's

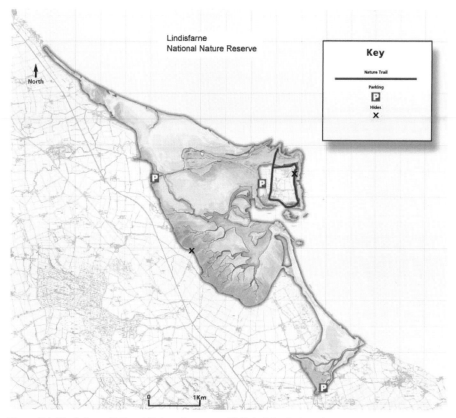

Figure 7.1 Lindisfarne National Nature Reserve with Holy Island at centre

Source: Natural England

finest mediaeval illustrated manuscripts, was written in his honour (Brown, 2003).

> *A hermit, prior and then bishop to the monastic community of Lindisfarne, Cuthbert became on his death in 687 one of the most important medieval saints in Europe and one of the foremost saints of Medieval England…The very physical presence of Cuthbert, in all areas of Northumbria both while alive and after his death, is a fascinating example of the way in which the corporal presence of a saint somehow helps sanctify a geographical region and affirms and strengthens it.* (Marner, 2000)

St Cuthbert had the reputation of having a close relationship and affinity with nature. For Christian preachers of the time this was not unusual. He was particularly fond of the seabirds and is attributed with establishing one of the first ever bird protection rules relating to the killing of wildfowl. 'He virtually

declared Lindisfarne a Nature Reserve 1300 years before the Nature Conservancy Council (now Natural England).' (Magnusson, 1984)

St Cuthbert's nature spirituality can be attributed to two sources: a Christian nature tradition and a pre-Christian Celtic nature spirituality. On the Christian side, St Cuthbert was one of a line of spiritual transmission from the 4th-century 'Desert Fathers' of the Middle East and North Africa, starting with the eremitic St Anthony. Many of the Celtic saints are connected with nature miracles, locating their centres based on signs from nature, or the appearance of specific animals. The Celtic pre-Christian religion was animistic and the Celts believed that all aspects of the natural world contained spirits. Evidence for the transition of the pre-Christian Celtic nature spirituality to a Christian form includes the nature images of the carved standing stones of the Picts (an indigenous tribe of linguistically Celtic peoples (Moffat, 2005))

Figure 7.2 Political divisions of northern Britain indicative of St Cuthbert's era

Source: Shepherd (1923)

that are found through central Scotland (Leatham, 1948; Fraser, 2008), the art of the Lindisfarne Gospels (Brown, 2003) and the folk religions of the Celtic countries (Carmichael, 1900).

Modern Lindisfarne Holy Island and commercial success

The Island is surrounded by coastal and marine habitats and supports internationally important wildfowl species. It is the only regular British wintering ground of the pale-bellied form of the Brent Geese (*Branta bernicla hrota*) population that breeds in Svalbard, Spitsbergen, high in the Arctic Circle (Natural England, n.d.). Six internationally important species of wildfowl and wading birds over-winter on Lindisfarne. It also has an outstanding assemblage of plants, with the dune grasslands being particularly rich. Due to these wildlife values the coastal area that surrounds Holy Island has been legally declared a National Nature Reserve (NNR). Lindisfarne is also a Wetland of International Importance under the Ramsar Convention.

Natural England (NE) is the statutory conservation institution empowered to declare and manage NNRs in England. It is managed by two full time managers and two seasonal wardens who are supported by local volunteers. Almost all of the area, including the mudflats, is under private ownership. It is registered as an IUCN category IV protected area in the World Database of Protected Areas (WDPA), considered a 'habitat/species management area'.

Spiritual values, churches and retreats

The Anglican or Episcopalian Church is the oldest church on the island and, in some regards, can be said to be the inheritor of the Lindisfarne tradition. The Church's main role, however, is that of a Parish Church. Few of the resident population are active church goers (a situation common in Britain) but the Church provides functions related to social events. The Parish Church is one of the key visitor sites, and often hosts large groups of several thousand people.

Due to declining parishioners on the island the United Reformed Church was closed as a functioning church and converted to St Cuthbert's Centre, open all year to visitors, and hosts a variety of religious, spiritual and cultural events. The Centre is sensitive to the environmental issues and hosts an annual retreat called 'Faith and Feathers' which combines birdwatching with spiritual considerations.

There is a Catholic church on the island and a resident Catholic Sister (Daughter of the Cross) who welcomes pilgrims and holds the key to the church. A Catholic organization, the St Vincent de Paul Society, runs an independent youth camp programme on the island. The Catholic church has no particular programme focused on environmental issues.

There are two retreat centres on the island, Marygate and The Open Gate. The former is an independent charitable trust not affiliated to any church or other body. The Open Gate is the headquarters of the Community of Aidan and Hilda, a dispersed ecumenical body of Christians who seek to cradle a holistic Christian spirituality that renews the church and heals the land. They focus on Celtic Christianity and run retreats, including one called 'God in Nature'. The various church groups meet together weekly to coordinate and Holy Island has a strong ecumenical movement.

Holy Island has, along with Iona in Scotland, been the node of a revival of a Celtic spirituality. Some argue that there never was an organized 'Celtic Church' as such and that the Church in Britain, Ireland, Dalriada and Pictland owes its origin to the Apostles, the Desert Fathers of Asia Minor and the Eastern Church; nor was there a distinctive Celtic spirituality (Bradley, 1999; Meek, 2000). However, many argue that a distinctive form of nature spirituality of the Celts was indeed incorporated into the early Christian Church as it became established in these islands in early medieval times. Based on this a rich, modern Celtic spirituality revival has developed, with an increasing number of books and inspirational Christian writings. David Adam, a native of the Northumbrian coast and vicar of Lindisfarne from 1995 to 2003, is one of the foremost proponents of Christian Celtic Spirituality, and the one most associated with Lindisfarne. He has written numerous books and prayers in the Celtic style (e.g. Adam, 1987, 1989, 1990, 1991). Numerous other books, including histories, lives of the saints, prayer books and anthologies rooted in Celtic Christianity, have been produced. A small sample includes Ray Simpson (Simpson, 1995) founder of the community of Aidan and Hilda, who lives on Lindisfarne; Philip Newell (Newell, 1999, 2001, 2008) and Anthony Duncan (Duncan, 1996). Celtic spirituality not only re-defines nature as part of a Christian ethic, but also aims to heal the division between mind and matter that occurred during the reformation (Duncan, 1996). While Celtic Christianity has its sceptics, it is clear from its remarkable popularity that it is filling a need for a form of Christianity with a clear concern for the Earth and its ecological community.

Holy Island has many heritage and community values that have brought commercial values to the island. The ruins of the 12th-century Lindisfarne Priory are managed by English Heritage. Immediately adjacent to the abbey ruins is the 12th-century Parish Church Saint Mary the Virgin (Figure 7.3), run by the Anglican Diocese of Newcastle. It is said to be on the site of the wooden church built by St Aidan in AD 635 and with extant parts dating to the 7th century (see www.stmarysholyisland. org.uk, last accessed 11 April 2010). Lindisfarne Castle is a 16th-century defensive fort and is run by the National Trust, the UK's largest heritage charity.

Lindisfarne is also a Northumbrian village that is typical of the area, with a small fishing harbour, old public houses and vernacular buildings. The traditional village community is made up of a number of long-established families who are mostly farmers and fishermen. They have deep-rooted cultural ties to the island and unique traditions. Unfortunately the local population has been declining over recent years, with people leaving to seek jobs elsewhere. Increasing demand from 'incomers' has increased house prices such that young people can no longer remain in their community. The resident population the island now stands at approximately 150 people, of whom fewer than 50 grew up on the island. The local islander community, who in common with most people in UK are generally not religious, has fears of the island becoming dominated by new religious groups that do not fall into the traditional and familiar Churches.

The island has two farms and retains six inshore fishing boats which operate from the island's harbour, primarily setting crab pots. While no official statistics are kept it is estimated that more than half a million visitors a year visit Holy Island, and increasingly much of the island's economy is built on tourism, which is now estimated at 70–80 per cent of the island's income (Tristram, 2009). The main heritage sites, the Lindisfarne Priory and Lindisfarne Castle, depend largely on entrance fees to maintain their properties and also operate retail outlets (gift shops and/or cafes). Other businesses on the island include four hotels and pubs, five guesthouses and several cafes, shops and kiosks. The island runs a website, which provides information on the island, and also a monthly e-magazine. The websites has experienced a significant increase in web hits from 1.5 million in 2001 up to 15.4 million in 2009 (www.lindisfarne. org.uk/webmaster/statistics1.htm, last accessed 11 April 2010).

The Crown Estate (government) retains about 30 per cent of land within the National Nature Reserve and the remainder falls within 17 private holdings of the intertidal area, over which lease agreements have been negotiated by Natural England. Property ownership on the island is

Figure 7.3 St Mary's Church on the site of St. Aidan's Church next to the ruins of the abbey also showing the edge of the village

Source: R. Wild

also private, including larger land holdings under the Church of England and the Crossman Estate. Within the village itself houses are owed by many people. Much of the personal wealth of modern Britons is dependent on land and property values, which is a critical element in understanding Holy Island. Property improvements and acquisition are seen as a key way to improve personal wealth. Rapid increases in house prices during the decade to 2008 within the UK means that households on low incomes and the young have been effectively priced out of their own communities. The young often move to larger towns where prices are lower and social housing is more readily available.

This situation, where young people are not economically able to establish themselves independently within their community is not unique to Lindisfarne and affects many villages in Britain: it is a politically dominant social and ethical issue facing the country. At least one village, Castle Combe in Wiltshire, has no local community members remaining at all (Margaret Hall, personal communication). Castle Combe, often voted Britain's prettiest village, and location for many film sets, has very high housing prices and presents a disturbing parallel for Lindisfarne. When no long-standing community members remain in a village it might be said to have lost its heart. On Lindisfarne the average house price is 17 times the typical income, (www.alanbeith.org. uk, accessed 7 April 2010) whereas the average for the North East of England is less than five times (NPAU, 2008). This disparity is fuelled by the fact that more than half of the 160 dwellings are owned by non-residents of the island with many used as second or holiday homes (www.alanbeith. org.uk, accessed 7 April 2010).

Discussion and recommendations
Conservation management

The National Nature Reserve staff engage in several management practices, including livestock grazing to maintain the species rich grasslands. The wildfowl are counted monthly as part of a national monitoring programme. Visitor management includes regulating the access to the most sensitive areas, especially the sand dunes. It hosts visiting groups on request, and about 200 school groups visit per year. Invasive alien species are monitored, the most notable of which is the New Zealand piripiri burr (*Acaena aserinifolia*) historically imported in wool for the region's cloth mills. The construction of a causeway (1954–64) has perhaps caused the biggest changes to the NNR, including a local rise in the sandflats in the vicinity of the causeway itself, and hastening the conversion of mudflats to sandflat and saltmarsh, thereby reducing the area of some habitats important for wildfowl grazing (Nature England, 2005). Car parking becomes limited during the peak season when cars park along the main access road by the dunes, which Natural England is under some pressure to prevent.

Community trust fund

In response to the lack of affordable housing the islanders established The Holy Island of Lindisfarne Community Development Trust in 1996. The Trust has established and owns the Lindisfarne Visitor Centre using the profits from sales for the benefit of the Holy Island community and to provide and regenerate village resources. The work of the Trust and the revenue from the Centre has been used to build seven community houses that are rented to community members who want to stay on the island. A further four houses have just been constructed. Dick Patterson, chair of the community development trust, recently said: 'The new homes will mean four families who may otherwise have had to leave will be able to stay on the island. This can only enhance the sense of community here, which is vitally important for the quality of life' (www.alanbeith.org.uk, last accessed 4 July 2010). This indicates the proactive way in which the island community is countering

some of the challenges brought about by high property values. The Trust was one of the earliest of the Community Land Trusts, a new movement within UK, where over 200 such trusts have been established in the past 10 years and are increasingly building up a set of community owned assets (The Countryside Agency, 2005). This action has been taken forward largely without the close integration of natural, spiritual and community values and while generally supportive, not all of the island's institutions are closely involved. Whether the community ownership of only 7 per cent of the housing stock will be sufficient to ensure community continuity remains to be seen and a higher target might be needed. To achieve this will require significant funds, but given the overall size of the economy generated by Holy Island, a mechanism to raise the necessary funding should be possible.

Managing tourism

Tourism is now the mainstay of the island's economy, providing 70–80 per cent of income (Tristram, 2009). Visitor types include day trippers, birdwatchers, pilgrims and retreat goers. The birdwatchers come mostly during spring and autumn, when the migrant birds pass through and the wintering wildfowl are in residence. Pilgrims come primarily over the summer, with a small but increasing number coming by foot (Figure 7.4). Some of these have used one of the newly established long-distance themed walks; these are not original pilgrim routes, but walks based on themes related to Lindisfarne. Bus pilgrimages of 2000 people in 60 buses are not unusual, and unannounced arrivals can overload the facilities, disrupting local traffic and putting a severe strain on car parking.

Hosting over half a million visitors naturally puts a strain on the 150 island residents. The tidal nature and limited accommodation on the island does, however, mean regular quieter times over the summer months. As most of the visitors stay in the central part of the village, it is relatively easy even in the busiest times to find quieter areas, while the winter is in any case much quieter. The NNR does not have as high a profile as other attractions and once one is away from the centre of the village,

Figure 7.4 Pilgrims crossing the sandflats of the Pilgrims Way

Source: G. Porter (www.lindisfarne.org.uk, last accessed 11 April 2010, with permission)

especially the Castle, Priory and the village centre, it can be relatively quiet. The NNR is therefore under less pressure than other elements of Holy Island as a whole.

Seeking balance between nature, religion, community and commerce

The Holy Island of Lindisfarne is managed by a wide range of institutions. Over the years this has been effective, but the increasing numbers of visitors are beginning to have some negative impacts. Agreeing to a common course of action is challenging, because the key players on the island have their own remits, and while there are common interests, each has a different job to do. Each is effective in what they do but each take action in their own sphere, so management is often compartmentalized. The remits and actions are based on different visions, not all of which are clearly articulated. Some of the players are very large national level government, church or charity organizations that have specialized mandates,

bureaucratic tendencies and remote and relatively inflexible decision-making mechanisms, while other key groups, especially the local community members, have no clear mechanism for decision-making or no formalized voice in the decision-making process. When asked the question 'who is in charge of Holy Island?', the universal response was 'no-one'. A single monolithic structure to provide direction would be both inappropriate and ineffective, though a greater collective sense of direction might be needed.

It is increasingly considered that a strengthening of community action is a key element in tackling some of the key social and environmental issues that face us today (McIntosh, 2008). By and large, however, holistic and integrated planning and working on community development process is not part of any of the remits of most island institutions: not within their staff skill sets, nor part of their institutional culture. As a consequence there is no overall shared and articulated vision how Holy Island will meet the challenges of the future. There have been efforts to work collectively in the past and the good will is in place. Given that the nature conservation values of the National Nature Reserve are less affected by visitor pressure than the heritages sites and village centre, Natural England is probably the least affected of the key players by visitor numbers, and it could legitimately remain within its own wildlife conservation focus. Reorganization of Natural England over the past three years has, however, followed a more outward looking approach, in line with international trends. The 2005 Natural England vision for Lindisfarne NNR put emphasis on a holistic and integrated approach (Natural England, 2005) and the organization is establishing a community team with a full-time staff member at Lindisfarne, in place in January 2010. The NNR has the capacity for increased visitor access which has the potential to reduce some pressure, at least in the short term, from other areas of the island. For its part, the Community Development Trust, after 13 years of establishment, is widening its remit and gaining in experience and is therefore better able to represent the community with larger institutions on a more equal footing. Likewise there is a willingness on behalf of other groups to work together and several have been operating for some time in this way.

Recommendations

A process of analysis, reflection and understanding followed by consensus decision-making would appear to be necessary bringing key players together in a more in-depth way than their current working patterns and communications allow. Decision-making staff need to be engaged in this process and be willing to commit to taking action on joint decisions.

The first steps are now being taken towards such a process with the formation of a proposed Holy Island partnership. This is in its very early stages, has not met and is not widely known among some of the key players. While a forum is likely to be essential it may not be sufficient, especially at the start. A consensus building process may need to be undertaken to engage with a wider group of people than the forum representatives. One approach to consensus building could be a series of facilitated workshops to bring ideas to the table that could be examined in a positive

light, generate a shared vision and develop an agreed work plan. A good understanding of visitor numbers seems fundamental. Asking questions of the Holy island economy, as posed by Brown and Garver (2009) might be useful. These include: What is the economy for? How does it work? How big is too big? What is fair? And, how is it governed? Understanding and building a 'whole island economy' that answers these questions could be an important effort. It is recommended that the key organizations active on Holy Island examine how they might serve community cohesion, a community of diverse interests unified by a strong sense of place.

The Holy Island of Lindisfarne is one of Britain's foremost Christian sacred natural sites and is the only one where national ecological values overlap with national religious and historical values. The rising tide of interest in the island is leading to a flood of visitor numbers. The island is the focus of a significant tourism and property economy, putting local community values at risk. To meet these challenges the key players on the island have been taking significant steps, including a greater understanding of the human ecology of the island and an increased level of collective action, to ensure that the island maintains its integrity and multiple values into the future.

References

Adam, D. (1987) *The Cry of the Deer: Meditations on the Hymn of St Patrick*, Triangle, London
Adam, D. (1989) *Tides and Seasons: Modern Prayers in the Celtic Tradition*, Triangle, London
Adam, D. (1990) *The Eye of the Eagle: Meditations on the Hymn 'Be Thou my Vision'*, Triangle, London
Adam, D. (1991) *Border Lands: The Best of David Adam's Celtic Vision*, Sheed and Ward, Wisconsin
Bede (AD 731) *An Ecclesiastical History of the English People*. Edited and with an introduction by McClure, J. and Collins, R. (1994) Oxford World Classics, Oxford University Press, Oxford
Bradley, I. (1999) *Celtic Christianity: Making Myths, Chasing Dreams*, Palgrave Macmillan, New York
Brown, M.P. (2003) *Painted Labyrinth: The World of the Lindisfarne Gospels*, The British Library, London
Brown, P.G. and Garver, G. (2009) *Right Relationship: Building a Whole Earth Economy*, Berrett-Koehler Publishers Inc, San Francisco

Carmichael, A. (1900) *Carmina Gadelica: Hymns and incantations, collected in the Highlands and islands of Scotland*, this arrangement published in 1992, Floris Books, Edinburgh

Duncan, A. (1996) *A Little Book of Celtic Prayer: A Daily Companion and Guide*, Marshall Pickering, London

Farmer, D.H. (1978) *The Oxford Dictionary of Saints*, Oxford University/Clarendon Press, Oxford

Farmer, D.H. (ed) (1998[1965]) *The Age of Bede*, Penguin Classics, London

Fraser, I. (ed) (2008) *The Pictish Symbol Stones of Scotland*, Royal Commission on the Ancient and Historical Monuments of Scotland, Edinburgh.

Leatham, D. (1948) *They Built on Rock: Stories of the Celtic Saints*, Hodder and Stoughton, London

Magnusson, M. (1984) *Lindisfarne: The Cradle Island*, Oriel Press, London

Marner, D. (2000) *St Cuthbert: His Life and Cult in Medieval Durham*, The British Library, London

McIntosh, A. (2008) 'Rekindling community: Connecting people, environment and spirituality', Schumacher Briefings 15, Green Books, Totnes

Meek, D. (2000) *The Quest for Celtic Spirituality*, Handsel Press, Kincardine

Moffat, A. (2005) *Before Scotland: The Story of Scotland before History*, Thames and Hudson, London

Natural England (n.d.) 'Lindisfarne National Nature Reserve', a visitor's guide, www.naturalengland. org.uk/ourwork/conservation/designatedareas/ nnr/1006092.aspx, accessed 4 July 2010

Natural England (2005) 'Management plan of Lindisfarne National Nature Reserve', Natural England, The Quadrant, Newcastle upon Tyne

Newell, J.P. (1999) *The Book of Creation: An Exploration of Celtic Christianity's Celebration of Creation and Creativity*, Paulist Press, New Jersey

Newell, J.P. (2001) *Listening to the Heartbeat of God: A Celtic Spirituality*, SPCK, London

Newell, J.P. (2008) *Christ of the Celts: The Healing of Creation*, J. Wiley and Sons, London

NPAU (2008) 'Affordability still matters', National Housing and Planning Advice Unit, Fareham, www.communities.gov.uk/nhpau

Shepherd, William R. (1923) available at www.lib. utexas.edu/maps/historical/shepherd/british_ isles_802.jpg (last accessed 4 July 2010)

Simpson, R. (1995) *Exploring Celtic Spirituality: Historic Roots for Our Future*, Hodder and Stoughton, London

The Countryside Agency (2005) *Capturing Value for Rural Communities: Community Land Trusts and Sustainable Rural Communities*, The Countryside Agency, Sheffield

Tristram, K. (2009) *The Story of Holy Island: An Illustrated History*, Canterbury Press, Norwich

8

Tourism Meets the Sacred: Khumbu Sherpa Place-based Spiritual Values in Sagarmatha (Mount Everest) National Park and Buffer Zone, Nepal

Jeremy Spoon

Summary

This chapter discusses how tourism influences Khumbu Sherpa place-based spiritual values inside Sagarmatha (Mount Everest) National Park and Buffer Zone, Nepal. The Khumbu Sherpa, who live inside the protected area, are Nyingma Buddhists who consider their homeland to be a beyul or sacred hidden valley and to contain yul-lha or protector deities that live on mountains. Inside this area, certain codes of conduct govern decision-making that has some environmentally-sustainable outcomes. These include taboos on killing animals, cutting live trees and polluting water sources. Tourism began in the 1960s and intermixed with subsistence herding and farming. It is now the cornerstone of the local economy, influencing how Sherpa view and interact with their homeland. The number of visitors continues to increase, totalling more than 25,000 for 2008. To gauge the influence of tourism on these place-based spiritual values, a stratified random sample of 100 households was selected and Multiple Regression Analysis comparing select demographics to knowledge of place-based spiritual values was conducted. The results showed that tourism appears to be changing these values, including those associated with sacred sites, especially for the more market-integrated and younger generations. These individuals appear to be ontologically dividing humans from the land – changes that may be the catalysts for less sustainable decision-making. Other values, such as the veneration of yul-lha and taboos on killing wildlife persist or are being transformed. This chapter concludes with a discussion on the potential causation for these market-driven changes.

The Khumbu Sherpa and Sagarmatha National Park and Buffer Zone

The Khumbu and Pharak landscape

The spectacular Khumbu and Pharak landscape contains some of the highest mountains on earth. The 1389km^2 region, located along the border

Figure 8.1 Map of Sagarmatha (Mount Everest) National Park and Buffer Zone (Khumbu and Pharak)

Source: Courtesy of the International Centre for Integrated Mountain Development

between Nepal and the Tibetan Autonomous Region of China in the SoluKhumbu District of Nepal, is almost entirely surrounded by mountain peaks – some more than 6000m (see Figure 8.1). These mountains cause a dramatic elevation range from 2800 to 8850m. Among these peaks are three of the ten highest in the world, including Mount Everest (8850m), known as Jomolangma to the Khumbu Sherpa and their Tibetan neighbours to the north, and Sagarmatha to the Nepalese government.

Khumbu vegetation roughly divides into three altitudinal zones – temperate (2800–3200m), sub-alpine (3200–4000m) and alpine (4000–6000m).

Centuries of grazing, harvesting, and burning also influenced the vegetation's distribution patterns (Sherpa, 1999; Byers, 2005). The wildlife of the area includes ungulates, predators, rodents, lagomorphs and diverse forest and migratory birds. The flowering plants support several butterfly, moth, bee and fly pollinators. Many also consider the Yeti or abominable snowman to be an inhabitant (Brower, 1991).

The Sherpa and agro-pastoralism

The migration of the Sherpa, 'people of the east', to the Khumbu region occurred around

Figure 8.2 View from Gokyo Ri (5357m) across Sagarmatha National Park and Buffer Zone at sunset

Jomolangma (Mount Everest) is the mountain on the far left.

Source: Jeremy Spoon

1533. Oral history suggests the homeland was a region in eastern Tibet in the province of Kham approximately 2090km away. Prior to Sherpa settlement, Khumbu was known as a vacant land without human settlement and was later used by hermits for meditation retreats (Ortner, 1989). Khumbu is almost entirely populated by Sherpa, including around 2800 that live there for more than three months each year. Most spend between 9 and 12 months in Khumbu annually, with the more affluent retreating to Kathmandu in the winter. It is also becoming increasingly common for the wealthy to send their children to boarding schools in Kathmandu for up to 10 to 12 months.

Khumbu Sherpa agro-pastoralism specializes in high-altitude varieties of crops and livestock and the collection of forest products. This specialization relies on the local ability to obtain agricultural and pastoral products through trade, the weekly market, Tibetan vendors and trips to Kathmandu. The Sherpa are not nomadic herders;

rather, shepherds migrate with their yaks, cows and yak/cow hybrids between specific lower and higher pastures at prescribed times of year. Although herding is declining, all households continue to farm, even those with significant income from tourism. Some households continue to collect forest products from the local temperate, sub-alpine and alpine ecosystems, while others hire or work alongside indigenous labourers from the south. Men typically carry out timber felling, and both males and females gather fuelwood, which in principle is dead wood. Women collect the bulk of leaf litter as well as mushrooms and incense. The most typical harvested food products are mushrooms; others are in decline.

The declaration of the protected area

Khumbu and Pharak share the same boundaries as a demarcated protected area called Sagarmatha National Park and Buffer Zone (SNPBZ) (see

Figure 8.1). It was created in 1976 under the National Parks and Wildlife Conservation Act (1972) and selected as a UNESCO World Heritage Site with a natural designation in 1979. With assistance from the New Zealand government, the protected area became one of the first national parks in Nepal where indigenous settlements and resource use were recognized. Indeed, there are many cases of protected area establishment where indigenous peoples were removed from their ancestral lands or their resource use was highly restricted or altered, including the barring of thousands of Tharu peoples from Chitwan National Park, Nepal (Ghimire, 1999). In SNPBZ, Sherpa land ownership and resource use afforded the opportunity for local landowners along the main tourist routes to develop their properties for tourism enterprises. In 2002, an additional 275km² area was added to the Park as Buffer Zone, which includes the adjacent area to the south. This area, called Pharak, leads from a small airport to the Park entrance, serving as the main tourism corridor (DNPWC, 2007). The Park's privately owned land and settlements, including some forests, croplands and homesteads, are all part of the Buffer Zone. Local residents also use some of the core Park areas for grazing and resource harvest. The core Park area is an IUCN Category II protected area, and the Buffer Zone areas are Managed Resource Protected Areas or IUCN Category VI. Khumbu Sherpa sacred sites exist in both the Category II National Park and Category VI Buffer Zone.

Park management and governance

Although the Sherpa were allowed to maintain their settlement in the Park, the first Management Plan lacked any mention of Sherpa spiritual values or resource management and did not have a strong tourism management policy (Garratt, 1981). In 2007, a new plan was ratified that places stronger emphasis on the integration of local spiritual values and practices into management. It also empowers the Sherpa to take a stronger role in resource management and has multiple regulations on tourism development (DNPWC, 2007).

The Chief Warden supported by a team of civilian park rangers, game scouts, administrative staff and the Nepal Army enforce SNPBZ management

objectives. Settlements not under National Park control are declared as Buffer Zone and are governed under the dual and overlapping control of the local Village Development Committee (VDC) and the Buffer Zone Management Committee (BZMC). Regulations allow settlers inside and at the boundary of parks to organize into different Buffer Zone User Committees (BZUC). Through these regulations the local settlements are eligible to receive 30–50 per cent of the National Park revenue for local development activities that they prioritise (Spoon and Sherpa, 2008). Most of these projects benefit local tourism in some way, such as improving trails and incinerating waste. The Buffer Zone has also funded programmes that promote the transmission of knowledge, including a Sherpa singing and dancing competition and prayer lessons.

Khumbu tourism
Escalating tourism

Nepal is one of the poorest countries in the world, subsistence agriculture is the mainstay of the economy (79 per cent) and most families earn under US$400 per year (Dahal, 2004). Tourism did not start to diversify the nation's economy until well after it opened up its borders in 1951. In Khumbu, aside from specific expeditions aimed at summiting Mount Everest, significant trekking and sightseeing activities did not begin until the late 1960s (Stevens, 1993).

The number of visitors continues to increase, reaching more than 25,000 in 2008. Quantitative and qualitative survey research on the Khumbu tourism economy and tourist perceptions conducted in the fall of 2006 and spring of 2007 found that most tourists trek along the main route towards Tengboche Monastery, Mount Everest Base Camp and Kala Patar in the Imja Khola Valley, and significantly fewer visit the Dudh Kosi and Nangpa Valleys (see Figure 8.2). The bulk of tourists originate from Europe, North America, Japan and Australia/New Zealand and travel in the spring and autumn seasons when the mountain views are clearer and frequent. Even though the Himalayas receive recognition as a prime mountaineering destination, most visitors are trekkers who do not climb peaks. The average trip length is around 14 days and most tourists stay and eat in locally owned lodges and teashops. The primary motivations for visits are beauty of the scenery/landscape and interest in the peoples/cultures.

The local and regional economies of Khumbu and the larger SoluKhumbu District are now rather dependent on tourism. Utilizing local estimates and data projections from research results, the local and regional profit and earnings from tourism (excluding trekking agencies and the airlines) in autumn 2006 and spring 2007 was roughly US$4.5 million. In that same period, the Khumbu Sherpa received approximately 29 per cent of these profits and earnings (US$1.4 million) with the remainder divided among a much larger population from ethnic groups in neighbouring districts and Kathmandu. Tourism also causes a significant amount of inflation in Khumbu; indeed, many goods at the local markets and stores cost more than double what they do in Kathmandu and exponentially more than in other rural locations. Khumbu Sherpa thus need to make more money to sustain their livelihoods and tourism enterprises, especially as their standard of living increases.

Sherpa tourism involvement and benefit

Khumbu Sherpa involvement and resulting benefit from tourism mostly derives from lodge and teashop ownership and providing tourism services. In spring 2007, a lodge survey showed that there were 180 lodges and 123 teashops in Khumbu with more than 80 per cent existing along the tourist route. Khumbu Sherpa owned and operated most of the lodges and teashops, which returned approximately US$1.2 million as profits in 2006; of these profits, more than 70 per cent benefited households on the tourist route. The disparity between households on and off the tourist route accounts for much of the difference in household economic capacity. The households living off the tourist route are also integrated into the tourism economy, but generally less strongly, serving as tourism service staff and seasonal porters. The remainder of the year these households engage more actively in farming and livestock herding.

Tourism service positions from all Sherpa households are on the decline because there is now a proliferation of outside ethnic groups serving in these roles. This is a significant change from the past where Khumbu Sherpa dominated the entire industry. Reasons for this shift in the tourist industry demographics include trekking agencies outsourcing labour for cheaper rates and the inability for some Sherpa to make enough money in these positions to afford the expenses of a Khumbu household. Many stigmatize lower-level tourism service positions, such as portering, as the work of poorer Sherpa and other indigenous groups from the south. As the number of tourists continues to increase, there will no doubt be an even larger representation of non-Khumbu Sherpa in the tourism industry for years to come.

Spiritual values, sacred natural sites and landscapes
Sherpa Nyingma Buddhism

The Sherpa are Tibetan Buddhists who follow the ancient Nyingma sect, incorporating Buddhist, Bon, and folk traditions (Tucci, 1988). As Buddhists, they assume the basic principles of sin and merit and of the reincarnation of various states of being. These reincarnations are positive or negative depending on the amount of sin or merit accumulated in the course of a lifetime. Ample good deeds and merit accumulation boosts one's chances of improved rebirth and the ultimate aim of ceasing the cyclic existence over a series of lives, deaths and rebirths. Importantly, the Sherpa consider the Indian saint Guru Rinpoche or Padmasambhava as the teacher of Buddhism and place him at a status near to the Buddha. Sherpa view the world as a place occupied by a diversity of supernatural beings, including deities, spirits and ghosts. Under the appropriate conditions, the deities and spirits protect the land, the people and their faith. In order to receive protection, the Sherpa regularly perform rituals and make offerings to please the deities and to ask for their forgiveness. Worship of these entities occurs in monasteries, homes or open spaces (Ortner, 1989).

The Khumbu Sherpa recognize two categories of sacred landscape: beyul or hidden valleys and yul-lha or sacred mountains. The spiritual values associated with these landscapes influence Sherpa decision-making regarding natural resources and connect to various sacred sites and species in the Khumbu landscape such as forests, trees, water sources, rocks, mammals and birds. These values generally encourage more environmentally-sustainable decision-making, such as taboos on cutting trees, polluting water sources and killing animals. Beyul and yul-lha spiritual values were most likely exported from other landscapes in Tibet to the Khumbu landscape upon the Sherpa migration.

Beyul

The Buddhist tradition teaches that in the 8th century Guru Rinpoche envisioned many hidden valleys of refuge, called beyul, in the Himalaya (Sherpa, 2003, 2005). Inside a beyul, people must refrain from negative actions that are inconsistent with Buddhist philosophy. Rules include not harming or killing any living things (from humans to animals to plants), refraining from violence in any way, not stealing or cheating another person and generally pleasing the local gods and spirits. All beyul lands are the same; however, it is the observation of these codes of conduct that make

them sacred and powerful. The beyul spiritual value helps to safeguard all living things through chaam and nyingje (kindness and compassion), which translates into the direct protection of mammals, birds and vegetation. Indeed, the beyul spiritual value places environmentally sustainable taboos on the hunting and killing of several animal species and the harvest of live wood (Spoon and Sherpa, 2008).

Yul-Lha

Yul-Lha are protector deities that live on mountains whose existence pre-dates the arrival of Buddhism in Tibet. They are part of an animistic tradition that intermixed with Buddhist and Bon spiritual tenets (Studley, 2005). In the Buddhist perspective, these deities were demons that Guru Rinpoche subdued and bound by oath to remerge as protectors of Buddhism. These deities must be pleased to offer protection from avalanches, landslides, floods, war and plane crashes (see Figure 8.3). Each deity has

Figure 8.3 Flags placed on the slopes of the sacred mountain for the protector deity Khumbu Yul-Lha during the annual Dumji ceremony

Source: Jeremy Spoon

its own associates or khor in the form of wildlife, livestock and other mythical creatures. People respect these associates and do not harm them. The deity appointed by Guru Rinpoche to protect Khumbu is Khumbu Yul-Lha or Khumbila, literally 'Khumbu country god'. This deity lives in the mountain directly above the Khunde and Khumjung settlements. Worship entails the burning of aromatic incense from multiple sub-alpine and alpine plants, placing white flags over the house on specific days and an annual ceremony. Tourism influenced the significance of the goddess Jomo Miyo Lang Sangma, who resides on Mount Everest and is the provider of wealth. Before tourism, this wealth was plentiful harvests and abundant pastures; after tourism, her gifts expanded to include tourists.

Generally, the climbing of a mountain that is the home of a protector deity is prohibited; however, there is a tradition of circumambulating sacred mountains. Mountain climbing became more common with the advent of tourism, affording income and reputation. Although the mountain climbing taboo was lifted for tourism purposes, Khumbila remains off limits. To ensure safety on expeditions, some climbers and their families offer the mountain deities incense and prayers before beginning a climb.

Sacred forests

Forests are sacred sites protected by spiritual values. There are two types; the first are forests that grow in areas considered sacred because certain spirits reside there and the second includes two types of protected groves, lama and monastery. Lama protected forests originated when a powerful lama sanctified or cursed a forest patch, where trees must not be used or felled by using cutting implements. Monastery forests are typically groves that surround or are nearby village monasteries. The oldest monastery forest of old growth Shugpa or tree juniper (*Juniperus recurva*) exists in Pangbuche, attributed to the sacred hair of the monastery founder (Stevens, 1993).

Sacred trees, water sources and rocks

Lu are another category of land protectors. Some live near homes under adjacent trees, in rocks and water sources, while others live inside the home in a constructed shrine. Lu can bestow wealth and long life to a family, but can also cause hardship, often in the form of physical ailments that can only be treated by the shaman. Women take care of Lu using knowledge passed down from female to female. Lu are upset by pollution, cutting trees, breaking boulders and digging land. These values thus influence environmental decision-making, such as taboos on polluting water sources and protecting various tree species.

Tourism and place-based spiritual values
Rationale

By and large, tourism and its resulting economic benefits appear to be reshaping perceptions of land, influencing decision-making regarding natural resources. The documented scrub and forest degradation in alpine areas (Byers, 2005) and on the periphery of the protected area (Stevens, 2003) may be evidence of this interaction. The households along the tourist route have generally received higher benefit from tourism than those off the route; these economic differences also appear to be translating into knowledge differences of place-based spiritual values. Additional drivers of change include western-style education in non-local languages, tourism and agro-pastoral involvement. With the number of tourists continually increasing, these dynamics will probably intensify for years to come.

Methodology

In order to learn how tourism influences Sherpa place-based spiritual values, field research was conducted over a period of 19 months between October 2004 and July 2007. A stratified random sample of 100 households was collected and demographically profiled. The sample was stratified to ensure that an even number of participants was selected from each local administrative district. One individual from each household was chosen for in-depth research on the following place-based spiritual values: beyul, yul-lha, kindness and compassion towards animals, monastery and other protected forests, and Lu spirits. Participants were all over 18 years old – an age whereby an individual had typically attended some school and conducted some agro-pastoralism or tourism, or both.

A photo recognition technique was used where participants were shown A4 size photos of deities, natural features and locations that have spiritual values associated with them. Participants were asked semi-structured interview questions that were identified through key informant interviews, focus groups and literature analysis. The results were based on 'scoring' the individual's knowledge of the selected spiritual values. Scored results and household demographics were then analysed applying multivariate Multiple Regression Analysis (McClendon, 1994) using SPSS statistical software (version 16.0). A hypothesis-driven model was applied based on independent and dependent variables.

Results

The results suggest that tourism is causing some placed-based spiritual values to erode and is influencing others to persist or adapt (see Figure 8.4). Proximity to the tourist route, age and gender were all significant predictors of general knowledge of selected spiritual values ($p<0.001$ and $p<0.005$). Individuals living off the route, elders and males were found to possess the most general knowledge. The significant predictors for beyul knowledge were proximity to the tourist route and age, and there was a tendency ($p<0.10$) for gender and tourism interaction. Individuals living off the route, elders, males and past tourism service providers hold more beyul knowledge. Yul-Lha knowledge results demonstrated that proximity to tourist route and age were significant predictors, and tourism interaction reflected a tendency. Individuals off the route, elders and present tourism service providers showed the most knowledge of these deities. The results for kindness and compassion towards wildlife knowledge were age and education level, and there was a tendency for tourism. Elders, the more educated, and past tourism service providers were more knowledgeable of these values. For monastery and other protected forests knowledge, proximity to tourist route, age and tourism interaction were significant predictors, and education level showed

a tendency for other protected forests. Participants living off the route and in one settlement on the route, elders, past tourism service providers and the less educated were the most knowledgeable. Finally, the significant predictors of Lu spirit knowledge were proximity to the tourist route, age and gender. Individuals living off the route, elders and males were found to have the most knowledge.

Descriptive statistics on the content of the structured and semi-structured questionnaires expressed that the most pervasive knowledge/practices were the taboo against climbing Khumbila, the belief in yul-lha in some/all mountains and values of kindness and compassion towards wildlife (protecting wild and domestic mammals and birds), Lu spirits and monastery forests were the next most common, followed by other protected forests. Beyul knowledge was the least known, especially among the younger generations.

Discussion

This research provides a snapshot into a particular time and place. Sherpa do not emerge from an unchanging static past. Knowledge of spiritual values is not monolithic; rather, it is heterogeneously distributed throughout a population and changes depending on what political and economic forces people experience in their day-to-day lives. At one point in time these values and the practices associated with them may be sustainable; at another time, they may not be. This case study shows how tourism is influencing the way the Sherpa see the land in general and sacred sites in particular. Apart from the protector deity Khumbila and general principles of kindness and compassion towards wildlife, individuals from off the tourist route had higher knowledge of these traditions. Knowledge transmission to the younger generations also appears to be declining. Spiritual values with sustainable practices connected to them thus appear to be eroding from a portion of the population because of market integration through tourism and the associated forces of globalization.

The findings suggest that the younger generations and households on the tourist route may be starting to ontologically divide humans

Variable/Place-Based Spiritual Value		General Place – Based Spiritual Value Knowledge	Beyul	Yul-Lha	Kindness and Compassion Towards Wildlife	Monastery Forests	Other Protected Forests	Lu Spirits
Market Integration	On the Tourist Route	–	–	p<0.05[b]	–	p<0.001–p<0.05[c]	–	–
	Off the Tourist Route	p<0.001–p<0.05	p<0.05	–	–	p<0.001–p<0.05	p<0.001–p<0.05	p<0.05
Age	Older	p<0.001–p<0.05	p<0.05	p<0.05	p<0.05	p<0.05	p<0.05	p<0.05
	Younger	–	–	–	–	–	–	–
Gender	Male	p<0.05	p<0.001–p<0.05	p<0.05	–	–	–	p<0.05
	Female	–	–	–	–	–	–	–
Education Level	Less Educated	–	–	–	–	–	p<0.10	–
	More Educated	–	–	–	p<0.05	–	–	–
Farming	Farmed in Past Year	–	–	–	–	–	–	–
	Did Not Farm in Past Year	–	–	–	–	–	–	–
Livestock Herding	Herded in Past Year	–	–	–	–	–	–	–
	Did Not Herd in Past Year	–	–	–	–	–	–	–
Fuelwood Collection	Collected Fuelwood in Past Year	–	–	–	–	–	–	–
	Did Not Collect Fuelwood in Past Year	–	–	–	–	–	–	–
Tourism Interaction	Past Tourism Service Providers	p<0.05	p<0.10	–	p<0.10	p<0.05	–	–
	Present Tourism Service Providers	–	–	p<0.10	–	–	–	–

N=100

Note: Sample period between 1 June 2006 and 30 April 2007.

[a] Results represent significant variables (p<0.001–p<0.05) and insignificant tendencies (p<0.10) for five or more models and do not have the six multiple dimensions of Location of Settlement and Age Group and three multiple dimensions of Education Level and Tourism Interaction.

[b] On the tourist route Pangbuche-Dingbuche and Khunde-Khumjung higher than off the tourist route Phurte-Samde.

[c] On the tourist route Pangbuche-Dingbuche higher than all other settlements.

Figure 8.4 Results of multiple regression analysis for Khumbu Sherpa place-based spiritual value knowledge

Source: Jeremy Spoon

from nature. Both entities are thus becoming separate and non-relational. This trend may be even more pervasive among individuals currently under the age of 18. Conversely, older generations generally consider humans and nature as interconnected and relational. The beyul concept serves as the umbrella that links humans to each other and the land. This perspective has obvious resource management implications, as it places taboos on harming or killing animals (livestock, mammals and birds) and restrictions on the harvest of live wood. Most of the sample under the age of 39 was unaware of this principle – evidence that it is falling away and being replaced by other knowledge that may divide people from place, such as information communicated in schools and in tourism's host–guest interaction.

The causation for the differences between elders and youth and the more market-integrated settlements appears to be the result of multiple interlinked factors. These include changes in standard of living caused by the lure of luxury goods, cross-cultural exchange between the tourists and the Sherpa and the general significance given to certain domains of knowledge that help to make money, such as English and mathematics. Most of the younger Sherpa have at least five years of education and are increasingly reaching the 10-year level. Many youth from more affluent families are being sent to boarding schools outside the area – a process that separates them from their elders and the land. As there is much information about practical and spiritual relationships with land coded in language, the lack of Sherpa language transmission by parents and elders, schooling taught in a non-local language and the outflow of students to boarding schools may be reinforcing the dissolution of place-based spirituality.

Men had more awareness of place-based spiritual values than women. Apart from researcher bias, causation for these findings may be that men rely more on protector deities that help in precarious situations, such as mountaineering. Women's lives are becoming more sedentary compared to men's, especially among lodge and teashop owners, which may also be causing a difference in knowledge. The result that present tourism service providers embody higher knowledge of protector deities on mountains may show that tourism is potentially remaking this domain. These individuals appear to be worshipping the deities for safety and/ or mountaineering, and trekking guides may be teaching the tourists about them. The belief that Jomo Miyo Lang Samba provides wealth in the form of tourists and not in agro-pastoralism is also evidence of these new innovations. These processes suggests that working on the land in tourism may perpetuate spiritual values; conversely, living more sedentary lives conducting business and not interacting with the land may be influencing their erosion.

Conclusion

This case study describes how tourism influences Khumbu Sherpa place-based spiritual values inside a protected area. Market integration through tourism and other associated forces appear to be causing the dissolution of some of these values, while reinforcing and remaking others. Some of these dynamics may purport an ontological separation between people and nature, especially among the households on the tourist route and the younger generations. Less environmentally sustainable decision-making is thus possible because some individuals are seeing the place differently. As the Khumbu Sherpa receive a significant benefit from tourism and related endeavours, the power, if desired, exists to reinforce their connection with their homeland through spiritual values. This process may in turn promote Sherpa associations with place while supporting environmental sustainability for future generations.

References

Brower, B. (1991) *Sherpa of Khumbu: People, Livestock, and Landscape*, Oxford University Press, Delhi

Byers, A. (2005) 'Contemporary human impacts on alpine ecosystems in Sagarmatha (Mt. Everest) National Park, Khumbu, Nepal', *Annals of the Association of American Geographers*, vol 95, pp112–140

Dahal M.K. (2004) *Nepalese Economy: Towards Building a Strong Economic Nation-State*, New Hira Books, Kathmandu

DNPWC (2007) 'Sagarmatha National Park management and tourism plan', Department of National Parks and Wildlife Conservation and Tourism for Rural Poverty Alleviation Programme, Kathmandu

Garratt, K.J. (1981) 'Sagarmatha National Park management plan', Department of Lands and Survey, Wellington

Ghimire, M. (1999) 'The Royal Chitwan National Park and its impact on indigenous peoples of Chitwan and Nawalparai, Nepal', in Colchester, M. and Erni, C. (eds) 'Indigenous peoples and protected areas in South and Southeast Asia', Proceedings of the Conference at Kundasang, Sabah, Malaysia, IWIGIA, Copenhagen

McClendon, M.J. (1994) *Multiple Regression and Causal Analysis*, Waveland Press, Inc, Prospect Heights

Ortner, S.B. (1989) *High Religion: A Cultural and Political History of Sherpa Buddhism*, Princeton University Press, Princeton

Sherpa, L.N. (1999) 'Human impacts on high-altitude forest structures in the Nangpa and Hinku, Sagarmatha and Makalu Barun National Parks, Nepal', PhD Dissertation, University of Washington, Washington, DC

Sherpa, L.N. (2003) 'Sacred Beyuls and biological diversity conservation in the Himalayas', Proceedings of the International Workshop on the Importance of Sacred Natural Sites for Biodiversity Conservation, Kunming and Xishuangbanna Biosphere Reserve, People's Republic of China, 17–20 February 2003

Sherpa, L.N. (2005) 'Sacred hidden valley and ecosystem conservation in the Himalayas', Proceedings of the International Symposium on Conserving Cultural and Biological Diversity: The Role of Sacred Natural Sites and Cultural Landscapes, Tokyo, Japan, 30 May–2 June 2005, UNESCO, Paris.

Spoon, J. (2008) 'Tourism in a sacred landscape: Political economy and Sherpa ecological knowledge in Beyul Khumbu/Sagarmatha National Park, Nepal', PhD Dissertation, University of Hawai'i at Manoa

Spoon, J. and Sherpa, L.N. (2008) 'Beyul Khumbu: The Sherpa and Sagarmatha (Mount Everest) National Park and Buffer Zone, Nepal', in Mallarach, J.-M.

(ed) *Protected Landscapes and Cultural and Spiritual Values*, Kasparek Verlag, Heidelberg

Stevens, S. (1993) *Claiming the High Ground*, University of California Press, Berkeley

Stevens, S. (2003) 'Tourism and deforestation in the Mt Everest region of Nepal', *The Geographical Journal*, vol 169, pp255–277

Studley, J. (2005) 'Sustainable Knowledge Systems and Resource Stewardship: In search of ethno-forestry paradigms for the indigenous peoples of Eastern Kham', PhD Dissertation, Loughborough University

Tucci, G. (1988) *The Religions of Tibet*, Routledge and Keagan Paul, London

9

The Road to the Future? The Biocultural Values of the Holy Hill Forests of Yunnan Province, China

Pei Shengji

If you cut down all the trees, you have only the bark to eat; if you destroy the forest, you destroy your road to future. (Dai folksong, Wang, 1988)

Summary

Yunnan Province is one of the most geographically, biologically and culturally diverse Provinces of China. Over a long period of time the diverse cultures of the area have developed holistic agricultural and forest livelihood systems. After 20 years of study of the biodiversity and culture of the Province, evidence is showing that the sacred forests or Holy Hills are as equally biologically diverse as government-established nature reserves despite their much smaller size. Recent development pressures have, however, led to the destruction of 90 per cent of the forests of the Holy Hills. With specific examples from the Dai and other communities in Xishuangbanna Dai Autonomous Prefecture the relationship between culture and nature is described and recommendations made for conserving biological and cultural diversity based on China's strong tradition of maintaining harmony between man and nature.

Introduction

Many traditional societies in Yunnan Province of southwestern China still recognize sacred forests and sacred mountains, engaging in traditional practices for the protection of species, natural ecosystems and geographic areas as social and cultural activities and as an expression of their worldview of the sacredness of nature.

Yunnan is a geographical region characterized by great biological and cultural diversity. Situated at the high altitude 'roof' of inland China the broader eco-region spans the upland areas of the Greater Mekong Sub-Region, it has six major watershed systems, including the upstream of Yangtze, Mekong, Selween, Irowadi, Red and Pearl Rivers and borders with Vietnam, Laos and Myanmar. The region plays an essential role as a 'water tower' for the large human population of much of south China and mainland of Southeast Asia. The topography has shaped a diverse and complex mosaic of microclimates, micro-environments and micro-sites leading to a broad range of land-use and farming practices even within small watersheds and villages.

Yunnan province has a land area of 389,000km², of which 94 per cent is mountainous. The topography of Yunnan can be broadly divided into three areas:

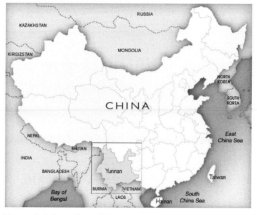

Figure 9.1 Location of Yunnan Province and of Xishuangbanna Autonomous Prefecture

Source: The Linden Centre, www.linden-centre.com

1   the high alpine mountains with deep valleys in northwest Yunnan;
2   the large temperate lakes in central Yunnan;
3   the hilly terrain and river valleys in tropical southern Yunnan.

Biological and cultural diversity

Yunnan has long been known for its outstandingly rich and diverse flora and fauna; representing 52 per cent of the plant taxa, and 54 per cent of the total vertebrates species, for all of China (Pei, 2003). Approximately 17,000 species of higher plants and 1737 species of vertebrates are found in Yunnan. Much of this biodiversity is due to the dramatic geographical variation of Yunnan from high alpine (6674m above sea level (asl)) down to tropical lowland (76m asl) to creating a wide variety of forest ecosystems such as tropical rain forests, mountain evergreen forests, alpine dark coniferous forests and savanna type of forest-grass land. Half of the 17,000 plant species of Yunnan are from forest vegetation types. Forest is the most important and characteristic biome of the province, where, at present, the forest cover is 44 per cent.

Yunnan is also well known for its high cultural diversity with cultural traditions of both Himalayan and southeast Asian societies. There are 26 ethnic groups, and many more subgroups, totalling 45 million people in the province. One-third of these are ethnic minorities that are distributed in a mosaic pattern across the province. These minority peoples include the Yi, Bai, Hani, Naxi, Dai, Yao, Miao, Zhuang, Lisu, Tibetan, Lahu, Hui, Mongol, Bouyei, Wa, Jingpo, Bulang, Primi, Achang, Nu, Deong, Jinuo and Dulong.

Nature and culture in Yunnan

Due to the extensive forest cover many cultural elements are forest related. There is no doubt, for example, that the mountain agriculture is directly supported by mountain forests. Yunnan rice terrace agriculture provides a large amount of China's rice, and therefore additionally has very high economic importance. The mountain forests also provide varied livelihood products, environmental protection, and cultural and spiritual needs for the mountain people themselves. Many ethnic groups are forest people, practicing gathering, hunting and cultivating forest resources. All ethnic groups have a high dependency on forest resources for their livelihoods including fuel, fodder, timber, medicine, supplementary food and the harvest of non-timber forest products (NTFPs), agroforestry, shifting agriculture and worship in sacred forests to meet their spiritual needs.

The worship of plants and animals is not new in China and has been practiced since ancient times. The 'Feng Chan' ritual of China's ancient emperor consists of worshipping a mountain to protect mountain forests (Wang, 1988). In Yunnan the worship of plants and animals by ethnic Yi, Lahu, Hani and Dai has been reported in a number of published papers (Liu et al, 2000, 2002; Pei 1991; Pei and Luo, 2002). All ethnic groups in Yunnan have established through history and culture value systems based on respect of the biological environment. As a consequence the rich genetic diversity is the result of both natural evolution and human manipulation of ecosystems through history. Cultural beliefs and practices of indigenous people has modified and changed the landscape creating a high diversity of landscape forms, one of which is the sacred forests. Often they are the tops of hills and are locally known as Holy Hills.

Sacred forests in Xishuangbanna, Yunnan Province, China

The biological and cultural diversity, the values of sacred forest in ethnic minority areas of Yunnan has been studied over the past 20 years using ethnobotanical approaches at Kunming Institute of Botany, Chinese Academy of Sciences. The rest of this chapter discusses one particular location of study.

The Xishuangbanna Dai Autonomous Prefecture is located in the south of Yunnan Province (24°10' – 22°40'N, 90°55' – 101°50'E). It borders the Lao P.D.R. in the south and Myanmar in the southwest (Figure 9.2). About 94 per cent of a total area of 19,220km² of Xishuangbanna consists of mountainous and hilly terrain, with river valleys making up the remaining area. Tropical forests

Figure 9.2 Map of Xishuangbanna in Yunnan

Source: www.chinaaps.info

are scattered across the area and account for 33.8 per cent of the total land coverage (Pei, 1993). Although it covers only 0.2 per cent of the total land surface of China, Xishuangbanna is in fact the richest area for biodiversity in the country (Wan and Chen, 2004). The 4669 species of vascular plants recorded in Xishuangbanna make up 18 per cent of China's total, while the 727 recorded vertebrate species number 20 per cent of the total.

Thirteen of Yunnan's ethnic groups live in Xishuangbanna with a total population of 817,000 (1995) of which 35 per cent are the Dai (who have a population of 1 million in Yunnan as whole). They mainly live in tropical and sub-tropical lowland areas. The Dai have a long history of traditional culture and nature conservation is part of their customary lifestyle (Pei, 1993). The Dai have developed a paddy – rice cultivation – oriented economy with the cultivation of tea, fruits and other economic crops.

Although the valley Dai people largely depend on rice cultivation for their livelihood, forests in the mountains and hills supply various plant and animal products to support their daily life and nutrient balance. More importantly, the water supply is guaranteed by the protection of forests in the hills and mountains (Figure 9.3). Meanwhile, the mountain ethnic groups are mainly dependent on forests for shifting agriculture and wild plant harvesting. The heterogeneity of economic systems and different survivor strategies adopted by the Dai and the mountain ethnic groups are interdependent and complement each other. Therefore, a relationship of harmony based on biocultural value systems of ethnic minorities in this region, is established between people and nature in Xishuangbanna. In this regard, traditional culture beliefs and practices play a key role in conservation, the sacred forests have made

Figure 9.3 Xishuangbanna landscape of settlement, paddy, agricultural land and natural forest on Holy Hills

Source: Pei Shengji

a great contribution to the forests and biodiversity conservation in Xishuangbanna.

Dai and other Holy Hills

The sacred forest or Holy Hill is known as 'Nong' in the Dai language. Traditionally, each village had its own Nong forested hill, where in the traditional concepts of the Dai, the gods reside. All plants and animals that inhabit the sacred forest are considered to be companions of the god and are 'sacred beings' living within the god's 'garden'. In addition, the Dai believe that the spirits of their ancestors and great and revered chieftains go to the sacred forest to live following their departure from the world of the living. Any violence to or disturbance of plants and animals in the forest will be punished by the gods. Therefore, hunting, gathering and cutting are strictly prohibited (Pei, 1985, 1991; Liu et al, 2002).

The Dai originally followed an animist religion which was heavily bound to the natural world and had a forest oriented philosophy. The Dai perception of the interrelationship of human beings with their physical environment is that it consists of five major elements: forest, water, land, food and humanity. They believe that the forest is humanity's cradle, water comes from the forests, land is fed by the water and rivers and food comes from the land. Human life is thus ultimately supported by the forests and the forests are one with the supernatural realm (Pei, 1985, 1991). Among Dai folk songs, there is one that says, 'Elephants walk with forests, the climate with bamboo'. Another Xishuangbanna folk song says, 'If you cut down all the trees, you have only the bark to eat; if you destroy the forest, you destroy your road to future' (Wang, 1988).

Other ethnic minority groups in Xishuangbanna are the Yi, Hani, Yao, Bulang, Lahu, Jinuo and Kemu people. These people are scattered over mountainous forested areas, and practice shifting agriculture and tea cultivation. The Yi people also have a long tradition of preserving forests in their surrounding mountain environment and have an extensive concept of holy trees and sacred forests religious beliefs, including indigenous shamanism, adaptive Buddhism and even Catholic practices, that are intrinsic to their daily life and the establishment of a

harmonious existence between people and nature. Other ethnic groups such as the Hani, Bulang and Jinuo in the prefecture have similar beliefs and sacred forest traditions. The Hani, the second largest minority group in Xishuangbanna, have a traditional classification system for sacred forests (Wang, 1998). For instance, there is the 'Earth Mother sacred forest', the 'water source forest' and the 'cemetery forest', maintained in the Hani's settlement area of the Mengsong Mountains. In the deep forest of the Mengyang sub-Nature Reserve, a small Bulang village, Kun-man, still maintain a well-protected sacred forest called Nong Deng or the 'horse-riding mountain'. This is about 200 hectares of evergreen mountain forestland with elephants, black bears, tigers and hornbills. Its trees and plants include Yunnan eaglewood (*Aguilaria yunnansis*), *Cycas siamensis*, wild mango (*Mangefera sylvestris* and *M. siamensis*) and medicinal orchids (*Dendronbium* spp.). The Jinuo people inhabit the Jinuo mountain of the Menglun sub-Nature Reserve of the Xishuangbanna Biosphere Reserve. All the 43 villages of Jinou, with a population of 17,735 (as of 1995), are located in forested areas, and more than half the villages are in the reserve or buffer zones. The Jinuo maintain god forests and water-source forests are near village sites along with traditional tea gardens. The Jinuo have established community regulations and do not allow the cutting down of religious trees (*Ficus altissima*), wild fruits and palms in swidden fields (Long and Pei, 2003).

Biodiversity research in the sacred forests

Liu et al (2002) investigated 28 sacred forests in Xishuangbanna's Holy Hills. In each sacred forest, all plant species were investigated and identified. Four samples (each 50m × 50m) were established in four sacred forest sites, within which five quadrats of 10m × 10m were selected at random. All individual plants above or equal to 5cm diameter at breast height (DBH) of tree species and shrub species were investigated in the sample and quadrats. The Shannon-Weiner index was used for comparisons of plant species diversity. The results show that most sacred forests are distributed in the regions below 900m asl, where the vegetation types are mainly dry evergreen seasonal rainforest and semi-evergreen seasonal rainforest. Because of the expansion of modern plantations, there are hardly any of these kinds of vegetation in other places, even in the national nature reserves. According to the study there are 268 plant species belonging to 92 families in the sacred forests investigated. 15 species are protected species listed in the 'Plant Red Data List of China' such as *Magnolia henryi*, *Homalium laoticum* and *Antiaris toxicaria*, and the sacred forests constitute 30 per cent of the total protected plant species. The indexes of plant species diversity in sacred forests are similar to those in the nature reserves. Therefore, the sacred forest can be considered as small forest reserves established by the Dai traditional beliefs (Liu et al, 2002).

Current status and causes of sacred forests of Xishuangbanna

It is believed that almost every village had a sacred forest before 1958, and all sacred forests were managed by the traditional institutions of each village, led by the village head man or Bimo (the village ritual specialist). At that time there were about 1000 of these sacred forests occupying a total area of 100,000ha of natural land, or about 5 per cent of the total land of Xishuangbanna (Gao, 1999). However, currently there are only about 250 Holy Hills in Xishuangbanna, occupying between 1000 and 1500ha (Liu et al, 2002). Some sacred forests are badly degraded while many have disappeared to be replaced by rubber plantations. In total, therefore 750 Holy Hill forests representing about 90 per cent the area of sacred forest has been destroyed in Xishuangbanna Prefecture in the last 50 years.

One of the reasons for the rapid loss of sacred forests over the last two decades is that rapid economic development and population increase has brought tremendous land use pressures. Rural communities converted large area of swidden fields below 900m asl to rubber plantations for income generation. As most of the Dai villages and sacred forests are located below 1000m and available land is limited for rubber, many villages consequently converted sacred forest land into rubber plantations. In addition the forest land management policy changed from community

management (1980s) to individual management (2000s) which created the option for villagers to lease their individual forest lands to others for rubber planting. Private sector involvement was allowed and this, coupled with an increased international rubber price during the 1990s, played an important role in accelerating the rapid expansion of rubber planting in Xishuangbanna. Economic pressures were coupled with major cultural changes since the 1950s, particularly the attempted eradication of all traditional cultural beliefs during the 1960s which severely weakened the culture of sacred forest care among local communities. All traditional worship and custodians activities towards sacred forests stopped until the 1980s. In conclusion, the overall socio-cultural change and economic development over the last two decades in China, plus the impact of economic globalization, are the main reason for the loss of 90 per cent of the sacred forests in Xishuangbanna.

Despite this dramatic loss of sacred forests in Xishuangbanna, traditional culture has been revived and continues in the remaining forests. Worship ceremonies are conducted in August and November every year and all members of the village participate, offering food: chickens, ducks and pigs (Figure 9.4). The activity lasts a whole day from morning to evening. Violation of the village regulations prohibiting disturbance of the sacred forest and cutting trees is punishable with a fine of US$20–40 for one tree. In addition nature reserves have been established in the area and sacred forests are now located in both the reserves and their buffer zones. These are managed jointly by the reserve managers and the village custodians using participatory management approaches. Community regulations on the sacred forest and traditional custom and worship activities can also be organized and implemented depending on the villagers' interests. According to interviews with people in four villages in the reserve, there was no case of cutting, hunting or harvesting activities carried out by local people in the sacred forest area over the past 20 years. This shows that community participation in sacred forest management in the reserve is effective and successful (Pei, 2006).

Figure 9.4 Votive offerings made within a Holy Hill forest

Source: Pei Shengji

Recommendations on the conservation and restoration of the sacred forests in Xishuangbanna

The following are some recommendations:

- **Restore degraded sacred forests by local communities under government reforestation programmes**. Technically, recovery of degraded sacred forests is possible as demonstrated by the restoration of a degraded Holy Hill at Meng-e village carried out by Xishuangbanna Tropical Botanical Garden, part of the Chinese Academy of Sciences. From 1988–1990 1.5ha of village-degraded sacred forest was protected and restored by the replanting of over 28 native tree species by the village conservation group and the village Buddhist Temple management unit, with financial support of the Ford Foundation.

- **Include sacred forests in the forest-corridors between protected areas in Xishuangbanna.** The remaining sacred forests can be included in an ongoing 'corridor' project that is establishing forest-corridors between different patches of the National Nature Reserve in Xishuangbanna.

- **Enhance policy support recognizing the social and conservation value of sacred forests and establish protective regulations.** This has been done by the local government in Guangdong Province, 2006–2008, to regulate protection of the 'Feng Sui Forests' at local 'Feng Sui' Sites.

Economic changes in Yunnan

As previously alluded to, the impact of rapid economic development and globalization over the past half century has brought about critical challenges to the environment, biodiversity and cultural traditions. Natural forests are declining, biodiversity is threatened, forest-land is being converted into other land uses, exotic and invasive species are increasingly occupying habitats of indigenous species. Additionally, traditional knowledge systems of forest management are being lost from indigenous communities in all ethnic groups. The sustainable use and management of forest resources is not only important for conservation, for combating global climate change, but also for maintaining traditional culture, and for rural poverty reduction, particularly in ethnic minority communities and marginal societies.

Conclusion

In many Asian countries, traditional sacred areas fulfill functions similar to those of legally protected areas. Due to access restrictions, these areas are natural ecosystems in a near-natural condition in an otherwise degraded landscape. Where they have survived the pressures of modernity they are well embedded in local cultures and traditional belief systems. They often provide sanctuaries to rare or endangered species and therefore play an important role as potential gene pools that can be used to restore degraded environment. They are also important reference places of cultural identity (UNESCO-MAB, 2005).

The conservation of nature through cultural value systems, especially the traditional belief in sacred forests, has made great contribution to biodiversity conservation, As reported in this chapter, the Dai people and other indigenous ethnic minority people in Xishuangbanna in Yunnan Province, in the long history of interaction with their natural environments, have established harmony and a balanced relationship with nature through the practice of traditional knowledge, technologies and cultural beliefs. Respect, recognition and learning from these cultural traditions would be of great benefit to the conservation of nature and biodiversity today as they are often more sustainable than those based solely on government legislation or regulation.

The indigenous approaches to resource management and conservation were, however, established for a relatively small population, large forest cover, rich biodiversity and subsistence economy basis. Today, the world faces the challenge of market pressure, globalization, population expansion, urbanization, new technologies, environmental degradation, land use change (in particular industrial crop plantation expansion in this region) and a decline in biodiversity. Therefore, a long process of promoting the wide use of indigenous knowledge, traditional culture and local practices in the conservation of biodiversity needs to be undertaken. The example of Xishuangbanna shows that 90 per cent of the sacred forests have disappeared in the past 50 years, while the sacred forests located in the biosphere reserve and its buffer zones were under protection through community participation in conservation and maintaining cultural biodiversity in the region as a whole. This suggests that in places with rich biological and cultural diversity, they should be considered as part of an integrated approach to conservation (Pei, 2006).

Within Yunnan a greater recognition of these cultural and biological components is emerging. For example the establishment of a bio-corridor between different nature reserves is being undertaken in Xishuangbanna. In the long run however, conservation policy reform is needed to better consider and to recognize traditional sacred forests as Community Conserved Areas (CCA) and establish community management organizations to protect, maintain and restore sacred forests.

Today, the problems of the degraded environment and the loss of biodiversity in many developing countries are mainly the result of guided development interventions and the overexploitation of natural resources for short-term economic development, rather than development based on the knowledge systems of indigenous communities which have maintained diverse resources for thousands of years (Pei, 1993). To improve the current situation of conservation strategy and approaches, it is important to recognize sacred forests and further strengthen cooperative local conservation action with support from government and international communities.

References

Gao, L.-S. (1999) *On the Dai's Traditional Irrigation System and Environmental Protection in Xishuangbanna*, Yunnan Nationality Publishing House, Kunming, Yunnan

Liu, A.Z., Pei, S.J. and Chen, S.Y. (2000) 'An investigation and study on plant worship in Chuxiong, Yunnan', *Chinese Biodiversity*, vol 8, no 1, pp130–136

Liu, H., Xu, Z., Xu, Y. and Wang, J. (2002) 'Practice of conserving plant diversity through traditional beliefs: A case study in Xishuangbanna, Southwest China', *Biodiversity and Conservation*, vol 11, pp705–713

Long, C.L. and Pei, S.J. (2003) 'Cultural diversity promotes conservation and application of biological diversity', *Acta Botanica Yunnanica*, Supplement XIV, pp11–22

Pei, S.J. (1985) 'Some effects of the Dai people's cultural beliefs and practices upon the plant environment of Xishuangbanna, Yunnan Province, Southwest China', in Hutterer, K., Rambo, T. and Lovelace, G. (eds) *Cultural Values and Human Ecology*, in S.E. Asia Paper No 27, Ann Arbor, University of Michigan

Pei, S.J. (1991) 'Conservation of biodiverstiy in Temple Yard and Holy Hills by the Dai ethnic minority of China', *Ethnobotany*, vol 3, pp27–35

Pei, S.J. (1993) 'Managing for biological diversity in Temple Yards and Holy Hills: The traditional practices of the Xishuangbannan Dai Community, Southwest China', in Hamilton, L.S. (ed) *Ethics, Religion and Biodiversity*, The White Horse Press, Cambridge UK

Pei, S.J. (2003) 'The role of ethnobotany in the conservation on biodiversity', in Lee, C. and Schaaf, T. (eds) Proceedings of the International Workshop on the Importance of Sacred Natural Sites for Biodiversity Conservation, www.unesco.org/mab

Pei, S.J. (2006) 'Biodiversity in the Sacred Forests of Xishuangbanna Biosphere Reserve, China', in Lee, C. and Schaaf, T. (eds) 'Proceedings of Tokyo Symposium: Conserving Cultural and Biological Diversity, The Role of Sacred Natural Sites and Cultural Landscapes', UNESCO, Paris

Pei, S.J. and Luo, P. (2002) 'Mountain culture in northwest Yunnan in China', in Shinwari, Z.K., Hamilton, A. and Khan, A.A. (eds) *Applied Ethnobotany*, Proceedings of Workshop on Curriculum Development, WWF, Pakistan

UNESCO-MAB (2005) 'Proceedings of the Tokyo Symposium: Conserving Cultural and Biological Diversity, The Role of Sacred Natural Sites and Cultural Landscapes', UNESCO, Paris

Wang, N. (1988) 'Preservation and development of minority culture in S.W. China: A case study on ethnobiology', Proceedings of the XIIth International Congress of Ethnological Sciences, Zagreb, Yugoslavia

Wang, J. (1998) 'Traditional culture and biodiversity management of mountain ethnic group in Xishuangbanna: A case study of Mengsong Hani community', MSc thesis, Kunming Institute of Botany, Chinese Academy of Sciences

Wan, Z. and Chen, M. (2004) 'The kingdom of animals: Nature conservation of Yunnan', *Journal of Yunnan Forestry*, vol 15

10

Uncovering the Intangible Values of Earth Care: Using Cognition to Reveal the Eco-spiritual Domains and Sacred Values of the Peoples of Eastern Kham

John Studley

Summary

This chapter introduces methods for uncovering the intangible values of earth care against the wider context of indigenous forest values. It is based on cognitive and geospatial mapping and augmented by barrier and overlap analysis. It is illustrated with data collected from Tibetan and Qiangic speakers in Eastern Kham. The research is predicated on 15 forest-related concepts and resulted in four cognitive categories and five well-defined geographical areas within which forest values were similar enough to warrant a particular conservation approach. Changes in forest values coincided with changes in underlying biophysical phenomena and there was a significant directional trend of forest value data along a NE to SW axis. This method can be applied to the care of natural sacred sites and forests for the enhancement of biocultural diversity. The chapter concludes by elaborating on the challenges posed by this approach and provides some policy recommendations for incorporating this approach into conservation practice.

Introduction

It is becoming increasingly apparent that the sacred dimension can and does play an important role in landscape care and nature conservation. Many societies attribute a special status to sacred natural sites because they:

- are presided over/embodied by a divinity (numina);
- are liminal thresholds to the supernatural/world of spirits;
- provide an ideal locale to 'pay ones respects to Buddha' (Studley, 2005; p 279);
- are associated with a temple or church, a geomantic feature or with the ancestors;

- have been blessed or consecrated by a priest, saint or prophet;
- are sites of supernatural phenomenon (trance, vision, vision quest, enlightenment, miracle);
- provide a symbolic site for rites of passage;
- are a conduit of blessing or healing for individuals who 'robe' site features (such as trees) with rags, clothes, thread or yarn;
- are related to the origin stories of a people.

Sacred traditions and nature

Explicit nature conservation is not necessarily embedded in all sacred traditions nor do the holders of all sacred traditions care responsibly for all their landscape. Although the majority of animistic/ shamanistic people exhibit explicit nature conservation on their sacred lands, this contrasts with some sacred traditions (such as Hinduism, Buddhism and Daoism) that reduce nature to symbolism and representation (Studley, 2005). This is illustrated among the environmentalist monks in Thailand who are Buddhists but are obliged to draw on animistic traditions and 'dharmic socialism' to conserve their forests (see Chapter 5).

While the symbolic tradition is finding increasing acceptance in the academic world (Studley, 2005), the animistic tradition in under threat in Asia because it is:

- regarded as a 'superstitions myth' by some states;
- considered an inferior or 'tamed' tradition by some clerics;
- considered invalid from the viewpoint of western epistemology and knowledge systems;
- being subjected to processes of Buddhization and Sanskritization.

It is evident that many sacred traditions such as Buddhism, Hinduism, Daoism or Confucianism do offer an ethic that supports the conservation of nature. Their view of the natural world, however often lacks explicit protection or 'bonds of affection' and at best only represents a deity or its divine aspect As a result these systems can just as easily provide the basis for the domination, exploitation and control of nature and humankind (Studley, 2005).

The 'bonds of affection' for the natural world exhibited by animistic/shamanistic peoples is evident in the complex reciprocal obligations surrounding life-taking and resource-gathering which characterize a community's relations with the local bioregion. The religious paradigms that constitute indigenous life are based on respect for the sources of food, clothing and shelter that nature provides, a sense of gratitude to the creator and to the spiritual forces in creation, ritual calendars coordinated with returning migratory birds, the blooming of certain plants or the movement of the planets (Posey, 1999).

Indigenous forest values

Most national forest management plans have been based on forest products, rather than on forest values or forest perception. Seeded, however by a post-modern paradigm shift (Trouvalis, 2000), former intangible forest values are being considered as a means of addressing multiple use forestry and incorporated into forest planning.

Anthropology provides a means of eliciting indigenous forest values and mapping them cognitively and geospatially. It produces results in a format comprehensible to policy-makers and reveals taxonomies based on locally relevant criteria. It provides a model for earth care based upon the environmental values of groups of people rather than only on silviculture or conservation criteria. This approach is illustrated in the following case study in Eastern Kham, in southwest China.

Case Study: Kham

Kham is one of the most distinctive biological regions on earth. It is situated at the eastern end of the Himalaya between Qinghai-Tibetan plateau and the Chinese provinces of Sichuan and Yunnan, comprising part of 'chol khar gsun' or 'Cultural Tibet'. The region constitutes about 4 per cent of China's land area, includes seven mountain ranges and comprises Western Kham and Eastern Kham.

External impact on the region is increasing and poses a threat to Tibetan culture and religion. This has included logging and resettlement by the Han Chinese. Logging between 1950 and 1998 resulted in flooding, climate change, erosion and snow

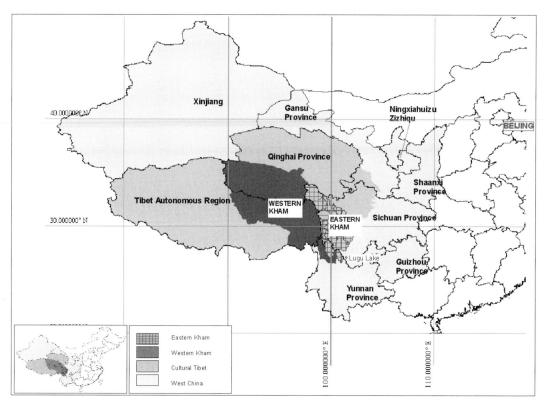

Figure 10.1 Map of the Kham region

Source: John Studley

disasters (Studley, 2005). Such activities threaten not only the diversity of flora and fauna, but also the survival of the indigenous cultures. The region bears the strong imprint of Tibetan Buddhism and animism, evident in the large temple complexes, chortens, prayer flags, festivals, shaman and numina associated with sacred landscape features. Sacred mountains punctuate the landscape and they are unique in that their forests have not been logged (Studley, 2005).

Of the nearly 5 million 'Tibetans' living in China, approximately 2 million speak Kham. They inhabit a vast area but are primarily concentrated for political and historic reasons in western Sichuan Province, a large portion of eastern Tibet Autonomous Region, parts of southern Qinghai Province and parts of Northern Yunnan (see Figure 10.1).

There are also about 250,000 Qiangic speaking peoples and 400,000 Nosu (Yi) peoples in Eastern Kham (Hattaway, 2000). The Qiangic speaking peoples are classified by the state as 'Tibetan' because

of their culture, customs and beliefs. In common with the Khamba they are animistic/shamanistic as well as Tibetan Buddhist, and burn incense and honour mountain gods at yearly festivals (Studley, 2005). They may speak Khamba as a second or third language, and are often matrilineal. Although the Nosu (Yi) live in Kham, they are not Tibetan or Qiangic speakers.

Traditional interactions with nature

There appears to be a strong tradition of natural resource care among the minority nationalities who live in Kham and unique linguistic ecologies bear testimony to these traditions. Kham's shamans and priests are often knowledgeable about trees, plants and animals and play an important role in environmental storytelling and mediation (see Figure 10.2). Many shamans and priests continue to have a role in environmental education (Studley, 2005).

Figure 10.2 A Mosuo shaman

While the priests are mostly interested in other-worldly phenomenon the shaman are liminal beings ensuring harmony on earth, between humankind, the natural world and the spirit world.

Source: John Studley

The Tibetans have three categories of sacred landscape. Two are Buddhist (Huber, 1999) and include neri mountains and beyul valleys. The other is animistic, namely yul landscapes which are embodied by a divinity with human personality and characterized by explicit nature conservation (see also Chapter 8 for Sherpa comparison).

Forest and environmental ritual

In common with many indigenous people, Eastern Kham has a tradition of spirit-placation or community restitution based on maintaining relational harmony. The Tibetan, Mosuo and Pumi describe the measures required to placate local numina and make restitution with the local community when trees or animals were killed in sacred areas (intentionally or by mistake).

Although Tibetan Buddhism is not insensitive to the natural world, its focus is much more on the purification of the mind and any ritual response to the natural world is secondary and/or symbolic (Eckel, 1997). This contrasts with the yul-lha

cults which are characterized by explicit nature conservation within sacred natural sites.

Although the Buddhist canon teaches that life is sacred and the Buddhist purgatory includes a special cold hell for souls who have killed animals, the Tibetans have always been avid hunters. However, they have accepted some taboos on some locations and species and they don't want to anger the local gods. Hunting appears to have been accepted by the establishment when game was plentiful, if there was a demand for furs in the monasteries or from the elite, or for trading purposes. Ancient dramas, such as Dunyudunju, are still performed in which the hero learns the art of hunting. Tibetan laymen still seek the blessing and protection of their territorial gods (yul-lha) when they go hunting. For all Tibetans the spiritual significance of conservation appears more important than the ecological significance.

Lartse, stone mounts, are annually constructed in ceremonies varying according to the lunar calendar. This is one of the oldest Tibetan customs and is found in all regions inhabited by Tibetans

Figure 10.3 Lartse (la btsas)

Among Tibetan laymen local territorial divinities (yul-lha or gzhi-bda) are honoured and appeased through the building of lartse (la btsas) which are wooden or stone cairns.

Source: John Studley

and some Qiangic peoples and has continued to the present day (see Figure 10.3).

The yul-lha theoretically 'tamed' by Buddhism are closer to Tibetan laymen in geography, identity and sensed presence. In the world of the lay Tibetan many landscape features point back to the worship of ancient gods. They are not only conscious of the constant scrutiny of the yul-lha when they go hunting but also they engage in rituals and place demands on their gods for protection and success in daily life. In common with the Tibetan Sherpa, they appear to recognize several different categories of earth care, from sacred and untouched to unmanaged and overexploited.

Tibetans who inadvertently remove material from a yul-lha habitat have an opportunity to make amends, usually by making offerings to the yul-lha. A more explicit form of restitution is replanting trees that have been cut down or taken away. The belief is that once the trees have grown back, the health and well-being of the culprit and the community will be restored. The replanting of trees is generally at the instruction of a Shaman.

The Tibetans do not appear to have any specific tree/forest consecration ceremonies, but lay people do recognize and protect trees within the territory of their yul-lha and sacred forests associated with monasteries are 'robed' in cloth or thread and trees are 'robed' to bring blessing or healing to the donor. These practices resonate with the 'robing' of forests in Thailand and tying rakhi (sacred bracelets) around trees during the Chipko movement (Studley, 2005; see also Chapters 4 and 5).

Methodology

Anthropologists typically try to measure attitudes, belief and perception (psychometrics) and use statistical techniques (multidimensional scaling) to build mental (cognitive) maps of intangible values. People do not react to the real world in real time, but to a mental environment filtered through traditional expectations and worldviews. They depend on mental maps to understand their world and socio-cultural factors influence the congruence of their maps with their actual environments.

Multidimensional scaling enables the researcher to study indigenous perception and cognition in order to better understand forest-related beliefs and attitudes and response to alien interventions. It has an advantage over other anthropological methods because dozens or even hundreds of values can be viewed simultaneously in a single 'picture', making it possible to see the interrelationships among beliefs and attitudes. This is important since changing one attitude or belief often changes others.

In order to prepare a cognitive map it is necessary to conduct a psychometric survey among local people and to enter the collected data into a multidimensional scaling programme. The result of this work is such that each value is represented as a point on a cognitive 'map'. Georeferenced psychometric data can also be displayed and extrapolated geospatially (Studley, 2005) and examined on the basis of barrier analysis directional trends and overlap analysis.

Results

Multidimensional scaling represented 15 forest-related concepts in four cognitive clusters or categories. On the basis of hierarchical cluster analysis, the juxtaposition of the concepts on the 'map' and the author's experience of the area it was deduced that the categories could best be described as psycho-cultural, biophysical, socio-economic and environmental and subsistence services (see Figure 10.4). The eco-spiritual domain comprises the psycho-cultural and biophysical categories and sacred values are largely synonymous with the psycho-cultural category.

Figure 10.4 shows, on the basis of multidimensional scaling (MDS), four cognitive domains (and one singleton) distributed along two dimensions (human and natural). It provides a picture showing values that are perceptually close, graphically and mathematically, and values that are not close. (The axes are meaningless and the orientation is arbitrary.) Although the four categories identified appear to be common in

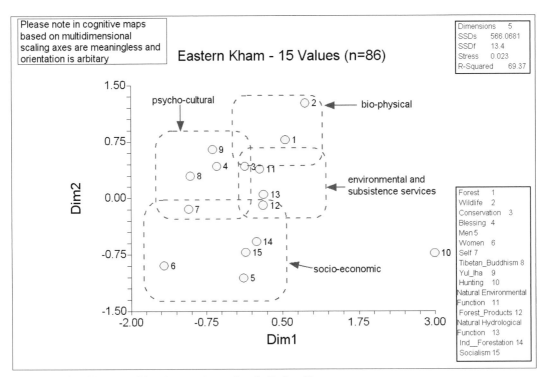

Figure 10.4 Cognitive map of forest concepts or values in Eastern Kham

Source: John Studley

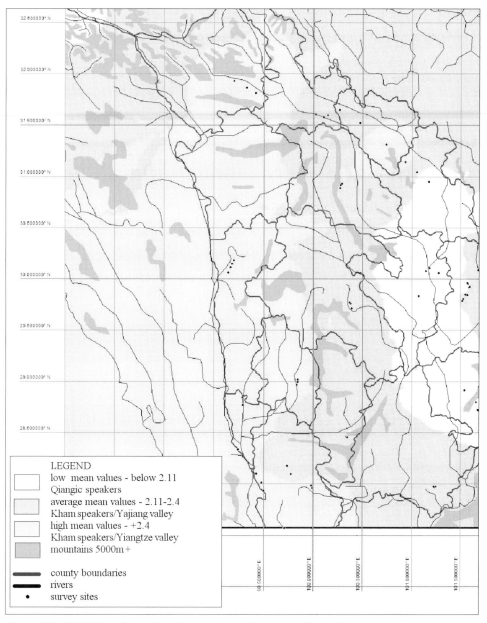

Figure 10.5 Distribution of mean forest concepts or values across Eastern Kham

Source: John Studley

Eastern Kham, category membership varies on the basis of gender, dialect, forest depletion, remoteness, watershed, market penetration, etc. There is also evidence of five well-defined geographical areas within which forest concepts are similar enough to warrant a particular forest or biodiversity care approach.

Figure 10.5 shows perceptual 'zones' that have been geospatially extrapolated from 86 sites across Kham on the basis of the same data set used for multidimensional scaling. Both the extrapolation (kriging) and the categories shown are based on psychometric means at each site. Figure 10.5 shows zones of similar mean perception by ethnicity and topography. Category 1 coincides with Qiangic speakers in the Eastern Yajiang watershed, Category 2 coincides with Kham speakers in the Western Yajiang watershed and Category 3 with Kham speakers in the Eastern Yangtze watershed.

Geospatial analysis

Geospatial analysis shows that some changes in forest-related concepts coincide with changes in underlying biophysical phenomena and overlap analysis reveals if the coincidence is statistical significant.

Figure 10.6 shows there is a significant overlap between changes in forest concepts/values (h) and dialects (g). Overlap statistics are based on nearest neighbour distances and is it the usual convention to term the overlap as 'O', one set of boundaries as 'G' and the other as 'H' (BLV = Boundary Likelihood Values).

Directional trend analysis

A significant directional trend of forest value data occurs along a NE to SW axis. This coincides with the migration patterns of the Khamba people and topographic influences.

In Figure 10.7, the data shows the direction of greatest correlation for Kham speakers to be at 50° (θ) north of the polar axis (East) and the

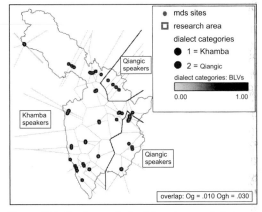

Figure 10.6 Overlap analysis of forest concepts/values and dialects in Eastern Kham

Source: John Studley

direction of least correlation to be 155° (θ) north of the polar axis (East). This indicates the direction of greatest change (in other words, NE–SW).

The mapping of forest values (cognitively and geospatially) provides a set of tools to:

*   understand the forest perception of specific local communities without compromising local social and cultural systems, gender relations or well-being;

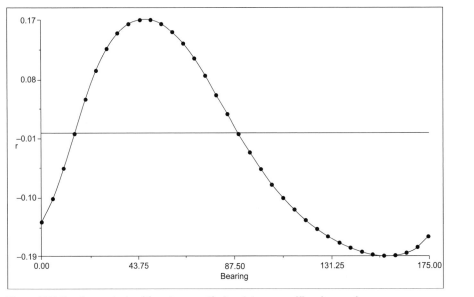

Figure 10.7 Bearing analysis of forest concept/value data among Khamba speakers

Source: John Studley

- identify areas or territories where people groups have similar environmental perception;
- enable geo-specific earth care predicated on indigenous or local beliefs and values;
- identify well-defined geographical areas within which forest values are similar enough to warrant a particular conservation approach;
- elevate and validate indigenous animistic values on the basis of science and geostatistics.

Mapping indigenous knowledge and values so they are comprehendible to scholars is only one step towards its adoption into natural resource planning, policy and care. There are many challenges which are explored in the next section.

Challenges

Post-modern approaches (Studley 2005) to earth care recognize the following:

- use values;
- whole systems that are open-ended;
- scientific uncertainty creating space for other sources of knowledge;
- adaptive management models;
- the recognition of indigenous knowledge through bottom-up approaches;
- local people as active participants in the system.

But despite this, progress is hindered by outmoded orthodoxies and paradigms. These include:

- perverse economic theory;
- narrowly conceived planning processes;
- the cultural elitism of western science;
- the imposition of a development agenda.

Perverse economic theory

Prior to the Enlightenment the intrinsic values of forests, and their sustainability, was a central tenet of many sacred traditions because forests were created by or presided over by a divine being. Intrinsic values were considered different from and superior to exchange value. Because intrinsic value was considered a 'metaphysical' concept by John Locke it came under increasing challenge and was eventually marginalized by scientism and explanations of exchange value and labour theories

of value from classical political economists, such as Karl Marx.

As a result forests were seen as only having economic importance in so far as they could support commercial timber or wood product extraction. Perhaps unsurprisingly, economic policy instruments and analysis of forest management options showed a clear tendency to favour commercial extraction, clearance for agriculture or modification for other seemingly profitable 'development' options. There seemed to be few economic benefits to be gained from forest conservation or sustainable management, and few economic costs associated with forest degradation and loss.

Yet forests yield economic benefits far in excess of their commercial values. Traditionally, classical economists have found these non-market benefits very hard to value or to express in monetary terms (Emerton, 2003) so they have tended to be ignored in decision-making. For 300 years neoclassical economics obscured sacred knowledge systems and the ethno-economies that supported them. The latter are rooted in personal and social relations and based on 'an equilibrium with the natural order and knowledge of biological diversity' that lends itself to the care of natural sacred sites (SAIIC, 1994).

Narrowly conceived planning processes

Traditional planning processes are failing to restore biocultural diversity or protect natural sacred sites. They tend to be (Studley, 2007) science-based, expert-driven, assume a consensus around a particular objective, cling to paradigms that are bio-centric and attempt to impose a green world order. Many are characterized by elite knowledge and processes of inquiry that view sense-perception as the only admissible basis for human knowledge. This compares with polyphasic cultures or with Hinduism which recognizes six senses (touch, taste, sight, sound, smell and mind) and six ways of knowing (Reagan, 2004).

Cultural elitism of western science

The cultural elitism of western science made it difficult for professionals to accept that indigenous people have any knowledge of worth. Much contemporary development still sees indigenous peoples as the ones who are to be 'developed' by those doing the developing. As a result, relations of dependency are established and maintained, during which indigenous cultures are crushed and indigenous knowledge marginalized. Many of the western attempts to prevent marginalization are either romantic (re-modelling indigenous peoples as always living in balance and harmony with nature) or they leave intact the dichotomy between western knowledge and indigenous knowledge (Studley, 2005).

Imposition of a development agenda

Many professionals have co-opted 'bottom-up' development and 'participation' and decentralization has also gained currency in the lexicon of mainstream development. While the rhetoric may appear to be endogenous, in reality, there is only recognition that local values are a desirable ingredient in the development process. The change agents remain mono-cultural, the development process is still exogenous and the agenda is authoritarian and the focus is on communities rather than individuals, actors or stakeholders.

The danger of focusing only on forest communities or territories, rather than stakeholders, is that it masks inequalities and power relations. This is exacerbated by employing a consensus perspective and participatory approaches that at best border on 'tokenism' and at worst are yet another 'western tyranny' (Hildyard et al, 1998). As a result differences according to class, ethnicity, wealth, age and gender are obscured and nothing is done to correct the subtle and widespread social processes of disempowerment.

Discussion and recommendations

Knowledge-brokers

A new 'post-modern forestry paradigm' (Studley, 2005) is allowing natural resource professionals to move beyond decision-making based around use values and adopt an adaptive approach. This approach has the potential of enhancing the forests and the well-being of the people who depend upon them. It provides a platform to address

pluriform forest management, sustainability, stakeholder needs, local and indigenous forest values, knowledge equity and synergy between formal and customary forestry knowledge systems.

This new approach offers potential for local people but raises challenges for natural resource professionals. For local 'forest actors' it offers the possibility of biocultural sustainability on their own terms, basis of knowledge and ways of knowing. For the natural resource professional, it may require capacity building. Knowledge-brokers are required because in spite of numerous attempts to integrate indigenous knowledge with formal forest/conservation management there is no conceptual framework for integration (Bennett and Zurek, 2006).

Although knowledge-brokers should be politically astute they are the antithesis of a typical expert as they approach indigenous cultures as an acolyte or learner. Typically they will demonstrate a willingness to become acculturated and to understand the worldview and values of all stakeholders and actors. Their modus operandi is bottom-up participation beginning with the worldviews, values and aspirations of indigenous people and subsequently as intermediaries with other stake-holders. Sillitoe et al (2002) sees the role of knowledge-brokers as mediating knowledge within 'globes of knowledge' with meridians representing aspirations interfacing with a network of different worldviews and paradigms. The aim of the knowledge-broker should be to enhance the well-being of indigenous people and their biocultural diversity and empower them to be able to broker for themselves.

Knowledge-brokers achieve this by bringing multiple worldviews and paradigms together around the problems or aspirations of their indigenous clients. They expose particular elements that are incompatible with their indigenous clients' worldview and look for synergy between alternative worldviews and paradigms (see Haverkort et al, 2003; Studley, 2007).

Policy support

The success of the approach outlined above is dependent on the political will of the state, staff capacity building and its incorporation into development plans. There is compelling evidence in the literature (see Studley, 2007) for increasing government support for a forest values approach to nature conservation in general and natural sacred sites in particular. To implement this vision conservation professionals need to:

- understand the concept of worldview as a foundation for inquiry and mediation and the processing of knowledge;
- engage cross-culturally as knowledge-brokers in order to bring multiple worldviews and paradigms together around problems or aspirations on the basis of synergy with that of their indigenous clients;
- understand how to bridge between cultures and alternative ways of knowing and perception;
- gain expertise in cognitive anthropology and the mapping of forest values.

Natural resource institutions should recognize traditional knowledge at the policy and planning level, but also secure bilateral aid to build the capacity of development professionals. They should use ethno-economists who would work with cultural mentors and conservation professionals until a team of professionals has been trained or mentored.

Incorporating the approach into development plans

The cognitive mapping approach outlined in this paper has the highest prospect of success when the forest values and eco-spiritual aspirations of the state resonate with those of the local people, though currently there is little resonance between the aspirations of the Chinese state and the indigenous peoples of Eastern Kham.

Progress is possible under the rubric of 'cultural differences' (Pei personal communication, 2001) through the ethno-botanic and sacred site literature, in the work of Centre for Biodiversity and Indigenous Knowledge and in bilaterally funded pilot projects (Studley, 2007). Hopefully this (post-modern) scientific approach can be adopted in countries where more convergence is possible, and China subsequently made to understand that its approach is outmoded.

Conclusions

The sacred dimension can and does play an important role in landscape care and nature conservation but eco-spiritual values continue to be ignored as a result of the mono-cultural myopia of dominant western research epistemologies. Intangible values only make sense when research epistemologies are predicated on pluralism, holism, multi-culturalism and post-modern logic and science.

Anthropology provides a means of revealing sacred values and eco-spiritual domains by mapping them cognitively and geospatially in a format comprehendible to scholars and field workers and revealing taxonomies and paradigms based on locally relevant criteria. Cognitive and geospatial mapping helps elevate indigenous animistic values from the 'superstitious and intangible' domain to the 'cognitively superior' realms of scientific validity and statistical probability. It provides a means of providing epistemological justice for the indigenous custodians of many sacred natural sites.

Governments should train their field staff as knowledge-brokers so they can bring multiple worldviews and paradigms together around the problems or aspirations of their indigenous clients and expose elements that are incompatible and look for synergy with alternative worldviews and paradigms. Governments need to adopt a new multi-cultural conservation paradigm that builds on the worldviews, cosmovision, epistemologies, forest values and ethno-economies of indigenous peoples. Furthermore they need to provide the resources and adaptive feedback channels to support endogenous conservation of natural resources.

References

Bennett, E. and Zurek, M. (2006) 'Integrating epistemologies through scenarios', in Reid, W., Berkes, F., Wilbanks T. and Capistrano, D. (eds) *Bridging Scales and Epistemologies: Linking Local Knowledge and Global Science in Environmental Assessments*, Island Press, Washington, pp275–293

Eckel, M. (1997) 'Is there a Buddhist philosophy of nature?', in Tucker M. and Williams, D. (eds) *Buddhism and Ecology*, Harvard University, Cambridge, MA, pp327–349

Emerton, L. (2003) 'Tropical forest valuation: Has it all been a futile exercise?', Congress Proceedings, Volume A, Proceedings of the 12th World Forestry Congress, World Forestry Congress, Quebec, Canada, 21–28 September 2003, pp103–110

Hattaway, P. (2000) *Operation China: Introducing all the peoples of China*, Piquant, Carlisle, UK

Haverkort, B., Hooft, K. and Hiemstra, W. (2003) *Ancient Roots, New Shoots: Endogenous Development in Practice*, Compas, Leusden

Hildyard, N., Hegde, P., Wolvekamp, P. and Reddy, S. (1988) 'Same platform different train: The politics of participation', *Unasylva*, vol 194, no 49, pp26–34

Huber, T. (1999) *The Cult of Pure Crystal Mountain: Popular Pilgrimage and Visionary Landscape in Southeast Tibet*, Oxford University Press, Oxford

Posey, D. (ed) (1999) 'Spiritual and cultural values of biodiversity', Intermediate Technology Publications and United Nations Environment Programme, UNEP, London

Reagan, T. (2004) *Non-Western Educational Traditions: Indigenous Approaches to Educational Thought and Practice*, Routledge, London

SAIIC (South and Meso American Indian Rights Center) (1994) 'Temuco-Wallmapuche Declaration on the North American Free Trade Agreement, Indigenous Peoples and their Rights', in North American Free Trade Agreement, Indigenous Peoples and their Rights Conference, Wallmapuche, Chile, 20 November and 1–2 December 1994

Sillitoe, P., Bicker, A. and Pottier, J. (2002) *Approaches to Indigenous Knowledge*, Routledge, London

Studley, J. (2005) 'Sustainable knowledge systems and resource stewardship: In search of ethno-forestry paradigms for the indigenous peoples of Eastern Kham', PhD thesis, Loughborough University, Loughborough

Studley, J. (2007) *Hearing a Different Drummer: A New Paradigm for the Keepers of the Forest*, IIED, London

Trouvalis, J. (2000) 'The dawn of post-modern forestry', in Trouvalis, J. (ed) *A Critical Geography of Britain's State Forests*, Oxford University Press, Oxford, pp179–204

11

Ancestral Beliefs and Conservation: The Case of Sacred Sites in Bandjoun, West Cameroon

Sébastien Luc Kamga-Kamdem

Summary

This chapter describes the ancestral management system of sacred natural sites in Bandjoun, Cameroon. It identifies stakeholders, presents a typology of these sites based on survey work which identified and mapped them and describes the ancestral management system as well as the threats they currently face. Recommendations are made for measures and actions for the sustainable management of Bandjoun's sacred natural sites and the promotion of ancestral conservation knowledge.

Despite various historical and more recent factors threatening their survival, many sacred sites are still present and the concept of sacred natural areas is deeply understood by the people of Bandjoun and is defined by functions, use and communal regulations. Faith plays a key role in respecting these sites alongside honesty, the respect for ancestors and the observance of long-held community values. Sacred areas are commonly considered to be 'the affairs of men' but this study has revealed that women play a significant role in their management. Sacred areas harbour animals and plants, many of which have largely disappeared from the surrounding areas and as such provide a genetic reservoir of locally important biodiversity, about which more needs to be understood. Despite strong community support the Bandjoun sacred sites are threatened by social and economic changes many stemming from the wider society.

Recommendations are made to safeguard Bandjoun's sacred areas, include the promoting of the traditional knowledge of conservation and the better recognition of the role of women. Further work should be carried out to gain a better understanding of their biodiversity and cultural values, the development of both guidelines and a national strategy for sacred natural site management.

Introduction

Sacred natural sites are widespread in the Bandjoun Kingdom of Western Cameroon. Many of these are small sacred forests that had, at least until recently, shown little or no signs of degradation, and were for many generations preserved without physical means of protection despite a high population density. The sacred forests, therefore, constitute a reservoir of ecosystem services and biodiversity which, through effective informal protection, are community protected areas (Kamga-Kamdem, 2003) a protected area category now recognized at the international level as Indigenous and Community Conserved Areas (Dudley, 2008).

In most cases the use of sacred areas for cultural purposes does not constitute a threat to their integrity or their biophysical components (Tahoux, 2002). Today's pressures, however, on these sacred areas result from various causes and the Bandjoun sacred natural sites are gradually losing their sacred character and being converted to other forms of land use. This constitutes a significant threat to their long-term existence and risks the loss of biodiversity and traditional knowledge. The traditional management system of sacred natural sites could be a successful approach to conservation in Cameroon rooted in local communities. For this to be achieved effective and appropriate state support is required, and urgent measures are needed to ensure the perpetuation of sacred natural sites, the promotion of ancestral conservation knowledge and experience and to reduce the loss of biodiversity and cultural values.

Study area

This chapter is based on research around the towns of Hiala, Soung and Tseghem in the Bandjoun Kingdom which covers a surface area of 274km^2 with 100,000 inhabitants (365 inhabitants/km^2) (ADB, 2007). The Bandjoun people belong to the Bamileke ethnic group and their language is Ghomala. The Bandjoun community constitutes all people under the authority of the Bandjoun King. That includes indigenous peoples, residents and even people journeying through the Kingdom. The Kingdom is subdivided into seven Jye (provinces) all converging on Hiala, the socio-political centre where the King resides (see Figure 11.1). Christianity is the principal religion, but traditional beliefs remain significant for numerous people.

Bandjoun lands are divided into two main categories: those that have been allocated for personal use (houses and farms) and those retained under the authority of the Kingdom which include sacred sites and government reserves. This customary use is overlain by national laws and the ownership of lands managed by the traditional authorities is vested in the state. Overall forest management is the concern the Ministry of Forests and Wildlife according Cameroonian legal statues (ADB, 2007).

Figure 11.1 Traditional subdivision of Bandjoun with Western Cameroon inset

Source: COE (2005)

Data collection and analysis

This chapter is based on a literature study and the use of participatory rural appraisal methods. These included interviews conducted with groups and individuals from different socio-cultural backgrounds. All of the 52 sites recorded were visited and the data collected included surface area, socio-geographical distribution, biological composition and management mechanisms. Workshops and direct field observations provided supplementary information. Data were collected for 16 sacred natural sites outside of the study area because of their great significance for the community or their strong connection with those within the study area. Finally, a feedback meeting was held in each locality to present and validate primary results while collectively drawing maps of identified sacred places. Although community reports of biodiversity values were recorded, plant and animal inventories were not carried out.

Results
Stakeholders in the management

Bandjoun interviewees distinguish the following groups with interests in sacred sites:

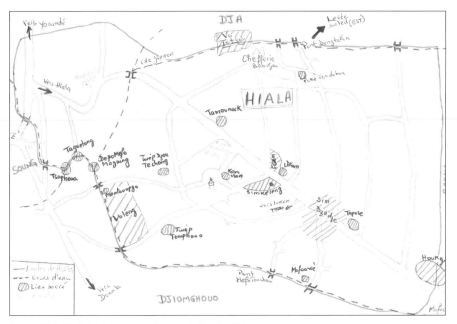

Figure 11.2 Participatory maps of sacred sites in Hiala

Source: Sébastien Kamga-Kamdem

- spiritual leaders (or diviners, MKamSi), who inform people of their past or future, advise on proper spiritual behaviour and act as intermediaries between people and their ancestors;
- traditional healers (Guèkè);
- secret societies (Mkem);
- twins (Po-mgne);
- the family (Tongdih);
- the quarter, a subdivision of the community (Mpfelack);
- the local community (Là);
- all human beings (Goung).

Interestingly the respondents ignored other stakeholders such as decision-makers or those involved in conservation and significantly the state was not listed among the interested groups. The role of women was completely ignored.

Sacred area concepts

Despite the various changes that have occurred since independence the tradition of sacred sites are on the whole still maintained by Bandjoun society.

The concept of a sacred area is well known to the local people. Fifty-two sacred sites were identified, including 37 in the study zone. The participatory maps drawn by the Bandjoun (e.g. for Hiala, Figure 11.2) matched the map constructed based of all the GPS data taken in the field.

Typology of sacred areas

Sacred areas were assessed by four main criteria: natural state, ecosystem, cultural function and key stakeholders (see Table 11.1).

A number of specific characteristics are noted:

- There are some large sacred areas (such as the forest of Voleng sacred site, see Figures 11.2 and 11.3) that are managed by multiple custodians
- All places of worship (excluding family shrines) are for everyone probably because God is universal
- Family shrines usually have the presence of a fig tree (*Ficus* sp.), peace trees (*Dracaena* sp.) and also rocks and can include the construction of a *Tock*, a small thatched shrine.

Table 11.1 Different criteria for considering sacred areas in Bandjoun

Criteria	No.	Description
Nature/state	3	
Type of ecosystem/biome/landscape	10	
Functions/uses	5	*Tchuép-Si* (Worship), *TsouckTcham* (secret meeting place), *Tookô* (making alliances or agreement), *TsouckTchim* (initiation centre), *Tse-sih* (cemetery), *Yoh* (ceremonial use)
Particularly interested social groups	10	*Tsouck-Dje-Goung* (everyone), *Tsouck-Dje-Lack* (Bandjoun community), *Tsouck-Dje -Tse* (chiefs), *Tsouck-Dje-Takdje* (province), *Tsouck-Dje-pfelack* (quarter), *Tsouck-Dje-mkem* (secret society), *Tsouck-Dje-mkam* (notable person), *Tsouck-Dje-Tongdih* (family), *Tchuép-Po-mgne* (twins)

Functions of sacred areas

The following functions, values and uses of sacred areas are recognized by all community members:

1 Spiritual and religious: worship places are places for prayer, expressing thanks to God and requesting his mercy.
2 Justice and customary law: some sacred places (e.g. Taamounock sacred site, Hiala Town, see Figure 11.2) constitute a community court. One can go there to protest one's innocence if accused of a transgression, complain about a known or unknown suspected wrong doer, and request justice of the supreme spirits (locally called *Ordelie*).
3 Cultural gathering and ceremonial places: some sacred places (e.g. Simdzedze sacred site, see Figures 11.2 and 11.3) constitute centres of traditional initiations to the community life, or places of public meetings.
4 Institutional: some sacred sites (e.g. Fam sacred site) are seats of socio-cultural and political institutions where specific initiated people retire to take decisions concerning the community's evolution and prosperity. Mystical rites may be practised at some sites.
5 Storage and refugium: private goods can be safely stored at certain sacred sites.

Other functions that were not identified by stakeholders include biodiversity conservation and healing which are connected to each other. Many natural sites conserve totems that are often animals that 'stand-in' for or 'represent' the site's owner.

They live (or once lived) in the forests and rivers of the sacred sites and their presence dissuades people from unauthorized access into sacred areas. Local people assert that certain plants and animals can now only be found existing in sacred natural sites, having become extirpated from other areas and that they also constitute a reservoir of medicinal products. Certain sacred areas contribute to the conservation of important ecosystems like water sources. Specific studies would enable better understanding of the biodiversity conservation of rare species and ecosystem services of these areas and these are recommended as a next step. Community education about biodiversity values is also recommended.

Ancestral management system of sacred area
Designation of sacred areas

The designation of a sacred area depends on its use and function. The location of natural and semi-natural sacred areas is identified by the initiated spiritual leaders (MkamSi). While most have been long-established the location of a sacred area it not immutable, it can be changed for certain reasons (road construction, socio–political reorientation). However, it is not advised to destroy one lightly, for example, to establish a residence.

Management of sacred sites

Generally, each sacred area comes under the responsibility of a custodian called Nongtchuép.

Figure 11.3 Coronation ceremony of a queen at Simdzedze place

'Queen' is a title reserved for the King's mother or sisters. It is transmitted through succession from mother to daughter.

Source: Sébastien Kamga-Kamdem

He is responsible for making offerings and sacrifices. He can mandate a representative or deputy (called Guèkô), who is usually a close friend, and is also succeeded by a custodian. The initiated elders are universal custodians, they have the right to work in all worship sites. Today, many people use sacred areas without informing their custodian, indicating the erosion of cultural norms.

Boundaries of sacred areas

Not all sacred areas have demarcated boundaries. According to local people, one can intuitively recognize a sacred site through the feelings experienced in its surroundings. Generally, they are impressive places marked by traces of sacrifice and offering. Sometimes sacred areas are delimited by roads, pathways, hedges and or raffia fibre boards

(called Kia) which are progressively being replaced by aluminium sheets (see Figure 11.4).

Use and protection rules

Uses depend on the area category. In all sacred sites orderlies are carried out, that is the practice of sacrificing and making offerings to give thanks to God and the ancestors or to request their assistance in case of difficulties or recurring misfortune. Certain people are allowed to collect non-timber-products, especially healing products. There are specific days and periods for access to sacred areas, generally, early morning and evening while activities at midday are very exceptional. Sacred areas are frequently used on three days (*Tamdze*, *Sèssou* and *Tamgo*) of the Bandjoun eight-day week, but not on the three prohibited days (*Tièpfo*, *Chekouk* and *Gosouo*).

Figure 11.4 Tchuép-Poumougne sacred site

Situated in the administrative centre of Bandjoun, Tchuép-Poumouge is a sacred area of high spiritual value. In the past, the area of its influence covered the whole Pete quarter. Because of urbanization, this has been drastically eroded to its really sacred portion, but only at the cost of losing natural values.

Source: Sébastien Kamga-Kamdem

Sacred areas have numerous proscriptions and their breach can bring serious consequences to the contravener, including death in former times, but also curses causing misfortunes or health problems. Communal penalties include suspending rural activities, for example for nine weeks if a stone is thrown at a *Tock* (shrine).

Clemency may be shown for taboo breakers, especially from ignorance, however, for certain very sacred places (e.g. Taamounock sacred site, Hiala Town, see Figure 11.2), there is no distinction between regulation breakers (natives, foreigners or simply the ignorant), so all are sanctioned accordingly. The situation can be very serious for those who consciously break the rules. For those who call for pardon, purification ceremonies are performed by customary experts. Some of the prohibited activities in Banjoun sacred areas include hunting, unauthorized entrance, starting bushfires, farming, using it as a toilet, lying, lewd or provocative behaviour, timber/wood collection without permission, smoking, making noise, tree planting without permission, stone throwing and claiming as private ownership.

Gender and management

Almost all the interviewees expressed the view that women have nothing to do with sacred areas, considering them 'male affairs'. However, further discussions revealed that women play an important role in the management of sacred areas, but this role is often hidden and ignored. For example, Megnesi (female equivalent of MkamSi) have the same capacities and duties as their male counterparts, notably, access and performing rites. Only the mothers of initiated twins can clean certain sacred sites. A woman can substitute the family chief and make offerings or sacrifices at a sacred place, of course with some restrictions. Furthermore, the traditional education is primarily given by women who enforce conservation regulations for sacred areas. In this respect, they refuse for example, to use firewood that has been collected from sacred places.

Threats to sacred areas

Traditional leaders stated that the survival of sacred areas is not threatened because these areas are strongly linked with the community identity; although they worry about the degradation of the attitude of young people who are becoming increasingly materialistic and dishonest. However, based on the changing attitudes and other reasons, representatives of government institutions and NGOs stated that the survival of sacred areas is threatened. The key threats were identified (Box 11.1) and some are discussed further in the following sections.

Box 11.1 Factors threatening sacred areas

- decline of traditional institutions;
- decrease of traditional basic education;
- insufficient transmission of knowledge to the younger generations;
- changing attitudes and lifestyle;
- development of individualism;
- administrative territory subdivision by the state;
- mixing of cultures;
- ignorance of the importance of sacred sites;
- human population growth;
- clearing for agriculture;
- encroachment by neighbours;
- expansion of Christianity;
- urban development.

Impact of the expansion of Christianity

Several villagers and Christian leaders (catechists and pastors) consider that evangelism has impacts on the conservation of sacred areas. There have been complaints that Protestant Christian leaders had a diabolic view of sacred sites and ancestral beliefs. In fact, one custodian stated: 'Because of the increasing dishonesty, many people rather prefer the Christian repentance whose effects would be only known after death, to the traditional justice system in sacred places whose consequences are (sometimes) immediate.'

Some people think that Christian influence on traditional beliefs is decreasing. They argue that some pastors have brought their faithful to sacred sites (e.g. Fovu sacred site in Baham village). If these visits are guided by the custodian who will highlight the importance of his sacred area, and also make sure that the trip objectives are in conformity with the sacred area rules, these should constitute an opportunity for their promotion and interfaith understanding.

Impact of infrastructure development

Infrastructure development, especially road construction and urban settlement, have caused the degradation of sacred areas in Bandjoun. When space is needed people turn to sacred areas because they do not belong to anybody. On several occasions, sacred areas have been proposed for building public services such as schools (e.g. in Voleng sacred site Hiala Town (see Figure 11.2) and Schoutapmekouk sacred site, Tseghen).

Impact of modern education

According to some, modern education can have a negative impact on local beliefs. Because of the modern school system, children spend little time with their parents in the villages. They do not therefore have enough opportunities to perform traditional initiations or to understand the background and functionality of the traditional system. This causes an intergenerational loss in traditional values.

Impact of changing attitudes and lifestyles

Almost all interviewees believe that changing attitudes and modern lifestyles have a negative influence on sacred sites. The increase of individualism is reported to be affecting collective responsibility. The great interest in money and individual property lead to changes in traditional value systems. Consequently, certain neighbours extend their lands by progressively clearing sacred areas.

Discussion: Conservation and measures for sustainable management

Although threats to sacred areas exist community leaders are convinced of their survival as long as Bandjoun exists as they are 'part of the heart of the community'. All interviewees were, however, explicit in their view that the long-term perpetuation and conservation of the sacred areas was a necessity. The principal measures suggested by community members consist of the following:

- raising public awareness of sacred site values at national and international levels;
- mapping and demarcating the boundaries of sacred areas;
- improving knowledge of sacred areas;
- reinforcing the capacity of customary managers of sacred areas;
- defining a legal status for sacred sites while recognising them as the property of the entire community;
- developing guidelines for the management of sacred areas;
- reviving traditional education while encouraging parents to transmit their conservation knowledge;
- involving all stakeholders especially women, young people, elites, state institutions, religious institutions and NGOs in all reflections related to the management of sacred areas in a participatory way and clearly defining the role of each.

The following sections give some details about opportunities to involve the state and women.

Participation of the state

People in Bandjoun did not identify the state as a sacred site stakeholder as these sites are not taken into account in national natural resources polices. Most interviewees were of the opinion, however, that the participation of the state is necessary for the conservation of sacred places particularly because of their legal recognition. This view, however, was not universal, and some think that 'the sacred places are relevant to ancestral tradition, spiritual belief and custom'; as such, it would be difficult for a civil servant to promote its conservation without a personal belief in local traditions. It was also a widely held view that the involvement of the state in the management of sacred areas could present risks and generate conflict due to:

- the appropriation of resources (wood exploitation, hunting, etc.) by government officers, which is not possible whilst they are protected by local tradition;
- weakening rather than strengthening the power of the elders;
- the prohibition of certain traditional rites or access to certain sacred places;
- the rapid turnover of individual government officers results in the fact they have little understanding and sympathy for local traditions and are poorly accountable for their actions.

Legal recognition of sacred natural sites might assist their conservation if done sensitively and at the national level two main options present themselves: a) to be community forests or b) as government protected areas. Neither of these is really suitable and both present risks. Some state involvement in sacred site management is, however, not only necessary but also unavoidable. Therefore, the question is not whether or not state participation is desirable but rather how to avoid potential conflicts. The development of specific, supportive and appropriate policy and laws offers the best solution.

Conclusion and recommendations

Sacred areas constitute an important component of the life of the people of Banjoun. Their existence is based on spiritual and cultural traditions. Sacred areas are considered to play important ecological roles, the details of which are however little known or understood either locally or at national level. There is a need for further studies to increase knowledge about the ecological functions of sacred sites as well as traditional conservation mechanisms.

The survival of sacred sites is threatened by a number of sources including population growth, cross-cultural mixing and the changing attitudes and value systems. Despite ongoing degradation, the disappearance of sacred areas is not foreseen in the short to medium term, as they are integral to the community identity. Their biodiversity and cultural values are, however, in decline. The greatest progress supporting the conservation of sacred areas would be a) their legal recognition, b) increased public awareness and wider appreciation, c) reduced negative changes in land use and d) better recognition of their socio-cultural and ecological importance. As a follow up to this study the following is recommended:

- Present the results of this study at national level in order to increase state and public awareness.
- Extend the pilot study to other parts of Cameroon as well as other countries in the Congo Basin sub-region many of which have similar sacred sites.
- Formulate a conservation strategy of sacred areas at national and sub-regional levels.

To achieve the above will require the involvement of all stakeholders at local, national and international levels.

References

ADB (2007) 'L'acuité des litiges fonciers dans les chefferies Bamiléké: Cas de Togodjo dans la Chefferie Bandjoun, Yaoundé, Cameroun', Association pour l'appui au Développement de Bandjoun

Biya, P., Sassou, N.D., Bongo, O., Obiang-Nguéma, M.T., Patasse, F.P., Kabila, L.D. and Deby, I. (1999) Sommet des chefs d'État d'Afrique centrale sur la conservation et la gestion durable des forêts tropicales: Déclaration de Yaoundé

CARFAD (2006) 'Bilan des acquis de la foresterie communautaire au Cameroun et nouvelles orientations', consultation commanditée par le Ministère des Forêts et de la faune, Yaoundé

CIPCRE (2000) 'Etude sur les stratégies de préservation et de protection des forêts sacrées de l'Ouest Cameroun', Bafoussam, Cameroun

COE (2005) Musée de Bandjoun, available at www.museumcam.org/bandjoun/royaume.php (last accessed June 2008)

CNUED (1992) Déclaration de Rio sur l'Environnement et le Développement Durable

Dudley, N. (ed) (2008) 'Guidelines for applying protected area management categories', IUCN, Gland

Kamga-Kamdem, S.L. (2003) 'Possibilities for the realisation of the ecological sustainable tourism concepts in the protected areas in Cameroon', Dissertation Goettingen Georg-August University, Verlag Dr Kessel, Remagen, Germany

Kamga-Kamdem, S.L. and Tiebou, J. (2006) 'Gestion décentralisée des ressources forestières: Cas des zones d'intérêts cynégétiques à gestion communautaire au Sud-est du Cameroun', in Mayaka T.B., Fotsing, E., de Lough, H. and Loth, P. (eds) 'Community based conservation of natural resources in dry and sub-humid savannas', Proceedings of the Second RNSCC International Seminar, 8 February 2006, Yaounde, Cameroon, pp61–82

Langhammer, P.F., Bakarr, M.I., Bennun, L.A., Brooks, T.M., Clay, R.P., Darwall, W., De Silva, N., Edgar, G.J., Eken, G., Fishpool, L.D.C., Fonseca, G.A.B. D., Foster, M.N., Knox, D.H., Matiku, P., Radford, E.A., Rodrigues, A.S.L., Salaman, P., Sechrest, W., and Tordoff, A.W. (2007) 'Identification and Gap Analysis of Key Biodiversity Areas: Targets for Comprehensive Protected Area Systems', Gland, Switzerland, IUCN

MINEF (n.d.) *A Compendium of Official Instruments on Forest and Wildlife Management in Cameroon*, Imprimerie Nationale, Yaounde, Cameroon

Nguekeng, C. (1998) 'Stratégies de conservation des forêts sacrées des chefferies Bamenyam, Bafoussam et Bahouan', Mémoire de fin d'études, FASA, Université de Dschang

Sobzé, J.M. (1993) 'Participation des populations de Dschang à la conservation de la faune et de la flore', Mémoire de fin d'études, INADER, Université de Dschang

Tahoux, T.M. (2002) 'Contribution au renforcement de la forêt sacrée en vue de la gestion durable des ressources naturelles: cas de la forêt sacrée de Zaïpobly dans le Sud-Ouest de la Côte-d'Ivoire', available at www.dakar.unesco.org/natsciences_fr/rapport_2002/rci.htm (last accessed May 2007)

Schaaf, T. (2006) 'Linking cultural and biological diversity: The UNESCO-MAB approach', UNESCO, Paris.

UNESCO-MAB (2006) 'Conserving cultural and biological diversity: The role of sacred natural sites and cultural landscapes', Proceedings of the Tokyo Symposium, UNESCO, Paris

Verschuuren, B., Mallarach, J.-M. and Oviedo, G. (2007) 'Sacred sites and protected areas: IUCN World Commission on Protected Areas', Summit on the IUCN categories in Andalusia, Spain, 7–11 May 2007

Wild, R. and McLeod, C. (eds) (2008) 'Sacred natural sites: Guidelines for protected area managers', Gland, Switzerland, IUCN

WWF-WARPO (n.d.) 'National strategy for the management of traditional conservation areas in Ghana, a proposal', WWF – West Africa Regional Programme Office, Accra, Ghana

12

The Crocodile is our Brother: Sacred Lakes of the Niger Delta, Implications for Conservation Management

E.D. Anwana, R.A. Cheke, A.M. Martin, L. Obireke, M. Asei, P. Otufu and D. Otobotekere

Summary

Communities in the Niger Delta have a close affinity with the surrounding wetlands which is exemplified by the interaction with plants and animals based on their world view. This interaction contains social codes and conservation ethics imbued with rules and meanings which have affected both the human community and aquatic resources. The two case studies presented in this chapter involve the Biseni and Osiama communities, both members of the predominant Ijo speaking group in the Niger Delta region of Nigeria. The belief structure of this group delineates natural landscapes into two categories, termed *aweýe* (forbidden) and *aweaya* (not forbidden). Forbidden freshwater lakes such as Lake Esiribi and Lake Adigbe have sacred species which are embodiments of gods and ancestral spirits and therefore have elevated status within these societies. These species, for example, the nationally threatened crocodile (*Osteolaemus tetraspis*), are revered and thus protected. The belief that the crocodile is the peoples' brother implies its protection within the *aweýe* (forbidden) lake.

If killed accidentally, it is given full obsequies akin to human funeral rites and when killed intentionally the culprit is made to replace a live crocodile for the dead one. Sacredness of these lakes means fishing when permitted is done in groups within specific dates and seasons, using fishing instruments prescribed by the group that are non-intrusive and selective. Common ancestry and social connectedness among neighbouring communities link the management of some of these lakes together, forming a network of lakes reserved for periodic fishing based on communal treaties. These culturally protected freshwater lakes provide insights into how the current rate of biodiversity loss in the Niger Delta can be tackled through the involvement of indigenous people in the management of threatened biodiversity and watershed areas. Sacred lakes, like their terrestrial counterparts, sacred groves, tend to be fragmented ecosystems as they are usually small habitat remnants preserved by indigenous people. However, the social cohesion amongst this group has an important role in conservation as it increases the chances of connectivity of sacred lakes within the region, thereby reducing small-island effects on the aquatic resources. Capacity building of indigenous groups and provision of appropriate legal instruments that protect the rights of indigenous groups within the region for sustainable wetland management are recommended.

Introduction

In many African communities, the concept of an ecosystem incorporates not just natural objects, but spirits of both animals and human ancestors (Dei, 1993; Greider and Garkovich, 1994; Neumann, 1998). Across the southern region of Nigeria, for instance, tribes belonging to the Niger-Congo family (e.g. the Ijos, Yorubas, Edos, Igbos and Efiks) share similar belief systems, culture and occupations (Osunade, 1988; Alagoa, 1999). Fishing as an occupation is a significant aspect of their lifestyle and communities have a close affinity with the habits of fish and are known to move seasonally in search of better fishing grounds (NEST, 1991). These communities, such as the Biseni and Osiama, are deeply spiritual and their belief systems and relationships with the environment are intimately connected as in many other African communities (Schoffeleers, 1978; Omari, 1990). Hence, indigenous practices can be viewed as socio-ecological entities (Berkes et al, 2003), where the landscape or seascape is protected by human behaviour influenced by spiritual value (Bisht and Ghildiyal, 2007). In this light, the two case studies discussed in this chapter examine the socio-ecological interaction of these communities and the wetland, with the view of building on the growing corpus of work on cultural belief and practices of indigenous peoples within the West African Guinea Forest of the Niger Delta region. In Nigeria, such evidence of socio-cultural practices is perhaps needed to drive useful decision-making processes on sustainable natural resource management and conservation.

Acclaimed to be an important tropical zone, the West African Guinea Forest is noted for its biological richness (Golubiewski, 2007). Likewise, the Delta region is regarded as a unique ecosystem and probably a Pleistocene refuge (Were, 2001) with holdings of several threatened IUCN Red List species (Hilton-Taylor, 2000), such as the Red Colobus Monkey (*Piliocolobus pennantii epieni*), Sclater's Guenon (*Cercopithecus sclateri*) and the Spotted-neck Otter (*Hydrictis maculicollis*). However, it has escaped close biological scrutiny,

with wildlife surveys not conducted until the late 1980s (Oates, 1989; Were, 1991), and lacks any state protected areas (McGinley, 2007). The rapid rates of ecosystem destruction in the Delta paint a bleak picture for the future of biodiversity except, probably, for areas maintained by indigenous institutions. These are institutions formed solely by local people. They embody the belief system, attitudes and practices of the community and are directly involved in making appropriate communal laws, enforcing sanctions and enunciating rules of engagement for natural resource use, and they have an accountability mechanism for monitoring agreed rules. In the past, governance of each community was by the oldest man in the community known as *Amaokosuowei* in Osiama and *Amadaowei* in Biseni. The *Amaokosuowei* was traditionally considered the chief priest to the gods of the community and in charge of carrying out the necessary rituals to the gods on behalf of the community. The *Amaokosuowei* ruled his village with a group, made up of the oldest male (*Amaokwens*) of each extended family unit and it was this group that governed the community's natural resources.

The indigenous conserved areas, such as the sacred lakes Adigbe and Esiribi found in Osiama and Biseni, respectively, exist in several coastal landscapes in the region (Powell, 1993). Overall, five categories of protected areas are nationally recognized (FME, 2006) including national parks, game reserves, forest reserves, biosphere reserves and special ecosystems/habitats (e.g. indigenous conserved areas).

Study area

The Niger Delta has played an important role in the global economy, through the slave trade, palm oil trade and now fossil fuels, over the last 400 years (Odukoya, 2006; McGinley, 2007). Currently in the Niger Delta, the oil and gas industry is the most important sector. Its crude oil and gas reserves are estimated at 25 billion barrels and 130 trillion cubic feet, respectively (Omene, 2001). These enormous reserves have attracted several multinational companies, whose activities have had negative impacts on the rich biodiversity of the region (Luiselli and Akani, 2003). Ironically, although the

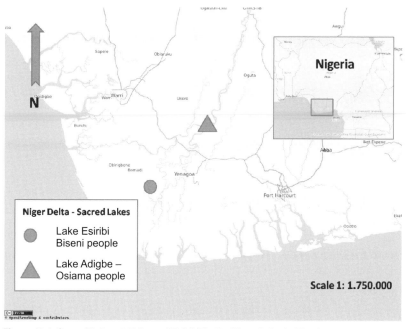

Figure 12.1 Sacred Lakes Adigbe and Esiribi in the Niger Delta in Nigeria

Source: Bas Verschuuren with Open Street Map ©

area accounts for over 85 per cent of the nation's GDP, it is the poorest region with its GDP per capita well below the national average (Aaron, 2005).

The region's main ecological division is between the southern tidal freshwater or Marsh forest zone and the inland Flood forest zone of the Eastern flanks (Powell, 1997; Oyebande et al, 2001). The Taylor Creek area where the Biseni people live is an example of the inland flood zone, while Osiama town lies within the Marsh Forest zone. Both Biseni and Osiama communities are in Bayelsa State, which is predominantly populated by the Ijo ethnic group. Its people speak four major dialects: Izon, Nembe, Ogbia and Epie-Atissa (Efere and Williamson, 1999).

Osiama town lies at 4° 53.147"N; 6° 02.635'E and Biseni at 5° 17.310'N; 6° 31.099'E. This chapter discusses the sacred lakes Adigbe and Esiribi (see Figure 12.1) and interviews conducted within the villages that have ownership rights to the lakes. Lake Esiribi belongs to the Biseni people (made up of four villages: Akpede, Egbebiri, Tuburu and Tein) and Lake Adigbe to the Osiama community (made up of four villages: Osiama 1, Awegbene, Ogbunugbene and Ogbubolama).

Methods

The research was multidisciplinary and involved the use of ethnographic tools (in other words, in-depth interviews, focus group interviews, participant observations) and assessment of the fish diversity. Fish sampling was done by observing catches of local fishermen in each project community. Local fish traps and netting sufficed for fish enumeration and diversity (Southwood and Henderson, 2000). Initial narratives obtained from the fishers showed that the people within these regions have a good knowledge of the species of fish within different wetland types. In addition, they recounted observing certain unusual occurrences within the wetland systems, for instance the appearance of a 'strange grass' (*Oxycaryum cubensis*) which previously was absent from Lake Esiribi. Hence, observing traditional methods of fishing creates room for comparison of local and scientific knowledge of the ecosystem.

Results

The context wherein words were used was important for exploring the research on sacred lakes. Therefore text is presented in several places as verbatim quotes from the interviews held with different groups (Ryan and Russell Bernard, 2003). These quotes exemplify the concept of sacred ecosystems and their relevance to conservation.

Cosmology and natural resources

In the cosmology (particular reference is made to aspects of cosmology that define the relationship of humans to the universe tied to beliefs and practices) of the two communities under study, there are two realms of reality: the visible world, generally in both communities referred to by the word *Kiri* and the invisible world or the land of spirits, *Teme*. The visible world is perceived with the natural senses and contains humans, plants and animals. The invisible world is composed of spirits which are not perceived by the physical senses. The interrelated nature of these two distinct entities brings on a separation of things and events into the categories of the 'forbidden' and the 'not-forbidden', evident in the social world or social unit. Areas and/or things which are said to be forbidden, denoted by the word *Aweýe* or *Toun* (forbidden), are treated specially in accordance with the world view of the people. Customary laws proscribe certain acts and conduct which regulates all individuals from within and outside the community in the way they treat and use these forbidden things and in violating these laws one is an anathema to the society. In contrast, areas and/or things which are not forbidden, recognized in local dialect as *Aweaya* or *Toun-áha* (not forbidden), can be used by eligible members of the community.

The spirits in invisible spirit world *Teme* appear to possess the ability to administer blessings or curses on human endeavours (here in *Kiri* – the physical or visible world) and these spirits are revered and make up the portfolio of gods that are worshipped in these societies. Spirits that are called gods have functional roles in the life of the people and majority associate gods with these specific functions or roles. Gods are perceived to exercise authority over Lake Esiribi, named after

the Esiribi god and Adigbe Lake named after the Adigbe god. In translating the beliefs into practices, indigenous institutions were developed that acted as proponents of the local belief systems.

The means of communication between the visible human medium and the invisible spirit realm (made up of a pantheon of gods and ancestor spirits) was via dreams. Shrines to these gods (see Figure 12.2), who speak to human mediums, dot the landscape of all of the communities. The shrine and everything that it embodies, including the statues, the sacrifices or methods of service and the human mediums, constitutes a visible force in each of these communities attributing an identity to them.

Although the majority seem to frown on the system of many deities and would not openly be counted as an adherent of this traditional belief system, they still maintain the rules/laws established by the same system that they scorn. Some people have attempted to break free of the behavioural boundaries imposed by this institution, adopting exogenous lifestyles that put pressure on the use of the ecosystem; some are seen to have escaped without obvious signs of punishment while others have not been as lucky as they are punished as shown in the narrative by the women's group in Biseni: '… people still enter the lake, if they are caught; the fish would be tied around the person's neck. For instance if they killed a crocodile, they would have to replace the dead with a live one'.

The other issue which touches on the social life of the people and their use of the natural system is the expression of their beliefs in celebrations to the gods, such as festivals and the observance of the Akinma day which is a sacred traditional day for worship of the gods. Akinma day as mentioned by the council of chiefs in Biseni was a traditional day of the week when people were barred from going into the forest and lakes for any activity. It is said that the Akinma day was holy and if one flagrantly disobeyed, the gods would punish the person while out in the forest/lakes, in most cases resulting in death. Festivals are aspects of Biseni and Osiama community life which serve to reinforce the traditional belief of these communities. These festivals are an expression of social connectedness and foster a strong kinship spirit amongst the groups as noted by the level of camaraderie

Figure 12.2 Priest and assistant in front of shrine erected for sacrifices to the lake god at Lake Esiribi (Biseni)

Sacrifices carried out in the shrine are mandatory and is an important function observed before and after the fishing festivities.

Source: E.D. Anwana

amongst participants. The celebration of festivals precedes the commencement of the group fishing.

Lake fishing and aquatic resources

The fishing expedition is characterized by sacrifices made to the gods, dances and fishing in the Lakes. In Osiama, fishing in Lake Adigbe is semi-annual, whereas in Biseni fishing in Lake Esiribi is a biennial event. The traditional implements used in these communities have the advantage that they result in selective fishing. The mesh sizes (35mm to 115mm) do not trap the protected reptiles in these lakes. In situations where the crocodiles get trapped, perhaps as a result of scavenging for trapped fish, fishermen painstakingly release them. We observed recently the practice of fishermen at Lake Esiribi releasing crocodiles, which had accidentally become caught in fishing nets. When asked why they did this (painstakingly releasing the crocodiles despite the potential harm), the response was: 'The crocodile is like a brother, and so cannot be hurt.

In Esiribi, where crocodiles and monitor lizards are protected, if you kill them, you are to bury the animal as you would a human being'.

Fish species from the two lakes have high economic value within the region and attract retailers from several communities within and outside the State (see Figure 12.3). Bigger fish are known to result in higher incomes and simultaneously result in vulnerability of the most reproductive of the species (*Gymnarchus niloticus*). However, in Biseni Gymnarchus are protected in Lake Asa, which serves as a sanctuary for these species. The sacred lakes Esiribi and Adigbe have higher fish species diversity in comparison to other lakes assessed within this study. In Lake Esiribi 231 fish species of 19 genera were recorded within two days of the survey. Similarly, Lake Adigbe had 416 fish species of 16 genera. Predominant within the two lakes is the Moon fish (*Citharinus citharus citharus*), locally named Afor or Apede (see Chapter 1 for comparisons of enhanced biodiversity in sacred groves).

Figure 12.3 Fishing activities on Lake Adigbe (Osiama)

The influx of people into the lake and community during each fishing festival is an added pressure on natural resources within the region illustrating the need for respect for the sacred dimensions of the lakes.

Source: E.D. Anwana

The West African Dwarf Crocodile (*Osteolaemus tetraspis*) and the Nile crocodile (*Crocodylus niloticus*) are not harvested from the two lakes (Esiribi and Adigbe), as a result of their emblematic representation in these communities. Although *Osteolamus tetrapis* is commonly found within the region, it is threatened and it is particularly hunted within the country for meat and for its skin (Crocodile Specialist Group Newsletter, 1999; IUCN, 2007). Also, in Lake Esiribi the monitor lizard (*Varanus niloticus*) is given protection from hunters.

Discussion on the relevance of sacred lakes to conservation
Inter-related lakes and social capital

Freshwater conservation planning is maintaining connectivity, particularly in data-poor regions such as those of the Niger Delta (Thieme et al, 2007). Fragmented ecosystems such as sacred groves and lakes influence viability of biological species, particularly animal populations that require large home ranges and could create what is referred to as an 'island-effect' on biodiversity (Triantis et al, 2006). To combat this effect and increase species biodiversity, Decher's (1997) recommendation for the preservation of a network of groves and forest remnants becomes relevant in linking the network of sacred lakes found in the Niger Delta. The social ties across communities (see Box 12.1) with common ancestry observed in the study area increases the success of this linkage, as these communities have shared rules and rotate periodical fishing of their collective lakes. Although these freshwater systems are not contiguous because of the meandering nature of the waterway, they can act to strengthen coordinated implementation of

---

Box 12.1 Biseni and Osiama as exemplars of Community Conserved Areas

Strengths:

- The acceptance of the legitimacy of communal rules and social sanctions which clearly define access to resources within these communities, help to reduce conflicts.
- The social ties amongst the different social groups and across communities reinforce traditional norms and helps builds strong resilience to interferences from exogenous cultures.
- Observance of rest from exploiting natural resources (this encourages rejuvenation of the system).
- The protection of threatened species in certain areas (this acts as sanctuaries for such species).

Weakness:

- Weakened communal governance, such as is beginning to happen in Osiama (weakened traditional leadership provides opportunities for power and influence to other social or political groups).

Opportunities:

- Communities who already have strong social capital create a good platform for capacity building and devolving of powers to community leadership.
- The willingness to work with government and other external bodies on natural resource matters outside the control of the community is an opportunity to building linkages for co-management of resources.

Threats:

- Migrants' influx into the region in search of job opportunities in the oil companies.
- Changes in religious orientation (conversion from traditional beliefs to dominant religions).
- Some current practices, such as using dynamite in fishing (this is in defiance of the set traditional norms).
- A further threat lies in the engagement of community members with livelihood opportunities derived from a different value system (such as opportunities arising from investment of private companies or government interests, as found in Osiama where the government is interested in making Lake Adigbe a tourist attraction).

Source: E.D. Anwana

---

conservation principles and may be connected during severe floods. These connected areas could become models of community conserved areas across large landscapes.

Conclusions and recommendations
Management of Sacred Lakes in the Niger Delta

Management issues within the Niger Delta communities are sensitive, as declarations containing elements of government involvement are viewed with suspicion. The discontentment with government intervention has roots in ethnic polarization and fiscal policies such as the cross-subsidization policy during British rule (Mustapha, 2006). Cross-subsidization meant that the allegedly richer south would subsidize developments and endeavours in the poorer north. But inequity in the distribution of revenues from the federation account has masked this goodwill policy and others, intended to unite the Nigerian state. As mentioned earlier in this chapter, crude oil is an important resource of the state. However, oil mining activities have had a devastating effect on the livelihood systems and socioeconomic arrangement of the Delta (Ibeanu, 2000). The communities pay for the high cost of oil production, as they are the most affected by oil drilling effects, such as incidences of pollution, gas flares, silting and turbidity caused by dredging (Saro-Wiwa, 1992; Niger Delta Human Development Report, 2006).

Also, the monopolistic powers of the state over land based on the 1978 Land Use Act further exacerbates the lack of trust between communities and the state. Land tenure rights in Nigeria have the propensity to benefit the state more than indigenous people. The principal interest of the state is to increase earnings by investing in projects and developments on land. This is in contrast to the perspective of indigenous communities on the land, who view land as both a spiritual and an economic entity. In addition is the lack of recognition of communal tenure system by the government and multiplicity of roles in natural resource sectors (SFM, 2005). However, villagers might be willing to allow the government to help in situations that are outside their capacity to manage whilst maintaining ownership and control over their resources. For instance, the water hyacinth (*Eichhornia crassipes*) is a major problem in some of these freshwater lakes and these communities requested government intervention to tackle problems associated with the invasion.

Sustainable management of these freshwater ecosystems will be achieved by adapting the stewardship model exemplified in these communities. Strategies should centre on maintaining the system of rotational fishing as the time lapse between fishing events encourages the rejuvenation of fishery and aquatic resources, leading to high productivity (Kalanda-Sabola et al, 2007) and perhaps accounts for the high biological diversity of these lakes (Alfred-Ockiya and Otobotekere, 1990).

Institutional networking and capacity building

Capacity building of active indigenous groups, such as the community development council and the council of chiefs within the region, will be important for knowledge sharing and monitoring of biodiversity. A strong recommendation is made for training of social groups with shared norms and values for wetland resource management. A caveat, however, is that care should be taken to avoid marginalization of other groups. Our study found that a high percentage (80 per cent) of indigenous livelihoods in the study area depend upon the natural system. Therefore group training can be stratified to accommodate all resource users. Building and forming useful networks both internally and externally is also important in the management of these freshwater systems.

Legal instruments

Policy reforms and legal instruments which recognize and legitimize these indigenous conserved areas are important to the issue of sustainability (Mgumia and Oba, 2003; Oviedo et al, 2005). Providing a legal framework that includes implementing Resolution 61/295 of the UN Declaration on the Rights of Indigenous Peoples is crucial. The state should give priority to fulfilling its obligations under both the CBD and Ramsar convention (e.g. Ramsar's Resolutions VIII/19 and IX/2, see also Papayannis and Pritchard, 2008; see also Chapter 17). Also important is the review of the nation's land-use Act, recently proposed to the National Assembly. However, to what extent the review will go to resolving tenure rights in the Delta is difficult to determine.

In conclusion, evidence from our research in the Niger Delta is indicative of the people's holistic view of the ecosystem. Their interaction with natural resources allows for constant observation and 'feedback' by traditional users in the form of responses and regulatory measures to meet the challenges of changes in the natural system. Hence, involving this group and other indigenous groups in monitoring and governance of wetland ecosystems is imperative, particularly in the current realities of climate change and global biodiversity loss.

References

Aaron, K.K. (2005) 'Perspective: Big oil, rural poverty, and environmental degradation in the Niger Delta region of Nigeria', *Journal of Agricultural Safety and Health*, vol 11, pp127–134

Alagoa, E.J. (1999) *The Land and People of Bayelsa State: Central Niger Delta*, Onyoma Research Publications, Choba, Port Harcourt

Alfred-Ockiya, J.F and Otobotekere, A.J.T., (1990) 'Biological studies of Ofonitorubuo Lake in the fresh water swamps of the Niger Delta, Rivers State, Nigeria', *Journal of Aquatic Sciences*, vol 5, pp77–82

Berkes, F., Colding, J. and Folke, C. (eds) (2003) *Navigating Social-ecological Systems: Building Resilience for Complexity and Change*, Cambridge University Press, Cambridge

Bisht, S. and Ghildiyal, J.C. (2007) 'Sacred groves for biodiversity conservation in Uttarakhand Himalaya', *Current Science*, vol 92, pp711–712

Crocodile Specialist Group Newsletter (1999) vol 18, no 3, IUCN-World Conservation Union, Species Survival Commission, available at http://iucncsg.org/ph1/modules/Publications/newsletter/CSG_Newsletter_www_183.pdf (last accessed August 2009)

Decher, J. (1997) 'Conservation, small mammals, and the future of sacred groves in West Africa', *Biodiversity and Conservation*, vol 6, pp1007–1026

Dei, G.F.S. (1993) 'Indigenous African knowledge systems: Local traditions of sustainable forestry', *Singapore Journal of Tropical Geography*, vol 14, pp28–41

Efere, E.E. and Williamson, K. (1999) 'Languages', in Alagoa, E.J. *The land and people of Bayelsa state: Central Niger Delta,* Onyoma Research Publications, Choba, Port Harcourt

FME (2006) Nigeria first national biodiversity report, Federal Ministry of Environment, Abuja, Nigeria

Golubiewski, N. (2007) 'Western Africa and forests and woodlands', in Cutler J. Cleveland, Environmental Information Coalition, National Council for Science and the Environment (eds) *Encyclopaedia of Earth*, available at www.eoearth.org/article/Western_Africa_and_forests_and_woodlands (last accessed July 2007)

Greider, T. and Garkovich, L. (1994) 'Landscapes: The social construction of nature and the environment', *Rural Sociology*, vol 59, pp1–23

Hilton-Taylor, C. (compiler) (2000) *2000 IUCN Red List of Threatened Species*, IUCN, Gland, Switzerland and Cambridge, UK

Ibeanu, O. (2000) 'Oiling the friction: Environmental conflict management in the Niger Delta, Nigeria', *Environmental Change and Security Project Report*, vol 6, pp19–32

IUCN (2007) *2007 IUCN Red List of Threatened Species*, available at www.iucnredlist.org (last accessed June 2007)

Kalanda-Sabola, M.D., Henry, E.M.T., Kayambazinthu, E. and Wilson, J. (2007) 'Use of indigenous knowledge and traditional practices in fisheries management: A case of Chisi Island, Lake Chilwa, Zomba', *Malawi Journal of Science and Technology*, vol 8, pp9–29

Luiselli, L. and Akani, G.C. (2003) 'An indirect assessment of the effects of oil pollution on the diversity and functioning of turtle communities in the Niger Delta, Nigeria', *Animal Biodiversity and Conservation*, vol 26, pp57–65

McGinley, M. (2007) 'Niger Delta swamp forests', in Cutler J. Cleveland, Environmental Information Coalition, National Council for Science and the Environment (eds) *Encyclopaedia of Earth*, available at www.eoearth.org/article/Niger_Delta_swamp_forests (last accessed July 2007)

Mgumia, F.H. and Oba, G. (2003) 'Potential role of sacred groves in biodiversity conservation in Tanzania', *Environmental Conservation*, vol 30, pp259–265

Mustapha, A.R. (2006) 'Ethnic structure, inequality and governance of the public sector in Nigeria', Democracy, Governance and Human Rights Programme Paper Number 24, United Nations Research Institute for Social Development, Geneva, Switzerland

NEST (1991) *Nigeria's Threatened Environment: A National Profile*, NEST Publications, Ibadan, Nigeria

Neumann, R.P. (1998) *Imposing Wilderness: Struggles over Livelihoods and Nature Preservation in Africa*, University of California Press, Berkeley, CA

Niger Delta Human Development Report (2006) United Nations Development Programme, UN House, Abuja, Nigeria

Oates, J.F., (1989) 'A survey of primates and other forest wildlife in Anambra, Imo and Rivers States, Nigeria: Report to the National Geographic Society, the Nigerian Conservation Foundation, the Nigerian Federal Department of Forestry and the governments of Anambra, Imo and Rivers States', The Nigerian Conservation Foundation, Lagos, Nigeria

Odukoya, A.O. (2006) 'Oil and sustainable development in Nigeria: A case study of the Niger Delta', *Journal of Human Ecology*, vol 20, pp249–258

Omari, C.K. (1990) 'Traditional African land ethics', in Engel, J.R. and Gibb, E.J. (eds) *Ethics of Environment and Development: Global Challenge, International Response*, University of Arizona Press, Tucson

Omene, G. (2001) 'Interim action plan and framework for development of the Niger Delta Region', Position paper on the First International Conference on the Niger Delta, Port Harcourt

Osunade, M.A.A. (1988) 'Nomenclature and classification of traditional land use types in south-western Nigeria', *Savanna*, vol 9, pp50–63

Oviedo, G., Jeanrenaud, S. and Otegui, M. (2005) 'Protecting sacred natural sites of indigenous and traditional peoples: An IUCN perspective', Gland, Switzerland

Oyebande, L., Obot, E.A., Bdiliya, H.H. and Oshunsanya, C.O. (2001) 'An inventory of wetlands in Nigeria', a report submitted to World Conservation Union (IUCN) West African Regional office, Burkina Faso

Papayannis, T. and Pritchard, D. E. (2008) 'Culture and wetlands: A Ramsar guidance document', Ramsar Convention, Gland, Switzerland, pp16–24

Powell, C.B. (1993) 'Sites and species of conservation interest of the central axis of the Niger Delta (Yenagoa, Sagbama, Ekeremor and Southern Ijo Local government areas)', A report of recommendations to The Natural Resources Conservation Council (NARESCON), Lagos

Powell, C.B. (1997) 'Discoveries and priorities for mammals in the freshwater forests of the Niger Delta', *Oryx*, vol 31, pp83–85

Ryan, G.W. and Russell Bernard, H. (2003) 'Data management and analysis methods', in denzin, K.N. and Lincoln, Y.S. (eds) *Collecting and Interpreting Qualitative Materials*, 2nd Edition, Sage Publications, Thousand Oaks, California, USA

Saro-Wiwa, K. (1992) *Genocide in Nigeria: The Ogoni tragedy*, Saros International, Port-Harcourt, Nigeria

Schoffeleers, J.M. (1978) *Guardians of the Land: Essays on Central African Territorial cults*, Mambo Press, Harare, Zimbabwe

SFM (2005) 'Nigeria', International Tropical Timber Organization (ITTO), pp112–118

Southwood, T.R.E. and Henderson, P.A. (2000) *Ecological methods*, 3rd edition, Blackwell Science, Oxford

Thieme, M., Lehner, B., Abell, R., Hamilton, S.K., Kellndorfer, J., Powell, G., Rivero, J.C. (2007) 'Freshwater conservation planning in data-poor areas: An example from a remote Amazonian basin (Madre de Dios River, Peru and Bolivia)', *Biological Conservation*, vol 135, pp484–501

Triantis, K.A., Vardinoyannis, K., Tsolaki, E.P., Botsaris, I., Lika, K., and Mylonas, M. (2006) 'Re-approaching the small island effect', *Journal of Biogeography*, vol 33, pp914–923

Were, J.L.R. (1991) 'A survey of the Taylor Creek forest area, Rivers State, Nigeria', Report to the Shell Petroleum Development Company of Nigeria, LTD and the Nigerian Conservation Foundation

Were, J.L.R. (2001) 'Terrestrial eco-regions: Niger Delta swamp forests', (AT0122) a peer review process document, available at www.worldwildlife.org/wildworld/profiles/terrestrial/at/at0122_full.html (last accessed October 2004)

13

How African-based Winti Belief Helps to Protect Forests in Suriname

Tinde van Andel

Summary

Suriname has many sacred forests, although none is officially recognized. However, many plants are considered sacred, regardless of where they grow. Based on ethnobotanical inventories, a market survey and interviews with traditional healers, the role of the Afro-Surinamese Winti belief in the use, commercialization and protection of sacred plants is discussed here. After centuries of being banned by the church, Winti is now more openly practised in Suriname. It provides an income to many people that collect, prepare or sell plants considered to have magic properties. More than half of the plants sold at the Paramaribo market are employed in supernatural rituals. Maroons, descendants of escaped slaves that live in Suriname's forested interior, are regarded as specialists in Winti and spiritual medicine. Their firm belief in forest spirits includes many taboos that prevent destructive extraction. Trees that house certain spirits are never felled, because the revenge of their 'inhabitants' will be dreadful. Some forests are sacred and no harvesting is allowed unless the spirits are paid with offerings and libations. Magic plants are often cultivated, which protects wild populations from overharvesting. With the exception of two species, the commercial extraction of magic plants seems ecologically sustainable. It is questionable, however, whether the belief in sacred plants and animals is strong enough to protect Suriname's forests in the future. Maroons do not have title to their traditional lands, tribal knowledge is threatened by missionaries and urban migration, and their sacred forests are preyed upon by mining and logging companies. Apart from official land rights, a greater respect for indigenous and Maroon culture from the church, the government and multinational companies eager for the country's natural resources, would certainly benefit the survival of sacred forests in Suriname.

Introduction

Traditional spiritual values have influenced human behaviour affecting the environment and continue to play a role in protecting sacred forests (Byers et al, 2001; O'Neal Campbell, 2005). Protection of vegetation at graveyards or other religious or spiritual sites is a common feature in many tropical countries and an important means through which biodiversity is protected (Cunningham, 1993; O'Neal Campbell, 2005). In some severely deforested countries like Haiti, sacred groves are almost the only remaining forest patches left (Boling, 1995). Deforestation rates tend to be much higher in areas where traditional leaders have lost much of their power, compared to areas where they still had much influence (Byers et al, 2001).

Sacred plants that grow outside such strictly protected groves are often less fortunate. Having magic properties does not guarantee that plants are treated with respect by commercial gatherers (Cunningham, 1993). Throughout the world, medicinal plants that play an important role in indigenous religion and magic rituals are being overharvested (Sheldon et al, 1997). The question arises whether magic plants can be efficiently protected once they have gained commercial value. This chapter will explain the role of the African-based Winti belief in the sustainable extraction and conservation of magic plants in Suriname.

As a country with less than half a million inhabitants and large stretches of dense tropical rain forest, Suriname is often seen as a great opportunity for nature conservation. Most of the country's diverse population live in the city of Paramaribo or along the coast. The interior is sparsely inhabited by Amerindian and Maroons. Amerindians (population 20,000) are found in the coastal savannah belt and in the southernmost part of the country. Maroons, descendants of escaped African slaves who created autonomous communities along the major rivers, are the third largest ethnic group in the country with 70,000 people. They are divided into different tribes, the largest being the Saramacca and Ndyuka. Most Maroons still reside in their remote forest villages, though during the last three decades they have migrated in great numbers to Paramaribo and the Netherlands (Kambel, 2006).

Maroons are culturally distinct from other sectors of Surinamese society and are regarded as specialists in Winti religion and traditional medicine (Price, 1990). For centuries, their religious system was regarded as witchcraft and idolatry by both missionaries and the colonial administration. In spite of the ongoing attempts to convert them to Christianity, Maroons have preserved much of their oral history, language, art and social organization. Much research has been done on Maroon culture (e.g. Price, 1990; Hoogbergen, 1990; Thoden van Velzen, 1995), as well as on Winti practices among coastal Creoles (e.g. Stephen, 1998).

Predominantly based on oral sources, stemming from multiple African origins and mixed to a varying degree with Christianity, Judaism and Amerindian beliefs, the Afro-Surinamese Winti religion is far from being uniform. Winti literally means wind, and refers to invisible, supernatural beings who by means of music, dance, prayers and specific herbs, can possess human beings and bring them into a state of trance. If neglected or not provided with regular offerings, the spirits are believed to cause disease and ill fortune (Stephen, 1998). In the Winti worldview, many diseases are caused by a disturbed relationship between human beings and (ancestor) spirits. Disturbance of the environment, such as river pollution, excessive hunting or cutting sacred trees can upset the spirits and cause disaster. Skilled Winti priests and complex rituals and offerings are needed to pacify such angry spirits (Stephen, 1998). In spite of the fact that most scholars agree that nature plays a major role in these beliefs, their anthropological focus has prevented them from looking further into the use of plants in Winti religion. How are plants used in Winti rituals? Does the Afro-Surinamese worldview allow for an effective protection of sacred plants? This chapter explains how Winti plays a role in the conservation of Suriname's rain forests.

Methodology

Data were drawn from an ethnobotanical inventory on medicinal plants, carried out between January and August 2006. Fieldwork took place around the capital, the Pará, Brokopondo and the Marowijne Districts. The inventory included a survey of three shipping agents and 15 per cent of the 432 market stalls selling medicinal plants. To assess the sustainability of the medicinal plant extractions, harvesters were accompanied to the forest to study extraction methods, harvesting sites, survival after extraction, growth form, plant parts harvested, volumes sold and scarcity of the plants. Herbarium vouchers were made of all plants employed in Winti rituals and deposited at the National Herbaria of the Netherlands. In total, 18 experts in Winti rituals were interviewed: eight in Suriname and ten in the Netherlands.

Results

How plants are used in magic rituals

Nature and plants play a paramount role in the Afro-Surinamese religion. During this inventory, which was limited to the coastal region of Suriname, a total of 269 plant species were recorded for use in Winti rituals. If we combine these data with the research outcomes of Ruysschaert (unpublished) who studied plant use among Saramacca Maroons deeper inland, we can distinguish 425 species employed for Winti purposes. This accounts for 10 per cent of the total flora of Suriname, which comprises 4443 species (Boggan et al, 1997). Herbal baths are the most frequently practiced Winti rituals. Sweet smelling leaves, mixed in countless numbers of recipes and combinations, are the main ingredients in herbal baths to strengthen one's personal spiritual well-being (Figure 13.1). People say these baths help them to gain more self-confidence, feel good, clean and with renewed energy.

Figure 13.1 A ritual herbal bath for happiness and good luck, Paramaribo

Source: C. van der Hoeven

Pungent smelling barks and herbs are mixed in herbal baths to purify the body from evil spirits and witchcraft. Women use a wide assortment of herbs to bathe their babies, with the aim to protect them from evil and to make them walk faster (Ruysschaert et al, 2008). Baths made from lianas with hooks and spines serve symbolically to attract men and prevent them from seeing other women (van Andel et al, 2008). Young palm leaves are folded open and hung like curtains in doorways or village entrances to prevent evil-minded people from entering. Broom-like herbs serve to sprinkle purifying decoctions around the village after burials and to sweep away evil from a sick person's body. Magic decoctions from plants and animal parts are said to prevent snake attacks.

Several war *obias*, magic objects or medicines that supported the Maroons in their struggle for freedom (Herskovits and Herskovits, 1934), but also popular during the civil war of the 1980s (Thoden van Velzen, 1995), are still being used today. Men bathe or rub their bodies with decoctions of magic herbs to protect themselves against machete attacks, broken glass or bullets. One of these herbs, the purple-brown forest creeper (*Psychotria ulviformis*) is thought to make things invisible. The herb is popular among cocaine traffickers, who hope to remain unnoticed by the Customs Officers on their flight to the Netherlands. Some wild forest species are planted in the yard to protect the household from misfortune and thieves, like *Philodendron melinonii*, *Alocasia plumbea* or *Piper aduncum*. Several large trees (*Parkia* spp., *Ceiba pentandra*), strangler figs (*Ficus* spp.), shrubs (*Piper* spp., *Costus* spp.) and the hemi-epiphyte *Clusia grandiflora* are believed to be the home of certain spirits. Few Surinamese will volunteer to cut down a *Ceiba* tree, fearing the dreadful revenge of its supernatural inhabitants (Figure 13.2). As its giant branches are often laden with epiphytes and provide a home for countless species of birds, small mammals, insects and even frogs, the protection of *Ceiba* trees automatically safeguards the habitat of the species that live in its crown. *Ceiba pentandra* is strongly held to be sacred over a wide area of Central and South America and also in Africa.

Figure 13.2 *Ceiba pentandra* **tree spared from felling along a public road in Paramaribo, Suriname**

Source: C. van der Hoeven

Winti as a significant economic force

Winti is one of the driving forces behind the medicinal plant trade in Suriname. More than 56 per cent of the 249 species sold at the medicinal plant markets had one or more applications in ancestor rites, herbal baths or protective *obias* (van Andel et al, 2007). This means that more than half of all Winti species recorded in this study have a commercial value in their unprocessed form. It should be noted, though, that many of these Winti plants are also sold for other, non-spiritual medicinal purposes. Animal products (e.g. feathers, skulls, anteater tails, toucan beaks, dried hummingbirds) are also sold, as well as many non-biological objects such as kaolin pipes, smoked by people possessed by ancestor spirits. Winti is a lucrative business, especially for those religious specialists who administer herbal purification baths for tourists or ritually prepare drug runners before they take on their flight. Approximately 55,000kg of fresh herbs are exported annually to the Netherlands.

Harvested sustainability

Assessing whether their popularity in Winti rituals leads to the overharvesting of certain plant species requires knowing the extracted quantities, their domestication state and their abundance in the wild. Three of the 10 magic plants that were sold in the greatest quantity at the Paramaribo markets in 2006 were domesticated exotics. Of the 249 commercial species (Winti- and non-Winti plants) recorded during the market survey, less than half was harvested exclusively from the wild. Many native species were being cultivated for the market (*Piper marginatum*, *Scoparia dulcis*). Others, like *Costus scaber* and *Lycopodiella cernua* were wild-harvested, but quite abundant in secondary vegetation. Most extraction took place in secondary forest or man-made vegetation close to the capital. Leaves were the main product. From all commercially, wild-harvested Winti species, only *Begonia glabra* and *Renealmia floribunda* are suffering from declining populations. Both occur in low densities in primary forest and are transported from increasingly distant sources to the market. *Begonia glabra* is used in herbal baths to calm anxious people, and is therefore popular among drug runners. Indiscriminate harvesting has doubled the price of this epiphyte in a few years (van Andel and Havinga, 2008).

Taboos that limit overharvesting

Almost all commercial wild species were subject to some form of domestication by Maroons: either tolerated as a weed, encouraged in their wild environment or planted in forest gardens or villages. The Maroon's firm belief in forest spirits includes many taboos that contribute to a respectful behaviour towards medicinal and magic plants. No harvesting is done after dark. People told us they would never ring-bark or cut down an entire tree to harvest its bark. They explained that they only slice the bark from the sunny side of the trunk, because of its greater medicinal power, leaving the shadow side intact. People can pick leaves from sacred trees for rituals, but they should first ask permission personally from the deities in question and never cut them down. Many people fear the magic power of plants like *Lycopodiella cernua* and *Dicranopteris flexuosa*, of which improper application can put the user in great danger.

Women do not handle plants during their menstrual period, because this will destroy the plant's healing power. Market vendors still take these cultural taboos quite seriously. When clients would suspect that these rules are not obeyed, they would immediately stop buying their products. Some Winti specialists prefer to obtain them directly from the hinterland to be sure that the plants are picked with respect to cultural traditions. Although some healers said they preferred plants harvested from the wild, the majority had no problems using cultivated herbs. The presence of home gardens full of sacred plants native to the Surinamese flora is important for potential conservation efforts.

Some forests are sacred and not accessible to outsiders. Harvesting of forest products is not allowed unless the local spirits are 'paid' with offerings and libations. Trespassing upon the territory of supernatural beings without a valid reason would

upset them and make them angry. Some traditional healers have lengthy conversations with forest deities before entering the bush trails, explaining the reason for their visit and the way they would pay them afterwards for this inconvenience. Some forests had less strict access rules, as they were only forbidden on Fridays or to people wearing black clothes.

Conclusions and discussion
Sacred plants and forests

Results of this study revealed that even though there is still some resistance from the religious side, the Winti belief is still very much alive in Suriname. With the exception of two primary forest species *Begonia glabra* and *Renealmia floribunda*, the commercial harvest of magic plants has not (yet) led to declining resources and species loss. With its low population density and market dominated by disturbance species, Suriname offers good possibilities for sustainable medicinal plant extraction. The protection of *B. glabra* and *R. floribunda* should be incorporated in nature conservation projects and their cultivation should be stimulated. In many African countries, people prefer plants collected from the wild, which leads to severe degradation of wild stocks (Cunningham, 1993). This is not the case in Suriname, where wild plants are cultivated in gardens, taking pressure from wild populations and contributing to their conservation. Both commercial and subsistence harvesters still respect cultural taboos regarding plant harvesting, which also limits habitat destruction. But is the belief in sacred plants and animals strong enough to protect Suriname's forests in the future?

Anthropologists have described several sacred Maroon sites where outsiders' presence was strictly prohibited. Examples are the Saramaccan spiritual centres of Dahome and Asidonopo on the Suriname River (Herskovits and Herskovits, 1934) and the Ndyuka witches' cemetery Saantigoon on the Tapanahoni River (Thoden van Velzen, 1995). Although recent studies briefly mention sacred Saramaccan forest zones (Hoffman, 2009), it is not clear how many such restricted areas still persist today, nor to what extent people protect them. Detailed mapping of currently existing sacred forests of Maroons and Amerindians is needed for the quantitative assessment of their importance for biodiversity conservation. The cultural reasons behind their sacredness should also be documented, as these sanctuaries often represent important moments in the tribes' oral history.

Land titles

At present, none of the Amerindian or Maroon communities in Suriname has formal title to their ancestral territories. All land and all natural resources are owned by the state, which means that they can be awarded by the government to third parties (Kambel, 2006). The country's pristine forests have drawn the attention of several multinational companies interested in tropical hardwood, precious minerals and other natural resources. The Surinamese government, eager to find solutions for its financial problems, regards the 'economic development' of the interior as a source of much-needed income. Faced with logging, mining and palm oil concessions that cover at least two-thirds of their territories, indigenous peoples and Maroons have begun to map their own territories in an attempt to seek a negotiated settlement with the government. The Amazon Conservation Team (www.amazonteam.org/index.php/235/Suriname, last accessed 25 May 2010) suppports Trio and Wayana Indians in mapping their traditional territories, including sites of historical and sacred significance. They also support Ndyuka Maroons in mapping their approximately 2 million hectares of traditional lands. Recently, an association of Maroon village leaders has been successful in their struggle for greater participation in decisions made on natural resource exploitation. Ecotourism, another booming business in Suriname, may offer some employment to several forest communities, but also causes conflicts when local people's access to forests is restricted. Recently, the proprietor of a luxurious jungle resort caused a huge conflict when without prior notice he prohibited local Maroons to enter their former territory, including an ancient burial ground (Azizahamad, 2008).

No sacred forests without bush spirits

From 1765, when the first Moravian Brethrens entered Saramaccan territory, the Maroons have been under pressure to leave their 'idolatry' behind and convert to Christianity. Even today, they still depend for their education and primary health care on Moravian and Catholic organizations, which generally ignore their culture and language (Price, 1990; Kambel, 2006). At the moment, several Pentecostal groups are increasing their influence in Maroon villages. Some of these groups tolerate the use of medicinal plants for physical ailments, but they all strongly condemn the worshipping of Winti spirits and ancestor shrines.

While Winti is gaining popularity among higher educated urban Creoles (Stephen, 1998), and urban Maroons maintain a flourishing market in magic herbs and objects, traditional Maroon culture is losing ground to the migration of their youth to the capital and evangelical pressure. This process of cultural destruction seems even more prevalent among Amerindians (Heemskerk et al, 2007). The original tribal knowledge on how plants received their magic power, who gave them their name, why each spirit prefers specific plants or animals and how certain areas became sacred, is maintained only by a small number of village elders. This specific oral history, largely undocumented and under great peril, forms the rationale behind sacred nature and its protection. Without forest spirits, people have no need to plant magic herbs, protect sacred trees, or remember wild food crops that fed their ancestors. A greater respect for Maroon and Amerindian culture, from the various churches, the government and multinational companies longing for Suriname's natural resources would certainly improve the survival of sacred plants and forests in Suriname.

Recommendations

With its low population density and vast tracts of undisturbed rainforest, Suriname is often named as a candidate for avoided deforestation initiatives, whereby developing countries prevent deforestation and consequently maintain the carbon storage capability of their tropical forest.

Suriname could earn considerable income by selling its 'carbon credits' to industrialized countries that fail to meet emissions limits imposed under international agreements like the Kyoto Protocol (Butler, 2006). Tribal communities trying to protect their sacred forests from exploitation by outsiders could profit from these future developments. If ancestral lands could become officially recognized carbon sinks, their protection would be ensured, as the cooperation of local people remains a key element to protecting nature. Maroon environmental and religious knowledge should from now on be taken into account by policy-makers when selecting protected areas and planning future development projects.

References

van Andel, T.R. and Havinga, R.M. (2008) 'Sustainability aspects of commercial medicinal plant harvesting in Suriname', *Forest Ecology and Management*, vol 256, pp1540–1545

van Andel, T.R., Havinga, R.M., Groenendijk, S. and Behari-Ramdas, J.A. (2007) 'The medicinal plant trade in Suriname', *Ethnobotany Research & Applications*, vol 5, pp351–373

van Andel, T.R., de Korte, S., Koopmans, D., Behari-Ramdas, J.A. and Ruysschaert, S. (2008) 'Dry sex in Suriname', *Journal of Ethnopharmacology*, vol 116, no 1, pp84–88

Azizahamad, Z. (2008) 'Afstammelingen Berg en Dal en nazaten roeren zich', *Dagblad Suriname*, 9 April

Boggan, J., Funk, V., Kelloff, C., Hoff, M., Cremers, G. and Feuillet, C. (1997) *Checklist of the Plants of the Guianas*, Smithsonian Institution, Georgetown, Guyana

Boling, R. (1995) 'Horticulture in hell: Protection of rainforest in Haiti', *American Forests*, Autumn

Butler, R. (2006) 'Carbon finance could net Guyana and Suriname tens of millions of dollars', available at www.mongabay.com (last accessed August 2008)

Byers, B.A., Cunliffe, R.N. and Hudak, A. T. (2001) 'Linking the conservation of culture and nature: A case study of sacred forests in Zimbabwe', *Human Ecology*, vol 29, pp187–218

Cunningham, A.B. (1993) *African Medicinal Plants: Setting Priorities at the Interface Between Conservation And Primary Healthcare*, UNESCO, Paris

Heemskerk, M., Delvoye, K., Noordam, D. and Teunissen, P. (2007) *Wayana Baseline Study*, Amazon Conservation Team, Paramaribo

Herskovits, M.J. and Herskovits, F.S. (1934) *Rebel Destiny: Among the Bush Negroes of Dutch Guiana*, S. Emmering, Amsterdam

Hoffman, B. (2009) 'Drums and arrows: Ethnobotanical classification and use of tropical forest plants by a Maroon and Amerindian community in Suriname', PhD thesis, University of Hawaii, Manoa

Hoogbergen, W.S.M. (1990) *The Boni Maroon wars in Suriname*, E.J. Brill, Leiden.

Kambel, E.R. (2006) *Policy Note on Indigenous Peoples and Maroons in Suriname*, Inter-American Development Bank, Washington DC

O'Neal Campbell, M. (2005) 'Sacred groves for forest conservation in Ghana's coastal savannas', *Singapore Journal of Tropical Geography*, vol 26, no 2, pp151–169

Price, R. (1990) *Alabi's World*, Johns Hopkins University Press, Baltimore, MD

Ruysschaert, S, van Andel, T.R, van de Putte, K. and van Damme, P. (2008) 'Bathe the baby to make it strong and healthy: Plant use and child care among Saramaccan Maroons in Suriname', *Journal of Ethnopharmacology*, vol 212, no 1, pp148–170

Sheldon, J.W., Balick, M.J. and Laird, S.A. (1997) 'Medicinal plants: Can utilization and conservation coexist?', *Advances in Economic Botany*, vol 12, pp1–104

Stephen, H.J.M. (1998) *Winti Culture: Mysteries, Voodoo and Realities of an Afro-Caribbean Religion in Suriname and the Netherlands*, Karnak, Amsterdam

Thoden van Velzen, H.U.E. (1995) 'Revenants that cannot be shaken: Collective fantasies in a Maroon society', *American Anthropologist*, vol 97, no 4, pp722–732

14

Seeking and Securing Sacred Natural Sites among Jamaica's Windward Maroons

Kimberly John, Collin L.G. Harris and Susan Otuokon

Summary

This chapter suggests broadening the management levers of human behaviour in Jamaica's protected areas beyond economic benefits and moral persuasion to include other drivers of behavioural change such as the spiritual. The indigenous Windward Maroon culture is examined for notions that parallel the western conservation concept of 'setting apart' areas for special uses and sacredness. The Maroons have occupied lands in the Blue and John Crow Mountains and Cockpit Country for more than three centuries. Only a few examples were found of sacred natural sites primarily associated with supernatural healing, burial and refuge. However, their sparse presence is significant in the Jamaican context of widespread ecological degradation and erosion of Maroon culture. Second, a discourse is initiated on how such sites can be integrated with, and even improve, protected area management by restoring and incorporating a sense of the sacred among protected area beneficiaries. The relationship between the protected area and sacred natural sites is seen to be synergistic since incorporating these sites into protected area management will help to preserve their knowledge and transmission within the Windward Maroon community and in turn reinforce the culture of Jamaica's only remaining indigenous group.

Introduction

Conservation efforts in Jamaica are faced with the dual task of restoring fragmented ecosystems and repairing or developing healthy linkages between people and nature. The latter usually focuses on sustainable livelihoods, where ecosystems are managed as commodities for wise use and profit. The discourse explores how this perspective can be broadened by including the sacred natural sites associated with Jamaica's Windward Maroons who occupied what is now the Blue and John Crow Mountains National Park (The Park) for some 300 years, and who had significant interactions with the indigenous Taínos before their extinction. The Park and the Windward Maroons are two entities which started and persist independent of each other, but which can each play a role in the other's success and survival as will be explored later.

Jamaica was first settled around 600 AD by the Taínos (described below) who were rapidly destroyed after the Spanish invasion of 1494. By 1513, Spanish settlers were compelled to import African slaves to replace the Taínos as a source of slave labour. Jamaica's population has grown steadily since the 600s AD from an estimated 60,000 people to the present 2.7 million people (STATIN, n.d.). The island's pattern of economic development and urbanization has contributed substantially to the destruction of biodiversity and indigenous artifacts (Atkinson, 2006).

Jamaica's indigenous people

The Taínos were an ethnic group whose pre-Columbian range included much of the Antilles. They inhabited Jamaica for about 900 years; however, within 30 years of contact with Europeans, most Taínos were extirpated and no longer existed as a separate group (Senior, 2003). Although some aspects of their culture remain in Jamaican food traditions, cultivated plants and the name 'Jamaica' which is derived from the Taíno word for 'land abounding in springs', many questions about Taíno spiritual beliefs and practices will remain unanswered. However, there are some clues about their spirituality in the archaeological records, the traits of related Amazonian groups from which the Taíno evolved and in the journals of contemporary Europeans. It is likely that the Taínos perceived sacred forests, trees, caves, rocks and rivers across Jamaica's landscapes (Saunders and Grey, 2006). For example, some tree species such as *Ceiba pentandra* (silk cotton) were used to make significant *zemís* (objects that possessed spiritual powers or spirits residing in trees, rocks, caves and other natural features) and has retained its spiritual relevance throughout the Antilles (see also Chapter 13). Is there a chance then, that in their brief interaction and eventual assimilation within the Maroons, the Taínos transmitted some of their spiritual knowledge?

Although predominantly West African in origin, the Maroons claim to have Taíno ancestry.

Maroons are characterized as communities in the Americas comprising a blend of indigenous Amerindian peoples and Africans who escaped slavery, formed viable communities within their territory and maintained their freedom by fighting off colonial attempts at control (Agorsah, 1994). Jamaica's Maroons first formed during Spanish occupation (1494–1655) when some slaves escaped to the hilly interior to join the remaining Amerindians. More slaves escaped as a result of the British invasion in 1655 and integrated into the existing Maroon settlements. By the early 1700s the Maroons became a problem for the British because of their growing numbers, raids on plantations and because their example of independence inspired plantation slaves to rebel. Several laws were passed and battles fought in unsuccessful attempts by the British colonists to rein in the Maroons.

The Maroons settled in two inaccessible areas: the Windward Maroons in the Blue and John Crow Mountains and the Leeward Maroons in the Cockpit Country. They owed much of their success in battle and long-term resilience to local ecological knowledge learnt from the Taínos in these high-biodiversity areas where the steep, rugged terrain and the almost impenetrable forest created natural fortresses. The Windward Maroons were almost completely dependent on the forests for food plants, clothing, shelter, household items, medicines and even toys for their children. They also had a close relationship with the streams and rivers which provided food, escape routes, hiding places, essential drinking water and even a guerrilla warfare technique that confused the British soldiers when groups of Maroons disappeared into waterfalls (Figure 14.1). This relationship is reflected in many of their centuries-old stories and songs which refer to 'following the river' to safety (Bilby, 2005).

After 80 years of conflict, the British requested peace. Two peace treaties were signed in 1739, by the Leeward and Windward Maroons respectively, granting the Maroons possession of the land they controlled. To this day, the Maroons are the only example of communal land ownership in Jamaica, with land holdings in the Rio Grande valley of more than 2000 hectares.

Traditional Maroon religion closely resembles West African and Taíno religions where the natural and supernatural worlds flow together. According to Agorsah (1994), this is characterized by the concept of a Creator God, the veneration of ancestors and rituals associated with both of the above. However, the peace treaties of 1739 marked the beginning of the Maroon's 'creolization' – the fusion and hybridization of different local cultural elements into one homogenous culture (Bedasse and Stewart, 1996). Bilby (2005) reports that by the mid-1800s, the presence of missionaries in Maroon settlements was firmly established. Within a few decades of the treaty, nearly all Maroons were converted to Christianity. A distinct Maroon culture still exists, particularly in the spheres of food, music, dance and the linguistic relic of West African dialects known as 'Kramanti', which along with other elements of Maroon culture is in decline and changing rapidly (Bilby, 2005). Bilby argues that the important markers of Maroon cultural identity are now the

Figure 14.1 Nanny Falls with the present Colonel of the More Town Maroons, Wallace Sterling, in the foreground

Source: Kimberly John

intangible, internal and private, not the tangible and public. The cultural distinctiveness and value of the Maroons was proclaimed in 2003 as an element of the Intangible Cultural Heritage of Humanity as being of outstanding universal value by UNESCO. Among the many pieces of literature that document the history and culture of the Maroons are two that call for an examination of significant sites. Bedasse and Stewart (1996) recommended identifying areas of cultural significance for ecotourism purposes and Harris (1994) advocated for the documentation of special areas before the knowledge of them is lost.

Blue and John Crow Mountains National Park

The Blue and John Crow Mountains National Park is Jamaica's first and largest national park, spanning 495.2km² and one third of the island's remaining natural forests (JCDT, 2005). Declared first as a Forest Reserve in the 1950s and subsequently as a National Park in 1993 its national and global importance is based on high levels of faunal and floral endemism, and the water and other ecosystem services provided to the wider society and economy.

Apart from its role in conserving biodiversity (JCDT, 2005) there has also been a growing recognition of the value of the cultural heritage of the Park. The Windward Maroons were described as 'frontline stakeholders' engaged in the formation and declaration of the Park. More recently, documents prepared for the World Heritage Site nomination emphasized the unique Windward Maroon culture and stressed the sacredness of the Park and buffer areas. The Park was nominated as a UNESCO World Heritage Site in January

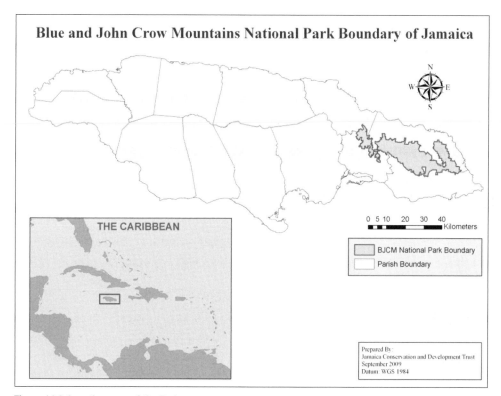

Figure 14.2 Location map of the Park

Source: Jamaica Conservation and Development Trust (JCDT)

2009, after a protracted consultation process which involved the Windward Maroons.

Sacred sites in Jamaica

Sacred connections between modern Jamaican culture and the natural environment are expected to be weak because the society is relatively young and because there has been a sharp disconnect between indigenous/traditional groups and most modern Jamaicans caused by the extinction of aboriginal Taínos, severe and prolonged slavery and colonization, creolization and now modernization. Consequently, the home-grown environmental culture is still in its very early stages.

The search for sacred natural sites in Jamaica started at the Jamaica National Heritage Trust (JNHT), whose mission focuses on the promotion, preservation and development of Jamaica's material and cultural heritage. All of the 29 'sacred' heritage sites in the JNHT database are churches

from mainstream Christian denominations, none is associated with significant groups such as the Taínos, Maroons or Rastafarians, and no sites are both 'sacred' and natural. This imbalance might reflect: the limited interest of Jamaica's overwhelming Christian majority in other worldviews; the Rastafarian focus on the African homeland; the paucity of tangible Taíno artefacts, and the secrecy of Maroon sacred knowledge and traditions. Maroons are regarded as the most secretive group in Jamaica (Bedasse and Stewart, 1996; Bilby, 2005).

Seeking sacred natural sites among the Windward Maroons

Given the more than 300 years of continuous occupation of the Blue and John Crow Mountains and their retention of vestiges of West African and Taíno cultural elements, Maroon sacred natural sites are a practical starting point for investigating the sacred values of the Park. This discourse aims to stimulate the discussion of the sacredness of nature in the Jamaican context through the following questions: What sacred natural sites exist among the Windward Maroons? Why are they sacred? How are they managed? And what are the management implications?

The findings are based on:

- key publications;
- participatory research such as focus group meeting and interviews conducted among the Windward Maroons;
- targeted interviews with Maroon elders;
- the draft World Heritage Site nomination dossier for the Park. Attempts were made to verify the data by independently consulting and cross-referencing with elders in the maroon community.

Maroon sacred natural sites

At first glance, the Maroons seem to have adopted a very modern and utilitarian view of nature, where forests, land and water are primarily resources for exploitation. However, many maroons recognize the mountains as a sacred landscape with significant areas of forest and streams which meet the accepted criteria for sacred natural sites. In times past, these were sites of refuge, places of healing and places where ancestors were buried. Many of these sites are found within the Park boundary and some are located in the buffer zone. Recalling and describing these sites is a source of great pride for elder Maroons.

Places of refuge

The main places of refuge that have been identified are Nanny Town, Pumpkin Hill and Stony River. Nanny Town, the original capital of Windward Maroon lands, is located within the Preservation Zone of the National Park at about 670m above sea level. Nanny Town is named after the great Maroon chieftain and national heroine Nya Nya, commonly called Nanny, who led the Maroon communities in warfare against the English in the early 1700s. Archaeological research by Dr Kofi

Agorsah on the 5000m² site, found *zemís* (see above) in the lower levels of the excavations, suggesting the site's original use by the Taínos as a sacred hill site before 1655. This period of Taíno occupation overlapped with what is described by Agorsah (1994) as the Maroon Phase. During the Maroon Phase the site was an important place of safety for the Africans because of its remote location, the thick forest and the treacherous water course of the Stony River, which borders the site. Bilby (2005) included Nanny Town, sometimes called Stony River (or Toni Ribba) as a major sacred site among Maroons and described the obvious 'awe' that Maroons feel when they speak about it. The area is regarded as the site where Nanny's spiritual power is still concentrated. According to Bilby (2005), Stony River is held sacred by the Maroons because it was a major escape route and source of water and food for the Maroon citadel at Nanny Town.

Pumpkin Hill is a former Maroon settlement where according to oral traditions, Nanny planted pumpkin seeds during an acute food shortage. The seeds sprouted and produced fruit on the same day and Nanny was able to provide food for her soldiers. Pumpkin Hill is a remote yet very visible promontory overlooking Rio Grande (Figure 14.3), which according to Bilby (2005) stands as a reminder to the Maroons of their special place in history.

Places of healing

The Maroons identified many riverine areas that have cultural significance including Sanda and Stony River. Sanda is a deep, narrow pool along the Wild Cane or Negro River that has existed for centuries. Sanda's healing properties were discovered in the 1700s when a maroon elder was completely healed from a potentially fatal wound by swimming along the pool. The name 'Sanda' is derived from the undisclosed song that the elder sang as he went to the river and has a very special meaning in Maroon oral traditions. These healing properties were useful for curing battle injuries during the long conflict with the British and more recently for healing after 'science works' (Maroon spiritual rituals during which some persons are cut with machetes). Another recent Sanda tradition is

Figure 14.3 River View in Rio Grande valley looking west at the Maroon sacred natural sites of Pumpkin Hill (highest peak) in the Blue Mountains

Source: Kimberly John

that persons about to get married bathe at Sanda on the dawn of their wedding day.

Places of burial

The Maroons have retained the West African and Taíno religious concepts wherein burial sites are viewed as the resting place of ancestors and where ancestral spirits reside and protect the living. The Blue and John Crow Mountains are home to several unmarked Maroon burial sites. Consequently, most of the area is regarded as a sacred landscape; a 'secure, natural citadel' (R. Ebanks, personal communication). This sacredness is accentuated because the ancestors buried in the mountains died while trying to protect the freedom and survival of the Maroon community. Bedasse and Stewart (1996) reported that the

Maroon elders spoke with 'reverence' about the 'Forest' which is understood to be the Park.

Places of cultural significance

Many special sites emerged in the study whose sacredness need to be verified. Sites that are proposed as sacred by some persons but not supported by others include Quao Falls, Dinnertime and Dinnertime Peak, the Rio Grande and Nanny's Boiling Pot.

Little consensus was found among the Maroons on the significance of Quao Falls, located on the Quao River. It is reputed that Quao, a Maroon captain and contemporary of Nanny, would lead Maroon women and children through the plunge pool into a cave at the back of the Falls which led them to an unknown exit.

To the British militia at the time, it appeared that the Maroons disappeared into the waterfall. The Dinnertime settlement and Dinnertime Peak refer to a former Maroon settlement where hundreds of Maroons were housed under one structure and probably served as a place of refuge (I. Harris, personal communication). Further inquiries into the intangible values of the Rio Grande are also needed. The Rio Grande is the main drainage in the Windward maroon territory and is the largest Jamaican river in terms of discharge. According to I. Harris (personal communication), in times past, Maroons revered the Rio Grande as a powerful force of nature and a source of food and inspiration. This agrees with 18th-century reports describing Rio Grande settlements as 'fishing communities' (Agorsah, 1994) and Bilby's description of the Rio Grande as a hallowed river among Maroons.

Another culturally significant site connected to the Rio Grande is Nanny's Boiling Pot. Nanny's Boiling Pot is a famous site where British soldiers were warned to beware of a large boiling pot, under which there were no flames, in which the Maroon heroine Nanny would kill their comrades. Bilby (2005) proposed that this boiling pot is near the turbulent confluence of the Stony River and Rio Grande along which was a narrow path. According to some accounts, Nanny placed soporific herbs in the river and soldiers walking on the path above the confluence would become drowsy, fall into the river and drown.

Management of sacred natural sites among the Windward Maroons

Maroons felt a sense of duty to maintain their sacred natural sites in times past. First of all, outsiders were not authorized to visit these sites otherwise they were 'bound for trouble' and as Bilby (2005) wrote outsiders would expose any collaborating Maroons to 'severe spiritual sanctions'. Furthermore, children were not allowed at many sacred natural sites, for their own safety and because many of the rituals were deemed to be inappropriate for children.

As a result, today there is no evidence of active management of sacred natural sites among the

Maroons, neither by formal management structures nor by social group norms and beliefs. Visitors are still discouraged from visiting some sites such as Quao Falls until they learn to communicate with the ancestors (R. Ebanks, personal communication). Moreover, Maroon culture has changed; it has retreated from the public to the private sphere. There are no Maroon community-based mechanisms for recounting or celebrating these sites and unfortunately, knowledge of Maroon sacred natural sites is no longer being transmitted to the younger generation through the oral traditions. Alarmingly, the knowledge of these sites seems to be stored in a few (academic) documents – such as this one – or it is held between a few Maroon individuals who in some cases cannot independently verify each other's stories.

Threats to Maroon sacred natural sites

The persistence of Maroon sacred natural sites in the Maroon community and wider Jamaican society is uncertain given several unfavourable conditions. These threats are the limited transmission of sacred natural site knowledge, the fact that many monuments and markers are impermanent and the risk of trivializing the sites among the Maroons.

The limited transmission of site knowledge is a recurring concern in Harris (1994), Bedasse and Stewart (1996) and Bilby (2005). This break in transmission of the oral history occurs between the remaining elders, many of whom are now in their 90s, and the young and middle-aged Maroons. This is partly due to the customary Maroon secrecy which prevented critical information from passing into the wrong hands. The 'wrong hands' in this case were outsiders, Maroons of mixed blood and rash Maroon youth who do not display the patience, perseverance and respect necessary to be stewards of the oral history. In fact some elders would prefer to go to their graves with the oral history kept to themselves rather than entrust this information to the unworthy.

In the 1960s and 1970s there was also a deliberate restriction in the expression and transmission of Maroon cultural heritage, which was believed to limit Maroon advancement through the educational system and to contradict Christian teachings.

Although this decision was later reversed, it was too late, and many Maroon traditions were driven underground and into extinction. This mirrors an incident in the 1930s described by Bilby (2005) among the Leeward Maroons in which a Maroon convert to Christianity burned down the sacred house of Kojo and other ancestors.

Many monuments and markers are impermanent. The markers of burial sites and other sacred areas might have been naturally destroyed because they were made of biodegradable materials. Agorsah's excavation found few artefacts of the Maroon Phase at Nanny town, whereas permanent artefacts were found from the Taíno and Modern Phase. Additionally, the Maroons were very mobile, and during clashes with the British, they elected to destroy the belongings left behind in abandoned settlements. As such, few permanent structures were left from the period preceding the peace treaty.

In the face of cultural extinction, there is an increasing willingness among the Maroons to partner with outsiders in the preservation of their cultural heritage and in the transmission of that knowledge to young people. There is however, a fear among many elder Maroons of the sacred natural sites becoming trivialized. Some interviewees were concerned that the recent interest in their cultural heritage might cause others to make unverified claims of sacredness in random places in an attempt to cash-in on visitors to the Park; others simply think that sacred knowledge is not for everyone.

Management recommendations

Jamaica's indigenous community has lost much of its traditional knowledge including sacred natural sites, and nascent but uncoordinated efforts are underway to document and protect the little that remains. This mirrors efforts to conserve what's left of Jamaica's biodiversity. The Park's management has fostered interest in both the natural and cultural heritage of the landscape using its cultural values as a major justification for nominating the Park as a World Heritage Site. Interest in Maroon culture and sacred natural sites is also pronounced among intellectuals and explorers who want to understand this semi-autonomous state in Jamaica, never conquered by the Europeans.

In light of the uncertain future of sacred natural sites in the Park they should be quickly brought into the management purview of the Park and the JNHT through existing legal, policy and institutional means. A framework is proposed based on the premise that legal designation in conjunction with a feasible management plan will enable the long-term protection and appreciation of the Maroon sacred natural sites. The framework consists of the following five actions.

Step 1: Develop a comprehensive and reliable database of sacred natural sites. This should be a participatory process involving the Maroons, park management, cultural researchers and archivists who will ensure that the survey is more than an academic effort or a hunt for sites to market for tourism. This can take the form of simply recording traditional stories about these sites as recommended by Putney (2005). This was illustrated in Bilby (2005) whose book is, to a large extent, a distillation of stories told by Maroon elders and faithfully recorded in the local vernacular. Above all, the documentation and dissemination of information about sacred natural sites should be done with respect for Maroon secrets and in close collaboration with the widest possible cross-section of the Maroon community.

Step 2: Develop and implement a robust verification process. This process will develop locally relevant indicators of sacredness and naturalness and assess the proposed sacred natural sites according to the agreed criteria. Furthermore, the sites should be 'ground-truthed' to ensure that the features do exist and to determine whether any information or artefacts have been preserved at the site.

Step 3: Integrate sacred natural sites into National Park Education and Awareness programmes. The goal of this programme will be to build awareness of the spiritual value of the Park among its stakeholders. This should be useful for buffer zone residents who might not relate to ecosystem services that are often realized in areas far removed from them. For example, the Park is described as a major source of water for the capital of Jamaica, Kingston, while it is geographically and culturally remote from the city. In particular, it will reinforce

---

the sense of belonging among buffer-zone residents and hopefully improve the stewardship of the Park. The value of this emotional link to the conservation movement was noted by Wilson (2002) who proposed that the human brain can only truly connect emotionally to a small piece of geography. A critical component of this education programme should be completely Maroon-centric, promoting Maroon heritage amongst Maroons. This will build on the work being done under the UNESCO/IOJ (Institute of Jamaica) project to record and promote Maroon cultural heritage.

Step 4: Include priority sacred natural sites for special protection in the Park. This will include management planning for the sites using frameworks such as the modified Conservation Action Planning tool developed by The Nature Conservancy (Secaira and Molina, 2005). UNESCO-IUCN guidelines for and New World examples of incorporating sacred natural sites in protected area planning are available in (Wild and McLeod, 2008). The next management planning period for the Park is 2010–2015 and the sites should be included in the planning process.

Step 5: Ensure legal recognition of sacred natural sites and seek protection through the JNHT. A legal mechanism already exists for protecting cultural sites in Jamaica. Under the Jamaica National Heritage Trust Act, a building, site or landscape can be declared 'protected national heritage' under criteria such as its historic, architectural, traditional or archaeological value. In addition to the World Heritage status being sought by the Park, verified Maroon sacred natural sites inside and outside of the Park should be declared as protected national heritage. The process for designating Protected National Heritage is clearly described in JNHT promotional materials (JNHT, n.d.). By seeking legal designation for the sacred natural sites, the portfolio of sacred sites under protection will more accurately represent the nexus between the natural and the sacred in Jamaica's heritage.

Based on this preliminary study of the Windward Maroons, sacred natural sites among the Leeward Maroons, some of which were introduced in Wright (2004), should also be examined and incorporated into the management of Cockpit Country, another high priority area for conservation.

Conclusions

The sacred natural sites of the Park present a compelling opportunity to highlight, protect and preserve the cultural values of Jamaica's protected areas. Sacred natural sites within the Park and its buffer zone showcase the deep-rooted, spiritual value of nature, having been places of refuge, healing and burial among the Windward Maroons and possibly Taínos. The presence of sacred sites can help to reinforce respect and appreciation for the Park as a repository of cultural and spiritual resources among the Maroons who inhabit the buffer zone, and the wider Jamaican public. Conversely, the Park clearly creates opportunities to conserve these cultural values and maintain them in the cultural domain. The involvement of the Park management and relevant authorities in managing these sites will further the conservation objectives by enriching the values base of the park and bolster the cultural heritage of the Maroons. Although they are few in number and in danger of being forgotten and completely lost, there are clear policy and institutional mechanisms for rapidly protecting Jamaica's sacred natural sites through protected area management plans, the Jamaica National Heritage Trust, the 2003 proclamation of Intangible Cultural Heritage and potentially, World Heritage Site status. A shared sense of urgency and collective will are now needed.

References

Agorsah, E.K. (1994) *Maroon Heritage: Archaeological, Ethnographic and Historical Perspectives*, Canoe Press, University of the West Indies, Kingston, Jamaica, pp163–186

Atkinson, L.-G. (ed.) (2006) *The Earliest Inhabitants, The Dynamics of the Jamaican Taíno*, University of the West Indies Press, Kingston, Jamaica

Bedasse, J. and Stewart, N. (1996) 'The Maroons of Jamaica: One with Mother Earth', in Redford, K.H. and Mansour, J.A. (eds) *Traditional Peoples and Biodiversity Conservation in Large Tropical Landscapes*, America Verde Publications, The Nature Conservancy, Latin America and Caribbean Division, Arlington, Virginia, pp57–73

Bilby, K. (2005) *True Born Maroons*, University Press of Florida, Gainesville, FL

Harris, C.L.G. (1994) 'The true traditions of my ancestors', in Agorash, E.K. (ed) *Maroon heritage: Archaeological, ethnographic and historical perspectives*, Canoe Press, University of the West Indies, Kingston, Jamaica, pp36–63

JCDT (Jamaica Conservation and Development Trust) (2005) 'Blue and John Crow Mountains National Park management plan (2005–2010)', Jamaica Conservation and Development Trust (JCDT), Kingston

JNHT (n.d.) 'Procedure for declaring a national monument or designating a protected national heritage', available at www.jnht.com/index.php (last accessed July 2008)

Putney, A. (2005) 'Building cultural support for protected areas through sacred natural sites', in McNeely, J.A. *Friends for Life: New Partners in Support of Protected Areas*, IUCN, Gland, Switzerland and Cambridge, UK, pp129–140

Saunders, N. and Gray, D. (2006) 'Zemís, trees and symbolic landscapes: Three Taíno carvings from Jamaica', in Atkinson, L.-G. (ed) (2006) *The Earliest Inhabitants, The Dynamics of the Jamaican Taíno*, University of the West Indies Press, Kingston, Jamaica

Secaira, E. and Molina, M.E. (2005) 'Conservation area planning for tangible cultural resources', Working document, The Nature Conservancy, Guatemala

Senior. O. (2003) *Encyclopaedia of Jamaican Heritage*, Twin Guinep Publishers, St. Andrew, Jamaica

STATIN (n.d.) 'Demographic statistics: Population, rate of increase, birth and death rates', available at www.statinja.com/stats.html (last accessed August 2008)

Wild, R. and McLeod, C. (eds) (2008) *Sacred Natural Sites: Guidelines for Protected Area Managers*, Gland, Switzerland, IUCN

Wilson, E.O. (2002) 'The bottleneck', *Scientific American*, vol 286, February, pp82–91

Wright, M.-L. (2004) 'The heritage of Accompong Maroons', in Agorash, E.K. (ed) *Maroon Heritage: Archaeological, Ethnographic and Historical Perspectives*, Canoe Press, University of the West Indies, Kingston, Jamaica, pp64–71

Sacred Natural Sites: International Recognition, Global Governance and Field Action

This section examines the response to the recognition of sacred natural sites from international agreements and institutions and the role that they have played in promoting their conservation. It then discusses programmes that have addressed sacred natural sites both in countries dependent on modern technologies and those based on more traditional agrarian ways of life. Some are multi-country programmes while others work within single countries (see Figure III.1).

Schaaf and Rossler (Chapter 15) discuss the contribution of UNESCO, which has a remit for both science and culture and has taken a lead in integrating these two domains, particularly through the World Heritage Convention and the Man and the Biosphere Programme. While exploring the use of international mechanisms for the conservation of sacred sites, Schaaf and

Rossler also report on important field studies that informed the international processes. As global change intensifies they call for strengthened collaboration and use of international partnerships for the conservation of sacred natural sites.

Techera (Chapter 16) explores how the international framework for sacred natural sites could be applied in the Pacific, focusing on the World Heritage Convention (WHC) and Convention for Safeguarding Intangible Cultural Heritage (CSICH). Despite the fact that these conventions are appropriate, applicable and potentially mutually supportive, they are largely unused for supporting sacred natural sites. In a region where traditional communities and their customary laws are still largely intact, natural heritage and intangible cultural heritage cannot be separated. Sacred natural sites present an ideal

Figure III.1 Local women meeting with the Applied Environmental Research Foundation in the temple at Janvale to discuss management strategies and governance for their local sacred groves in the Western Ghats, Maharastra, India

Source: Archana Godbole

opportunity for the application of international agreements to good effect, but the lack of capacity in Small Island states mean that this potentially powerful approach is lying idle, in face of increasingly damaging anthropogenic change.

Papayannis and Pritchard (Chapter 17) provide a summary of the steps that the Ramsar convention has taken over the past 20 years to incorporate a cultural element. From an early stage the convention laudably took a much broader approach to society, through the 'wise use' of wetland resources, than the more narrowly focused protected areas approach (especially IUCN categories I–IV). Some time ago, Ramsar begun to address cultural issues via a cultural working group. Its strong base in natural science has, however, meant that, despite the spiritual significance of fresh water for many societies as 'giver of life', steps towards the recognition of sacred natural sites under this broader cultural milieu is still in the early stages.

Various organizations have learned that sacred natural sites are key components of their work and have developed international and national approaches. An example is the field-based work of the COMPAS network in seven countries in Latin America and Africa (Delgado et al, Chapter 18). Focusing on 'well-being', this chapter introduces endogenous development as an approach that addresses the various dimensions of sacred natural sites: sacred seasons, sacred space, mythical origins, historic origins and special energies. Relating the various cultural meanings and uses of sacred natural sites to human well-being this chapter looks at the roles of sacred natural sites in agriculture, natural resource management, rural livelihoods and traditional leadership amongst others.

The Delos Initiative (Mallarach and Papayannis, Chapter 19) engages with the conservation of sacred natural sites in technologically developed countries, through the development of case studies. The case studies include over 30 protected areas from all IUCN categories, found in 16 countries across Europe, North America, Asia and Oceania. They relate largely to mainstream religions but

also to several traditional spiritual spiritualities, folk or ethnic religions. The authors emphasize a rights-based approach where in addition to basic human rights, the rights of indigenous and faith custodians of sacred natural sites are respected. The Delos Initiative provides recommendations for the management of sacred natural sites and now aims at producing complementary guidelines for sacred natural sites related to mainstream religions as well as specific guidelines for managing sites.

Otegui-Acha et al (Chapter 20) describe a methodology for conducting the systematic inventory of sacred natural sites based on ecosystem types, developed by Pronatura Mexico, a civil society organization. This inventory aims to empower Mexican indigenous and local communities and provides a tool for relevant national conservation authorities and agencies. The methodology's testing phase started several years ago by initiating community consent (FPIC) and involvement across four indigenous territories of the country. The methodology is currently in the latest phases of being tested and preliminary results are presented here.

Godbole et al (Chapter 21) of the Applied Environmental Research Foundation (AERF) in India have been running a programme for the conservation of the sacred natural sites of the Western Ghats region for over 15 years (see Figure III.1). From 1985 to 1990 about 35 per cent of the sacred groves from one of the region's districts were clear-felled based on government policy. The chapter explores how, despite these losses, the spiritual and cultural underpinnings of sacred groves can be used for long-term biodiversity conservation programmes and, at least to some extent, income-generation for marginalized groups. As part of their efforts AERF has recorded the conservation status of 250 sacred groves, carried out biodiversity inventories of 142, developed management and restoration plans for 26 and revived traditional management in a further 13. This consistent and long-term effort has developed many lessons for the conservation of sacred natural sites in India and elsewhere.

15

Sacred Natural Sites, Cultural Landscapes and UNESCO's Action

Thomas Schaaf and Mechtild Rossler

Summary

The introduction of sacred natural sites to the international arena more than a decade ago has led to major actions by the international community concerned with environmental conservation. Beginning with research pilot projects on sacred natural sites, and discussions about definitions, key conferences and workshops involving concerned stakeholders have also taken place in India, Mexico, China, Japan and Mongolia. These have helped to formulate the IUCN-UNESCO Guidelines for the Conservation and Management of Sacred Natural Sites. This chapter discusses inscription of sacred natural sites and landscapes within the regulatory framework of the World Heritage Convention and the UNESCO Man and Biosphere (MAB) Programme. Despite legally protected area status, core areas of biosphere reserves are not always respected by local people, who are often compelled to revert to poaching or illegal logging even in the protected core areas so as to satisfy their immediate livelihood needs. In search for solutions this chapter outlines experience based on a UNESCO MAB research project in Ghana which studied sacred groves and the importance of sacred natural sites for biodiversity conservation and local livelihoods. The project employed an interdisciplinary approach for establishing baselines based on scientific knowledge of the natural world for the planning of restoration activities. These revealed higher biodiversity levels at the edges of sacred groves than inside the groves but also more birds, reptiles and mammals within the sacred groves than outside. Socio-cultural values and belief systems were also assessed in combination with the development of environmental educational programmes. Traditional beliefs regulating hunting activities helped to provide insight into traditional leadership enforcing the respect of responsibilities and taboos regarding the sacred groves. Income-generating activities beyond the confines of the sacred sites were developed in consultation with and for the benefit of local people. Because of their biodiversity values sacred natural sites can signal potential restoration sites for the elaboration of integrated conservation strategies. These should be supported by modern and legal instruments. The recognition of the importance of safeguarding sacred natural sites will not only serve the protection of species and the environment at large, but also the spiritual and qualitative well-being of humankind.

Introduction

In the United Nations Educational, Scientific and Cultural Organization (UNESCO), the topic of sacred sites and cultural landscapes with strong associative values has come to the foreground through the following developments:

- the recognition of cultural landscapes under the 1992 World Heritage Convention, including associative landscapes and those related to belief systems;
- collaboration between IUCN, WWF and UNESCO on the conservation of biodiversity and sacred natural sites through various joint workshops and conferences, for example Mexico City (2001), Kunming (2003) and Tokyo (2005);
- the publication of the IUCN-UNESCO, World Commission on Protected Areas Best Practice Guidelines No.16; 'Sacred Natural Sites: Guidelines for Protected Area Managers' (Wild and McLeod, 2008);
- a growing collaboration amongst UN agencies (including UNESCO, FAO, UNEP, UNPFII, UNU), international conventions (such as the Convention on Biological Diversity) and other bodies such as the International Union for Conservation of Nature (IUCN), the International Council on Monuments and Sites (ICOMOS) and the International Centre for the Study of the Preservation and Restoration of Cultural Heritage (ICCROM).

In this chapter, we provide a brief overview of these key developments and exemplify the integrative approach of the UNESCO-MAB Programme using a project undertaken on sacred groves conservation in northern Ghana. We summarize the major achievements and discuss them in relation to future challenges.

World Heritage Convention

The World Heritage Convention 1972 (ratified by 186 countries and covering 890 sites of outstanding global value) is the leading global legal instrument in heritage conservation (Francioni and Lenzerini, 2008; UNESCO, 1972; WHC, 2009). While people often live in and around World Heritage sites, their role in the heritage conservation process and management of the sites has changed considerably to one of much greater inclusion since the 1992 decision to recognize these landscapes as a category of heritage for World Heritage listing (Rössler, 2000). The fundamental nature of the new category of cultural landscapes bringing together

biological and cultural diversity (Rössler, 2005), was crucial to increasing this inclusion. Today 66 cultural landscapes of outstanding universal value are listed and protected at the global level.

Many of these cultural landscapes and the sacred natural sites located in them are however, threatened by significant and ongoing changes, including continuous degradation, intense use, hostile agricultural policies, unregulated tourism, population shifts, economic factors, urban encroachment, pollution and climate change (Rössler and Mitchell, 2005; Schaaf, 1999; UNESCO, 2003a). Each of the three categories of cultural landscape defined in the Operational Guidelines for the Implementation of the World Heritage Convention (designed landscapes, continuing evolving/relic and associative cultural landscapes) poses specific issues for their protection and conservation, including the question of the acceptance of traditional protection and customary law under the 1972 World Heritage Convention (UNESCO, 2008). In many cases the sites previously had no formal legal protection. Examples are the Sacred Mijikenda Kaya Forests (Kenya), inscribed in 2008, which was only gazetted as a protected area through the World Heritage nomination process and the recent (2009) inscription of the 'Sulaiman-Too Sacred Mountain' in the Central Asian Republic of Kyrgyzstan (UNESCO, 2009). Here, sick people sit in the caves on the mountainside hoping to be cured, and there's a natural rock slide that women use to promote fertility (see Figure 15.1). Their inclusion on the World Heritage List enhanced their protection, but the local elders are now facing new challenges including very limited resources and pressure for access to these forest and mountain areas by visitors and tourists. One of the key challenges for the future will be deciding how to protect these natural places – which are often influenced by strong belief systems, linked closely to rituals, stories and legends of local communities and indigenous people – while ensuring adapted use.

Links with other culture conventions

The case of the Kaya Forests, which have been recognized as a World Heritage cultural landscape with its associative values, also demonstrates the strong links between the 1972 World Heritage

Figure 15.1 The Sacred Suleiman Mountain (Kyrgyzstan) inscribed on the UNESCO World Heritage list in 2009

Source: Fedde Jorritsma for UNESCO

Convention and the 2003 Convention on the Safeguarding of Intangible Cultural Heritage (UNESCO, 2004). In 2009 the traditions and practices associated to the Kayas in the sacred forests of the Mijikenda were included in UNESCO's List of Intangible Cultural Heritage in Need of Urgent Safeguarding (UNESCO, 2009) (see Figure 15.2). In addition to their inscription on the World Heritage List in 2008, the Kayas were recognized in 2009 as intangible heritage under the 2003 Convention (UNESCO, 2003b). This notion of 'sacred spaces' and 'relations with nature and the universe' opens further avenues for the recognition of the heritage of indigenous people and for capacity-building in the important area of safeguarding some traditions.

Man and the Biosphere (MAB) Programme

The UNESCO Man and the Biosphere (MAB) Programme is an international and intergovernmental environmental research and conservation programme. One of its objectives is to study and improve the relationship between people and their environment; another objective is to conserve the environment through the sustainable use of natural resources (Schaaf, 2003). This is primarily accomplished through the biosphere reserve concept. Biosphere reserves, with their multiple zonation patterns (which include one or several legally protected core zones for environmental conservation, buffer zones to reduce adverse impacts on the core zone(s), and transition zones, which are economically used for activities that do not jeopardize species and their habitats) are contributing to sustainable development in line with conservation objectives. Many biosphere reserves include sacred natural sites.

According to the Statutory Framework of the World Network of Biosphere Reserves, a core area should be legally constituted and be devoted to long-term protection according to the conservation objectives of the biosphere reserve (Article 4,

Figure 15.2 Kaya Rabai Elders in procession (Sacred Mijikenda Kaya Forests World Heritage property, Kenya)

Source: Bakonirina Rakotomamonjy/UNESCO

paragraph 5a of the Statutory Framework refers; see UNESCO, 1996). However, despite their legally protected area status, core areas of biosphere reserves are not always respected by local people, who are often compelled to revert to poaching or illegal logging even in the protected core areas so as to satisfy their immediate livelihood needs.

MAB pilot project on sacred groves

The need for an interdisciplinary approach

The far from satisfactory situation in place led us to consider how environmental conservation could be based on other means in addition to the (sometimes weak) legal protection. One approach believed to be worthy of exploration was the idea that the locally and culturally accepted belief systems of particular sacred natural sites could be used as an effective means of conserving their surrounding

environment (Schaaf, 1996). Moreover, the national and international recognition of such sites could instil a sense of pride for local communities in charge of sacred natural sites and help preserve their cultural integrity.

Based on this approach, the UNESCO-MAB Programme implemented a pilot project on sacred groves in northern Ghana (West Africa) from 1993 to 1997. Entitled 'Cooperative Integrated Project on Savannah Ecosystems in Ghana' (CIPSEG), the project endeavoured to put environmental conservation in an inter-disciplinary context, drawing on the expertise of natural and anthropological scientists.

Sacred groves in Ghana

In Ghana, as in most other African countries, rapid population growth and expansion of economic activities have led to deforestation and degradation of the environment. In some parts of northern Ghana, the natural population increase between 1960 and

1984 had reached some 490 per cent (Republic of Ghana, 1984). This has had increasingly distressing socio-economic consequences for people who have been compelled to widen their resource base, which has in turn been to the detriment of environmental conservation. In many parts of the country, the natural vegetation has also been seriously affected by bush fires, agricultural cultivation, overgrazing, fire wood cutting, urbanization and village sprawl.

Although environmental degradation is widespread in northern Ghana (which is a dry sub-humid savannah of the Guinea type), however, small pockets of closed canopy forests remain near human settlements. Many of these forest pockets are 'sacred' or 'fetish' groves which have survived environmental degradation because of religious beliefs. The groves cover small areas and may vary from 0.5 to 20 hectares each. Village communities have actively protected their sacred environments and thus, without realizing, have contributed to environmental conservation objectives.

Establishing baselines and planning restoration

The project focused on three different sacred groves – Malshegu, Tolon and Yiworgu – which were selected as both study and intervention sites. One of the aims of the project was to assess whether sacred groves could be indicator sites for the original (and potential) natural vegetation of the savannah area. In other words, could they give an idea of how the Guinea type savannah looked before human pressure increased to current levels. The project's overall goal was to develop a baseline of scientific knowledge on the groves' ecosystems and their plant and animal species composition.

Based on these findings, the aim of the second stage of the project was to restore the adjacent and degraded savannah areas by using native plant species from the sacred groves' gene-pools. The project, therefore, had both a scientific and a development orientation.

In order to address these two main objectives, several scientific teams were mobilized for an interdisciplinary approach. The Botany and Geography Departments of the University of Ghana carried out in-depth plant inventories and

looked into the overall land use systems. The University of Science and Technology in Kumasi was concerned with assessing the area's edaphic, climatic and socio-economic conditions, while the newly established University of Development Studies in Tamale undertook a detailed study of vertebrate and invertebrate wildlife and their socio-cultural and economic dimensions.

Socio-cultural belief systems and education

The Centre for National Culture in Tamale undertook in-depth studies of the traditional beliefs which had led to the protection of the sacred groves, and analysed the sacred groves' functions for ceremonial purposes. These studies focused on traditional resource use of the areas by village communities (for example the planting, ownership and marketing of forestry products) and were particularly important for culturally appropriate savannah restoration.

Environmental education and the involvement of local people in all stages of the project were considered essential for its success. The project's main counterpart institution (the Environmental Protection Agency of Ghana) carried out multi-level education programmes. For example, seminars were organized on the control and prevention of bush-fires, and on the establishment of shelter belts around the groves; women were trained in tree planting, men were trained on the usage of fodder banks to reduce browse pressure; environmental awareness and sustainable land use seminars were geared towards the general public. In addition, the Ghana Broadcasting Corporation made several national television programmes about the project to promote environmental conservation practices using sacred groves. A 'docu-drama' was produced for video presentations using villagers of the sacred groves as actors.

One of the project's goals was to test the working hypothesis that the biodiversity within a sacred grove would be much higher than in the adjoining non-sacred areas. This proved to be the case for the diversity of animal species. Birds, reptiles and mammals were more abundant within the sacred groves than outside. This was not surprising, as hunting is prohibited in groves, and breaking this customary law invokes sanction by the custodian. An antelope, for example, can be hunted outside the grove, but as it enters the sacred grove, hunting has to stop.

Surprisingly, however, a greater diversity of plant species was found at the edges of the sacred groves than within them. It is believed that this occurs because the edges of the sacred groves function like eco-tones of high diversity where two different environmental settings meet.

Research on the cultural significance of the three groves also proved fascinating. Through interviews with the village elders and extrapolation of historic events, it was estimated that some of the sacred groves were at least 300 years old. The three study groves originated as the respective abodes of a python god, a leopard god and a monkey god that could command abundant or lean harvests. Other sacred groves in the study area still serve as burial grounds of ancestors and have become taboo. In some cases, it was possible to identify the occasion when a sacred grove became taboo – for example, a chief once sought shelter in a grove, during tribal warfare, the deity made him invisible and he was saved. Since that time, the grove has been venerated.

Traditional leadership and taboos

The power of a chief is intrinsically linked with his function as supreme custodian of a sacred grove. No matter whether the chief is a practising Muslim or Christian, his power over the community derives from his role as protector of the sacred grove. Should he relinquish this function, his power as chief would be forfeited.

Some interesting taboos were brought to the fore. For example, it was considered taboo for a young man to plant a tree during the day: should the shade of the tree fall on the young man, he would be doomed to die. This view was widely held which may explain why many forestation and rehabilitation projects failed in the savannah areas of Ghana. However, the taboo can be circumvented by planting trees at sunrise or sunset.

The taboos and obligations vary from one sacred grove to the other, but there are several common features. For instance creating shelterbelts around the groves through communal labour is a community obligation. The strict observance of the sacred grove rules also cannot be compromised.

Perhaps one of the most interesting lessons learned from the project was that the grove has, first and foremost, a spiritual significance as the abode of a god. The god could dwell in a single tree or rock and still exert his/her power. This is a view held by many young people who would wish to extend their agricultural lands even if this would cut into the sacred grove. As long as the sacred tree or rock still exists, no harm is done to the religious integrity of the sacred grove.

The project abandoned the idea of solely using plant genetic resources of the sacred groves for restoration activities on its periphery, but focused on agro-forestry methods which permitted cash-crop production (e.g. cashew nuts, mango, etc.). These cash-crops provided an income to local people, especially women and young men, and permitted the restoration of a vegetation cover in particularly degraded areas. The establishment of woodlots and fodder banks were additional means to create a 'buffer zone' around the sacred groves which in turn reduced the pressure on the sacred site itself.

Some conclusions of the CIPSEG project

The CIPSEG project has shown that the rehabilitation of degraded areas is more sustainable if based on cultural beliefs which tie in well with the religious and spiritual views shared by a specific community. Spatial extensions of sacred groves and other sacred natural sites may well foster environmental conservation and integrity.

In a follow-up project entitled 'Natural Sacred Sites – Cultural Integrity and Biological Diversity', UNESCO identified natural sacred sites (including many sacred mountains) in Africa, Asia and Latin America in order to launch a worldwide comparative study on culture-based environmental conservation. Building on the earlier project, the working hypothesis for this research was that sacred natural sites contain important areas for biodiversity conservation. They can also be interesting as indicator sites for potential natural vegetation, and as such can serve as reference areas for environmental restoration.

The natural sacred sites were considered in a wider spatial context (beyond the sacred areas themselves) for the elaboration of integrated conservation and development schemes. Income-generating activities beyond the confinements of the sacred sites were developed in consultation with and for the benefit of local people. The project clearly demonstrated that one should seek to combine people's traditional concepts of natural sacred sites with modern and legal instruments to enhance the conservation of the environment as follow-up studies showed in China, India and Madagascar (Schaaf and Lee, 2006).

Setting the international arena for Sacred Natural Sites

Following the pilot project in Ghana, the MAB Programme and the World Heritage Convention organized several major events that contributed significantly to the international recognition of sacred natural sites and their intrinsic value. In December 1997, the UNESCO Office in New Delhi organized a sub-regional workshop on 'The Role of Sacred Groves in Conservation and Management of Biological Diversity' (Ramakrishnan et al, 1998) which among other things evidenced the high species diversity in temple groves. Following this, a 'UNESCO Thematic Expert Meeting on Asia-Pacific Sacred Mountains' (hosted by the Government of Japan) took place in Wakayama City 5–10 September 2001. Organized by the UNESCO World Heritage Centre, the Agency for Cultural Affairs of Japan and Wakayama Prefectural Government, this expert meeting formulated a number of recommendations pertaining to the identification, significance and values of sacred mountains (UNESCO, 2001).

In February 2003, the UNESCO MAB Secretariat organized an international workshop which focused on the theme 'The Importance of Sacred Natural Sites for Biodiversity Conservation'. It was held in Kunming and Xishuangbanna Biosphere Reserve (China) and was attended by experts from Africa, Asia, Latin America, Northern America and Europe (Lee and Schaaf, 2003).

A landmark event in the recognition of sacred natural sites and their intrinsic value was the international symposium on 'Conserving Cultural and Biological Diversity: The Role of Sacred Natural Sites and Cultural Landscapes' (Schaaf and Lee, 2006) at which the IUCN-UNESCO Guidelines on sacred natural sites (Wild and McLeod, 2008) were further discussed and refined. The symposium also benefited from the support of other international organizations and previous work, including the 2004 Akwe Kon Guidelines on sacred sites (Secretariat of the Convention on Biological Diversity, 2004). The Secretariat of the Convention on Biological Diversity (CBD), the United Nations Permanent Forum on Indigenous Issues (UNPFII), the United Nations Food and Agriculture Organization (FAO), and IUCN participated. Within UNESCO, the MAB Programme was the principal organizer of the entire event, in collaboration with the Secretariat of the World Heritage Centre. This input from such a range of international organizations clearly demonstrated that the issue of sacred natural sites had moved into the international arena and had become a topic of interest for experts from the natural and socio-cultural sciences.

UNESCO's work in the international arena on the recognition of the values of sacred natural sites indicated the importance of legal mechanisms for helping to conserve biodiversity in protected natural areas. Furthermore, their recognition can help to preserve the cultural integrity of particular societies and communities.

IUCN-UNESCO guidelines

The IUCN-UNESCO Best Practice Guidelines (No.16) 'Sacred Natural Sites: Guidelines for Protected Area Managers' (Wild and McLeod, 2008), were launched at the Barcelona World Conservation Congress in October 2008. In 2009 they were translated into Russian and Spanish and respectively launched at the CBD meeting on article 8j in Canada and the World Wilderness Conference in Mexico.

They were the result of many years of collaborative work between UNESCO, IUCN, indigenous communities and the Specialist Group on the Cultural and Spiritual Values of Protected Areas (CSVPA), within the World Commission on Protected Areas (WCPA) of IUCN. These guidelines represent an important milestone in recognizing the biological and cultural importance of sacred natural sites.

The origins of the guidelines date back to the UNESCO Kunming workshop in 2003. The draft guidelines which arose from this meeting were prepared by a team of conservation experts from different world regions, people from various international agencies, and were presented for further discussion at a side event held at the World Parks Congress in Durban (South Africa) in September of the same year. Most importantly, discussions were held with a number of indigenous people, as well as with a broad range of stakeholders. Complex problems (for example, regarding the revealing of the location of sacred sites and breaching the seal of secrecy and of issues relating to access and appropriate behaviour for tourists and national visitors) were discussed at length. The extensive consultation period of several years was required to ensure that all stakeholders (in particular local people, indigenous groups and elders who have maintained those sites over centuries) were satisfied with the outcome. An additional process of testing the guidelines and translating the core of the guidelines into other languages is currently being facilitated through CSVPA.

Conclusions

From the Rio Conference on Environment and Development in 1992 to the Johannesburg Summit in 2002, global debates on sustainability and development have advanced. At the same time local people and indigenous communities have increasingly become involved in protected area management. The voices of indigenous people and local stakeholders are essential to future conservation strategies, and the recognition of sacred natural sites which form part of their heritage is a crucial part of this. Significant collaborative efforts have been made by international agencies, local people and indigenous communities in this field of research, and this has led to the increasing international recognition of the value of sacred natural sites – precious places of high biodiversity and cultural integrity. Throughout the process, the intrinsic link between cultural and biological diversity was demonstrated: investing in cultural diversity is closely linked with investing in biodiversity conservation of the priceless heritage of humankind.

However, sacred natural sites and cultural landscapes also face significant threats. Among the key threats, climate change is paramount – impacting those sacred places and landscapes located in vulnerable environments especially mountains, islands, coastal areas and drylands. Global change including climatic change may seriously alter the integrity of sacred natural sites, especially the composition of species and their habitats.

In a world marred by unprecedented species loss and marked by increasing globalization, the conservation of biological and cultural diversity becomes an imperative. Sacred natural sites provide both the basis for the life of current and future generations and for their spiritual fulfilment. In this situation the safeguarding of cultural diversity is essential to remind us of our identities. Therefore, a new enhanced and strengthened collaboration must be developed making full use of international partnerships and networks.

Environmental conservation thinking has shifted from a purely quantitative and materialistic approach to a more qualitative view which also takes into account cultural identities of non-western belief systems and spiritual values. In fact, the intrinsic linkage of human beings with their environment cannot be considered by materialistic justifications only. The qualitative interdependence between nature and humankind is well demonstrated in sacred natural sites and cultural landscapes with associative values. The recognition of the importance of safeguarding sacred natural sites will not only serve the protection of species and the environment at large, but also the spiritual and qualitative well-being of humankind.

References

Francioni, F. and Lenzerini, F. (eds) (2008) *The 1972 World Heritage Convention: A Commentary*, Oxford University Press, Oxford

Lee, C. and Schaaf, T. (eds) (2003) 'The importance of sacred natural sites for biodiversity conservation', Proceedings of the international workshop, Kunming and Xishuangbanna Biosphere Reserve, China, 17–20 February 2003, UNESCO, Paris

Ramakrishnan, P.S., Saxena, K.G. and Chandrashekara, U.M. (eds) (1998) *Conserving the Sacred for Biodiversity Management*, Science Publishers Inc., USA/India

Republic of Ghana (1984) 'Population Census of Ghana, 1984', Central Bureau of Statistics, Republic of Ghana

Rössler, M. (2000) 'World Heritage cultural landscapes', in The George Wright Forum, Special issue, 'Landscape stewardship: New directions in conservation of nature and culture', *The Journal of the George Wright Society*, vol, 17, no 1, pp27–34

Rössler, M. (2005) 'World Heritage: Linking biological and cultural diversity', in Hoffmann, B. (ed) *Art and Cultural Heritage Law for the Twenty-First Century: Policy and Practice*, Cambridge University Press, Cambridge

Rössler, M. and Mitchell, N. (2005) 'Landscape linkages without boundaries?', in World Heritage at the 5th IUCN World Parks Congress, Durban South Africa, 8–17 September 2003, World Heritage reports No 16, UNESCO World Heritage Centre, Paris, pp23–26

Rössler, M., Mitchel, N. and Tricaut, P.M. (eds) (2009) 'World Heritage cultural landscapes: A handbook for conservation and management', World Heritage papers 26, UNESCO, World Heritage Centre, Paris

Schaaf, T. (1996) 'Sacred groves: Environmental conservation based on traditional beliefs', in *UNESCO, Culture and Agriculture, UNESCO World Decade for Cultural Development*, UNESCO, Paris

Schaaf, T. (1999) 'Environmental conservation based on sacred sites', in Posey, D. (ed) *Cultural and Spiritual Values of Biodiversity: A Complementary Contribution to the Global Biodiversity Assessment*, UNEP, pp341–342

Schaaf, T. (2003), 'Biosphere reserves: Tangible and intangible values', in Harmon, D. and Putney, A.D. (eds) *The Full Values of Parks: From Economics to the Intangible*, Rowman & Littlefield Publishers, Inc., Lanham, Boulder, New York, Oxford

Schaaf, T. and Lee, C. (eds) (2006) 'Conserving cultural and biological diversity: The role of sacred natural sites and cultural landscapes', Proceedings of the International Symposium 30 May–2 June 2005, Tokyo, Japan, UNESCO, Paris

Secretariat of the Convention on Biological Diversity (2004) *Akwé Kon: Voluntary Guidelines for the Conduct of Cultural, Environmental and Social Impact Assessment regarding Developments Proposed to Take Place on, or which are Likely to Impact on, Sacred Sites and on Lands and Waters Traditionally Occupied or Used by Indigenous and Local Communities*, CBD Guidelines Series, Montreal, p25

UNESCO (1972) 'Convention concerning the protection of the world cultural and natural heritage adopted by the General Conference at its seventeenth session', UNESCO, Paris

UNESCO (1996) 'Biosphere Reserves: The Seville Strategy & the Statutory Framework of the World Network', UNESCO, Paris

UNESCO (2001) 'Final report of the UNESCO Thematic Expert Meeting on Asia Pacific Sacred Mountains', 5–10 September 2001, Wakayama City, Japan, UNESCO World Heritage Centre, Agency for Cultural Affairs, Japan, Wakayama Prefectural Government, Tokyo

UNESCO (2003a) 'Cultural landscapes: The challenges of conservation', Proceedings of the International Workshop (Ferrara, Italy 2002), World Heritage Papers No 7, UNESCO, Paris

UNESCO (2003b) 'Convention on the safeguarding of the intangible cultural heritage', available at http://unesdoc.unesco.org/images/0013/001325/132540e.pdf (last accessed January 2009)

UNESCO (2004) 'Proceedings of the international conference on the safeguarding of tangible and intangible cultural heritage: towards an integrated approach', Nara, Japan, 20–23 October 2004, available at http://unesdoc.unesco.org/images/0014/001470/147097M.pdf (last accessed January 2009)

UNESCO (2008) 'Operational Guidelines for the implementation of the World Heritage Convention', available at http://whc.unesco.org (last accessed February 2009)

UNESCO (2009) 'Nomination files for inscription in 2009 on the list of intangible cultural heritage in need of urgent safeguarding (point 14 on the agenda)', available at www.unesco.org/culture/ich/index.php?pg=00246 (last accessed February 2009)

WHC (2009) available at http://whc.unesco.org (last accessed 11 October 2009)

Wild, R. and McLeod, C. (eds) (2008) 'Sacred natural sites: Guidelines for protected area managers', IUCN Best Practice Protected Area Guidelines Series No. 16, IUCN, Gland

16

Synergies and Challenges for Legal Protection of Sacred Natural Sites in the South Pacific

Erika J. Techera

Summary

The South Pacific islands are home to a diversity of peoples with a rich culture and areas of outstanding biodiversity. While monumental heritage is found in some parts of the region, all of the Pacific Islands have a wealth of customs, practices and traditional knowledge linked to natural places. Globalization, modernization and population growth are placing increasing pressure upon this culture and the associated sacred natural sites. In the past, international and domestic attention has focused heavily upon management of protected areas for biodiversity conservation rather than their intangible cultural heritage values. However, more recently attention has turned to safeguarding intangible cultural heritage. Nonetheless, law in this area remains fragmented: independent international treaties protect natural and cultural sites and intangible heritage, and in most cases domestic approaches to heritage protection separate natural areas from cultural elements. This chapter considers the international law in this area and suggests a way forward for the better protection of sacred sites in the South Pacific.

Introduction

The indigenous peoples of the South Pacific Small Island Developing States (SIDS) have cultural and spiritual values closely connected with nature. These relationships are particularly evident in sacred natural sites, which range from places of local significance to natural landscapes relevant to the region as a whole. This powerful heritage has helped to ensure an abundance of equally rich terrestrial and marine biodiversity. However, globalization, modernization and urbanization have resulted in shifting value systems with population growth, invasive species, natural resource exploitation and land degradation all contributing to the pressure placed upon natural and cultural heritage.

The independent South Pacific SIDS have an abundance of both natural and cultural heritage yet have only two listed sites under the World Heritage Convention (WHC) (see Figure 16.1). Whilst 11 SIDS are state parties to the WHC only two of these countries have ratified the Convention on the Safeguarding of Intangible Cultural Heritage (CSICH), (UNESCO, 2003).

The Pacific Island states have developing economies and in most cases little technical expertise and financial resources to devote to heritage

Figure 16.1 Chief Roi Mata's Domain World Heritage Area, Efate, Vanuatu

Source: Erika J. Techera

protection. However, in many other respects they are well placed to protect sacred natural sites: they tend to have high percentages of indigenous peoples, widespread incidences of customary land tenure and large populations still living a mainly traditional lifestyle. Furthermore, this region experiences less conflict than in other parts of the world where displacement and loss of traditional tenure have resulted in tension over multiple uses of lands. Whereas in the past the success of protected area management has been linked to economic development, the conservation of sacred natural sites provides a cultural motivation, with the added benefits of providing opportunities for sustainable livelihoods, reinvigorating local cultures and strengthening traditional governance structures.

For the SIDS of the South Pacific implementation of the above mentioned conventions alone will not

ensure their protection. This chapter draws attention to the need for further research to identify best practice programmes and legal frameworks which would both satisfy international obligations and meet the needs of local communities. Particular attention is given to mechanisms for the treatment of intangible cultural heritage that may offer appropriate tools for helping to protect sacred natural sites.

Background to the South Pacific region

The South Pacific region encompasses thousands of islands extending across a great ocean expanse. The region has enormous biological diversity including a high level of endemism due in part to the small land areas and isolation of the islands (Gerbeaux et al, 2007). However the region is often termed a biodiversity hotspot with one of the highest extinction rates in the world (CEPF, 2007). The South Pacific region also provides examples of many categories of intangible cultural heritage, representing a 'significant enrichment of the global heritage catalogue' (Smith and O'Keefe, 2004, p12). Today the safeguarding of this intangible heritage is of particular importance to the peoples of the South Pacific as they historically have had no writing and any physical (archaeological and architectural) record of their culture is mostly not of the monumental kind. In addition this is one of the few regions in the world where sites of cultural heritage demonstrate continuous human interaction with the environment (Smith and Jones, 2007). In some cases sacred natural sites continue to be used and therefore their heritage values are evolving; in others they are the surviving remnants of past times.

The uniqueness of the South Pacific region has been internationally recognized and well-documented by the World Heritage Centre of UNESCO (UNESCO, 1997), the International Council on Monuments and Sites (ICOMOS) (Smith and Jones, 2007), the International Union for Conservation of Nature (IUCN) (Gerbeaux et al, 2007) and others. While each of the countries is different, the cultural heritage has become intertwined at a regional level over many years 'through common voyaging, kinship, trade and other relationships' (Smith and Jones, 2007, p6). Today the majority of these countries are independent, post-colonial societies with developing economies. Whilst most of the people no longer live an entirely traditional lifestyle, customary laws and practices still play an important part in everyday life. Thus while each nation, and indeed in many cases each island, may have its own specific natural and cultural heritage, many commonalities support the regional approach taken in this study.

Links between intangible heritage and natural sites

The lives of indigenous peoples in the South Pacific were, and still to a great extent are, dependent on nature, not only through their physical reliance upon

natural resources but also their spiritual connection with land and marine areas. Their inseparable link with the environment is evidenced by the rich histories, oral and life traditions, customary laws and practices associated with biodiversity. An example of this is the Uafato conservation zone, Fagaloa Bay and Ti'avea area in Samoa. The area is notable within Samoa for its considerable biodiversity and for illustrating an ongoing relationship between a community and the environment. The Fagaloa-Uafato area is geologically one of the oldest in Samoa and also one of the earliest settled areas, having been occupied for approximately 3000 years. Early settlers used local clay to make the well-known Lapita pottery and today many legends surround the areas where the clay was collected. Lapita is an ancient culture believed to be the common ancestor of several societies in the Pacific.

The local people of the area maintain close links with the environment involving traditional ways of life and conservation practices which continue to benefit the area. The 1400-hectare Uafato Conservation Area includes the village, the largest area of virgin rainforest in Samoa, the coastline, coral reef and adjacent marine areas. It is located on traditionally-owned land based upon the matai system, a village agreement which includes conservation measures. The matai are traditional Saman chiefs or heads of families. The area contains many sacred natural sites: the resting place of the ancestral god Moso; and the mountain where the Ancestral God Tagaloa lived (Equator Initiative, n.d.) as well as the sacred ifelele tree. The area has been placed on the WHC tentative list (UNESCO, 2009).

This inseparable connection between Pacific Island people and the natural environment has long been the subject of research (Smith and Jones (2007) is a recent example). There is no doubt that in the South Pacific, the involvement of local communities as custodians of sacred sites has been essential to their survival to date. But today tensions can arise between customary uses of land and more contemporary demands (for example, tourism). Whilst some conventional modern approaches to heritage protection may not be appropriate in this context, the IUCN-UNESCO Sacred Natural Sites Guidelines are significant as they recognize the primacy of traditional custodians and promote cooperation between them and official area managers (Wild and McLeod, 2008). Of particular importance in the South Pacific is the need to identify legal and policy frameworks for traditional sacred natural sites in ways which protect the heritage while meeting the contemporary needs of indigenous and local communities.

International law and policy context

Several international heritage conventions are relevant to the protection of sacred natural sites. The WHC represents a shared commitment to preserve areas of natural and cultural heritage of 'outstanding universal value'. Article 1 of the WHC includes as cultural heritage 'combined works of nature and man'. Within this category is the sub-group of 'cultural landscapes' (see Chapter 15). Sacred natural sites fit well within this category which is particularly appropriate to the South Pacific where local communities have maintained traditional knowledge, tenure and relationships with the natural environment (Smith and Jones, 2007). Specifically, two sub-categories are most apposite: first, the 'continuing landscapes' where places retain an active and continuing social role associated with traditional ways of life; and second, 'associative cultural landscapes' involving a link between people and places based upon traditional stories, knowledge, ideas and beliefs.

Although the WHC covers both natural and cultural heritage it does not protect intangible heritage directly. This deficiency has been addressed with the adoption of the CSICH which protects intangible heritage in its own right. The CSICH aims to 'safeguard' oral traditions and expressions, social practices, rituals, festivals, traditional knowledge and craftsmanship as well as the associated spaces within which these activities take place. The principal protection mechanisms involve the preparation of national inventories and an international representative list of intangible cultural heritage (Article 12). While these provisions are similar to the WHC, in CSICH, local communities are the centre of attention and their participation in the safeguarding of living culture is emphasized. The treaty facilitates

the continuation of traditional cultural processes and practices by encouraging national 'Living Human Treasures' systems which both honour the custodians and encourage the transmission of intangible cultural heritage (UNESCO, n.d., 2003). Other measures include the establishment or strengthening of institutions for training people in the management and transmission of intangible cultural heritage and developing documentation repositories and facilitating access to them.

The international focus on intangible cultural heritage has continued with the recent adoption of the Convention on the Protection and Promotion of the Diversity of Cultural Expressions. This Treaty again indicates international concern to protect cultural diversity from the processes of globalization. In many cases cultural expressions, such as celebrations and ceremonies, are linked with natural areas. Therefore this treaty contributes to international law supporting the protection of sacred natural sites.

Both WHC and CSICH provide mechanisms for conserving sacred natural sites, and in some respects they overlap (Verschuuren, 2007, p80). In particular CSICH has added to the toolkit of mechanisms that can be utilized to protect important elements of sacred natural sites. In the South Pacific the separation of the tangible and intangible is artificial and almost all of the culturally important sites embed intangible values (Smith and O'Keefe, 2004). Given the high level of intangible heritage it is thus important that countries in this region consider ratification of both treaties to ensure conservation of their culture.

South Pacific implementation of international heritage law

Eleven of the South Pacific SIDS are state parties to the WHC: Cook Islands, Fiji, Kiribati, Marshall Islands, Federated States of Micronesia, Niue, Palau, Samoa, Solomon Islands, Tonga and Vanuatu. Other parties geographically located in the region include Australia, New Zealand and Papua New Guinea.

Both Australia (Uluru-Kata Tjuta and Kakadu National Parks, Willandra Lakes and the Tasmanian

Figure 16.2 Eretoka Island, Chief Roi Mata's Domain World Heritage Area, Vanuatu

Source: Erika J. Techera

Wilderness area) and New Zealand (Tongagriro National Park) have cultural sites listed under WHC. But of the South Pacific SIDS only two states have inscriptions. East Rennell, in the Solomon Islands, was inscribed in 1998. It is the largest raised coral atoll in the world (Smith and Jones, 2007) and, while inscribed for its natural values, its conservation management also respects customary ownership and management by indigenous peoples. In 2008 Chief Roi Mata's Domain in Vanuatu became the second such World Heritage (WH) property and the first inscribed for cultural heritage values. As well as including archaeological remains such as Roi Mata's residence and burial site the WH area is a focus of much oral tradition.

This lack of representation on the World Heritage list has been the subject of research and investigation (The World Heritage List, 2005). The promotion of the WHC in the Pacific was initially

undertaken by UNESCO at the World Heritage Global Strategy meetings. In 2005 ICOMOS published a report, 'The World Heritage List: Filling the Gaps – An Action Plan for the Future'. The report found that despite associative cultural landscapes being common in the Pacific region, few sacred sites and places of symbolic significance had been acknowledged. More recently the World Heritage Committee has developed the Pacific 2009 Programme and Action Plan (Smith and Jones, 2007). The Action Plan recognizes the importance of intangible heritage and the objectives and scope of CSICH but sets out no particular provisions. However, it does acknowledge the need to integrate natural and cultural World Heritage work with other conservation efforts in the region (UNESCO, 2004).

In contrast to the WHC, none of the South Pacific SIDS has yet ratified CSICH or the Convention on Cultural Expression, although Vanuatu is in the process of doing so and other ratifications are expected in the future (UNESCO, 2007). At the regional level the Asia/Pacific Cultural Centre and UNESCO have worked to promote CSICH including conducting workshops and seminars and publishing relevant documentation through the Asia-Pacific Database on Intangible Cultural Heritage (ACCU, 2009).

In terms of strategic policy, the Mauritius Plan for SIDS 2005–2015 calls for the development of measures to protect natural and tangible cultural heritage and increase resources for the development and strengthening of national and regional cultural initiatives. At the sub-regional level the Pacific Islands Forum Secretariat (PIFS) has included intangible heritage protection within the Pacific Plan. In particular the PIFS is committed to developing a regional cultural strategy for the protection of traditional knowledge and cultural expressions. In addition several items of South Pacific intangible cultural heritage have been proclaimed Masterpieces of Oral Tradition and these have been transferred to the first representative list of intangible cultural heritage under CSICH. These include the Lakalaka Dances and Sung Speeches of Tonga and the Vanuatu Sand drawings.

The CSICH places considerable emphasis on local communities and their involvement in heritage protection and so domestic initiatives are of significance. Despite the fact that CSICH has not been ratified, two South Pacific examples illustrate work that is currently being done to safeguard intangible heritage. The Vanuatu Cultural Centre (VCC) runs the fieldworkers' network programme which involves local community members collecting and documenting oral histories, genealogies, practices and performances (Abong, 2007). The success of the programme has been attributed to the fact that the fieldworkers are volunteers and the Vanuatu Cultural Centre maintains an ongoing relationship with them. In Fiji a National Culture and Heritage Policy is being developed. The Ministry of Fijian Affairs, Culture and Heritage together with the Institute of Fijian Language and Culture (IFLC) has commenced cultural mapping in preparation for an inventory of intangible cultural heritage. The

Fiji Arts Council, in conjunction with UNESCO, has instigated a project to establish a national Living Human Treasures programme with the aim of providing support to custodians of traditional knowledge and skills that are in danger of disappearing (UNESCO, n.d.).

Challenges of protecting sacred natural sites

The protection of sacred natural sites poses specific challenges due to the blend of the tangible and intangible values in these places. One of the principal risks involved is that one aspect will be protected at the expense of the other. For example, conventional 'fortress conservation' (Brockington, 2002, 2004) approaches may be a means to protect biodiversity and natural elements but will risk inhibiting or preventing continued cultural use of the site. Simply recording or documenting the intangible heritage, away from sites, may cause it to be fossilized.

From the international legal perspective taken in this chapter, the conservation of both aspects could be achieved by combining the protection mechanisms under WHC and CSICH. Nonetheless, translating these international laws into local action can present significant challenges. ICOMOS has identified two relevant issues underlying the paucity of World Heritage representation in the South Pacific: firstly, the lack of documentation and investigation of cultural heritage in the region and, secondly, the absence of appropriate conservation legislation (ICOMOS, 2005). Both of these are required by the WHC but also equally apply to the protection of intangible cultural heritage (UNESCO, 2008). These are significant stumbling blocks for many SIDS who lack capacity to address these issues.

The reasons for these deficiencies were considered in the Pacific Action Plan. Government heritage management agencies are small and have limited resources while the small land areas, relative isolation of communities and poor infrastructure makes communication with local people extremely difficult (UNESCO, 2004). This last point is significant as community consultation and involvement is particularly important and lies at the heart of CSICH. Therefore, capacity issues remain central to the problem: as well as consultation with local communities, considerable resources are needed for mapping sacred natural sites and documenting intangible cultural heritage. Further financial resources and expertise are needed for the preparation of action plans, policies, institutions and legislation. The Pacific Action Plan seeks to address lack of expertise through capacity building in the region involving workshops to provide practical guidance on identification of sites, writing of nominations and management plans. Such information has been made available through the Asia Pacific Focal Point (APFP). Regional cooperation is also important and has worked effectively in the past. For example, Australia has provided advice to Vanuatu and assistance to Papua New Guinea and Kiribati in relation to their WHC site nominations.

A further challenge is to safeguard the practices and processes associated with sacred natural sites in ways that respect indigenous and local community values. For example, in circumstances where elements of secrecy are associated with the heritage, documentation would not be appropriate. This would also be the case where indigenous intellectual and cultural property rights are involved. When drawing upon intangible cultural heritage protection mechanisms, initiatives must provide for the culturally sensitive transmission of knowledge rather than preservation of specific tangible records of it.

The legal protection of sites also poses significant challenges as none of the SIDS currently has specific legislation to protect sacred natural sites. Only a limited number of countries have legislation designed to safeguard heritage more broadly and many do not have environmental management legislation. More common are laws that provide for the declaration of natural heritage areas, although even here national legislation for integrated protected area management networks is limited.

In many cases the laws that do exist are based on western legal systems that do not reflect the values of indigenous communities. Experience has shown that such laws are unlikely to be effective as indigenous peoples will continue to utilize customary laws and practices. The challenge

remains to identify legal frameworks which involve local communities in environmental and cultural management. This is justified on many grounds but particularly where indigenous peoples are the landowners, holders of intangible cultural heritage and community custodians of sacred natural sites. Furthermore, international law including the WHC, CSICH, Declaration on the Rights of Indigenous Peoples and Convention on Biological Diversity (CBD) all require local community involvement.

Recommendations

To meet the challenges of preserving sacred natural sites, priority must be given to their identification and protection through integrated policies and plans which recognize the link between cultural and natural heritage. In the South Pacific, attention has been paid to biodiversity conservation through two key regional environmental treaties, the Noumea Convention and Apia Convention. But these do not address the links between cultural heritage protection and the natural environment. For example, they make no specific reference to sacred sites or the cultural aspects of protected areas.

The Action Plan 2009 refers to government agencies in the region being small, but other significant impediments come from the fragmentation of administration. This has been identified as a problem in Vanuatu, for example, where the Vanuatu Cultural Centre and Vanuatu Cultural and Historic Sites Survey have the potential to manage heritage but a number of other agencies are also involved, complicating efficient management (Smith and O'Keefe, 2004). Therefore at the national level, strategies, policies and administrative agencies must become more integrated and harmonized.

There is also a necessity to engage with local communities to a much greater extent. Stakeholder consent, participation, inclusion and collaboration are recognized key principles for best practice management of sacred natural sites (Wild and McLeod, 2008). Local communities must be involved at all stages from research, identification, cultural mapping, documentation, planning and management, through to monitoring, compliance and enforcement. By ensuring voluntary involvement and providing educational workshops, as in Vanuatu, local community members can be trained and encouraged to collect and document heritage data and information. A living human treasure programme could also be tailored to meet community needs where the recording of cultural heritage associated with a sacred site would not be appropriate.

A further issue is the formal recognition and legal protection of sacred natural sites. In the past, traditional landowners have acted as custodians, managing these areas through customary law, informed by traditional knowledge and enforced by local governance institutions. However, globalization, modernization and urbanization are putting increasing pressure on land areas and the authority of traditional village-based institutions. In this situation national governments and local communities must work together to protect sacred natural sites. New legislation must take into account customary laws and practices, indigenous values, communal land tenure and the cultural diversity of the region. This is where UNESCO's work in relation to CSICH may be of value. Through the UNESCO website and databases, models are shared, leading to the development of best practice. This could be continued throughout perhaps through a South Pacific sub-regional body, as individual states begin implementing initiatives and laws that address tangible and intangible heritage issues.

As the distinction between cultural and natural heritage is artificial in most South Pacific communities, the future of legal protection may lie in combining the protection of both. Potential models for this may be found in the recent community-based environmental management regimes successfully adopted in the region. In many cases these bottom up approaches rely upon customary laws and traditional practices as a foundation for local management and regulation. For example, the Locally Managed Marine Area (LMMA) initiative involves community-initiated management of inshore marine areas combining western science and traditional ecological knowledge, village governance and modern adaptive management techniques, and customary laws such as taboos.

Legislation could also provide for and strengthen the utilization of traditional governance institutions. For example, in Samoa, the customary village institution has been legally recognized and re-invigorated under the Village Fono Act of 1990. A 'fono' is a Polynesian term for national as well as local village councils. Furthermore the Samoan Fisheries Act, 1988, empowers the fono to pass local fishery by-laws which are then enforceable in state courts. In Vanuatu the Environmental Management and Conservation Act of 2002 provides for the registration and enforcement of Community Conservation Areas (CCAs), which may include sites with 'unique cultural resources' or those which merit protection under the WHC (section 35). Conservation goals include the 'preservation and protection of natural resources and heritage' (section 2) and once a site is registered it is an offence to contravene any term of a Community Conservation Area (section 41).

These community-based initiatives could be utilized for the protection of sacred natural sites and may already be having an indirect impact in this area. For example in the Fijian village of Ucunivanua, funds raised through an LMMA project were used to build a sea-wall to protect their sacred burial ground (Aalbersberg et al, 2005, p148).

Community-based environmental management has been found to be effective in protecting biodiversity and providing for sustainable livelihoods. If this approach were applied to sacred natural sites they may be even more successful, as the cultural element provides an additional conservation incentive.

Conclusion

The profound connection that the South Pacific people have with nature is undisputed and the region contains many sacred natural sites. But despite a long history of indigenous stewardship of these places, many of them remain unprotected in any formal or legal sense. Sacred natural sites lie at the intersection of cultural and natural heritage and provide the context for oral traditions, stories and spiritual beliefs. They illustrate one material form of 'living' intangible culture and their multiple values provide the basis for giving high priority to their protection.

In circumstances where natural and intangible cultural heritage are significantly interconnected the CSICH and WHC combined offer a range of tools for the international recognition, protection and management of sacred natural sites. However, greater harmonization is needed between these conventions, as well as other international standards such as those in the Declaration on the Rights of Indigenous Peoples.

At the domestic level many of the SIDS in the South Pacific region have taken some steps towards conserving intangible heritage. But the policy and legislation in the region seldom include specific reference to sacred natural sites, nor detailed provisions for the safeguarding of associated intangible heritage. In the long term *sui generis* laws may be needed that reflect the unique aspects of this heritage and specific countries' needs. *Sui generis* laws constitute an independent and unique legal framework. In the shorter term, efforts must be made to overcome administrative and legal fragmentation.

This chapter has attempted to set the priorities for more detailed research and work in relation to the protection of sacred natural sites of the South Pacific. Vanuatu's recent World Heritage inscription and moves to ratify CSICH may give impetus to this undertaking. It is essential to ensure that these sites, and the associated living heritage, are internationally recognized, domestically protected and locally managed. Only then will the cultural diversity of these rich and varied islands continue to 'live' for many generations to come.

References

Aalbersberg, W., Tawake, A. and Parras, T. (2005) *Village by Village: Recovering Fiji's Coastal Fisheries, The Wealth of the Poor: Managing Ecosystems to Fight Poverty*, UNDP, UNEP, The World Bank and WRI, Geneva

Abong, M. (2007) 'The experience of safeguarding of the intangible heritage in the Republic of Vanuatu', Paper presented at the International Symposium on Safeguarding and Preservation of the Oral and Intangible Heritage of Humanity, 10–13 December 2007, Nadi, Fiji

ACCU (2009) 'Asia/Pacific Cultural Centre for UNESCO, Asia Pacific Database for Intangible Cultural Heritage', available at www.accu.or.jp/ich/en/ (last accessed August 2008)

Brockington, D. (2002) *Fortress Conservation: the Preservation of the Mkomazi Game Reserve, Tanzania*, Bloomington, Indiana University Press, Indiana

Brockington, D. (2004) 'Community conservation, inequality and injustice: Myths of power in protected area management', *Conservation and Society*, vol 2, no 2, pp411–432

CEPF (2007) 'Critical Ecosystem Partnership Fund, Ecosystem Profile: Polynesia–Micronesia biodiversity hotspot', available at www.cepf.net/Documents/final.polynesiamicronesia.ep.pdf (last accessed August 2009)

Equator Initiative (n.d.) 'Equator Initiative award nomination: Uafato', available at www.equatorinitiative.org/knowledgebase/files/2002-0224_Nom_UafatoConservationAreaProject_Samoa.doc (last accessed 20 August 2008)

Gerbeaux, P., Kami, T., Clarke, P. and Gillespie, T. (2007) 'Shaping a sustainable future in the Pacific', IUCN Regional Programme for Oceania 2007–2012, IUCN Regional Office for Oceania, Suva, Fiji

ICOMOS (2005) 'Filling the gaps: An action plan for the future', The World Heritage List, ICOMOS, Paris

Smith, A. and Jones K.L. (2007) 'Cultural landscapes of the Pacific Islands', ICOMOS Thematic Study, ICOMOS, Paris

Smith, A. and O'Keefe, D. (2004) 'Training workshops in cultural heritage management in the Pacific Island Nations Interim Report', Workshop 1, Levuka, Fiji, UNESCO, Paris and ICOMOS, Australia

UNESCO (1997) '3rd Global Strategy Meeting: Identification of World Heritage properties in the Pacific, findings and recommendations', UNESCO World Heritage Centre in association with the Fiji Museum, Suva, Fiji, 15–18 July 1997

UNESCO (2003) 'Convention on the safeguarding of the intangible cultural heritage', available at http://unesdoc.unesco.org/images/0013/001325/132540e.pdf (last accessed January 2009)

UNESCO (2004) 'World Heritage, Pacific 2009 programme action plan', 17–22 October 2004 Tongariro National Park, New Zealand

UNESCO (2007) 'Report of the sub-regional meeting in the Pacific on the convention for the safeguarding of the intangible cultural heritage', 12–14 December 2007, Nadi, Fiji

UNESCO (2008) 'World Heritage operational guidelines', available at http://whc.unesco.org/en/guidelines/ (last accessed August 2008)

UNESCO (2009) 'World Heritage tentative List, Fagaloa Bay – Uafato Tiavea conservation zone', available at http://whc.unesco.org/en/tentativelists/5090/ (last accessed August 2008)

UNESCO (n.d.) 'Guidelines for the establishment of national living human treasures systems', available at www.unesco.org/culture/ich/doc/src/00031-EN.pdf (last accessed August 2008)

Verschuuren, B. (2007) *Believing is Seeing, Integrating Cultural and Spiritual Values in Conservation Management*, Earth Collective (FSD), The Netherlands and the IUCN, Gland

Wild, R. and McLeod, C. (eds.) (2008) *Sacred Natural Sites: Guidelines for Protected Area Managers*, IUCN and UNESCO, Gland, Switzerland

17

Wetland Cultural and Spiritual Values, and the Ramsar Convention

Thymio Papayannis and Dave Pritchard

Summary

In many traditional societies, people have lived in close proximity to wetlands and made good use of their resources and services, while incorporating them in their culture. These links, while still in existence, have been damaged and weakened in contemporary, technologically developed societies, rendering the conservation of wetlands more difficult.

That is why the Parties to the Ramsar Convention have decided to encourage the incorporation of cultural aspects in the management of wetlands, including recognizing sacred natural sites. By reconnecting people to wetlands through culture, conservation efforts can secure greater public support. Moreover, better understanding of cultural practices, including the concept of sacredness, can reveal sustainable approaches to the 'wise use' of wetlands. Combining culture with nature may also create a novel product for sustainable tourism, with benefits for local communities.

Introduction

The concept that the conservation of both cultural/ spiritual and natural heritage can benefit from an integrated approach has been gaining ground at all levels among governments, specialists and the public, although in places it also remains the subject of significant controversy. In this process, multilateral agreements are playing a major role, both as arenas of debate and as promoters of more holistic policies concerning the environment and human heritage.

The Ramsar Convention

The idea of a convention on the conservation and wise use of wetlands arose in the 1960s on the initiative of dedicated ornithologists and other conservationists. These origins explain why, when it was adopted at the city of Ramsar (Iran) in 1971, it was named the 'Convention on Wetlands of International Importance especially as Waterfowl Habitat'. However, its founders had broader views, expressed in the preamble of the Convention, inter alia through the following phrase:

> … *Being convinced that wetlands constitute a resource of great economic, cultural, scientific and recreational value, the loss of which would be irreparable…*

During subsequent decades, the Convention broadened its concerns well beyond waterfowl, to cover other taxa (such as fish and invertebrates) and aspects including water management, health, human subsistence, poverty alleviation and cultural aspects. Thus, its mission has in more recent times been defined as 'the conservation and wise use of all wetlands through local, regional and national actions and international cooperation, as a contribution towards achieving sustainable development throughout the world'.

As of late 2009 the Convention's 159 Contracting Parties have designated 1880 sites totalling 185 million hectares for inclusion in the Ramsar List of Wetlands of International Importance. A number of Ramsar sites overlap with or are considered sacred natural sites, and examples in this volume are in Chapters 7 and 12.

Wetlands, people and culture

In the framework of the Ramsar Convention, the interpretation of 'wetland' covers a broader range of ecosystem types than is commonly realised. Wetlands are defined (in Article 1.1 of the Convention) as:

areas of marsh, fen, peat land or water, whether natural or artificial, permanent or temporary, with water that is static or flowing, fresh, brackish or salt, including areas of marine water the depth of which at low tide does not exceed six metres.

The main characteristic is the presence of water – even temporarily – as an element essential for the existence of most if not all living species, including *Homo sapiens*. In addition, water and wetlands provide a multitude of services, both material and non-material, to human beings (Millennium Ecosystem Assessment, 2005). This is perhaps the reason why human societies have historically been associated so closely with wetlands, starting with Neolithic lacustrine settlements and continuing with entire cities built in or around wetlands.

Figure 17.1 Fishing communities on Lake George, a Ramsar site in Uganda, have a strong fishing culture and live closely with wildlife

Source: Robert Wild

Human beings have exploited wetland resources for millennia, especially water, and great civilizations, such as ancient Egypt and Mesopotamia, were built around wetlands, with high dependence on their services. As a result, wetlands and water have been the focus of spiritual interests in many societies, and they feature strongly in several faiths and religious practices. For example, the blessing of the waters is a common element of numerous major faiths.

This intimate relationship between people and wetlands has however diminished over time, for a number of reasons. The onslaught of malaria, with Anopheles mosquitoes as a vector, has been an important factor in generating negative attitudes to wetlands. In many places, traditional activities that made use of wetland resources, such as harvesting of fish, salt and reeds, are becoming less attractive financially or have been abandoned. The need for inexpensive flat land, often drained without much difficulty, has led to the destruction of wetlands and to a change of land uses towards urbanization, agriculture, aquaculture, industry, tourism facilities and large scale infrastructure such as roads, airports, harbours and sewage treatment plants, particularly in lowland and coastal areas. Not surprisingly, the resulting decline in the extent of wetlands and the increasing estrangement from them of local populations has led to an associated loss of wetland cultural values.

Growing sensitivity to the multiple values of wetlands (for flood control, storm protection, nature conservation, water supply and many others), and to the need for sustainable use of natural resources, has led to significant initiatives for the protection of wetlands at various levels from the local to the international, many of them catalysed by the Ramsar Convention. This positive trend has been strengthened by an appreciation of the impacts of global climate change on water scarcity, sea-level rise, extreme climatic phenomena, loss of coast protection functions and the functions of wetlands as carbon sinks. These are all related in various ways to the water cycle and hence to wetlands, further strengthening the case for the conservation of wetlands (Millennium Ecosystem Assessment, 2005) and a wider appreciation of their values.

Use of wetland resources

All human activities – to a greater or lesser extent – have a cultural dimension, although this is not always fully perceived or valued. With regard to wetlands, two points should be clarified. The first concerns the distinction between the potential cultural value of any activity and its desirability in terms of wetland conservation and wise use. Aquaculture, for example, if practised in an unsustainable manner, can seriously damage wetlands, especially mangroves. The same is true of quarrying, salt extraction and hunting. At the same time, however, an understanding of relevant cultural values can help in developing guidelines for the sustainable use of the resource concerned.

The second point concerns the realization that the strong cultural aspects of traditional productive activities are being eroded, as those activities become replaced by more modern ones. Options for addressing this problem could include attempting to maintain these activities and their cultural aspects through subsidies, as in the case of traditional boats in wetland fishing, preserving them under museum-like conditions or modifying them and incorporating them in viable contemporary activities such as tourism. Contemporary activities of course also have their own cultural context, which may not be immediately evident to the casual observer.

Cultural landscapes

The importance of water for human survival, health and well-being has among other things given rise to spiritual values associated with wetlands and their connected landscapes. These values are respected by many societies, from ancient Egypt (e.g. with the Nile) to ancient Greece (with its sacred springs and groves) and as evidenced in the teachings of the Qur'an and the traditions seen in many Buddhist countries. In addition, wetland cultural landscapes have provided inspiration for many art forms, including painting, literature, music and others, throughout human history.

The example of the River Nile

Nowhere is the intricate relationship between water, wetlands and human survival better illustrated than in the case of the Nile River and ancient Egypt.

The cyclical ebb and flow of the river waters which were considered to be controlled by the gods determined the fortunes and fate of the powerful civilizations that grew in this region and left their weighty marks.

During Akhet, the season of inundation, the Nile flooded 'the black land', which included most of the flat plains along its banks. This allowed planting of wheat and barley in September, during the season of Peret, and these were harvested in March or April. Shemu, the summer season of drought followed, and the life-sustaining cycle was repeated. During the Old Kingdom, in the 3rd millennium BC, the kings were expected to maintain Ma'at, the cosmic order, and guarantee the continuity of the Nile cycle.

The Nile was so important to the Egyptians that they assigned to the god Hapi responsibility for the river's annual inundation. Hapi and the Pharaoh were believed to control the flooding of the Nile. The river was also considered a causeway from life to death and the after-life.

Goddesses and gods took the shape of the Nile's creatures, such as the crocodile and the hippopotamus, which were considered sacred especially in relation to fertility and childbirth. Botanical signs featuring species such as the lotus and papyrus (which grow on the Nile's banks) figured prominently, while in architecture, the structure of temples emulated the sandy mounds in the Nile and its waves.

Spiritual and other non-material values

In addition to Hapi, the God of the Nile, other great rivers have often been viewed as deities, e.g. Acheloos in western Greece, who was depicted with the head of a bull and the body of a snake. The Great Ganges, despite its ecologically degraded state, is still considered sacred by hundreds of millions of people.

In spite of the secular trends of our times, religious beliefs are still an important medium for reaching and motivating large numbers of people throughout the world. Spiritual attitudes, usually rooted in ancient traditions, are often favourable to the natural world, by incorporating beliefs either in its inherent sanctity (as in the case of many indigenous peoples) or in a divine creation (as in the major monotheistic faiths). The teachings

which flow from these beliefs often include strong admonitions to use the natural world wisely, with humans seen as stewards of creation (Bragader et al, 1994; see also Chapter 4). On the other hand, over a lengthy period, such teachings have become misunderstood and distorted into a rationale for human dominion over the Earth and supposed justification for inequitable exploitation of its natural resources, extending to inequitable treatment of indigenous peoples.

During the past few decades, the major faiths and their churches and communities have started to reassess their position concerning the natural world, and to interpret their teachings in a more environmentally enlightened manner. A characteristic example is the Christian Orthodox Ecumenical Patriarch, who has led a movement for considering the destruction of nature and the environment as a sin – a view which has since been adopted by the Catholic Church and other Christian faiths. The environmental sensitivity of Buddhism and, in a contemporary context, of the Dalai Lama in particular, is also well known and has perhaps been a motivation for other religious leaders as well as their followers.

An especially important opportunity is being created with joint efforts for the conservation of 'sacred natural sites', bringing together the spiritual custodians of these sites and those responsible for their scientific and administrative management as a component of protected area systems. The IUCN Specialist Group on Cultural and Spiritual Values of Protected Areas has been working on providing appropriate guidance (see Wild and McLeod, 2008) and on developing an integrated approach of this kind in technologically developed countries through its Delos Initiative (see Chapter 19).

To promote such collaboration in relation to wetlands, the following priority actions have been suggested within the framework of the Ramsar Convention (Papayannis and Pritchard, 2008), by its Culture Working Group:

- for each religion and belief system, study in detail its links with nature, water and wetland resources, drawing on the active participation of religious institutions and leaders and the custodians and practitioners of the belief systems in indigenous and local communities;

Figure 17.2 Patriarch Bartholomew visits an indigenous village, Santarem, Amazon, Brazil

Note: During his River Amazon Symposium where representatives of the indigenous people of Amazonia, western religious leaders, scientists, environmentalists and policy-makers came together to examine the ecological reality in the Amazon basin, the global impact of deforestation and, importantly, to propose sustainable solutions to preserving the forest for the future.

Source: Ivy Nanopoulou

- use this knowledge to present the conservation and sustainable use message in appropriate forms;
- work with churches and/or religious leaders and leading members of indigenous and local communities to encourage them to convey these messages and to participate actively in efforts for environmental conservation as an integral part of respectful management of the Creation.

Close collaboration between those responsible for both the spiritual/cultural heritage and the natural heritage can create synergy that benefits both groups.

The example of Doñana and the El Rocío pilgrimage

Of all the cultural aspects of the Doñana National Park in Spain (one of the major wetlands of the Mediterranean region, and a Ramsar site), perhaps the most important are the celebrations in honour of the Virgin Mary (La Madre) of El Rocío, a village in the junction between the area's beaches and marshes. Initially of interest only within neighbouring populations, in more recent decades this major religious event has acquired a growing regional significance in Spain. Among other elements, it includes a procession on foot, horseback and carriages through the Doñana National Park as far as the village of Nuestra Señora del Rocío (Our Lady of the Dew).

One hundred and four fraternities take part, from all over Spain and from abroad, and the number of participants reaches an estimated 1 million people. All of the fraternities make the pilgrimage to Almonte town on foot, in carts drawn by oxen or on horseback along well-worn dusty tracks in the natural landscape, through the National Park. The El Rocío Pilgrimage, also known as El Rocío Grande, is held each year on Whitsun Saturday, Sunday and Monday, 50 days after Easter Sunday.

Along with their positive social and spiritual impacts, the El Rocío events cause a number of environmental problems, especially littering and trampling of the vegetation. The challenge for the organizers and for the management of the Park is to make use of these events and their spiritual context for a better appreciation of the Doñana wetlands, strengthening conservation efforts through popular support (Novo and Cabrera, 2005).

Ramsar and culture

Multilateral agreements among sovereign states reach consensus through patient and lengthy negotiations. Incorporating cultural and spiritual aspects into the work of the Ramsar Convention is a process that started in the late 1990s and is continuing to move forward with small but positive steps (Pritchard, 2008).

Initial work

Not until 1990, almost 20 years after the signing of the Ramsar Convention, was an information field included in the datasheet for Wetlands of International Importance which related to data on social and cultural values. In 1992, the cultural values of Greek wetlands were presented in a workshop in Thessaloniki (Papayannis, 1992). In 1999, the seventh meeting of the Conference of Parties (COP7, in San José, Costa Rica) broached the issue of culture in its theme 'People and Wetlands: the Vital Link'.

At the same time, the Ramsar Bureau (now 'Secretariat') produced a series of Culture Sheets which were widely disseminated (Ramsar Bureau, 2001) and published a pertinent technical article (Davidson, 2001).

Deliberations at Ramsar conferences

As the issue was maturing, in 2001 the Standing Committee of the Convention decided to have 'a broad-ranging discussion on the role of cultural and socio-economic issues in the Convention, and ways to enhance that role (including the question of a potential site selection criterion)'.

As a result, an information document was prepared and a draft resolution on culture was included in the working documents of the eighth meeting of the Conference of Parties in 2002 (COP8). The two documents created considerable interest during the COP, but also strong disagreements and reactions, requiring the establishment of a Contact Group that was chaired by the Spanish delegation. In the lengthy debates that followed, the main argument against dealing with cultural aspects in the framework of the Ramsar Convention was that these were the responsibility of other international bodies, such as UNESCO and the World Heritage Convention, and that involvement in culture might undermine responsibilities of states under the World Trade Organization. It was only through the strong support of African and European Union countries that a resolution on 'Incorporating cultural values in the management of wetlands' was eventually approved by consensus (Resolution VIII.19).

The resolution included statements on the rationale for incorporating cultural values in wetland work, the need for a broad and substantial collaboration with organizations and institutions responsible for cultural heritage and the recognition of the rights of indigenous peoples and local communities. It encouraged the Contracting Parties of the Convention to take into consideration cultural values in managing their wetlands wisely and in designating relevant sites as Wetlands of International Importance.

Subsequent Conferences (COP9 in 2005 and COP10 in 2008) have continued to give attention to these issues, including the adoption of a further decision at COP9 (Resolution IX.21) and the launch of a new guidance document at COP10.

Plans and perspectives

The Ramsar Standing Committee has agreed to the continued operation of the Convention's Culture Working Group during 2009–2012, to focus on providing further guidance and on the analysis and presentation of case studies.

During the coming three or four years, the Ramsar Convention will attempt to deepen and extend its activities on the cultural values of wetlands. This will involve guidance by the Secretary General, systematic work by the Culture Working Group and expert support from members of the Scientific and Technical Review Panel. The active involvement of interested Contracting Parties will be sought, especially in promoting and supporting cultural initiatives at the regional level.

Towards an integrated approach to nature and culture in relation to wetlands

The main goal of all these efforts is to achieve a more integrated approach to nature and culture in all work related to wetlands, and particularly in management planning. This will necessitate a move away from unduly sectoral approaches and towards adopting a more holistic frame of mind in dealing with wetlands.

A first step in this direction is to recognize that wetlands generally cannot be viewed without their human context, and that the relevant biological processes and human actions are usually closely interrelated. The second step is to comprehend that nature is also part of the human heritage, with all that this implies (Howard and Papayannis, 2007). Even in the case of the most supposedly non-utilitarian 'intrinsic' or 'existence' values that may be ascribed to nature, the fact that humans are ascribing them makes these values of utility to humans. It may not be a question of consumptive exploitation, but nonetheless it could be said that people 'use' nature in this way, for example to serve our moral sensibilities. In the language of the Millennium Ecosystem Assessment, which has also been adopted by Ramsar, this is an example of 'cultural ecosystem services'.

Developing a common currency for understanding between those responsible for the cultural and spiritual heritage – in particular custodians of sacred sites – and those charged with the management of wetlands, is essential for the collaboration required. Common 'language', in this sense, can lead to a common approach and methodology, for example in the management of sites.

Hopefully, such collaboration may result in better-integrated policies for the conservation and wise use of both the cultural and the natural heritage.

Providing guidance into the future

In the years to come, the Ramsar Convention intends to assist its Contracting Parties – and all those interested and concerned – by providing guidance on ways to incorporate culture in work related to the management and conservation of wetlands. This will be done through the activities of the Culture Working Group, in partnership with a broad array of organisations and institutions, and will include the following:

- drafting a strategy for the Convention concerning cultural matters in wetlands, including sacred natural sites;
- further elaboration and refining of the general and specific objectives included in the current Guidance document (Papayannis and Pritchard, 2008);
- proposal of additional actions for the implementation of the stated objectives;
- identification of case studies and actions of Contracting Parties that illustrate successful practices that could be emulated by others;

- preparation of a guidance manual to be launched in 2012.

In addition, communication efforts will be strengthened, mainly through publications and a website. Particular emphasis will be placed on sacred wetland sites in collaboration with the Delos Initiative of the IUCN Specialist Group on Cultural and Spiritual Values of Protected Areas, by selecting and analysing relevant case studies throughout the world.

Conclusions

In the near future, the intangible aspects of culture and spirituality are expected to gain increasing importance. In parallel, the intangible aspects of nature will follow a similar path. In the current context of a rapidly changing planet (characterized by climate change and its impacts, scarcities and high prices of natural resources and intensifying economic uncertainties), the ensuing turmoil gives rise to a search for certainties and for spiritual support. This takes many forms, including a rise of New Age spiritualism and often futile efforts to return to ancient faiths, such as the Greek Dodecatheon.

What is needed today, however, is a flourishing respect for this world, for its beauty and its beings, as divine creation if one is a believer and as an integral part of existence for all; a respect that may give rise to fewer destructive practices and actions and may even encourage new initiatives for conservation.

A growing sensitization of people and societies may lead to a new view of nature and biodiversity, and may create a new culture with both secular and spiritual benefits.

References

Bragader, A.A. et al (1994) *Environmental Protection in Islam*, IUCN, Gland, Switzerland and Cambridge, UK

Davidson, N. (2001) *Wetlands and Cultural Heritage Conservation*, Ramsar Bureau, Gland, Switzerland

Howard, P. and Papayannis, T. (2007) *Natural Heritage: At the Interface of Nature and Culture*, Routledge, London, UK

Millennium Ecosystem Assessment (2005) *Ecosystems and Human Well-being: Wetlands and Water Synthesis*, World Resources Institute, Washington DC, USA

Novo, F.G. and Cabrera, C.M. (2005) 'Doñana: water and biosphere', Doñana 2005 Project, Spanish Ministry of the Environment, Madrid, Spain

Papayannis, T. and Pritchard, D.E. (2008) *Integrating cultural aspects in the management of wetlands: A Guidance document*, Ramsar Convention, Gland, Switzerland

Pritchard, D.E. (2008) 'Nature and culture in the coastal zone; the role of the Ramsar Convention on Wetlands', Public lecture given during course/symposium: 'Coast', convened by Cambridge Centre for Landscape and People, Cambridge University, 28 July–1 August 2008

Ramsar Bureau (2001) 'Culture sheets', Gland, Switzerland

Wild, R. and McLeod, C. (eds) (2008) *Sacred Natural Sites: Guidelines for Protected Area Managers*, IUCN, Gland, Switzerland

18

Sacred Natural Sites, Biodiversity and Well-being: The Role of Sacred Sites in Endogenous Development in the COMPAS Network

Freddy Delgado, Cesar Escobar, Bas Verschuuren and
Wim Hiemstra

Summary

This chapter reviews the sacred natural sites of COMPAS partners found in seven different countries in Africa and Latin America. The sites are of importance for community well-being and for global biocultural teachings in nature conservation. Focusing on 'well-being', this chapter introduces endogenous development, or development from within, as an approach to address the various dimensions of sacred natural sites: sacred time, sacred space, mythical origins, historic origins and special energies. These dimensions are important to well-being as they are key components of the worldviews of indigenous and local communities. Sacred sites and spiritual values are not only important in livelihood activities such as food security and providing medicinal plants, but they are also significant in maintaining a people's mental health and socio-cultural life. A methodology for measuring and monitoring the material, social and spiritual importance of sacred natural sites is presented making use of a set of indicators and indicator criteria which address the importance of biodiversity and well-being. The chapter provides evidence that high biodiversity values are maintained through sacred natural sites and that these constitute vital links between community well-being and nature conservation. The chapter also signals the need for recognition of the importance of sacred natural sites in policy formulation. It provides examples of how the COMPAS network assists local and indigenous communities to conserve sacred sites and facilitate policy dialogue at the national level in Latin America and Africa.

Introduction

Sacred natural sites and spiritual values are not only important for the conservation of wild and domestic biodiversity and ecosystem health, but also for spiritual well-being, physical health, housing, education, food security and human well-being. In essence, sacred natural sites are socially constructed places where the spiritual dimensions of human-nature interactions are an expression of distinct worldviews (Verschuuren, 2007a). Worldviews of indigenous and local communities are often based on a sophisticated understanding of the web of life, which includes the divine with which people interact during rituals and meditation, at different times and places, including sacred natural sites (Medina, 2006).

This chapter is based on the natural resource management experiences of the COMPAS network. In Latin America, COMPAS partnerships are active with indigenous and local communities in seven countries: Quechua (Ecuador, Peru and Bolivia), Aymara and Uru (Bolivia), Mapuche (Chile), Mayan (Guatemala), Nahuat (El Salvador) and Mestizo (Colombia). In Africa, COMPAS partnerships are active in Ghana, Uganda, Tanzania, Zimbabwe, South Africa and Lesotho.

Whereas the importance of participatory approaches and of integrating local knowledge into development interventions has become broadly recognized, many of these approaches still experience difficulties in overcoming an implicit materialistic bias. The members in the COMPAS network are working to overcome this bias through building in the spiritual links between biological and cultural diversity. Biocultural diversity is increasingly believed to be able to contribute to successful nature conservation strategies (Cocks, 2006; Persic and Martin, 2008; Verschuuren, 2010). 'Successful' in this context means that human use of nature has remained within the control of cultural systems over long periods of time and as such has assisted in conserving both cultural and biological diversity.

Sacred natural sites and sacred plant and animal species, through their spiritual function, play an important role in the maintenance of biocultural diversity (Bhagwat and Rutte, 2006; Posey, 1999; Sponsel, 2001). In this chapter, arguments are proposed for taking endogenous development approaches to nature conservation strategies that link sacred natural sites, cultural practices and biodiversity. In Latin America, well-being indicators have been developed for monitoring the role of sacred natural sites in human well-being and biodiversity conservation, based on experiences with well-being indicators for food security and food sovereignty.

Sacred natural sites, biodiversity and well-being

The aim of endogenous development is to empower local communities to take control of their own development process. By revitalizing ancestral and local ways of knowing and learning, endogenous development helps local people to select external resources (COMPAS, 2007).

Different cultures have different ways of knowing and learning. In the Andes, the spiral notion of time is not separated from space (territory). The first ordering principle is 'relationship': everything is related and this leads to a reciprocal relationship between people, animals, plants, rocks, water, wind, sun, moon and stars. The relations are re-lived in rituals and festivals (Rist et al, 1999). In African worldviews, the world is made up of ancestors, the living and the as yet unborn. Nature is sacred and there is a hierarchy between divine beings, spiritual beings, ancestors, living human beings and nature. Nature provides a habitat for human as well as spiritual entities (Millar, 2006).

'Well-being' is a relatively new concept used in development discourses but is also central in the 'economics of happiness' as in Gross National Happiness approaches in Bhutan. White (2009) defines well-being using three key dimensions: material, relational and subjective. The 'material' comprises assets, welfare and standards of living, the 'relational' dimension deals with social relations and the 'subjective' relates to perceptions of well-being and cultural values, ideologies and beliefs.

COMPAS defines well-being as 'real life', where material, social and spiritual well-being coincides. The endogenous development approach is in essence an intercultural dialogue between indigenous and local communities on the one hand, and outsiders on the other hand. To agree on well-being outcomes, such as strengthened biocultural diversity, the endogenous development approach creates an interface of communication between different worldviews. 'Real life' is in fact comparable with what the Millennium Ecosystem Assessment (MA) has called 'freedom of choice and action' based on the balance of security, basic material for good life, health and social relations (MA, 2003). According to the MA, well-being exists on a continuum with poverty, which has been defined as 'pronounced deprivation in well-being'.

The questions this chapter seeks to answer are the following:

- How are sacred natural sites related to human well-being?
- Does applying an endogenous development approach to sacred natural sites contribute to improved management of biodiversity?

The linkages between sacred natural sites, well-being and support activities are clarified in Figure 18.1. Results in terms of well-being outcomes are improved livelihoods (food security, increased health, availability of traditional varieties, lower expenditure), increased biodiversity (conserved forests, wetlands, rare animal species, medicinal plants available for effective health care) and respect for cultural heritage (legitimizing and revitalizing ancestral wisdom, special plants available for religious ceremonies and festivals). As the COMPAS programmes are based on participatory approaches, increased empowerment is a key outcome. The strengthening of cultural identity is labelled '**intra**culturality' and the exchange with external knowledges and technologies that fit the local context as '**inter**culturality' (Delgado et al, 2006).

Sacred natural sites and biodiversity management

In some of the sacred natural sites mentioned in Figure 18.1, human activity related to biodiversity is practically nonexistent or banned. In Amerindian and other indigenous cultures, spirituality is generally animistic, which means it is expressed through living beings. In this case, the sacred manifests itself as a living entity embodied by wild plant and animal species. Here the cultural practices at sacred natural sites are optimal for biodiversity because they are carried out according to natural cycles, in which human action is oriented towards conservation and care. The examples from Uganda, Chile, Zimbabwe and Ghana (Figure 18.1) show how sacred places allow for human interaction and consequently, how they represent an expression of biocultural diversity.

Incaraqay in Bolivia is a sacred natural site based around a fort built in the Inca cultural period (1400–1450 AD). Although archaeological data do not report a ritual use, it is currently a sacred natural site and rituals are carried out periodically because Incaracay has come to represent the ancestors. During rituals, people living in the 21st century ask their ancestors for protection and well-being.

Santa Vera Cruz in Bolivia is a festival celebrated at an ancient sacred natural site, which now provides the location for a Catholic church. An astrological calendar indicates the beginning of the reproduction of plant and animal species and is therefore considered sacred, see Figure 18.2. The sacred time, the evening and night between 2nd and 3rd May each year, is exclusively dedicated to asking for blessings from Pachamama (Mother Earth), (San Martin, 2001).

Auzangati in Peru is an example of a sacred natural site with special energies. The inhabitants of the Andes believe that the highest places such as mountains, but also trees and water sources, are the source of energies that radiate to living beings. When the energy is positive and beneficial, rituals are performed in exchange for the favours received. When the place radiates negative energies and hinders material and social relationships, rituals are performed to positively realign the energies in question.

The Ruins of Petén and Tikal World Heritage Site in Guatemala are an example of a site held sacred due to its mythic origin. The site was abandoned after the mystical collapse of the Mayan kingdom around 900 AD. Currently, Petén is regarded by the state as a simple tourist attraction and its management lies in private hands. The Mayan peoples of Guatemala have access to the place as tourists and are allowed to perform ritual practices or spiritual training at certain times during the year. However, their current and potential role in managing the site is not acknowledged.

In **Marange** (Zimbabwe), the Gwindingwi sacred forest provides necessary spiritual services to the local inhabitants. The chiefs and spirit mediums

Country	Character of the Sacred natural site	Biodiversity		Well-being		Activities
		Within the sacred natural site	Outside the sacred natural site	Within the sacred natural site	Outside the sacred natural site	Community support through COMPAS and partners
Bolivia	*Historical origin:* Incaraqay Ruins	Ruins represent the ancestors; wild plants and animals are protected	Wild plants and animals are used in farmers' fields	Request well-being from the ancestors	Enhanced food security; balanced social relations and spiritual life; improved health	AGRUCO has community workshops to recover the meanings of sacred natural sites
Bolivia	*Sacred time:* Santa Vera Cruz festival	A specific time to request the spirits to bless fertility of crops, animals and people	Crops and animals thrive well in farmers' fields	Maximum opportunity for developing human spirituality	Healthy people, plants, animals; social relations strengthened	AGRUCO supports the revitalization of the Santa Vera Cruz festival in one community
Chile	*Sacred time:* Guillatun ritual	A special area has a wooden altar, decorated with specific tree leaves from the region	Reinforces harmony through ritual dance, prayer, food preparation and domesticated animal sacrifice.	Request for rains, seed germination, plant and human health, and living spirituality.	Continued health of people, plants, animals; balance of food safety, social relations, health and spiritual life	KUME FELEN staff participate in rituals which creates mutual respect and dialogue
Peru	*Special Energies:* Tata Auzangati mountain	No human activity permitted: wild animals and plants reproduce naturally	Crops and animals thrive well on farmers' lands	A quest to re-establish the harmony of the spiritual dimension with nature	Balance of food safety, social relations, health and spiritual life	CEPROSI conducts periodic rituals; organizes visits with traditional authorities to the sacred mountain
Uganda	*Special energies:* Sacred Shrine in forest of a traditional healer	Herbal garden of traditional healer Haji Zakariya Nyanzi conserves medicinal plants	Prescribed medicines are obtained from medicinal plants	Clients engage in spiritual counselling to diagnose illnesses and administer therapy	Ministry of Health's laboratory validates traditional medicine derived from medicinal plants and assists in marketing.	CCFU documented the experiences of the healer and organized national meetings to discuss findings
Guatemala	*Mythic origin:* Ruins of Petén	Natural reproduction of wild plants and animals. Human exploitation is banned	Domesticated plant and animal species thrive well on farmers' lands	Reaffirmation of religious beliefs; quest to re-establish balance in the spiritual, material and social dimensions	Attending festivals and rituals helps Mayan people to balance material, social and spiritual demands	OXLAJUJ AJPOP formulated a legislative proposal for a Law on Mayan sacred natural sites (see below).
Zimbabwe	*Sacred time & special energies:* Annual rainmaking ceremony in sacred forest	Conservation of wildlife and sacred wetlands; rainmaking ceremonies performed under specific *Mukuyu* tree (*Parinari catifloia*).	The Shona people request ecosystem safety: adequate rainfall for their food crops	Flora and fauna mediate between ancestors and the living. Sacred wetlands harbour rainmaking spirits.	Rare medicinal plants; fruits for food and medicine. Fresh and uncontaminated water from the wetland to brew beer for ceremonies.	SAEDP encourages Traditional Institutions to reinstitute the traditional bylaws in bio-cultural diversity and supports rainmaking ceremonies
Ghana	*Sacred time & special energies:* Sacred groves and wetlands in the Tanchara	Higher density of trees; wild fruits, medicinal plants, mammals, reptiles in sacred wetlands	Indigenous tree seedlings from the sacred forest planted in farmers' fields; medicinal plants for healers.	Flora and fauna communicate between the ancestors and the living. Hunting of totem species is prohibited; hunting of other species only after sacrifice by spiritual leaders.	Cultural and clan identity maintained, as totem species are conserved. Livelihood security increased, as indigenous trees are replanted on farmers' land. Herbalists have their herbs secured.	CIKOD stimulates traditional authorities to revitalize their roles in today's context.

Figure 18.1 Sacred natural sites, biodiversity and human well-being

Source: Information derived from the authors' own studies, narrative reports from COMPAS partners in Latin America and Africa and discussions at COMPAS regional partner meetings

Figure 18.2 Santa Vera Cruz festival, Bolivia

Asking for a fertile and prosperous year for plants, animals and people by burning dried animal dung, drinking maize beer and being joyful in a sacred place during a sacred time.

Source: COMPAS

go to spiritually selected places to perform rituals. Traditional medical practitioners procure medicines from the forest used in the cure of diseases. The COMPAS partner Southern African Endogenous Development Programme (SAEDP) has helped the people of Marange to reintroduce the nature conservation traditional bylaws that were used by their ancestors to keep nature and people interconnected. The chiefs and spirit mediums of Marange lead all community based processes based on the principles of their Shona culture. SAEDP's major role in this regard is to facilitate the process by providing additional financial resources to organise ceremonies, rituals, meetings and workshops to strengthen the Marange community in managing their biocultural diversity in the Gwindingwi forest. Community to community exchange visits are also facilitated by SAEDP where indigenous nature conservation expertise is shared. A Plan of Action to establish indigenous tree nurseries in Marange has already been ratified by the traditional authorities. The seedlings will be used to rehabilitate the degraded forest's tree species that used to benefit the communities in various spiritual ways. An additional three sacred forests have been identified for revitalization.

Improved biodiversity?

The conclusion from Figure 18.1 is that human well-being and biodiversity is intimately related in sacred natural sites and imbued with spiritual values. An endogenous development approach as applied by the COMPAS partners leads to understanding, legitimization and maintaining this relation and thus to improved biodiversity management. Yet, in many countries, the national government neglects the importance of sacred natural sites. Governments are mainly driven to supply material and social well-being through eco-tourism, industrialization, modern farming, infrastructure and urbanization. Therefore, COMPAS partners also engage in policy dialogue processes to emphasize the importance of conserving sacred natural sites. Below we describe and analyse one example of lobbying in the management of sacred natural sites at a national level.

Guatemala: Policy dialogue on sacred natural sites

In Guatemala many sacred natural sites have been expropriated by the state because they lie in areas marked for road construction, housing, or tourism, or, in the case of Tikal, a protected area with World Heritage status. For this reason, Mayan community and spiritual leaders, united by the organization Oxlajuj Ajpop (conference of spiritual Mayan leaders), have formulated a 'Legislative proposal for a Law on indigenous peoples' sacred sites'. The initiative was developed in the context of Agreement 169 on Indigenous and Tribal Peoples in Independent Countries of the International Labour Organization and the Law for Peace Agreements (Peace Agreements, 2008). The Peace Agreements acknowledge the rights of indigenous peoples to live their culture on a specific territory and thereby implicitly acknowledge sacred natural sites as part of that territory.

The aim of getting the law passed is to achieve recognition for and management of use, conservation, administration and access to Mayan sacred natural sites. The law proposal, accepted by the Guatemalan Congress on 19 August 2009, expresses many elements of the Mayan worldview. Once accepted by the government, the law will also create jurisprudence in other areas such as education, health and justice, all rooted in Mayan identity.

The law proposal focuses on the integral quality of the sacred natural site as a source of spirituality, territory, knowledge management and reproduction of a social vision of the world. In other words, it expresses the importance of the sacred natural site to Mayan culture and Mayan 'well-being'. The law will also allow for the institutionalization of sacred natural sites as part of the Guatemalan state and legal structure. This is an important step towards the construction of a plural society within Guatemala and development according to the Mayan perception of well-being. Through the law's implementation, the Mayan worldview complements the contemporary western state-based system currently adopted by the Guatemalan government. By placing the management of sacred natural sites in the hands of indigenous Mayan organizations and assisting them with capacity building and biodiversity management of sacred natural sites, these places will become more aligned to the local cultural worldview.

The Guatemalan experience shows that it is possible to develop policy proposals based on indigenous worldviews which are accepted by congress members. A similar openness is currently (2009) seen in Bolivia, Ecuador and El Salvador. COMPAS Latin America is part of these policy dialogue processes which aim to reverse the marginalization of indigenous peoples. Policy is influenced in the fields of education (Bolivia), health (Chile), land ownership (Chile) and natural resources management (Peru, Bolivia). Initial experiences have been gained and the COMPAS network is working on a publication in 2010 to highlight these lessons.

How to monitor biocultural diversity management of sacred natural sites?

The COMPAS programme has developed tools for participatory monitoring of well-being since 2006. For example, in Bolivia field activities and monitoring has been in the area of food security and food sovereignty. In 2006, Agroecologia Universidad Cochabamba (AGRUCO) and community members living in the Jatun Mayu watershed developed the

well-being monitoring tool together (COMPAS Latin America, 2007). Sacred sites are also important for the purpose of receiving blessing for the work of the University Staff and the Community members (see Figure 18.5).

A total of 400 families live in seven communities at altitudes between 3200 and 4000 metres above sea level, cultivating on slopes of up to 60 per cent. It was agreed to conserve natural resources (through soil conservation and water harvesting) and implement agroecology (agroforestry, organic vegetable production, small animal production) in three of the seven communities. From the well-being perspective, social and spiritual dimensions of natural resources were also discussed and a set of eight indicators were agreed upon. Monitoring is done in quantitative and qualitative terms.

Figure 18.4 lists the indicators and the quantitative progress assessment carried out in mid-2009. Each indicator has agreed criteria. For example, community-based ritual practices related to soil conservation and agroecology (indicator 4) are: participation in the annual regional festival (to exchange food items from highlands and lowlands), ritual practices during sowing and harvesting and the blessing of roads.

The approach and lessons learned can also be applied to sacred natural sites. In Figure 18.3, indicators are given for monitoring well-being dimensions at sacred natural sites from the perspective of material, social and spiritual well-being. The indicators focus on community biodiversity conservation practices related to sacred natural sites.

Discussion and recommendations

Sacred natural sites are protected by the people, intimately related to biodiversity, part of a living ecosystem and play a key role in the well-being of indigenous and local communities as they reaffirm and strengthen cultural identity. The sacred natural site intentionally contributes to these tasks and endogenous development as employed by the COMPAS network is an approach that strengthens biocultural diversity at sacred natural sites (Dudley et al, 2005; Haverkort and Reijntjes, 2006).

Sacred natural sites may also attract increasing recognition, funding and other support in contrast

Dimension	Indicator	Indicator criteria	Importance of the sacred natural site	Importance for biodiversity
Spiritual dimension	1. Existence and valuation of sacred natural sites	• Number of sacred natural sites used for rituals • Degree of valuation for sacred places: 1 (low) to 5 (high)	Promotes respect for cultural identity and spiritual renewal Promotes the interaction between humans and spiritual world	Plant and animal biodiversity reproduces naturally, since hunting or cultivation is prohibited
	2. Use of plants for spiritual food, drinks and medicine	Percentage of plant species used as spiritual food, drinks and medicine	Regulates and balances human beings, physically and spiritually	Many plant species have diverse uses, including ritual uses, which demand conservation and reproduction
	3. Teaching and revitalization of spiritual knowledge	• Degree of teaching of knowledge of rituals: 1 (low) to 5 (high) • Degree of revitalization of knowledge of rituals: 1 (low) to 5 (high)	Promotes the sharing and revitalization of spiritual knowledge.	The transmission of knowledge in the ritual use of plants and animals guarantees the future regeneration of these species.
	4. Revitalization and innovation of ritual celebrations	• Number of rituals • Percentage of families practicing rituals • Degree of teaching of ritual celebrations: 1 (low) to 5 (high) • Degree of revitalization of rituals: 1 (low) to 5 (high) • Number of rituals that have been innovated	Promotes the re-establishment of harmony and communication between society, nature and the spiritual world.	A sacred human–nature relationship guarantees worldviews with an important role for biodiversity
Social Dimension	5. Existence of historical awareness	Degree of knowledge and valuation of one's own history: 1 (low) to 5 (high)	Historical awareness revitalizes cultural identity	History reveals how biodiversity is one of the sources of a holistic vision of society
	6. Valuation of local knowledge on the sacred use of plants and animals	Degree of valuation of local knowledge: 1 (low) to 5 (high)	Legitimizing local knowledge strengthens cultural identity	Agroecology, human health and food sovereignty also depend on local knowledge concerning the sacred use of plant and animal species.
	7. Recovery of cultural expression	Degree of recovery of cultural expression:1 (low) to 5 (high)	Cultural expression strengthens collective identity and cohesion	As a part of cultural expression, indigenous seed fairs are important for cultivated biodiversity
Material Dimension	8. Diversity of plant species and wild animals	• Number of species • Species inventory	Presence of plant and animal species at sacred natural site make it possible to verify their availability and reproduction in time	Biodiversity is important for ecosystem health
	9. Presence of endemic plant and animal species	• Species inventory • Levels of density	The sacred natural site is important for the conservation of endemic species	Endemic plant and animal species require special care due to their significance for biodiversity
	10. Traditional and introduced plant varieties and animals	• Number of traditional varieties managed • Number of introduced varieties managed	Agricultural practices are not wholly banned from sacred natural sites	Agro-biodiversity needs monitoring to verify whether introduced species have negative results

Figure 18.3 Endogenous development indicators for biodiversity management at sacred natural sites

Source: Indicators for sacred sites developed from the agreed framework for planning, monitoring and assessment of the COMPAS Latin American programme (COMPAS Latin America, 2007)

Well-being dimension	Nr	Indicator	Baseline (2006)	Progress (2009)
Conservation of natural resources (material)	1	% of families which implement soil conservation measures	30%	60%
	2	% of families which implement agroecological practices	35%	64%
Ritual practices performed in relation to soil conservation and agroecology (spiritual)	3	% of families which implement family-based ritual practices related to soil conservation and agroecology	50%	58%
	4	% of families which participate in community-based ritual practices related to soil conservation and agroecology	25%	27%
Social organizational strength for self-management of natural resources (social)	5	% of families which apply local norms for the self-management of natural resources	60%	86%
	6	% of families which assume roles in the social organization of the community	60%	77%
	7	% of families which engage in community-based reciprocal labour sharing	55%	77%
	8	% of families which engage in traditional markets and festivals, within and outside the community	27%	27.5%

Figure 18.4 Indicators and quantitative progress for material, social and spiritual well-being comparing 2006 and 2009

Source: COMPAS 2009, Mid-Term Review

Figure 18.5 Community members and university staff join in a ritual to ask for protection from the ancestors at Incaracay, an Inca fort which now represents the ancestors, therefore a socially constructed sacred natural site, Bolivia

Source: COMPAS

to secular places. The weaknesses are that the sacred natural sites are often not adequately recognized and appreciated by the government and public. To preserve sacred natural sites it is not enough to invigorate cultural identity and local worldviews; rather, it is necessary to enforce public policies to support local efforts. Thus, the experience in Guatemala and the forthcoming Law on Sacred

Natural Sites represents an important step towards greater recognition of the indigenous Mayan peoples in a nation state.

Sacred natural sites may be semi-natural instead of pristine nature or wilderness. In some cases sacred natural sites may be too small or fragmented to possess much, if any, value for biodiversity conservation. Furthermore, sacred natural sites may be vulnerable to changes taking place in the associated culture and religion or to economic values being allowed to supersede religious ones. Traditional custodians may wish to keep sacred natural sites secret when there is a risk that knowledge and control may be reduced or removed from its traditional users.

Worldviews, as a key to understanding the web of life, and the ability to re-create relationships between biodiversity and cultural identity, are important elements of well-being and, thus, of endogenous development. Especially at sacred natural sites, the dynamic balance between material, social and spiritual dimensions can be understood, legitimized and maintained, leading to improved biodiversity management of the sacred natural site as well as the surrounding natural and (agri)cultural landscapes.

It is necessary to establish monitoring mechanisms in order to understand the development of biodiversity and the role of the indigenous and local communities at sacred natural sites. Linking cultural and biological diversity, the COMPAS programme proposes using well-being indicators, generated through a participatory process in line with a community's vision for endogenous development. This is an example of systematic research requested by an increasing number of international organizations and researchers (Sponsel, 2001; Verschuuren; 2007b, Wild and McLeod; 2008).

References

Bhagwat, S.A. and Rutte, C. (2006) 'Sacred groves: potential for biodiversity management', *Frontiers in Ecology and the Environment*, Ecological Society of America, vol 4, Issue 10, pp 519–524

Cocks, M.L. (2006) 'Moving beyond the realm of "indigenous" and "local" people"', *Human Ecology*, vol 34, no 2, pp185–200

COMPAS (2007) *Learning Endogenous Development, Building on Biocultural Diversity*, Intermediate Technology Publications Ltd (trading as Practical Action Publishing), Bourton on Dunsmore, Rugby, United Kingdom, available at www.compasnet. org/afbeeldingen/Books/Lendev/lendev.html (last accessed January 2010).

COMPAS Latin America (2007) 'Planning, monitoring and evaluation of well-being in COMPAS Latin America', COMPAS Leusden, available from www.compasnet.org/publications/articles (accessed November 2009)

COMPAS (2009) 'Mid-term review', unpublished document, COMPAS, Leusden

Dudley, N., Higgins-Zogib, L. and Mansourian, S. (eds) (2005) *Beyond Belief: Linking Faiths and Protected Areas for Biodiversity Conservation*, WWF, Equilibrium and ARC, Gland, Switzerland

Haverkort, B. and Reijntjes, C. (eds) (2006) *Moving Worldviews Reshaping Sciences, Policies and Practices for Endogenous Sustainable Development*, COMPAS series on Worldviews and Sciences, No 4, ETC/ COMPAS, Leusden, Netherlands

Medina, J. (2006) *Suma Qamaña. Por una convivialidad postindustrial*, Garza Azul Editores, La Paz

Millar, D. (2006) 'Ancestorcentrism: A basis for African sciences and learning epistemologies', in *African Knowledges and Sciences*, COMPAS Series Worldviews and Sciences, COMPAS-UDS-CTA, Leusden, Netherlands

Millennium Ecosystem Assessment (MA) (2003) 'Ecosystems and human well-being: A framework for assessment', Island Press, Washington, DC

Peace Agreements (2008) 'Congress of the Republic Of Guatemala,' Sixth Legislature, 2008–2012, Ciudad Guatemala

Persic, A. and Martin, G. (eds) (2008) 'Links between biological and cultural diversity-concepts, methods and experiences', Report of an International Workshop, UNESCO, Paris

Posey, D. (ed) (1999) 'Cultural and spiritual values of biodiversity, a comprehensive contribution to the UNEP Global Biodiversity Assessment', Intermediate Technology Publications, London

Rist, S., San Martin, J. and Tapia, N. (1999) 'Andean cosmovision and self-sustained development', in Haverkort, B. and Hiemstra, W. (eds) *Food for Thought*, ZED Publishers, pp177–190

San Martín, J. (2001) 'Conociendo a quienes afectan y guian el clima y la vida – el caso de los Andes', in AGRUCO-COMPAS, *Cosmovisión Indígena y Biodiversidad en América Latina*, Ediciones AGRUCO, La Paz, Bolivia

Sponsel, L.E. (2001) 'Do anthropologists need religion, and vice versa?: Adventures and dangers in spiritual ecology', in Crumley, C. (ed) *New Directions in Anthropology and Environment: Intersections*, Altamira Press, New York, pp177–200

Verschuuren, B. (2007a) *Believing is Seeing: Integrating cultural and spiritual values in conservation management*, Foundation for Sustainable Development, The Netherlands and IUCN, Gland, p100

Verschuuren, B. (2007b) 'An overview of cultural and spiritual values in ecosystem management and conservation strategies', in Haverkort, B. and Reijntjes, C. (eds) *Moving Worldviews Reshaping Sciences, Policies and Practices for Endogenous Sustainable Development*, COMPAS series on Worldviews and Sciences, No 4, ETC/COMPAS, Leusden, Netherlands

Verschuuren, B. (2010) 'Integrating biocultural values in nature conservation: Perceptions of cultural significant sites and species in adaptive management', in Pungetti, G., Oviedo, G. and D. Hooke (eds) *Sacred Species and Sites, Guardians of Biocultural Diversity*, Cambridge University Press, Cambridge

White, S. (2009) 'Well-being in development practice: Well-being in developing countries', working paper 09/50, available at www.welldev.org.uk (last accessed January 2010)

Wild, R. and McLeod, C. (2008) 'Sacred natural sites: Guidelines for protected area managers', Best Practice Protected Area Guidelines Series No 16, IUCN, Gland, Switzerland

19

Sacred Natural Sites in Technologically Developed Countries: Reflections from the Experience of the Delos Initiative

Josep-Maria Mallarach and Thymio Papayannis

Summary

This chapter discusses the conservation of sacred natural sites in technologically developed countries, from the viewpoint of the Delos Initiative, an international initiative launched in 2004 by the Specialist Group on Cultural and Spiritual Values of Protected Areas of the IUCN World Commission of Protected Areas. Case studies of the Delos Initiative include over 30 protected areas from all six IUCN management categories, found in Europe, North America, Asia and Oceania. They relate to mainstream religions and several traditional spiritual traditions, folk or ethnic religions. These cases combine outstanding natural, cultural and spiritual values.

The chapter presents the approach adopted by the Delos Initiative, including key developments on science, policy and mainstream religions. The second part distils the five years' experience of the Initiative, explaining the systematic approach adopted for the case studies and presenting some results at global, bioregional, national and site level and presenting some of the key strategic lines of work and summarizes the lessons learned.

Introduction

Sacred natural sites can be found in most of the world's countries, in different sizes and densities and with differing levels of significance. They are found in all major ecosystems and encompass all the IUCN categories of PAs (Verschuuren et al, 2008). Sacred sites constitute the oldest known form of nature conservation, and in some countries may be quite extensive. Management of sacred natural sites displays a variety of forms, some of which have proved amazingly effective and resilient over centuries, adapting to subsequent civilizations.

In technologically developed countries full recognition of their sacred natural sites has been hampered by reductionist and materialist ideology stemming from the belief that only the material world is real, and that only modern western science provides a valid understanding of reality (Smith, 1984). This has posed psychological barriers to the inclusion of cultural and spiritual values in conservation management. In legally established PAs where the management focus has normally been on natural heritage and biodiversity values, other important values related to the intangible cultural heritage have often been disregarded. In addition, the influence of religions and spiritual traditions on society in many technologically developed countries has been declining during the last decades and many western societies have an erroneous but widespread impression that only indigenous traditions possess a sacred view of nature and have sacred natural sites.

The western conservationist community has largely merged from within and embraced a scientific materialistic paradigm, failing to acknowledge that its reductionist concepts do not exist in the vast majority of the world's cultures nor expressed in their languages (Mallarach, 2008). Despite the positive results obtained, this has prevented, in many instances, the acceptance of the full spectrum of values that link human beings with nature. This essential factor for involving local populations and attaining the conservation and safeguarding of many outstanding natural areas that have been held in high esteem for reasons quite different from natural heritage values, is proven by many of the contributions included in this book. Recognition of sacred natural sites in technologically advanced countries had been overlooked and is now being addressed by the Delos Initiative.

Background: Some key developments

This chapter discusses three significant changes regarding the growing acceptance of the sacred dimension in nature: the scientific evidence of the limits of western science; the recognition of the need to account for governance factors and their implications, and the growing interest of mainstream religions in the environment and the conservation of biodiversity.

Impact of scientific discoveries on scientism

During the 20th century the impact of scientific discoveries showed the intrinsic limitations of modern western science. This has produced waves of effects in many different disciplines, such as the philosophy of science, physics, cosmology and theology. Significant milestones include Heisenberg's uncertainty principle (1926), Gödel's theorem (1931), Gibson's theory of visual perception (1950) and Dembski's theory of design (1998). As the physicist Wolfgang Smith (2003) puts it, 'hard science…is ultimately destructive of scientist myth'.

Many scientific research organizations have made significant contributions to the recognition of the diversity and richness of the spiritual and intangible aspects and values of nature, usually from the viewpoint of humanities (Gardner, 2003). A significant milestone was the series of conferences on religions and ecology organized by the Centre for the Study of the World's Religions of Harvard University, in which large numbers of scholars participated, issuing a remarkable collection of reference works (Tucker and Grim, 2000). Another was the publication of the comprehensive Encyclopaedia Religion and Nature (Taylor and Kaplan, 2005).

In academia, the field of 'religion and ecology', or 'ecological spirituality', is based on the convergence the philosophical (theoretical or structural) and the moral (ethical or spiritual). Many academic institutions offer specialized studies through the departments of religion and anthropology, where diverse contemporary worldviews are being taught without prejudice.

The governance component

Four main types of PA governance are now internationally recognized: sites managed by governmental agencies; PAs run and managed by shared governance; private PAs designated and managed by individual landowners, non-profit organizations or for-profit organizations, and sites owned and managed by indigenous and local communities (Borrini-Feyerabend et al, 2004; Dudley, 2008).

Governance arrangements are usually site-specific. In addition to human rights, IUCN has underlined seven basic principles for good governance which include: legitimacy and voice, subsidiarity, fairness, avoiding harm, direction, performance, accountability and transparency. These principles have been included in the latest version of guidelines for IUCN categories of PAs (Dudley, 2008) and are significant for the conservation of sacred natural sites.

Positive developments by mainstream religions

It is known that some branches of Christianity have maintained that human beings have the inherent and inalienable right to conquer and exploit nature and its resources, including indigenous peoples, which has contributed to the impact of the western colonization over the world (LaDuke, 2005). In addition, most Protestant churches opposed the sanctity of nature and abolished the old Christian sacred natural sites, including pilgrimage trails, hermitages, holy springs, etc., which are still very significant in Orthodox, Catholic as well as the Eastern Christian churches (see also Chapter 5).

During recent decades mainstream religions have demonstrated an increased interest and concern in environmental matters in response to growing awareness and disquiet regarding environmental matters by their followers (Palmer and Finley, 2003). Best practice case studies related to the major world religions have been documented in a number of works, for example the Chartered Institution of Water and Environmental Management (2008). The Ecumenical Patriarchate of the Christian Orthodox Church has led environmental interfaith initiatives focusing on water bodies and on broader environmental issues, mainly through shipboard symposia held in critical regions of the world. Since the 2002 joint declaration on the environment of Pope John Paul II and Ecumenical Patriarch Bartholomew I, several high level statements from Christian authorities have been calling for an 'ecological conversion' and new respect for nature (Bartholomew I, 2003). Simultaneously, good practices have been developed on most Christian monastic lands and are currently expanding.

Some achievements

At different levels dialogue developed between conservation organizations and mainstream religions has produced promising results. Dudley et al (2005) document the role that mainstream religions and indigenous spiritual traditions have played in 100 examples of SNS (Sacred Natural Sites) around the world. Bagader et al (1994) provide a good example on how a specific religious law can provide the basis for improved environmental policies in Islamic countries.

Multilateral agreements and programmes – such as UNESCO and its conventions (especially the Man and Biosphere Programme, World Heritage and Living Heritage Conventions), the Convention on Biological Diversity and earlier, the Ramsar Convention on Wetlands – have been instrumental in promoting a more holistic view of nature and in encouraging their member states to implement such an integrated approach (Bridgewater et al, 2007; see also Chapters 15 and Chapter 17).

At the 2003 World Parks Congress in Durban, South Africa, indigenous people, local communities, a number of working groups (including CSVPA) and major international organizations recommended that all PA systems should recognize and incorporate spiritual values and culture-based approaches into their conservation efforts.

Two out of many examples of positive achievements at the national level come from Europe and North America. Estonia shows that efforts at the policy level can be very effective. Estonia has more than 2000 ancient pre-Christian SNS, named *hii*. Only one-quarter of them are legally protected and this lack of legal protection, coupled with the weakening of traditional beliefs, puts many SNS at risk. Civil society organizations have taken to court public and private developers that are promoting projects that could potentially harm SNS. Maavalla Koda, a national NGO, is lobbying to achieve recognition for the native religion of Estonia and giving appropriate protection to SNS. In 2008 they convinced the Estonian government to promote an official inventory and research of SNS. Once completed, the Estonian Ministry of Culture will be responsible for the implementation of the conservation strategy (Kaasik and Valk, 2008).

The Sacred Mountains Programme in North America includes a number of national parks with Native American values and visions of nature. The programme demonstrates that for assurance of long-term sustainability, conservation programmes need to be grounded in deeply held values and beliefs and use careful, sensitive and inclusive language (Bernbaum, 2007).

Uneven results and new challenges

Nature-oriented conventions faced strong opposition to sensitization to cultural and spiritual values from countries that feared problems of national issues with indigenous peoples and local communities. Other concerns are global trade and major economic agreements, which contribute to the continuing loss of biodiversity. The most comprehensive assessments that have been made globally and in European technologically developed countries show unabated biodiversity losses continue (Hassan and Scholes, 2008; EEA, 2009).

Growing secularization has weakened the power of the institutionalized religions and the social influence of the traditional custodians resulting in the dimming of the intrinsic values and decreased protection of SNS. In fact, most PAs are managed as secular areas and there is a largely unspoken assumption that they do not have religious or spiritual significance (Byrne et al, 2006). Ignorance, indifference and neglect of sacred values result in cultural, religious and spiritual weakening or breakdown as well as the loss of the cosmic dimension of the religion. Close collaboration between the custodians of SNS and the managers of PAs is necessary to face these new challenges and to establish synergies for the benefit of conservation of both spiritual and natural heritage. This requires overcoming old mistrusts and prejudices, and learning each other's languages and values. These challenges are found in most of the world, including in technologically developed countries, despite the fact that they have the capacity and resources to manage their heritage. The reasons for that are complex and a few are mentioned here.

In some technologically developed countries, sites sacred to indigenous peoples are not respected

sufficiently against development, or are simply ignored. The US Forest Service expansion of a ski resort (and the use of waste water to create artificial snow) on the San Francisco Peaks in Arizona – sacred to 17 Native American Nations – is a case in point (Hamilton and Benally, 2009). The outstanding film *In the Light of Reverence* produced by the Sacred Land Film project documents this and other similar flagship cases in the US.

Major shrines and centres of Christian pilgrims located in natural areas are subjected to the pressures of intense mass tourism, which often undermine their spiritual functions. A typical example is the Meteora site in Thessaly, Greece, with its monasteries on rocky pinnacles. The site is subjected to heavy visitor flows and uncontrolled urbanization of the surrounding natural area (Lyratzaki, 2007). In other SNS that have been incorporated in PAs, the collaboration between their custodians and the PA management is weak, leading to conflicts and malfunction. At times, events related to mainstream religions may pose threats to protected natural areas. This is the case of the Virgin of El Rocío sanctuary in the Doñana National and Natural Parks, Andalusia, Spain. At certain times of the year, the sanctuary attracts over 1 million pilgrims who travel through the dunes and marshlands by foot or on horseback while praying, chanting and celebrating for several days (Falgarona, et al, 2007). Another example is the arrival – usually by car – of over 2 million visitors per year to the monastery of Montserrat, nested in a Nature Reserve in Catalonia, Spain (Mallarach, 2007).

The Vanatori-Neamt Nature Park in Moldavia includes the largest concentration of Christian Orthodox monasteries in Romania, receiving a continuous number of pilgrims. The monasteries are located in a mountain forested landscape with very diverse fauna, including healthy populations of top predators such as wolf (*Canis lupus*) and brown bear (*Ursus arctos arctos*), with a successful reintroduction programme for the European bison (*Bison bonasus*). The area is also considered one of the richest in Romania from a traditional culture point of view (Catanoiu, 2007).

A recent phenomenon related to the global movements and migration of people is the emergence of new SNS related to mainstream

Figure 19.1 Orthodox monastery of Rila, spiritual and cultural heart of Bulgaria, nested in the middle of a natural park managed as a nature reserve created by the Orthodox Church of Bulgaria

Source: Josep-Maria Mallarach

religions settling in new places. A well-documented case are the parklands around Sydney, Australia, where new SNS related to Buddhism and Mazdeism (Zoroastrianism) are being established by migrants from different religious backgrounds (Byrne et al, 2006). European examples include the Hinduization of some parts of the mountain landscape of the National Park of Snowdonia, Wales, or the Holy Arran Island in Scotland, a long-abandoned Celtic Christian sacred site, which has been re-sanctified as an interfaith centre led by a Tibetan Buddhist organization (Soria, 2007).

The approach of the Delos Initiative

The Delos Initiative was launched in 2004 to improve the management of the natural, cultural and spiritual values of PAs in developed countries. It was named after the Aegean island of Delos,

a sacred site during the classical times for both Greeks and Romans dedicated to Apollo, the god of light. Delos Island has no links to any single living faith and was the centre of a long-lasting Athenian Alliance, home to religious and political functions during the Hellenic civilization.

The Delos initiative approach is twofold and complementary. In technologically developed parts of the world, specific natural sites sacred to mainstream faiths or indigenous peoples were chosen (see Table 19.1) to reach a balance between regions, cultures and faiths. These sites were analysed and assessed – usually by local experts – focusing on their natural, cultural and spiritual values in order to understand their specificities and to identify threats and opportunities. The case studies were then discussed with local stakeholders, to reach a deeper comprehension of the issues. Recommendations to overcome the identified obstacles were elaborated with the main stakeholders where possible. The resulting

Table 19.1 Case studies of The Delos Initiative

SNS name	Protected Area name	IUCN category	Religion/spiritual tradition	Country
Äjjis/Ukonsaari	Lake Inari – Natura 2000 site	V	Sámi	Finland
Athos Holy Mountain	Athos Peninsula WHS	III	Christian Orthodox	Greece
Buila Vinturarita	Buila Vinturarita National Park	II	Christian Orthodox	Romania
Casentine Forests	National Park of the Casentine Forests	II	Christian Catholic	Italy
Dhimurru	Indigenous Protected Area	–	Yolngu Spirituality	Australia
Ein Gedi Oasis	En Gedi Nature Reserve and En Gedi Antiquities National Park	Ia	Judaism and Christianity	Israel
Holy Circle of Karamats-Cape Town	Table Mountain National Park and other PAs, including CCA	II–IV	Sunni Islam	S. Africa
Holy Island of Lindisfarne	Lindisfarne National Nature Reserve	IV	Celtic/Anglican Christianity	UK
Kii Mountain Range	Several National Parks	II–V	Shinto, Buddhism, Shugento	Japan
Kolovesi	Kolovesi National Park	II	Pre-historic	Finland
Numerous diverse names	National Park della Majella	II	From Pre-historic to Christian Catholic	Italy
Mani-san Mountain	Mani-san Mountain National Tourist Area	V	Folk religion	South Korea
Maulây Abd al-Salâm ibh Mashish	Jbel Bouhachen Site of Biological and Ecological Site. Intercontinental RoB of the Mediterranean	V	Sunni Islam	Morocco
Meteora	Meteora WHS	III	Christian Orthodox	Greece
Monastery of Chrysopigi	Chania WHS	–	Christian Orthodox	Greece
Monastery of Mileseva	Uvac-Milesevka Special Nature Reserve	IV	Christian Orthodox	Serbia
Monastery of Rila	Natural Park of Rila	III + V	Christian Orthodox	Bulgaria
Montsant	Serra del Montsant Natural Park	V	Christian Catholic	Spain
Montserrat	Muntanya de Montserrat Natural Park	III–V	Christian Catholic	Spain
Mount Nantai	Nikko National Park WHS and Ramsar sites	II	Shinto	Japan
Oconaluftee River	Great Smoky Mountains National Park	II	Native American (Cherokee)	USA
Poblet Monastery	Poblet Natural Area of National Significance + WHS	IV	Christian Catholic	Spain
San Francisco Peaks	Coconino National Forest	VI	Native American (Navajo)	USA
Santuario del Rocío	Doñana National Park and Doñana Natural Park	II	Christian Catholic	Spain
Solovetsky Islands	Solovetsky Archipelago WHS	V	Christian Orthodox	Russian Federation

Table 19.1 continued

SNS name	Protected Area name	IUCN category	Religion/spiritual tradition	Country
Tashi Ling Monastery	Park of Garraf	V	Tibetan Buddhist	Spain
The Holy Island of Arran	Arran Island Marine Reserve	–	Celtic – Buddhism	UK
Vanatori Neamt Natural Park	Vanatori Neamt Natural Park	V	Christian Orthodox	Romania
Via Lauretana	Several National Parks	Several	Christian Catholic	Italy

Source: J.-M. Mallarach and T. Pappayanis

case studies were presented to a peer group in international workshops and debated among its members. Lessons were extracted from them, and shared with others.

In parallel, theoretical work applied the fundamental principles that all spiritual traditions share, namely a belief in the symbolic character of nature and in the sacredness or holiness of natural celestial manifestations. Thus, they profess awe and profound respect for the natural order as a terrestrial reflection of a divine order. Hence the Initiative attempts to better characterize the main principles and practices of different spiritual traditions, to assess their relevance and influence in various contexts, based on the common ground with ecology and nature conservation (Tucker and Grim, 1988).

The initiative has led to conclusions encapsulated in the Montserrat Statement (Mallarach and Papayannis, 2007) and the Ouranoupolis Statement (Papayannis and Mallarach, 2009; also Wild and McLeod, 2008). These conclusions are being further evaluated, refined and completed with the analysis of additional case studies so that guidance can be provided, initially to the managers of protected natural areas that include sacred sites, but which can also be of use to the custodians of these sites, and other concerned stakeholders. These conclusions can be the basis for developing a specific set of guidelines for protected area managers.

Actions at international, regional and national levels

Although the Delos Initiative has been presented at many international congresses, symposia and

workshops in Europe, Asia and Africa, most of the work has been at European, either bioregional or national, levels with organizations such as Europarc, Eurosite, the Convention of the Carpathian PAs, Mediterranean Ramsar sites, the Spanish Section of the Europarc Federation and the Romanian Service of Natural Parks. For instance, the 11th and 12th Conferences of the Spanish Section of Europarc agreed to integrate cultural and spiritual values in planning and management of PAs in the Programme of work for PAs of Spain 2009–2013 (Europarc España, 2009). Another example was the first Conference of the Carpathian Convention on Protected Areas in Romania in 2008, which approved the identification and characterization of the Carpathian cultural identity in the PAs – including spiritual, cultural and natural values – in the Programme of Work, and established a working group for tangible and intangible cultural heritage of protected areas.

The Delos Initiative is planning complementary guidance for dealing with the issue of overlapping of sacred sites from different religions and spiritual traditions. This is a common phenomenon in regions where SNS have been used by successive religions and spiritual traditions. Mount Sinai is just one example of this (Grainger and Gilbert, 2008).

In Europe, only a few countries have SNS related to living indigenous traditions. Instead many ancient SNS are now archaeological monuments or places of cultural heritage. However SNS related to mainstream religions are found in PAs belonging to all IUCN categories. In some countries entire systems of PAs have been established on lands belonging to religious organizations. For instance,

Figure 19.2 Fire-lighting ceremony in a temple of the Kii Mountain Range, a Buddhist-Shinto pilgrimage complex protected by several national parks, south of Kyoto, Japan

Source: Edwin Bernbaum

the National Parks of South Korea are owned or managed by religious organizations. Many religious organizations are significant landowners of natural areas of outstanding quality in various countries, including Romania, Bulgaria, Serbia and Greece.

Lessons learned

General conclusions have been drawn from the work carried out during the Delos workshops at Montserrat, Spain, and Ouranoupolis, Greece.

The sacred remains potentially one of the most powerful drivers for conservation, inspiring feelings of awe, veneration and respect. This is demonstrated by SNS, sacred landscapes or particular sacred features that have been an effective form of nature conservation over the ages, even in most technologically developed countries. Some SNS are of local importance, while others have a broader significance, for wider groups, cultures, traditions and religions. Along with the current neglect of many SNS, there is interest and even a revival of a small number of them.

In most cultures nature has significant intrinsic values and meanings – including cultural and spiritual – which are still considered key values for society. In fact, followers of mainstream religions often understand nature as a manifestation or sign of some deeper, unseen, sacred reality, in whatever form that may be considered.

The spiritual aspects of nature can contribute greatly to the conservation of a country's natural heritage. They do so directly through inspiring people and involving them in conservation actions. Taking intangible values into consideration has in many different countries contributed to a significant broadening of the social support for nature conservation.

Certain rights should be inalienable. The traditional rights of the custodians of sacred sites must be safeguarded from insensitive public or private development interventions and from misguided conservation efforts, while their participation in determining the future of the PA in which they are concerned is ensured.

All measures and initiatives concerning the natural, cultural and spiritual aspects of SNS must respect the universal rights of people, as defined in numerous well-known conventions, and be grounded on sound and equitable participatory approaches.

Particular respect and recognition should be addressed to sites in PAs that are sacred for indigenous peoples, local communities and minorities, including new immigrants. These people often lack the capacity and means to defend their SNS. In places where multiple religions and/or spiritualities, or multiple branches of the same religion, co-exist, it is necessary to recognize their different approaches to nature and their implications for conservation, promoting the identification of common elements, so that interfaith collaboration can be encouraged for the conservation of the natural heritage.

An integrated management approach of PAs must include cultural and spiritual values in the planning processes. This requires the preparation, approval and implementation of integrated management plans for PAs that include or affect sacred sites. This encompasses the establishment of appropriate systems for evaluation and feedback, which incorporate natural, cultural and spiritual aspects, giving balanced weight to each of them. Such plans must be established with the participation of all stakeholders concerned, custodians of local communities and religious organizations alike.

It is necessary to ensure close and equitable collaboration between the custodians of the sacred sites and those responsible for the management of PAs (including related policy-makers), with mutual respect of their different mentalities and prerogatives. Dialogue should be encouraged so that better understanding of each other's position and requirements can be reached and a unified or coordinated approach satisfying both sides can be attained. However, synergy between spiritual and conservation approaches should not be limited to sacred sites in officially designated PAs only, but should extend to broader landscapes.

Capacity building is needed so that custodians of sacred sites can be exposed to the practices of nature conservation – including integrated management – and PA managers become better able to appreciate the spiritual approach and requirements of the custodians of the religious or spiritual heritage. Intercultural dialogue, joint education, research and art activities can play a positive role in bridging the gap between cultural/spiritual concerns and conservation initiatives of SNS and facilitate collaboration between the two. Achieving complete synergy would be the ideal. The resulting benefits are already evident in sites where such holistic approaches have been implemented.

It is time for those making policy and management decisions to give more recognition to the inspirational values, healing powers and other values of SNS. This will enable a stronger and deeper relation to nature by modern societies, and less to the material short-term and short-sighted profits. This would be a crucial contribution to correct a materialistic values system that has over-exploited nature and to help redress the trends that have led to the global ecological crisis.

References

Bagader, A.A., El-Chirazi El-Sabbagh, A.T., As-Sayyid Al-Glayand, M. and Izzi-Deen Samarrai, M.Y. (1994) 'Environmental protection in Islam', IUCN Environmental Policy and Law Paper No. 20. Gland Switzerland and Cambridge, UK

Bartholomew I (2003) *Cosmic Grace, Humble Prayer: The Ecological Vision of the Green Patriarch Bartholomew I*, William B. Erdmans Publishing Company Grand Rapids, Michigan

Bernbaum, E. (2007) 'Great Smoky Mountains (shagonage) and Qualla Boundary: Tennessee and North Carolina, Southern Appalachian Mountains, United States of America', in Mallarach, J.-M. and Papayannis, T., *Nature and Spirituality in Protected Areas: Proceedings of the 1st Workshop of the Delos Initiative*, Abadia de Montserrat and IUCN, Sant Joan les Fonts, Spain

Borrini-Feyerabend, G.A., Kothari, A and Oviedo, G. (2004) *Indigenous and Local Communities and Protected Areas: Towards Equity and Enhanced Conservation*, Best practice protected area Guidelines Series No 11, IUCN, Gland and Cambridge

Bridgewater, P., Arico, S. and Scott, J. (2007) 'Biological diversity and cultural diversity: The heritage of nature and culture through the looking glass of multilateral agreements', *International Journal of Heritage Studies*, vol 13, no 4–5, July–September

Byrne, D., Goodall, H., Wearing, S. and Cadzow, A. (2006) 'Enchanted parklands', *Australian Geographer*, vol 37, no 1, pp103–115

Catanoiu, S. (2007) 'Vanatori-Neamt Natural Park. A Romanian Jerusalem', in Mallarach, J.-M. and

Papayannis, T., *Nature and Spirituality in Protected Areas: Proceedings of the 1st Workshop of the Delos Initiative*, Abadia de Montserrat and IUCN, Sant Joan les Fonts, Spain, pp289–309

Chartered Institution of Water and Environmental Management (2008) *Faiths and the Environment*, London

Dudley, N. (ed) (2008) *Guidelines for Applying Protected Area Management Categories*, IUCN, Gland, Switzerland

Dudley, N., Higgins-Zogib, L. and Mansourian, S. (2005) *Beyond Belief: Linking Faiths and Protected Areas to Support Biodiversity Conservation*, WWF, Equilibrium and Alliance of Religions and Conservation, Gland, Switzerland

EEA (2009) 'Progress towards the European 2010 biodiversity target: Indicator fact sheets', EEA Technical report No 5/2009, Copenhagen

Europarc España (2009) *Programa de trabajo para las Áreas Protegidas 2009–2013*, Fungobe, Madrid

Falgarona, J., García-Varela, J. and Estarellas, J. (2007) 'Doñana National and Natural Parks, Sanctuary of La Virgen del Rocío', in Mallarach, J.-M. and Papayannis, T., *Nature and Spirituality in Protected Areas: Proceedings of the 1st Workshop of the Delos Initiative*, Abadia de Montserrat and IUCN, Sant Joan les Fonts, Spain, pp175–199

Gardner, G. (2003) 'Invoking the spirit: Religion and spirituality in the quest for a sustainable world', *Worldwatch Paper*, vol 164

Golser, K. (1995) *Religion and Ecology: Responsibility Toward Creation in the Great Religions*, EDB Bologna

Grainger, J. and Gilbert, F. (2008) 'Around the sacred mountain: The St Katherine protectorate in Mount Sinai, Egypt', in Mallarach, J.-M. (ed) *Protected Landscapes and Cultural and Spiritual Values*, IUCN, GTZ and Obra Social de Caixa Catalunya, Heidelberg, pp13–21

Hamilton, L. and Benally, J. (2009) 'Holy San Francisco Peaks, California, USA', in Papayannis, T. and Mallarach, J.-M. (eds) *Proceedings of the 2nd Workshop of the Delos Initiative, Ouranoupolis 2007*

Hassan, R. and Scholes, R. (eds) (2008) *Current Status and Trends, Millennium Ecosystem Assessment*, Island Press, Washington, DC

Kaasik, A. and Valk, H. (2008) 'Looduslikud pühapaigad: väärtused ja kaitse', Maavalla Koda, Tartu Ülikool, Õpetatud Eesti Selts, Maalehe Raamat (includes English translation)

LaDuke, W. (2005) *Recovering the Sacred: The Power of Naming and Claiming*, South End Press, Cambridge, MA

Lee, C and Schaaf, T. (2003) *International Workshop on the Importance of SNS for Biodiversity Conservation*, UNESCO, Kunming and Xishuangbanna Biosphere Reserve, People's Republic of China

Lyratzaki, I. (2007) 'Meteora World Heritage Site', in Mallarach, J.-M. and Papayannis, T., *Nature and Spirituality in Protected Areas: Proceedings of the 1st Workshop of the Delos Initiative*, Abadia de Montserrat and IUCN Sant Joan les Fonts, Spain, pp251–261

Mallarach, J.-M. (2007) 'Montserrat', in Mallarach, J.-M. and Papayannis, T., *Nature and Spirituality in Protected Areas: Proceedings of the 1st Workshop of the Delos Initiative*, Abadia de Montserrat and IUCN, Sant Joan les Fonts, Spain, pp151–162

Mallarach, J.-M. (ed.) (2008) *Cultural and Spiritual Values of Protected Landscapes: Values of Protected Landscapes*, Vol 2, IUCN, GTZ, Caixa Catalunya

Nasr, S.H. (1996) *Religion and the Order of Nature*, Oxford University Press, Oxford, UK and New York

O'Brien, J. and Palmer, M. (2007) *The Atlas of Religions: Mapping Contemporary Challenges and Beliefs*, Earthscan, London

Palmer, M. and Finley, V. (2003) *Faith in Conservation: New Approaches to Religions and the Environment*, The World Bank, Washington DC, Part 2, pp67–145

Papayannis, T. and Mallarach, J.-M. (eds) (2009) *Proceedings of the 2nd Workshop of the Delos Initiative – Ouranoupolis 2007*, IUCN and Med-INA, Gland and Athens

Putney, A. (2008) *Sacred Dimensions: Understanding the Cultural and Spiritual Values of Protected Areas*, IUCN-WCPA, Gland, Switzerland

Schaaf, T. (ed) (2006) *International Symposium on Conserving Cultural and Biological Diversity: The Role of Sacred Natural Sites and Cultural Landscapes*, UNESCO, Tokyo, Japan

Smith, W. (1984) *Cosmos and Transcendence: Breaking through the Barrier of Scientistic Belief*, Sherwood Sugden and Company, Peru

Smith, W. (2003) *The Wisdom of Ancient Cosmology: Contemporary Science in Light of Tradition*, The Foundation for Traditional Studies, Oakton, VA

Soria, I. (2007) 'The Holy Island, Arran, Scotland', in Mallarach, J.-M. and Papayannis, T., *Nature and Spirituality in Protected Areas: Proceedings of the 1st Workshop of the Delos Initiative*, Abadia de Montserrat and IUCN, Sant Joan les Fonts, Spain, pp219–234

Taylor, B.R. and Kaplan J. (2005) *Encyclopedia of Religion and Nature*, Continuum, London

Tucker, M.E. and Grim, J. (1988) 'Religions of the world and ecology: Discovering the common ground', *Earth Ethics*, vol 10, no 1

Verschuuren, B., Mallarach, J.-M. and Oviedo, G. (2008) 'Sacred sites in protected areas', in Dudley, N. and Stolton, S. (eds) *Defining Protected Areas: An International Conference in Almeria, Spain*, IUCN, Gland, pp164–170

Wild, R. and McLeod, C. (eds) (2008) 'Sacred natural sites: Guidelines for managers', UNESCO-IUCN, Gland, Switzerland

20

Developing a Methodology and Tools for Inventorying Sacred Natural Sites of Indigenous Peoples in Mexico

Mercedes Otegui-Acha, Gonzalo Oviedo,
Guillermo Barroso, Martín Gutiérrez, Jaime Santiago,
Bas Verschuuren

Summary

The methodology presented in this chapter is the first systematic approach at a national scale to develop, test and implement a methodology and tools for inventorying sacred natural sites based on an ecosystem and habitat types approach. The methodology has been developed based on data from around Mexico and is currently being tested in the states of Sinaloa, Sonora and Chihuahua in northwestern Mexico. This chapter presents the methodology in steps and also introduces the tools to accompany and implement each of them. The steps include guidance on the identification of the main stakeholders involved, the time frame suggested and the benchmarks to monitor a progress leading to a successful implementation of the proposed methodological framework. The chapter closes with the main findings drawn from implementation of the initial part of the methodology illustrated by two emblematic case studies of indigenous sacred natural sites. These examples can assist with making recommendations for further

developing the criteria used in the methodology for the identification and distribution of sacred natural sites and sets an optimistic tone for future exercises of a similar nature. Lessons learned from this and other similar exercises will, with no doubt, render an ameliorated and enriched methodology.

Introduction

Sacred Natural Sites can be considered an expression of Mexico's biological and cultural richness. The country is considered biologically mega-diverse, with approximately 10 per cent of all living species. It is one of the top five countries in species richness of vascular plants and of vertebrates such as mammals and reptiles. Levels of endemism are high, often similar to those of island countries, ranging from around 10 per cent for birds to more than 60 per cent for amphibians and some groups of plants (Mittermeier et al, 1997). In terms of ethnic diversity, Mexico harbours at least 62 different indigenous peoples and is home to America's largest population of indigenous communities (Toledo, 2003) or, using ethnolinguistic criteria, around 230 endemic indigenous languages.

Despite external threats and challenges, sacred natural sites in Mexico show resilience and continue to protect natural, cultural and spiritual values of the communities and their environment. Little is known about their numbers, and distribution, or their state of conservation and the management approaches maintained by their custodian communities. These knowledge gaps do not allow for appropriate planning, action and support of their conservation and legal protection. Although many formal protected areas in Mexico include sacred natural sites within their boundaries, the vast majority is left without protection and many of them are bound to be lost before their importance is properly understood. Therefore, there is a need to prioritize registration, documentation and recognition of sacred natural sites currently lacking support. Recognition of the cultural and spiritual dimensions of sacred natural sites, and the rights of their custodian communities, is urgently needed and will contribute to the conservation of biodiversity inside and outside protected areas.

Defining sacred natural sites and landscapes

A careful bibliographical review shows, among other things, that there is not a widely accepted definition of sacred natural sites (Jeanrenaud, 2001; Dudley et al, 2005; Wild and McLeod, 2008).

The term 'sacred natural site' is used in a generic sense as to include those sacred entities (e.g. 'spatially disperse and definable sacred landscapes', 'sacred natural physiographical features' and communities of 'sacred floral and faunal species') that are venerated and held in awe by the communities involved. Thus, while the term may refer to sites of spiritual importance, it also encompasses places that are of symbolic significance – where space, place, memory and spiritual meaning come together (Jeanrenaud, 2001; Verschuuren, 2007). Based on the above, a classification of Sacred Natural Site has been developed according to spatial scales as follows:

- Spatially disperse sacred landscape: having an extensive geographical influence zone; transcending geopolitical borders, usually unified and connected through sacred pilgrimages routes or symbolic sacred natural physiographical features such as rivers.

- Spatially defined sacred landscape: having well-defined and cohesive spiritual and cultural norms and practices as well as geographic limits; extension and geographical limits.
- Sacred natural physiographical features: include a wide array of manifestations that can be contained within spatially disperse or defined sacred landscapes, ranging from mountains, oasis, valleys, rivers, lakes, caves, forest groves, coastal waters, islands, wetlands, trees, groves of shrubs, stone arrangements, quarries, caves, ponds, outcrops, gorges, ravines, hills, rock holes, creeks, waterholes, sand hills, dunes, termite mounds, etc.
- Sacred floral and faunal species: include those communities of species that are attributed a sacred, ritualistic and/or medicinal use by the indigenous and traditional community. Their presence confers a sacred status to either a landscape or a sacred natural physiographical feature.

A proposed framework for developing an inventory of sacred natural sites

The proposed framework for implementing the methodology and tools is divided into five distinct steps, see Figure 20.1.

The initial situational analysis was based on a literature review and interviews in order to establish an updated status quo of sacred natural sites among key stakeholders. In the next step, an overlay of protected areas, indigenous territories and the intactness of the original vegetation types and hydrological data provided by Mexico's National Commission for the Knowledge of Biodiversity (CONABIO) were conducted using a GIS-based methodology (see Table 20.1). Combining these sources of information provided an initial basis for carrying out situational analysis in the field in order to confirm the existence of sacred natural sites and their viability for conserving biodiversity together with their need for protection.

Step1: Baseline information

In this phase bibliographic research was combined with open-ended interviews conducted with key

Proposed Implementation Framework of a Methodology an Tools for Inventorying Sacred Natural Sites						
Methodological Steps proposed	1. Baseline Information		2. Distribution and Identification		3. Site Specific Inventory	4. Information Analysis and Compilation of Results	5. Dissemination and Communication of Results
			Coarse Filter Criteria	Fine Filter Criteria			
Tools to be used	• Bibliographical review • Key stakeholders questionnaires • Open-ended interviewing • Development of Research Protocol		• GIS mapping	• GIS mapping	• Registration Template • MoU • FPIC	• Excel Database	• Guidelines on how to apply the methodology • Webpage • Publications • Bulletins • Magazines
Key stakeholders involved	Spiritual and traditional indigenous authorities; National environmental and cultural authorities; State and local authorities; Private owners; Indigenous, community - based and non - governmental organizations	Representatives	Conservation Actors; GIS Specialists; Researcher(s)	Conservation Actors; GIS Specialists; Researcher(s)	Indigenous and Traditional Rightful Representatives Researcher(s) Government Authorities	Researcher(s) and associated institution(s) Data base expert Indigenous and traditional rightful representatives Government Reps	Spiritual and traditional indigenous authorities; National environmental and cultural authorities; State and local authorities; Private owners; and NGO's
Duration	3 months		3 months		12 months	2 months	6 months plus long term dissemination activities
Benchmarks	• Questionnaires completed and evaluated • Protocol developed and ready for implementation		• Thematic GIS maps produced and final map detailing potential distribution of SNS resulting from applying coarse and fine filters		• SNS information captured • MoU accorded upon and implemented • FPIC accorded upon and implemented • Community rightful reps. participating in project	• Database on registered SNS	• Dissemination tools implemented

Figure 20.1 A proposed framework for developing an inventory of sacred natural sites

Source: Otegui-Acha (2007)

stakeholders such as representatives of indigenous and traditional peoples organizations, conservation and cultural governmental authorities, national conservation organizations representatives and academia representatives. Identification of the institutional context and the stakeholders involved is key in this step. In addition the development of research protocols are needed in this phase. They are essentially guidelines to foster positive and mutually-beneficial working relationships by promoting good, ethical and responsible research, as well as equitable exchanges among the communities and institutions/individuals conducting the research. This methodology includes a wide diversity of cultural, social, political, economic and geographic situations in which indigenous and traditional peoples live. Based on this experience the development of a universally applicable draft protocol requires a flexible, adaptive and sensitive approach.

Research protocols are confirmed by formal written agreements of various natures. The agreement has important benefits for all parties, as it provides clarity on the project. Indigenous and traditional communities are often hesitant about working with outside researchers, but communities can also be empowered through a well-negotiated agreement. For researchers, an agreement defines the expectations of the community and makes

clear the role of the researcher(s) in the project and should include the stakeholders involved, propose a timeframe and have mutually agreed benchmarks. These benchmarks – to be established over a three-month period – include a completed bibliographical review, the identification of stakeholders, the development of questionnaires, interviews being conducted, the completion of questionnaires and protocols for future collaboration evaluated under consultation.

Step 2: Distribution and identification

A methodological approach based on Ordoñez (1999) and Oviedo and Maffi (2000) was executed in combination with the use of a Geographic Information System (GIS). The GIS allowed for the application of a 'coarse filter' and a 'fine filter' process summarized in Table 20.1. The coarse filter process focuses on sacred natural sites of indigenous and traditional peoples with rich cultural, spiritual and biodiversity traits.

Coarse filter

For the biodiversity component, the Terrestrial and Hydrological Priority Regions established

Table 20.1 Step 2: Analysis of potential distribution of sacred natural sites

Step 2: Distribution and Identification		
COARSE FILTER		
Terrestrial Priority Sites, Hydrological Priority Sites	Indigenous and Traditional Regions	Protected Areas Distribution
Potential SNS Distribution Sites (Coarse Filter)		
FINE FILTER		
Primary Vegetation %, Cover of Potential SNS distribution sites		Sacred Natural, Physiographical, Features
Potential SNS, Distribution Sites (Fine Filter)		

Source: Otegui-Acha (2007)

by the National Commission for Knowledge and Use of Biodiversity (CONABIO) were used (Arriaga et al, 2000). These 'priority' regions were determined in an inclusive participatory process in which all the main conservation actors in the country intervened; hence, these regions are widely acknowledged as the most accurate and representative when depicting those areas with a high and priority conservation value in Mexico. The component of indigenous and traditional peoples was represented by 'traditional space', a geographical display of areas historically occupied by indigenous and traditional groups before and after the Spanish conquest that show unique linguistic and cultural expressions, cosmovision, as well as physical and natural traits, altitude and climate conditions according to the National Commission for Indigenous Development (CDI) (Serrano Carreto, 2006). For this purpose, three different information sources were combined:

1   a map of 77 per cent of the indigenous and traditional regions of Mexico which constitute around 8 million people (CDI, 1998);
2   filling in the information gaps, additional data from Toledo (2003) was used which resulted in a more comprehensive and complete representation;
3   field research enabled the inclusion of indigenous and traditional sites and pilgrimage routes that are used seasonally.

These results were overlapped with federal and state protected areas which show that there is a significant coincidence between these areas and those lands with an indigenous and traditional presence.

Fine filter

The fine filter further reveals the potential distribution of indigenous peoples' sacred natural sites with high biodiversity value. The degree of conservation of the potential sacred natural sites distribution areas was determined by using percentages of primary vegetation occurrence as an indicator of the sites conservation status. The smaller percentages denoting a 'disturbed to highly disturbed environment' while the higher values (above the 34 per cent mark) were associated with areas in a 'pristine/almost pristine state'.

Areas with higher percentages of primary vegetation are presumed to contain sacred natural sites in a pristine or almost pristine state. Distribution areas under the 34 per cent mark indicate highly degraded environments that may still contain sacred natural sites as the last surviving nodes of resilience and genetic reservoirs and regeneration sites. Their value cannot be underestimated and a further in-depth analysis must be conducted.

Types of physiographical features

In a new attempt to narrow down further the potential areas of sacred natural sites with high biodiversity values, it was decided to focus on and locate the most 'popular' of these sacred features:

- Mountains higher than 2500 metres are included because field experience shows that it is the higher mountains that usually elicit reverence as well as mountains displaying distinct features such as geometrical and humanoid forms, coloured strata, etc.
- Water bodies: in desert-like environments to be found in the northwestern and northeastern regions of Mexico, most water bodies (from creeks and ponds to oasis) are sacred entities revered by the local communities.
- Caves play a key role in the spirituality of Mesoamerican indigenous and traditional groups. At the national level the distribution of caves, caverns, cavities and subterranean features has not yet been compiled. Therefore in this analysis they have been substituted using a proxy of karstic strata which most commonly contain these geological features.
- Sacred species of plants and animals exist and would need to be identified along with their distribution. In Mexico there are several endemic species – such as the 'peyote', the Huichols' sacred cactus – that have been conferred a sacred status and that are to be included in this analysis (Otegui-Acha, 2003).
- Indigenous and traditional pilgrimage routes and destinations usually unify distantly spatially disperse and defined sacred landscapes and are dotted with many sacred natural physiographical features along their way. The final map of potential distribution of sacred natural sites is to be used as the basic starting point to conduct a site-specific inventory of biodiversity rich sacred natural sites (Step 3).

Preliminary testing of the methodology and tools

The following section illustrates the results obtained in a first run of Step 2 of the methodology, and the tools proposed; it proves the effectiveness and accuracy of the methodological approach developed in three Mexican Sacred Natural Sites case studies while identifying a potential distribution area of additional sacred natural sites for a future site-specific inventory.

Figure 20.2 Seri Indian 'Comcaac' singing and praying in ceremony with Tiburon Island in the background

Source: Alonso Martínez

Case Study 1: Seri Territory

The Seri indigenous region has one of the highest percentages (56–91 per cent) of primary vegetation cover at the national level resulting from the sound traditional management system implemented by the Seri community. The author's previous field work has shown that indeed the Seri territory, including the peninsular and insular (Isla Tiburon) extensions, is dotted with sacred entities varying in size, importance and significance. The Seri territory as a whole can be categorized as a 'Spatially Defined Sacred Landscape' dotted by various sacred natural physiographical features (water ponds, rock formations, coastal mangroves, etc.) that are revered by the community due to their spiritual significance (see Figure 20.2).

The Seri territory also contains communities of sacred floral and faunal species, because diverse sacred species with a medicinal use converge in its waters and dry lands. These findings confirm the soundness of the criteria used in both the coarse and the fine filters to delimit a potential SNS distribution area.

Case Study 2: Wirikuta

Wirikuta is the final destination of an annual pilgrimage ritual performed by the Huichols and was not initially included in the coarse filter analysis that only registered indigenous regions with a permanent indigenous and traditional presence. This site, being visited only during the fall by the Huichol pilgrims, was to be included though, via the fine filter that contemplates the inclusion of these cyclic sacred destinations.

Wirikuta is a spatially defined sacred landscape (approximately 140,000 hectares) that is dotted with sacred natural physiographical features, such as water bodies (as identified in the map), mountains (above 2500 metres), rock formations, etc. Wirikuta has a community of sacred floral cacti, formed by the 'peyote', the revered cactus of the Huichols, which they use in their communications with their gods. The Huichol spatially disperse sacred landscape is united by this pilgrimage route, of which a fraction crosses the Wirikuta area. The total route extends 800 kilometres through Central Mexico.

Step 3: Site-specific inventory

The researcher is now ready for the site-specific inventory of the selected sacred natural sites: to locate them on the ground and to conduct their inventory. This step is based on building local trust from the offset.

Field trips will be made to collect information available and to confirm the biocultural richness of the selected sites. In this phase, the researcher will get to know the selected sites and closely work with the indigenous people and their organizations. The main steps of this phase include:

- selection of site/community specific inventory;
- vision and common goals assessment;
- socio-cultural assessment;
- inventorying strategy development;
- inventorying implementation.

Any initial accords between the researcher and the communities should be formalized via a Memorandum of Understanding (MoU) to clarify and formalize the working relationship as outlined in Step 3. MoUs, while not creating binding or legal obligations on either party involved, provide the basis of their relationships and are a public agreement of the collaborative arrangements which they have, and intend to have, with each other. The registration template is a key tool for this step. After extensive bibliographic research and in accordance with the working premises set up in this research project, the following template is proposed for an initial site-specific inventory:

In addition, and to ensure a broad acceptance and commitment to the sacred natural sites inventorying strategy, a free, prior and informed consent agreement must be agreed and signed by all parties involved (see Box 20.1 and Figure 20.3).

Step 4: Information compilation

The recorded sacred natural sites information is to be filtered and condensed into several fields depicting the sites most relevant cultural and natural features – to be made compatible with various international databases such as UNEP's World Conservation Monitoring Centre (WCMC) – and should include the following information:

- name of sacred entity (native and western denominations);
- indigenous and traditional peoples;
- location (indigenous and traditional region);
- coordinates (if available);
- size (in hectares);
- sacred entity category;
- in/out terrestrial/hydrological priority sites;
- percentage of primary vegetation cover;
- in/out formal protected area;
- degree of threat: high, medium, low.

Step 5: Results dissemination

It is recommended that diverse methods of disseminating the project results be considered to ensure maximum and widespread use of the project findings. Given the delicate nature of the research subject, the dissemination of its results must be guided by an overall pervading ethical responsibility on the part of the researcher and the institution he/she represents, including careful reviewing of copyright issues.

Research results are often highly technical, captured in foreign languages and not widely available. Therefore the materials need to be made accessible, understandable and useful to the communities and custodians of sacred natural sites in the following ways:

- writing up project results in local languages;
- elaboration of appropriate documents, posters and multimedia for distribution of information among concerned communities and custodians;

Table 20.2 Sacred natural sites proposed registration template

Sacred natural sites proposed registration template

1 Name of the site (native and western denominations)

Name:
Origin and significance, spiritual and cultural context:
Indigenous and/or traditional groups involved:

2 Location and size

Geographic location (country, province/state/department/latitude/longitude):
Extension in hectares:
Spatial classification of sacred entity:

3 Protection status

If within the limits of a protected area, specify which:
Current authority (government, community, religious or spiritual group). Historic evolution of management authority:
Management instruments, if any (management plan, co-management model, community agreement, land use plan, other):
Land tenure status:
Monitoring and Evaluation System (if any):
Relationship to formally declared protected areas or other Sacred Natural Sites:
Relationship to international categories (World Heritage Site, Biosphere Reserve, Cultural Landscape, etc.):

4 Environmental significance

Site ecosystem type/uniqueness:
Priority terrestrial region – CONABIO:
Hydrological terrestrial region – CONABIO:
Type of vegetation (primary, secondary):
Degree of conservation:
Watershed protection:
Other:

5 Cultural significance

Importance of site for indigenous and traditional communities:
Societal role, meaning:
Secrecy status:

6 Current situation

Strengths, weaknesses, opportunities, threats:
Government and NGO involvement:
Financial support, if any:

7 Information sources

References/bibliography:
Videos:
Graphic materials/visual aids:

8 Lessons learned that might help other sacred natural sites custodians or managers and planners

9 Annexes (if pertinent, decrees, pertinent legislation, etc.)

Source: Otegui-Acha (2007)

- engaging into ongoing processes and international meetings promoted by IUCN and UNESCO (see for example Lee and Schaaf, 2003);
- posting project results on national and international websites;

- production and publication of guidelines on how to implement step by step the methodology and tools developed;
- articles on major research findings in scientific, and cultural journals;

Figure 20.3 Signing a free, prior and informed consent agreement with the Mayo Community in Mexico

Source: Jaime Santiago

Box 20.1 Free, Prior and Informed Consents (FPIC)

Free, Prior and Informed Consents (FPIC) is based on a legal commentary prepared for the Working Group on Indigenous Populations. FPIC is a way of formally documenting that the people taking part in a research project understand what the project is about and what they will be asked to do, and to give permission for their knowledge to be used for the project. The main objective is to ensure that anyone who participates in a given research project is informed about:

- how you propose to conduct the research;
- what you are asking the participants to do;
- what the research products will be;
- who will own them and rights to reproduce them;
- how you will protect personal or culturally restricted information;
- what will happen to any raw data;
- how the researcher will communicate to the participants the results;
- how to record the indigenous and traditional communities involved consent to all of the above before participating in the inventorying process.

Source: CRC (n.d.)

- writing up project highlights in accessible languages in general information magazines.

Conclusion

Organizations such as UNESCO, WHC, IUCN, WWF and WCPA have prioritized the conservation of sacred natural sites over the last decade (see Chapter 15). The work of Pronatura's Biocultural Unit presented in this chapter has been part of this stream of development but has focused on operationalizing a methodology for conserving sacred natural sites at the national level. The WCPA Specialist Group on Cultural and Spiritual Values of Protected Areas has since produced specific guidance on sacred natural sites (e.g. Wild and McLeod, 2008) that will allow for development of synergies with the outstanding research projects that, as in this case, further explore and elaborate on the conceptual issues related to the validation of Sacred Natural Sites as effective biocultural conservation mechanisms.

This methodology is currently being tested and a careful and extensive review of its core contents and tools proposed will be carried out once the lessons learned in the field are compiled, analysed and conclusions drawn from them. This methodology is thought to be the first to rapidly assess sacred natural sites at a national scale. Once revisions are made based on field testing this methodology it is expected to become a useful adaptable generic model ready to be applied in other countries. As such it is hoped that this methodology will offer a practical tool to assist countries to undertake work on sacred natural sites on a nationwide scale.

On a final note, we reiterate the need to pay attention to those indigenous and traditional conservation methods that – by respecting the inherent sacredness of nature – have proven successful and viable conservation methods throughout the ages: sacred natural sites are in fact a 'living' proof of it.

References

Arriaga, L., Espinoza, J.M., Aguilar, C., Martínez, E., Gómez, L. and Loa, E. (2000) *Regiones Terrestres Prioritarias de México*, Comisión Nacional para el Conocimiento y uso de la Biodiversidad, Mexico

CDI (1998) 'Mapa de conaculta y otros, la diversidad cultural de México, Colección Pueblos Indígenas de México', Instituto Nacional Indigenista, Mexico

CRC (n.d.) 'Prior Informed Consent Form', Desert Knowledge Cooperative Research Center, Alice Springs Australia, available at http://desertknowledgecrc.com.au/socialscience/downloads/Informedconsenttemplate.pdf (last accessed January 2010)

Dudley, N., Higgins-Zogib, L. and Mansourian, S. (2005) 'Beyond belief: Linking faiths and protected areas to support biodiversity conservation', Research report by WWF, Equilibrium and the Alliance of Religions and Conservation, WWF, Gland Switzerland

Jeanrenaud, S. (2001) *An International Initiative for the Protection of Sacred Natural Sites and other Places of Indigenous and Traditional Peoples with Importance for Biodiversity Conservation*, WWF, Gland, Switzerland

Lee, C. and Schaaf, T. (eds) (2003) 'The importance of sacred natural sites for biodiversity conservation', Proceedings of the international workshop, Kunming and Xishuangbanna Biosphere Reserve, China, 17–20 February 2003, UNESCO, Paris

Mittermeier, R.A., Goettsch, C. and Robles Gill, P. (Coordinators) (1997) 'Megadiversidad: Los países biológicamente más ricos del mundo', CEMEX, S.A. de C.V. México

Ordoñez, J.A.B. (1999) 'Captura de carbono en un bosque templado: el caso de San Juan Nuevo, Michoacan, Instituto Nacional de Ecologia', México, Secretaria del Medio Ambiente, Recursos Naturales y Pesca SEMARNAP, Mexico D.F., p72

Otegui-Acha, M. (2003) 'Wirikuta: The Wixarika/Huichol sacred natural site in the Chihuahuan Desert, San Luis Potosí', in Harmon, D. and Putney, D.A. (eds) *The Full Value of Parks: From the Economics to the Intangible*, Rowman and Litchfield Publishers, London

Otegui-Acha, M. (2007) *Developing and Testing a Methodology and Tools for the Inventorying of Sacred Natural Sites of Indigenous and Traditional Peoples*, Pronatura Mexico, Mexico

Oviedo, G. and Maffi, L. (2000) *Indigenous and Traditional Peoples of the World and Ecoregion Conservation: An Integrated Approach to Conserving the World's Biological Diversity*, WWF, Gland, Switzerland

Serrano Carreto, E. (2006) 'Comisión Nacional para el Desarrollo de los Pueblos Indígenas y Programa de las Naciones Unidas para el Desarrollo', Comisión Nacional para el Desarrollo de los Pueblos Indígenas (CDI) y, Programa Naciones Unidades de Desarrollo (*PNUD*), p147, México.

Toledo, V. M. (2003) 'Ecología, espiritualidad y conocimiento: Dela sociedad del riesgo a la sociedad sustentable', Programa de Naciones Unidas para el Medio Ambiente, Oficina Regional para América Latina y el Caribe y Universidad Iberoamericana, México

Verschuuren, B. (2007) 'An overview of cultural and spiritual values in ecosystem management and conservation strategies', in Haverkort, B. and Rist, S. (eds) *Endogenous Development and Bio-cultural Diversity, The Interplay of Worldviews, Globalisation and Locality*, Compas/CDE, series on Worldviews and Sciences, No 6, Leusden, The Netherlands

Wild, R. and McLeod, C. (2008) 'Sacred natural sites: guidelines for protected area managers', Task Force on Cultural and Spiritual Values of Protected Areas, UNESCO Man and Biosphere Programme, IUCN, Gland, Switzerland

21

Culture-based Conservation of Sacred Groves: Experiences from the North Western Ghats, India

Archana Godbole, Jayant Sarnaik and Sameer Punde

Summary

A sacred grove is a traditional multipurpose religious common shared by one or more villages and is managed by the communities and priests. For many generations they have been guarded according to strict but non-written regulations. India has well over 13,000 documented sacred groves. These sacred sites have provided an opportunity to maintain flora and fauna and habitats in near natural conditions. Since time immemorial the deities and the vegetation had equal importance and therefore many rare and endangered species have been protected in sacred groves, even though they have disappeared elsewhere. Sacred landscapes and sacred sites are facing enormous challenges in today's globalizing era. The synergies between people and nature have been disturbed due to processes of infrastructure development and market mechanisms leading to urbanization. It is a challenge for conservation researchers, thinkers, policy-makers and practitioners to help protect these sites for posterity, to protect the species therein and to relate local communities to them through the revival of cultural norms. The spiritual and cultural basis of sacred groves can be used for developing and implementing the long term biodiversity conservation programme for the Western Ghats region of India.

In the northern part of the Western Ghats region the sacred groves are owned by the state revenue department and are managed by local communities. Sacredness has traditionally been attributed to these forest patches for many centuries. Worshipping the gods or ancestors, their abodes and forests surrounding them, explains why they are considered sacred. Cultural practices including religious ceremonies, folk art forms, spiritual ceremonies and individual linkages with the guarding deities are common in the area. Through modernization and migration of local people to urban centres, the cultural ties with the abodes of deities and the vegetation/forests have faded. In the process, biodiversity conservation has also suffered. Through participatory work with communities the Applied Environmental Research Foundation has revived the tradition of sacred groves and has successfully incorporated biodiversity conservation into the practice of maintaining the sacred groves in the region.

Introduction

Since time immemorial indigenous societies all over the world have developed their own concept of the sacred. Through understanding the natural, local knowledge-holders have defined the sacred for a community, village or region. Accordingly the sacred species, groves and landscapes became an integral part of culture. The sacredness attributed to natural systems and nature later took the form of tangible symbols, images, effigies and elaborate structures for deities. However, the worship of natural elements like lakes, rivers, forests, mountains, animals and trees remained the basis of any such worship of symbols. Conservation practitioners, policy-makers and planners have now recognized the concrete relationship between these cultures and their epistemology that could be used for slowing the rapid depletion of nature and natural resources (Godbole et al, 2005). In India the tradition of sacred groves can be observed all across the country, though in each state and region the rules and regulations, cultural as well as social attributes, are diverse. In Maharashtra state, they are referred to as Devrai or Devrahati which means abode of the gods or forest deities.

The Applied Environmental Research Foundation (AERF) has been working on sacred groves conservation in north Western Ghats for over 15 years. Western Ghats is a mountain range running parallel to the west coast of India with biodiversity rich forests locally known as Sahyadris which means 'the mountain that tolerates'. The northern part of the mountain system runs from Navapur in Gujarat to Goa in the south. In India each district is divided into several blocks which are smaller administrative units composed of a number of villages.

AERF's participatory conservation work is concentrated in Sangameshwar block of Ratnagiri district (see Figure 21.1). In Sangameshwar block, AERF has revived the tradition of sacred groves and involved local people in planning as well as implementation, for long-term conservation of the sacred groves. With AERF's facilitation, the local people have again become fully responsible for managing their sacred groves (Godbole and Sarnaik, 2005a, b). These community forests harbouring the region's valuable biodiversity are under tremendous pressure. Threats include encroachment for agriculture, grazing, development of roads, dams and canals as well as urbanization. The concentrated efforts of the AERF have ensured habitat protection through the restoration of degraded sacred groves and rehabilitation of rare and endangered plant species of the region.

During 2007 AERF worked specifically on scaling up and replication of the long-term management of sacred groves with community involvement. Consequently, more sites were incorporated into long-term management. The experiences of involving local people and understanding the perceptions underpinning the spirituality of these areas provided more clues for effective long-term conservation and a space for learning new lessons for practicing biodiversity conservation on the ground (Godbole et al, 2008). This chapter describes the work of AERF in north Western Ghats region of India, seeking to understand the tradition of maintaining the sacred groves and building on cultural perspectives for long-term conservation of biodiversity.

Geographical and ecological context

The north Western Ghats of India is an ecoregion forming a part of the Western Ghats and a global biodiversity hotspot. The region has high biological diversity, complemented by diverse local traditions. Traditional conservation practices such as sacred forests are an important component of the landscape in three districts of the north Western Ghats Maharashtra state. With only about 0.6 per cent of the land in north Western Ghats being formally protected for conservation, such traditional conservation areas are important in filling gaps within the existing regional protected area network.

Almost every village in the Sahaydri-Konkan region has at least one sacred grove ranging from just a few hectares to hundreds of hectares (see Figure 21.2). In the absence of statutory protected areas, and in the wake of mass deforestation, sacred groves form important repositories of forest biodiversity. They provide refuge to many plant and animal species of conservation significance

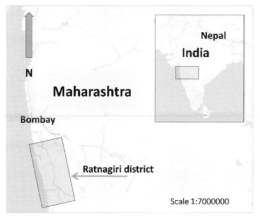

Figure 21.1 Map of Maharashtra State in India with Ratnagiri District

Source: Bas Verschuuren with Open Street Maps ©

(Gadgil and Vartak, 1975). Together these groves created a network of patches within the landscape.

Moist deciduous and semi-evergreen forests are natural vegetation types within the north Western Ghats. Though these forests have been degraded, the original forest type could be easily identified within the sacred groves. Research had previously been concentrated in the southern part of the Western Ghats. However, from a biodiversity perspective, the northern part is equally important.

Ecological importance and biodiversity of the sacred groves

In India, the earliest documented work on sacred groves is that of Brandis (1897). Later, in 1973 Vartak and Gadgil conducted floristic and ethnobotanical studies on the sacred groves of Maharashtra (Vartak and Gadgil, 1973). Sacred groves have survived for many hundreds of years and today act as reservoirs of much local biodiversity. The 40 contiguous groves studied by Bharucha (Posey, 1999) account, as a whole, for most of the plant species present in the Maharashtra region. The forest structure is also unique, representing the least disturbed islands of old growth. AERF's work on sacred groves started in 1996 when botanical inventories were made for sacred groves from the Sangameshwar block. This baseline was also used for refining ecological understanding and prioritization for conservation.

Figure 21.2 Sacred grove of Sayale village and renovated temple

Source: Archana Godbole, AERF

Table 21.1 Criteria used for the Forest Intactness Rating (FIR)

Criteria	Rating		
	1	2	3
Average no. of (richness) of canopy forming trees per 0.5 acre of forest area	<5 species/plot	6–10 species/plot	>10 species/plot
Population structure of dominant trees (Type 1, 2, 3)	Type 3	Type 2	Type 1
Canopy layers (height classes)	1–2	3	4
Canopy cover (%)	20–35	50–60	75 and above
Species and regeneration guild	Secondary	Late Secondary	Primary
Presence of rare or endemic plant species	none	Present	Significant population

Source: Godbole et al (2008)

The identification of priority sites was based on a set of criteria and indicators. To define a set of criteria and indicators for the prioritization and selection process, the AERF referred to two globally accepted prioritization schemes:

1   the Important Plant Area (IPA) programme launched by Plant Life International (Anderson, 2002);
2   the High Conservation Value Forest (HCVF) network launched by the Forest Stewardship Council (FSC) (Poiani et al, 2001).

Based on the botanical surveys and ecological data collection from the sacred groves after initial screening for minimum size, a Forest Intactness Rating (FIR) system was used to allocate scores to each surveyed site. Table 21.1 shows the criteria used for rating.

A higher score indicates the high conservation priority. It is clear from the assessment that once-common local flora, especially trees, have disappeared from surrounding lands and can now only be seen in sacred groves.

In the Sangameshwar block the high plant diversity is clearly visible from the number of species from just 10 sacred groves within an area of 30km². The recorded plants species are restricted to flowering plants only. These sacred groves range from 0.5 to 7 hectares in size. Therefore sacred groves are important sites both for regional biodiversity and for vital ecosystem services to local communities. Streams and rivers often originate from sacred groves, supplying water to an entire village. Sacred groves are important components of larger village landscapes.

Risks and threats to the sacred groves

Threats to sacred groves stem mainly from acculturation and globalization. Many sacred groves have been destroyed, with only the temple remaining. These include the grove at Humbrat, destroyed due to the construction of a railway line, and another grove at Dewle, destroyed due to the construction of a dam. Such small sacred groves are often considered as small negligible patches of forests that hinder development work. Many sacred groves have succumbed to the internal pressures within the communities, resulting from the modernized world forcing change on culture and social norms. The conservation significance of these community conserved areas is decreasing.

From 1985 to 1990 about 35 per cent of the sacred groves from Sindhudurg district were clear felled. The state Social Forestry Directorate, a section of the Department of Forests, replaced them with plantations of exotic species such as Australian Acacia (*Acacia auriculiformis*). This practice contributed to the widespread loss of species and habitats. Logging and forest conversions took place with the consent of local people, initiating a process of acculturation and weakening of religious beliefs throughout the region. In recent times the temple often gained more importance than the vegetation of the sacred groves. Acculturation and changing faith and belief systems may be the greatest threats to these valuable sacred sites. It is a challenge to rebuild on the faith, culture and spirituality of traditional systems for reinforcing the values responsible for maintaining biodiversity and conservation.

Sacred groves in the social and cultural life of people

In Ratnagiri district and parts of Sindhudurg district every village has one or more sacred groves. In Raigad district small, sacred groves can be seen around villages with a large amount of privately owned land. Such land historically belonged to the rulers like Siddi and King Shivaji. Sacred groves are maintained in such villages because the land needed for other uses is readily available. The ownership of sacred groves remains with the State Revenue Department, with the District Collector taking decisions over their use for other than traditional purposes. However these small forest patches are not generating any revenue. Godbole et al (2008) provide the following characteristics of Sacred Groves:

- In the districts of Raigad, Ratnagiri and Sindhudurg the legal ownership is with the state revenue department.
- Management of the sacred grove including religious functions and protection is supervised and monitored by a group of village elders.
- The size ranges from 0.1ha to about 140ha.
- Cultural significance is high and most of the community festivals are celebrated in the sacred grove temple.
- Some groves are burial grounds or crematoriums and some are abodes of ghosts.
- The protection of sacred groves in the region cannot use the same legal system as that for forest protection because the rules for management are different, based on the cultural and social attributes.
- Resources in the sacred groves, except water, are not used by people.

- Sacred groves are common lands but are not used for grazing or NTFP collection as in other regions of India.

The rules and regulations defined by the wise ancestors for the management and protection of sacred groves are not written down and at times could be twisted easily according to the needs of the village, or greedy individuals within the community. Therefore reinforcing the rules and regulations in village management systems is an important issue while designing the conservation strategy for sacred groves.

Sacred groves form an integral part of collective decision-making process. Temples within the grove are often important meeting places. In most villages monthly meetings are organized to discuss the issues of the community or just for worshipping the deity of the grove. Decisions like new development works, implementing the watershed programme of the government or building a school are made in such meetings. Decisions such as seeking permission for using sacred groves' resources for village well-being are generally taken in the temple. In many villages the local priests are involved in matters of religious importance. The open degraded areas of the groves are used to cultivate crops. The produce is for deities and it is often provided to the needy and poor in the village with minimal costs.

Most of the festivals and fairs take place in the sacred grove and its surrounds. The two important festivals, Navratri and Holi, are closely linked to the sacred groves and have significant impact on the traditions practiced. Navratri is the local nine-day festival in which the temple within the grove is important. The silver idols of the deities are brought from the village to the temple where they are worshipped and guarded by the villagers. Holi is the festival of fire celebrated at the end of winter, in March. In Konkan (north Western Ghats), a pile of wood is set alight in front of the sacred grove's temple. Silver idols and masks of the deities of sacred groves are worshipped and worn during ceremonial dances. During the Holi festival a Palkhi – a wooden palanquin to carry the silver masks and images of deities – is carried on the head or shoulders during dances. Holi is otherwise celebrated as a festival of colours in the rest of India. Though the sacred groves are important in the social and cultural life of people, use of sacred groves for livelihoods or income generation is not a common practice.

Using culture for conservation purposes

Cultural norms and the legends associated with the sacred groves deities are important for developing an in-depth understanding of the sacred grove's importance for conservation. In the sacred grove of Janavale the myth of a chicken-hunting leopard is well known. The sacred grove of Janavale is about 3 kilometres away from the village and has a good canopy cover and a small renovated temple. According to the legend the guarding deity of the grove, Janai, occasionally gives permission to the leopard to hunt chickens. The leopard requests permission of the deity overnight and can be seen

the next day by marks made by his tail. Villagers don't have any objections to occasional chicken hunting because the leopard is permitted by the deity. The myth tells many things about the belief system. The people believe the leopard represents other living beings which share resources and this right has been legitimized by the deity of the grove. Stories of the past and such myths attract the young generation and are the best tools to enforce the cultural norms being followed by the ancestors.

In Nandlaj village, another myth is associated with the Holi festival celebrated in the sacred grove. The gods and goddesses of the grove are placed in the Palkhi (see Figure 21.3) and people dance all afternoon. Finally, at sunset when the fire is lit, children dressed like wild boar bathe in mud around the fire. People believe that wild boar will not harm the crops in the subsequent cropping

Figure 21.3 Gods and goddesses are placed in Palkhi during the Holi festival

Source: Archana Godbole, AERF

season and hunting the wild boar is banned; this myth has resulted in hunting restrictions. Myths help to develop a common understanding about the linkage of culture and conservation.

The AERF approach

Through AERF's work on culture-based conservation in the region, various approaches have been used to engage communities, to generate awareness and to link the actions to reinforcing the cultural norms.

Capacity building and awareness generation

The stakeholder groups are enthusiastic and curious about sacred groves. Bridging the gap between the research and its use for reviving the cultural practices can lead to better conservation on the ground. Efforts of awareness generation are often in isolation and need a common platform where all stakeholders can understand, learn and contribute more to the process of conservation of sacred groves. The media play an important role in building consensus and generate awareness about local environmental issues, but they need to be fed with more information about the sacred groves.

AERF has organized stakeholder sessions at both block and district levels. During the deliberations, it was clear that the age-old relationship of culture and conservation needs to be restored by making the cultural perspective more rational and relevant. While reviving sacred groves for healthy forests, the roles and responsibilities of stakeholders are important. Understanding the importance of sacred groves in today's context and the possibilities for culture and resource conservation varies considerably among the stakeholders. Special capacity building sessions for planning and managing the sacred groves have been repeated periodically for maintaining enthusiasm and securing participation.

Local stakeholders such as communities, priests, temple trusts and government line departments need to be empowered to enhance their responsibility in the process of biodiversity conservation. Awareness will not automatically trigger the conservation action alone. In addition, specific capacity building sessions for planning and managing the sacred groves are essential and need to be repeated periodically.

Co-management through long-term action

Re-establishing cultural norms could lead to co-management. Co-management includes activities like cleaning the water resource in the grove, augmentation plantations using the indigenous species, removing invasive species, developing mechanisms to connect sacred sites with the adjoining forest patches within the region, promoting certain dispersers like hornbills as flagship species, creating spaces for continuous stakeholders' dialogue within the management framework, redefining the rules and regulations, reinforcing mechanisms for protection and control over free grazing and using sacred groves for ecotourism to provide livelihoods. Strong facilitation and continuous financial support are prerequisites for the success of such long term co-management.

Institutional empowerment

In most villages local Panchayati Raj Institutions (PRI) are strong, or the local NGO has been engaged in rural development activities. PRI is the legally elected body at village level responsible for the governance and implementation of government aided development programmes. The election is carried out by a *Gram Sabha* (a meeting of all members of the village called by the PRI head).

However, conservation activities often take a back seat on the agenda. These institutions may not have the capacity to implement conservation projects. There are many community-based organizations formed for various developmental programmes like watershed management, self-help groups of both men and women and youth groups engaged in sports and voluntary labour work for development. These groups could be engaged for the implementation of both sacred groves and forest conservation activities. However, generating awareness, motivating the groups and building the capacity to act on the ground to secure long-term conservation need facilitation and financial support to maintain their enthusiasm.

Local conservation leadership

The most important way to sustain the efforts of conservation of sacred groves at village level is to develop and strengthen the local conservation leadership. The educated youth in the village can shoulder the responsibility. Such leadership needs to be nurtured and a livelihood within the village for a local leader is a prerequisite. AERF has identified local youth and involves them in conservation activities and building their capacity to become the local conservation leaders.

Linking conservation of sacred sites to livelihoods

Ecotourism is a very well developed approach and could be used in sacred groves. It could be an income generation activity and could be linked to the livelihoods of the community maintaining the sacred grove. Local communities' capacity building is an issue of concern. Once the initiative begins, the linkages to markets and control on the numbers of visitors/tourists, through institutional mechanisms, are other important aspects.

In some sacred groves limited extraction of specific Non-Timber Forest Products (NTFP) is allowed. In Nirom the flowers of Surangi (*Mamea suriga*) are collected and sold with a seasonal lease. However, there is no provision to plant new trees on the degraded area of the sacred grove or use profits for the management of sacred groves. The sacred groves like Ajiwali and Tungi are used by tribal families for the extraction of Madi, the juice of a palm (*Caryota urense*) and they have specially maintained the populations of this palm in the sacred groves. Such tree cover and cooler surroundings is conducive for Madi production (Godbole, 1994). However, the challenge is how to involve non-beneficiaries in the process of conservation and how to exert checks on overexploitation.

Key results

AERF has studied and initiated work within 250 sacred groves from the region. Through various small projects, AERF has improved the status of about 100 sacred groves within the last 15 years. Key results are thorough research and documentation

of sacred groves from north Western Ghats using set ecological and social criteria; cultural understanding; biodiversity inventories of 142 sacred groves and the conservation status of 230 sacred groves has been recorded.

Through the continuous facilitation and involvement of communities, AERF revived the traditional practice of protecting and managing 13 sacred groves from the region.

Long term co-management plans have been prepared for 10 large sacred groves (greater than 5 hectares) and a restoration process initiated in 16 sacred groves. Community awareness about the sacred groves and their role in culture as well as conservation has increased among the local people and other stakeholders.

Conclusions

Human societies and natural systems are co evolving. They interact so closely that each exerts a strong selective force on the other. Such a co-evolution can be either benign or hostile and if we intend to guide our future course along the former path, then we need to involve other species and the natural systems and processes that provide us with many ecosystem services free of cost. (Cairns, 1995)

Ancestors of the communities that are maintaining the traditions related to sacred groves may have established such traditions from an anthropocentric viewpoint, but over time, the philosophy of protection ran much deeper to extend intrinsic values to all organisms and even non-living entities (Gupta and Guha, 2002). Our present day experiences with protected areas like sanctuaries and national parks are ample reminders of the fact that no matter how foolproof our legislation is, exercises in conservation rarely meet with success unless accompanied by the right ethos, which in turn is dictated by the positions and activities adopted by the local people. The same is true for research and its use and adoption by the local people to ultimately revive the tradition and to ensure the long-term future of sacred groves and other sacred sites (Godbole et al, 2008).

While many local stakeholders are determined to retain sacred groves, they are often vulnerable to outside political and economic forces (Laird,

1999). Therefore it is all the more important to constantly work with communities to maintain the culture and tradition that has contributed greatly to biodiversity conservation and to provide a more scientific understanding of biodiversity and ecology.

Long-term programmes using community-based approaches and the alliances of various stakeholders and institutions to combat the serious losses of species and ecosystems could be effective means to pass on the sacred groves and their biocultural importance to later generations.

References

Anderson, S. (2002) *Identifying Important Plant Areas*, Plantlife International, Salisbury

Brandis, D. (1897) *Forestry in India*, Government Press, Shimla

Cairns, J. (1995) 'Eco societal restoration: Reexamining human society's relationship with natural systems', *Annals of Earth*, vol 13, no 1, pp18–21

Gadgil, M. and Vartak, V.D. (1975) 'Sacred groves of India: A plea of the continuous conservation', *Journal of Bombay Natural History Society*, vol 72, no 2, p313–320

Godbole, A. (1994) 'Ethno botanical studies of Mawal taluka, district Pune, Maharashtra', PhD Thesis, Pune University, Pune

Godbole, A. and Sarnaik, J. (2005a) 'The Future of sacred groves conservation through collaborative management and benefit sharing', in Kunnikannan, B. and Gurudev, S. (eds.) *A Strategy for Conservation of Sacred Groves*, IFGTB, Coimbatore, pp182–188

Godbole, A. and Sarnaik, J. (2005b) 'Tradition of sacred groves and communities contribution in their conservation. A monograph', AERF, Pune

Godbole, A., Anitha, V. and Chandrashekhara, U.M. (2005) *Integrating Cultural and Biological Diversity into the Conservation of Agasthyamalai Biosphere Reserve*, UNESCO, New Delhi

Godbole, A., Punde, S., Sarnaik, J., Pashte, S. and Gokhale, K. (2008) 'Revival of traditional forest conservation practices from northern Western Ghats, India', Final project completion report of the project supported by Whitely Nature Fund, UK

Gupta, A. and Guha, K. (2002) 'Tradition and conservation in North eastern India: An ethical analysis', *Eubios Journal of Asian and International Bioethics*, vol 12, pp15–18

Laird, S. (1999) 'Trees, forests and sacred groves', in Posey, D.A. (ed) (1999) *Cultural and Spiritual Values of Biodiversity: A Comprehensive Contribution to the UNEP Global Biodiversity Assessment*, Intermediate Technology Publications, London

Poiani, K.A., Merrill, M.D. and Chapman, K.A. (2001) 'Identifying conservation-priority areas in a fragmented Minnesota landscape based on the umbrella species concept and selection of large patches of natural vegetation', *Conservation Biology*, vol 15, no 2

Posey, D.A. (ed) (1999) *Cultural and Spiritual Values of Biodiversity: A Comprehensive Contribution to the UNEP Global Biodiversity Assessment*, Intermediate Technology Publications, London

Vartak, V.D. and Gadgil, M. (1973) 'DevRahati: An ethno botanical study of the forests preserved on grounds of religious beliefs', Proceedings of Indian Science Congress, Chandigarh, 3–9 January, p341

In Our Own Hands: Living Culture and Equity at Sacred Natural Sites

This section presents inspiring cases where action for the conservation of sacred natural sites is being taken by communities themselves (see Figure IV.1). It reports how they have taken their own action to conserve and protect their sacred sites, in some cases with the help of external organizations. It has become increasingly clear that the wise use and protection of natural resources is best secured at the local level. Increasingly, sacred natural sites are becoming part of strategies for conservation of the environments and ecosystems which they embody. The fact that they are respected and even venerated by local people offers a good starting point for the successful local level conservation of nature and culture.

Tafi Atome Monkey Sanctuary in Ghana is a good example of community driven ecotourism operation at a sacred site (Ormsby and Edelman, Chapter 22). The sacred monkeys and the festival in their honour form the essence of a tourist experience in the sacred grove that adjoins the village. The shared revenue from the ecotourism operation provides an incentive to the villagers to maintain their traditions of forest conservation, and so protect the monkeys which are the only intact, protected population of this subspecies of mona monkey in Ghana. Overall the community reaction is positive and the monkey population is growing.

Dobson and Mamyev (Chapter, 23) describe the development of a management strategy for the state-recognized Uch-Enmek Indigenous Nature Park in the Altai Republic of Russia, based on cultural and sacred traditions. The indigenous custodians of the Karakol valley in the Golden Mountains of Altai consider their sacred natural

Figure IV.1 Soliga and Ashoka Trust for Research in Ecology and the Environment are mapping sacred sites using a handheld GPS in the Biligiri Rangaswamy Temple Wildlife Sanctuary, India

Source: Sushmita Mandal

sites to be places for maintaining and healing human relationships with the landscape. Indigenous spiritual leader and park manager Danil Mamyev believes sacred sites to form a network with nearby sites that ultimately spread across the earth to form a global network. The work of the site custodians in this global network is to maintain a correct human-nature relationship, but as the sacred natural sites and their custodian cultures come under increasing pressures the network is faltering. Despite the positive developments at the Uch-Enmek Indigenous Nature Park, the indigenous way of life is threatened by imminent land tenure change, road and pipeline development, archaeological excavation, tourism and climate change.

Coron Island in the Philippines was once host to a diverse and ecologically intact marine ecosystem but modernity has brought coral reef destruction. In a move to stop the illegal and destructive fishing activities in their traditional fishing grounds, the indigenous Calamian Tagbanwa have successfully asserted their rights over their ancestral waters and marine sacred sites (Sampang, Chapter 24). There are plans to reinstate the traditional fish sanctuaries and sacred marine areas. The fishing practices of recent immigrants are, however, damaging fish resources and the Council of Elders is faced with the challenge of extending the traditional enforcement responses to immigrants as well as addressing the changing behaviour of younger generations. The formulation of the Ancestral Domain Sustainable Development and Protection Plan is regarded a potential instrument to achieve this.

In India, where government policy often mandates the removal of indigenous people from forest reserves, a similar culture-based process is under way where the Soliga people, with the support of the Ashoka Trust, are mapping their sacred natural sites in order to establish evidence of their long association with the area now incorporated into the Biligiri Rangaswamy Temple Wildlife Sanctuary (Mandal et al, Chapter 25; see Figure IV.1). The Soliga consider mapping as a political process and they plan to use maps to gain rights of access and management to sacred natural sites and forested areas within the reserve under new Indian laws. Documenting and mapping also leads to a better understanding of traditional knowledge systems, including practices such as fire management and techniques for controlling invasive species that can be incorporated into co-management plans. It is considered that this will not only lead to more effective management of the sanctuary but also promote intergenerational and cross-cultural transmission of indigenous knowledge.

In a strong demonstration of the adaptable nature of culture, Indian women of a number of Adivasi or tribal peoples have united under a grassroots movement identified with Sarna Matha, the Indian goddess of sacred groves (Borde and Jackman, Chapter 26). This movement of marginalized Indian women is, over a large area of the country, reclaiming an ancient spirituality, reviving neglected sacred groves while newly establishing others. They are challenging the current social and religious order and taking practical actions for environmental restoration.

22

Community-based Ecotourism at Tafi Atome Monkey Sanctuary, a Sacred Natural Site in Ghana

Alison Ormsby and Craig Edelman

Summary

For generations, communities in Ghana have protected small forest areas for cultural reasons. Many of these forests, deemed sacred, are considered to house local gods, also called fetishes. The sacred grove at Tafi Atome Monkey Sanctuary in Ghana provides an example of how economic incentives can link with traditional protection for successful natural resource conservation. For centuries, traditional law protected this sacred forest and the natural resources it housed, including a species of sacred mona monkey (*Cercopithecus mona mona*) that was taboo to hunt. As newly-introduced religion began to erode traditional beliefs, the incentive to protect the forest and monkeys was weakened. It was not until the introduction of ecotourism, and the benefits that followed, that traditional protection was reaffirmed and incentives to use and destroy the forest were replaced by incentives to protect it. Ethnographic research conducted in 2004 and 2006 at Tafi Atome revealed the history of the sacred site, purposes for its protection, taboos relating to natural resource use and community attitudes toward the forest and ecotourism. A qualitative, ethnographic research methodology was used, including semi-structured, open-ended interviews. Results indicate that participation in management, level of community involvement in the ecotourism project and ecotourism profit sharing are key to effectiveness of the forest's protection. Tafi Atome represents the potential of community-based ecotourism to combine the objectives of community development and natural resource conservation of sacred forests.

Introduction

Ghana has a long history of community protection of sacred forests. For centuries, communities secured these forests for religious practices, burial grounds, and water resources (Campbell, 2005; Chouin, 2002; Lebbie and Freudenberger, 1996; Dorm-Adzobu et al, 1991; Castro, 1990; see also Chapter 15). The size of groves varies from small plots (less than one hectare) to several thousand hectares (Ntiamoa-Baidu, 1995). Ghana has over 1900 sacred groves (Ntiamoa-Baidu, 1995). Within these sacred forests, often referred to as fetish groves, taboos on hunting particular species offer protection to the natural resources housed by the forests (Amoako-Atta, 1995). Traditional fetish beliefs and a taboo therefore serve as incentives to conserve natural resources. However, such sacred forests are vulnerable to the changing values and practices of the people around them. The fetish is a local god often associated with a sacred grove and looked after by a fetish priest who communicates with the local god and conveys messages to the local community. The fetish chief also cares for the fetish shrine, makes appropriate offerings or sacrifices and performs rituals associated with the fetish. The chief is a member of the fetish family, who are the clan or family group historically associated with the sacred species.

The sacred forest at Tafi Atome Monkey Sanctuary in Ghana provides an example of shifting traditional beliefs and how the introduction of ecotourism to the community helped reaffirm traditional conservation practices. For approximately 200 years, local beliefs have protected the sacred forest that contained a subspecies of sacred mona monkey that was taboo to hunt. However, as the influence of Christianity eroded traditional beliefs, protection of the monkeys was weakened. Ecotourism initiatives have helped to provide economic incentives for forest protection.

Ecotourism is a promising method by which the demands of both conservation and local development can be met. In general, ecotourism can provide the necessary incentives for people to conserve a resource by providing an alternative and/or supplementary means of livelihood (Furze et al, 1996; Honey, 1999). The concept diverges greatly from the potentially destructive movement of mass tourism that can be harmful to both culture and natural resources (Asiedu, 2002). The International Union for the Conservation of Nature (IUCN) and Ceballos-Lascurain (1996, p20) define ecotourism as:

> *environmentally responsible travel and visitation to relatively undisturbed natural areas, in order to enjoy and appreciate nature (and any accompanying cultural features − both past and present), that promotes conservation, has low visitor impact, and provides for beneficially active socio-economic involvement of local populations.*

The Tafi Atome Monkey Sanctuary illustrates how the introduction of ecotourism and the economic incentives that follow can link with traditional protection for successful natural resource conservation. Research at Tafi Atome investigated the community's perception of the ecotourism project and its cultural impacts, documented changes in use of forest resources, tourism benefits distributed within the community and the level of monkey protection since the inception of the ecotourism project in Tafi Atome in 1996.

Site description

The village of Tafi Atome has over 1000 residents and is located within the Hohoe District of the Volta Region of Ghana (see Figure 22.1). The language widely spoken in Tafi Atome and throughout the region is Ewe. The village is surrounded by a sacred grove of approximately 28 hectares (see Figures 22.2 and 22.3). The grove is a dry semi-deciduous forest and lies within the forest-savannah transitional zone (NCRC, 1997; Gocking, 2005). Both grassland and cultivated farmland immediately surround the sacred grove. The grove most closely fits into IUCN protected area Category IV, a habitat and/or species management area (Dudley, 2008). The area is protected by a 2006 Hohoe District bylaw for its main value as a habitat for its sacred monkeys. The grove supports the only protected population of true mona monkeys (*Cercopithecus mona mona*) in the whole of Ghana (see Figure 22.4). The monkeys are found in the lower and middle layers of the forest, usually in troops of approximately 12 monkeys, feeding on fruits and leaves (Switzer, 1996). They have a reddish brown back and two white spots on their tail, with a bluish face.

History

According to residents interviewed about the history of the sacred grove, approximately 200 years ago, the ancestors of the residents of the Tafi Atome area migrated from Assini in central Ghana. They brought with them an idol or fetish that was placed in the sacred forest in Tafi Atome in order to keep it safe. The fetish family resided near the forest of Tafi Atome, reasoning that the gods would desire a cool place to stay within the forest. Following this settlement by the fetish clan, the forest was immediately considered sacred and therefore protected. A short time after their arrival in the area, the village residents began to notice monkeys that they believed they had seen in their original

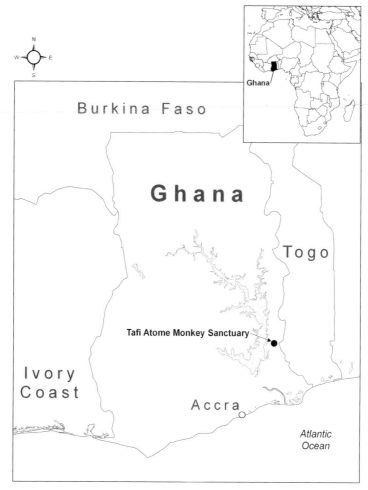

Figure 22.1 Map of Tafi Atome Monkey Sanctuary within Ghana

Source: M. Hibbard

region of Assini, and therefore believed that the monkeys had followed them to Tafi. The monkeys were considered 'representatives of the gods' and therefore protected as sacred. The fetish priest of Tafi Atome acts as the messenger between the village residents and the idol. Because the monkeys are associated with the idol, it is taboo to kill them. A festival to celebrate the monkeys takes place every February, managed by the fetish priest who kills a goat and pours libations at the forest shrine.

The influence of Christianity brought opposing views to traditional law, which led to the deterioration of spiritual connections with the fetish forest, and erosion of traditional protection. Particularly during the 1980s, there were several

incidents of a local priest encouraging the killing of monkeys in an attempt to display the falsities of traditional religion. Whereas traditional law strictly prohibited any use of the sacred forest (except for limited usage by the fetish family for traditional rituals), with the erosion of tradition residents began to cut down economically viable trees. Clearing the forest for use as farmland also began to place particular pressure on the forest boundaries (NCRC, 1997). It was not until the arrival of ecotourism that incentives to conserve the forest began to outweigh pressures to degrade the forest.

The economic prospects from ecotourism supplied the community of Tafi Atome with new

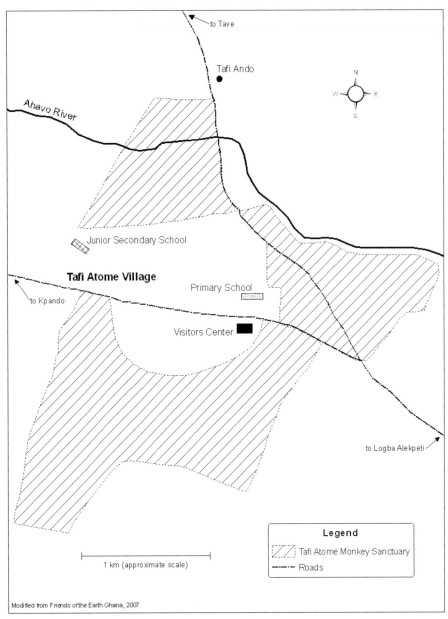

Figure 22.2 Map of Tafi Atome Monkey Sanctuary, a sacred forest

Source: M. Hibbard

motivation to practice conservation of the forest. In 1995, John Mason of the Accra-based Nature Conservation Research Centre (NCRC) visited the village of Tafi Atome after hearing about the area and its particular species of interest, the true mona monkey. Upon arrival, Mason saw the sacred forest in a state of degradation; the larger trees were being felled, the grove was shrinking due to pressures from farmland expansion and bushfires had destroyed portions of the area. Mason reasoned that the introduction of tourism into the community could provide a plausible and practical solution to the impending problem. The NCRC has played a crucial role in the establishment of the

Figure 22.3 Main road through Tafi Atome village with sacred grove on the left

Source: S. Symon

sacred forest as a tourism destination, affording it an additional level of protection to support local tradition.

In 1996, a community-based ecotourism project began in the village of Tafi Atome. Through the decision of the community itself and support from the other project stakeholders including NCRC and the Ghana Tourist Board, the project became a reality and the Tafi Atome Monkey Sanctuary and Cultural Village was created. The project began with the goal of providing an alternative incentive to protect the forest and its rare subspecies of mona monkey, and is now further evolving to promote community development.

In 1997, mahogany trees (*Khaya senegalensis*) were planted to demarcate the boundary of the sanctuary in order to halt future encroachment of farmland upon the forest edge. In 1998, a tourist welcome centre was built to serve as the first point of contact for tourists arriving at the village. The community members funded and built the centre themselves, with only partial funding from external partners. Visitor fees are collected at the centre, which contains a small gift shop, but has limited interpretive or educational material for visitors. A guesthouse was built by community member labour.

Rationale and methods

Edelman and Ormsby conducted surveys with the residents of Tafi Atome in 2004 and 2006. A total of 63 community members living within the study area were surveyed; Edelman interviewed 30 residents (18 men and 12 women) and Ormsby interviewed 33 (17 men and 16 women). This research investigated the following issues:

- use of the resources in the sanctuary forest;
- perception of tourism and its cultural impacts;
- perception and protection of the mona monkeys;
- potential benefits of tourism and project stakeholders.

A qualitative, ethnographic research approach was used, including interviews, participant observation and focus groups (Bernard, 1988; Creswell, 1994; Krueger, 1994; Weiss, 1994; Morgan, 1997). Ormsby conducted a focus group interview with the Tafi Atome Tourism Management Committee. She used a stratified sampling method for individual interviews to include representatives of each clan in the research sample. In Tafi Atome, residents generally live in the vicinity of their family members or clan group.

Edelman administered questionnaires in October and November 2004; Ormsby conducted interviews in June and July 2006. The questionnaires were administered individually, in the company of a local community member who served as a translator, and by whom the questions were read in Ewe; answers were translated back into English for the interviewer to write the responses. The interviewees were assured upon introduction of the confidentiality of their responses. Along with asking basic demographic information, the questionnaires consisted of open-ended and closed-ended questions. A wide variety of ages and occupations were targeted for the interviews.

Results
Sanctuary forest use

Interviewees identified three main possible threats to the sanctuary forest: the felling of trees (73.3 per cent), farming in and near the sanctuary (56.7 per cent) and bushfire (40 per cent). One respondent stated that 'our lands are not so big, so we farm on the same place every year'. Another resident explained that 'there used to be a lot of land to grow on, but now we depend on the same area for a long time because of increased population.'

Asked about their use of the forest before and after the arrival of tourism, the majority of respondents (66.7 per cent) claimed to have never taken any form of forest products from the sanctuary forest before the promotion of tourism, with many interviewees referring to the sacredness of the forest and lack of ownership of the land. It did appear that there was some level of use of the sanctuary forest before the promotion of tourism, when a substantial percentage of community members were able to find the products and animals (NTFPs) they needed. None of the residents interviewed in 2004 admitted to be taking materials from the forest, whereas in 2006, 15 per cent of respondents said they took products from the forest.

Perceptions of tourism and cultural impacts

Community members were asked about their perceptions of tourism at the sacred forest. Asked in 2004 whether or not the arrival of tourists has caused any harm to the community, the forest or the monkeys, all respondents said no. During a 2006 focus group, the Tourism Management Committee (TMC) was asked if there could or should be a maximum number of tourists per week (a visitor carrying capacity) to which the TMC responded 'there is no limit', basically, there is no such thing as too many tourists.

With the arrival of tourism, it is possible that changes to the cultural cohesion and traditional values of the community may have occurred. This appears to be the case within the study area, in that 93.3 per cent of the respondents interviewed in 2004 recognized some level of change, predominantly positive – that the cultural values of the community have improved as a result of tourism promotion. Only 3.3 per cent of interviewees believed that tourists had worsened the community's cultural values. As one resident stated: 'When tourism was not established we did not mind our culture too much. But now when tourists come, we display and practice our culture.' It appears that because tourists come to visit a 'cultural village,' they wish to see displays of culture, which are performed to them by the community in the form of dancing, drumming and storytelling. This seems to have rejuvenated some cultural practices that were beginning to be eroded. According to one respondent, 'before tourists came here we nearly forgot our culture. We now display our culture to them.'

Species protection and perceptions of the mona monkeys

Residents were asked in 2006 to identify taboos associated with the sacred forest. Hunting was identified as forbidden by 52 per cent of respondents. When asked whether they would kill the monkeys if the animals were not protected by a taboo, 83 per cent of the respondents stated that they would not.

The monkey population in the sacred forest area appears to be growing with the renewed protection of the forest as a monkey sanctuary. In 1996, the total mona monkey population was estimated at 47–52 (Switzer, 1996). In 2004, although no scientific study had been carried out,

Figure 22.4 True mona monkey

Source: M. Scace

each guide working at the sanctuary said there were approximately four troops, each having a total of 65 monkeys. In recent years, guides feed the monkeys to lure them close for tourist photo opportunities, changing the monkeys' natural behaviour.

Benefits of tourism and stakeholders

The main decision-making body governing the tourism-related issues of Tafi Atome Monkey Sanctuary is the Tourism Management Committee. The TMC was first created in 1996 and the members had a leading role in creating rules and deciding the distribution of revenue throughout the community. The TMC is concerned with all issues pertaining to tourism development and implementation, and is made up

of 10–14 elected members, with representatives from each of the eight clans within Tafi Atome. Since the commencement of the project, the TMC meets weekly to discuss a broad range of issues including accounting, revenue disbursement, village development projects, rules and any problems that arise. This committee collaborates with the chiefs, elders and the fetish family, and holds community meetings to make decisions and implement efforts for tourism development.

Distribution of revenue was originally decided by the TMC, chiefs and elders (see Table 22.1). Tourism income is disbursed by the TMC to the different groups quarterly before accounts are openly posted in the visitor centre.

Residents were asked if they received a personal or family benefit as a result of tourism. A common benefit noted was a sponsorship programme whereby donors pay the school fees of some students in Tafi Atome. Thus far, over 100 students have been sponsored within the community, mostly from visiting tourists or secondary connections through the tourists. Other benefits mentioned included the renovation of the primary school, interactions with tourists, the arrival of electricity and gifts given by tourists. As one resident explained about the benefits received, 'I have never gone abroad before, but now that my stories are taken with the visitors, my voice has been able to go.'

Of residents interviewed in 2004, 23.3 per cent claimed to have received no benefit from the tourism project. This is important to note, in that the benefits received by the community may not be

Table 22.1 Distribution of tourism revenue at Tafi Atome Monkey Sanctuary

Stakeholder and portion	Intended use
50% community development	Used for community development, e.g. re-roofing the tourist guesthouse, general construction materials, chairs for the welcoming center, and cement electrical poles.
20% landowners	Paid to the six families who were original owners of the land within the sanctuary forest.
12% educational fund	Helps with local students' school fees.
8% fetish priests	Given to the fetish family for traditional purposes such as rituals and sacrifices.
5% chiefs	Given to the traditional chieftaincy.
5% tourism management committee	Paid to the TMC as compensation for their work with the sanctuary.

Source: Alison Ormsby and Craig Edelman

well distributed throughout the entire community. In 2006, 45 per cent of residents interviewed said they receive a personal benefit from tourism and 61 per cent of residents said the community benefits, for a variety of reasons ranging from education to community development.

Management and policy responses

Originally, unwritten laws protected the fetish forest, with any acts of non-compliance taken to the chief and the fetish family, whereupon the offender would be fined to help pay for a sacrifice or offering to pacify the unhappiness of the gods. The fetish forest is the core area of the larger sacred forest and is where the fetish shrine is located. Entry into the fetish forest is strictly forbidden, except by the fetish priest. When tourists visit the monkey sanctuary, the trails that they use do not go near the fetish forest.

The rules governing the forest and the tourism project have been fairly consistent since the beginning of the project; however, specific rules have been further emphasized. The original TMC created the rules pertaining to the sacred forest, with the approval of the chiefs and secondary approval from the community. There is no official written management plan for the sacred forest. The Hohoe District passed official bylaws in 2006, which include the following:

- No person shall enter the forest Reserve or Sanctuary without the permission of the management committee.
- No person shall fell, set fire, or otherwise damage any tree\timber\ property within the grove.
- No one shall make or cultivate a farm within any protected area.
- No hunting, shooting, snaring, capturing, destroying, or setting traps for any animal in the grove.
- No one shall catch or kill monkeys and other animals in the grove.

In 2006, residents were asked the open-ended question, 'What do you think should happen to the grove in the future?' The main responses were: expand the forest (36 per cent); protect the forest (29 per cent); plant trees (16 per cent)

and development projects for the community (8 per cent), such as a health clinic. When residents were asked in 2004 for suggestions to improve the ecotourism project with Tafi Atome, a wide variety of responses were given. Many desired to expand the forest with more trees for the monkeys, while others wanted stronger punishment for anyone who disobeyed the rules and some suggested improving the road to Tafi Atome (currently a dirt road) to facilitate access for both tourists and community members. Expansion of the forest would be a very difficult undertaking as the sacred forest is surrounded on all sides by farmland.

Discussion and recommendations

Perceptions of the tourism project are largely positive, as the residents of Tafi Atome seem generally happy with tourists coming to the village. The distribution of revenue and benefits along with the rules seem generally acceptable. It appears that support for the influx of tourism into Tafi Atome is high, as perceptions of tourism are optimistic. This is consistent with Doxey's (1975) model of typical stages of tourism development. Doxey proposed that tourism initiatives progress through four main stages: euphoria, apathy, annoyance and antagonism. Tafi Atome may still be in the initial tourism stage, euphoria.

In 1997, mahogany trees were planted to demarcate the boundary of the forest to prevent encroachment of farmland and minimize disagreements regarding land ownership. These trees are generally visible; however, in some areas the demarcation of the border seems rather unclear. It is possible that once the trees grow to substantial sizes the boundary will become clearer, but farming has occurred in some areas within this demarcation. Pressure on the forest can arise from the fact that the farmland lies directly adjacent to the forest, with no buffer zone to reduce impacts. With help from Friends of the Earth Ghana, the boundary was officially demarcated with cement boundary markers and surveyed in 2006. Overall, because farmland and forest lie directly adjacent to one another, multiple threats including bushfire, farmland encroachment and tree felling can potentially still occur to negatively affect the sanctuary forest through the intentional or unintentional actions of landowners.

Although the sacred forest at Tafi Atome cannot be considered a completely open-access resource, free for the use of any community member, Ostrom's (1990) principles about sustainable management of a community resource are a useful tool to test the potential sustainability of this site. Ostrom identified seven conditions for sustainability:

1 clearly defined boundaries;
2 congruence between rules and local conditions;
3 those affected by rules can help change and modify them;
4 right to organize;
5 graduated sanctions;
6 monitoring;
7 conflict resolution mechanisms.

Following Ostrom's principles, the demarcation of the sanctuary boundary is of crucial importance to the project. The progress in demarcation bodes well to prevent future degradation of the forest. Tafi Atome appears to have worked through most of the constraints in this area, but the boundaries must remain clearly defined to all members of the community to ensure the protection of the forest. The community has created rules that are consistent with long-held beliefs to protect the sacred forest. However, because these rules are not publicly posted, residents may not be completely aware of the rules. Therefore the rules should be posted in the Visitor Centre.

Related to the Tafi Atome project and crucial to Ostrom's design principles is the idea that communities must have the right to organize on their own without control by outside forces, such as governmental powers. The District Assembly based in Hohoe has requested 40 per cent of the tourism revenue on numerous occasions and at one point was given 20 per cent for a period of four months in 2002. The community discontinued this payment following the support of non-governmental organizations for their cause and after realizing that the District Assembly was not giving any aid in return. This issue is one that needs careful attention as the project becomes more profitable, with increasing external interest.

Protective monitoring of the sanctuary is quite difficult to measure. No group of people is specifically in charge of monitoring the sanctuary; however, the TMC does have the duty of protecting the forest. The level of monitoring the changes within the forest is limited and needs improvement. In particular, the population status of, and behavioural responses by, the mona monkeys as a result of tourism impact needs to be researched. Ostrom emphasizes low-cost, easily accessible mechanisms to solve problems. In the study area, these criteria are met by general community meetings as well as sub-meetings with the chiefs, elders and the TMC. Current levels of communication seem to be effective.

Out of the seven design principles that can help construct the sustainability of a project, it appears that for Tafi Atome Monkey Sanctuary, monitoring and the right to organize are the most important as they are currently the weakest.

Conclusions

Sacred groves are a tradition that exists in West Africa, particularly in Ghana (Sheridan and Nyamweru, 2009). Tafi Atome Monkey Sanctuary is an interesting case of a sacred forest in Ghana that was traditionally protected for nearly 200 years, but subsequently needed outside intervention to reaffirm traditions and maintain the integrity of the sacred site. It is a place where conservation traditions have combined with an ecotourism initiative, to mutually beneficial ends. The tourism project has served to strengthen the cultural values of the site. It remains to be seen if tourism is a truly compatible use of a sacred site in the long term.

The community has already benefitted specifically from philanthropic tourists. Over 100 schoolchildren are now being sponsored and the primary school has been renovated, which are evidence of the successes that have arrived in the community from the tourism project at this sacred grove. The community also gains general benefits from the social, political, economic and psychological empowerment from a community-based project such as this (Asiedu, 2002). Furthermore, the negative cultural impacts along with the costs imposed on the community for changing their livelihoods appear to be low thus far, although this is typical of the early stages of development of a tourism project (Doxey, 1975). The cultural tradition of conserving the forest does need to remain strong, as full reliance on tourism can backfire if events occur that prohibit or reduce tourism for any length of time.

Underlying the apparent and displayed positive aspects of the project also lie issues of concern that may limit its success. The community's capacity to sustain the project is important. Non-governmental organizations and other interested parties and individuals have supported this project; in the future, however, the extent to which they influence the grove management will need consideration. The community has had to adapt a system that works for them, instead of being forced to follow a set of rules governed by an external authority or stakeholders. Also, the community has had to deal with the problems that can arise with this type of community-based project. In particular, Tafi Atome struggles from the conflicts that can arise as a result of money influx to a project, particularly in terms of tourism revenue distribution. It is important to realize the sensitivity of this issue in that once money starts coming into a community, more people can start getting interested, and that is when problems can arise (Lindberg et al, 1998). In particular, this case and others like it in Ghana (see Ormsby, 2011) demonstrate the issues surrounding the reading of accounts and the distribution of revenue and benefits from tourism endeavours. Guidelines for sacred sites and suggestions for strengthening stakeholder participation, acknowledging management rights and recognition of the sacred site should be followed (Wild and McLeod, 2008). Overall, with the limited extent to which external support can be attained, the community of Tafi Atome and other community-based ecotourism projects must have the cohesion, determination, resilience, ingenuity and desire to partake in such a venture so that the objectives of rural development along with conservation of a sacred site may be satisfied.

References

Amoako-Atta, B. (1995) 'Sacred groves in Ghana', in van Droste, B., *Cultural landscapes of universal value*, Gustav Fischer Verlag, New York, pp80–95

Asiedu, A.B. (2002) 'Making ecotourism more supportive of rural development in Ghana', *West African Journal of Applied Ecology*, vol 2, pp1–16

Bernard, H.R. (1988) *Research Methods in Cultural Anthropology*, Sage Publications, Newbury Park, CA

Campbell, M.O. (2005) 'Sacred groves for forest conservation in Ghana's coastal savannas: Assessing ecological and social dimensions', *Singapore Journal of Tropical Geography*, vol 26, no 2, pp151–169

Castro, P. (1990) 'Sacred groves and social change in Kirinyaga, Kenya', in Chaiken, M.S. and Fleuret, A.K.(eds) *Social Change and Applied Anthropology*, Westview Press, Boulder, CO, pp277–289

Ceballos-Lascurain, H. (1996) *Tourism, Ecotourism, and Protected Areas*, IUCN, Cambridge, UK, Gland Switzerland

Chouin, G. (2002) 'Sacred groves as historical and archaeological markers in southern Ghana', *Ghana Studies*, vol 5, pp177–196

Creswell, J.W. (1994) *Research Design: Qualitative and Quantitative Approaches*, Sage Publications, Thousand Oaks, CA

Dorm-Adzobu, C., Ampadu-Agyei, O. and Veit, P.G. (1991) *Religious Beliefs and Environmental Protection: The Malshegu Sacred Grove in Northern Ghana*, World Resources Institute, Washington, DC

Doxey, G.V. (1975) 'A causation theory of visitor-resident irritants; methodology and research inferences', Proceedings of the Sixth Annual Conference of the Travel Research Association, Travel and Tourism Research Association, Lake Orion, MI

Dudley, N. (ed) (2008) *Guidelines for Applying Protected Area Management Categories*, IUCN, Gland, Switzerland

Furze, B., De Lacy, T. and Birckman, J. (1996) *Culture, Conservation and Biodiversity: The Social Dimension of Linking Local Level Development and Conservation Through Protected Areas*, Wiley and Sons, Chichester, UK

Gocking, R. (2005) *The History of Ghana*, Greenwood Press, Westport, CT

Honey, M. (1999) *Ecotourism and Sustainable Development: Who Owns Paradise?*, Island Press, Washington, DC

Krueger, R.A. (1994) *Focus Groups: A Practical Guide for Applied Research*, Sage Publications, Thousand Oaks, CA

Lebbie, A.R. and Freudenberger, M.S. (1996) 'Sacred groves in Africa: Forest patches in transition', in Schelhas, J. and Greenberg, R.S. (eds) *Forest Patches in Tropical Landscapes*, Island Press, Washington, DC, pp300–324

Lindberg, K., Eppler-Wood, M. and Engeldrum, D. (eds) (1998) 'Ecotourism: A guide for planners and managers, Volume 2', *The Ecotourism Society*, North Bennington, VT

Morgan, D.L. (1997) *Focus Groups as Qualitative Research*, Sage Publications, Thousand Oaks, CA

NCRC (1997) 'Reforestation plan for the bio-diversity reforestation project', Unpublished report, Nature Conservation Research Centre, Accra, Ghana

Ntiamoa-Baidu, Y. (1995) *Indigenous vs. Introduced Biodiversity Conservation Strategies: The Case Of Protected Area Systems in Ghana*, African Biodiversity Series, 1, Biodiversity Support Program, Washington, DC

Ormsby, A. (2011) 'Cultural and conservation values of sacred forests in Ghana', in Pungetti, G., Oviedo, G. and Hooke, D. (eds) *Sacred Species and Sites: Guardians of Biocultural Diversity*, Cambridge University Press, Cambridge

Ostrom, E. (1990) *Governing the Commons: The Evolution of Institutions for Collective Action*, Cambridge University Press, Cambridge

Sheridan, M.J. and Nyamweru, C. (2009) *African Sacred Groves: Ecological Dynamics and Social Change*, Ohio University Press, Athens, Ohio

Switzer, D. (1996) 'Tafi Atome monkey forest sanctuary primate population assessment', Unpublished report, Nature Conservation Research Centre, Accra, Ghana

Weiss, R.S. (1994) *Learning from Strangers: the Art and Method of Qualitative Interview Studies*, The Free Press, New York

Wild, R. and McLeod, C. (eds) (2008) 'Sacred natural sites: Guidelines for protected area managers', IUCN, Gland and UNESCO, Paris

23

Sacred Valley, Conservation Management and Indigenous Survival: Uch Enmek Indigenous Nature Park, Altai Republic, Russia

Joanna Dobson and Danil Mamyev

Summary

For the Altai indigenous people the Karakol valley represents the spiritual heart of the Republic. The sacred mountain which stands at the head of the valley is so revered that the replacement name 'Uch Enmek' meaning 'three fontanel' is used to avoid speaking the mountain's true name. The valley supports a wide range of characteristic wildlife including rare and endemic species and is filled with enigmatic ancient monuments, rock art sanctuaries and the world renowned Bashadar kurgan complex. These monuments are placed in a specific relationship to the natural landscape. They reflect centuries of sacred knowledge which has transformed the valley into a shrine. A naturally formed ring of magnetite located at the centre of the valley is believed by the indigenous population to represent the 'navel' of the valley which together with the kurgans surrounding it brings a life force and knowledge through the sun's rays to the middle world of man. The indigenous culture encodes the sacred knowledge of the ancients while the local people continue to guard the valley's secrets. The rock art sanctuaries are the people's 'sudur bichik', their sacred text for the future. The epic spiritual giants of the past are said to rest in the kurgans offering their strength to future generations. Threatened by a rapidly growing tourist industry, archaeological excavation motivated by the perceived threat of global warming to permafrost burials and the uncertainty of new land and tenure laws the people of the valley have responded by creating their own nature park in an attempt to preserve their land, heritage and culture. Combining traditional sacred knowledge with contemporary scientific methods of research, the indigenous community attempt to formalize their knowledge and to deepen understanding of the ritual function of kurgans. After generations of keeping the valley 'closed' to outsiders local spiritual leaders now offer initiation and pilgrimage in the hope of raising a broader awareness of their spiritual worldview. Concerned for the status of sacred lands the world over, the Karakol indigenous leaders dream of creating a model territory in their sacred valley for the study and harmonious development of such sacred places and for the well-being of humanity.

Introduction

The Altai Republic borders Siberia, Mongolia, China and Kazakhstan and is home to the 'Golden Mountains' UNESCO serial natural world heritage site. It has great historical and spiritual meaning as 'the homeland of all humanity', 'the cradle of the world' and 'the source of wisdom' (Roerich, 2001). 'Uch Enmek' Indigenous Nature Park was set up to protect the Sacred Karakol Valley and is situated in the Ongudai region at the heart of the Altai Republic, (see Figure 23.1).

The Park encompasses 60,551 hectares and is bordered by the Ursul and Karakol rivers and the Ongudai and Ust-Koks regions. The landscape is characteristic of different altitude belts in the Central Altai and consists of high-mountain, mid-mountain and mountain valley landscapes. The main ridges of the Terektinskii mountain range are influenced by glacial activity with major geomorphologic features such as moraine hillocks, ridges and traces of creep and avalanche with an elevation between 900 and 3000m. Vegetation ranges from tundra, moss, lichen, (sub)-alpine meadow to mountain steppe, marsh and meadow landscapes. The territory is rich in rare, endemic, relic and endangered species of flora and fauna such as the Maral Root (*Rhaponticum carthamoides*),

Black Stork (*Ciconia nigra* L.), Demoiselle Crane (*Anthropoides virgo*), Altai Snowcock (*Tetraogallus altaicus*), the snow leopard (*Panthera uncia*), Altai argali (*Ovis ammon ammon*) and at least 14 other species of butterflies, reptiles and birds, which are Red Book listed.

Approximately 2500 indigenous people live in six villages administered by three municipalities. The majority depend on raising livestock (cattle, sheep, goat, cows and horses), hunting and deer farming. The Park is under jurisdiction of the municipalities and the Forestry Commission. Tourism in the park is jointly managed by the park body and local tourist company 'Ongudai Tour' which offer excursions, horse-riding treks, 'pilgrimages' and cultural tourism.

'Uch Enmek' was created by decree of the Altai Republic in 2001 based on legislation termed: 'Specially Protected Nature Territories and Sites in the Altai Republic' and 'The historical and cultural heritage of the peoples' of the Altai Republic'. It was an initiative of the indigenous organization 'Tengri – Soul Ecology' and represents a specially protected nature territory that includes both natural and historical features, cultural complexes of high recreational, aesthetic and economic value. It was established for the purposes of nature and cultural conservation and for recreational activities. The park territory has been divided into three zones based on indigenous notions of land use and function:

- Zone A: Reserve area – 'the nucleus': includes the sacred peaks of 'Uch Enmek', 810 hectares, including summer and winter pasture with no hunting or farming
- Zone B: Buffer zone – includes 'kurgans' and other historical and cultural monuments; strictly regulated visitation for shamanic ritual, scientific research and recreational purposes as well as limited agricultural use (4776 hectares)
- Zone C: Development zone – provides for the protection and preservation of natural complexes, monuments of historical and cultural heritage. It includes villages and farming lands, hunting and recreation areas (54,964 hectares).

Figure 23.1 Location of Altai Republic and Uch Enmek Indigenous Nature Park

Source: Bas Verschuuren

Cultural and historical heritage of the sacred Karakol valley

The philosophy of the Altai worldview considers natural objects (plants, stones, stars and planets) to be living beings endowed with the same functional organs as a human being and accordingly Mount Uch Enmek is traditionally considered the 'navel'. The earth is believed to receive vital energy and knowledge through this navel in the same way that a foetus receives nourishment in the mother's womb.

The natural peculiarity of the Karakol valley lies in its geological formation. The valley is unique for its widespread outcrops of gabbro and dolerite which are high in magnetite mineral content. In the centre of the valley these outcrops form what is essentially a ring of magnetite that is considered to attract the energies of the ether to the earth (see Figures 23.2 and 23.4).

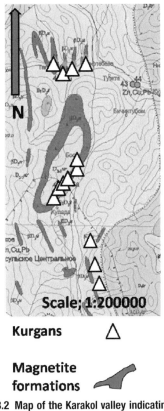

Scale: 1:200000

Kurgans

Magnetite formations

Figure 23.2 Map of the Karakol valley indicating magnetic magnetite outcrops and approximate locations of Kurgans

Source: Mamyev (2008), adapted by Bas Verschuuren

Perhaps as a response to the unique geology the valley is home to a whole system of sacred archaeological complexes including a Stone Age dwelling, petroglyphs, runic inscriptions, standing stones and kurgans (burial chambers) characteristic of the Karakol (see Figure 23.5), Afanasiev, Scythian and Turkic cultures. The Bashadar and Tuekta kurgan complexes researched in the 1950s by S.I. Rudenko, dated to the Scythian period and attributed to the Pzyryk culture (5th–7th century BC) are renowned the world over. The permafrost burials of the Scythian period situated in the south of the Altai Mountain are unique for their highly ornamental burial inventory made of gold, felt, leather and wood, mummified human remains of the tribal elite and sacrificial horses (Soenov, 1998). It is strongly believed by the current indigenous custodians that the true uniqueness of these archaeological monuments lies in their layout and magnetic qualities which repeat the form and structure of the 'magnetic ring' described above (see Figure 23.4). As a result the Karakol valley represents a shrine created consecutively over a period of several millennia. Of particular significance are the kurgans, a burial type construction with characteristic stone, or earth cover. Locally kurgans are treated with immense reverence. They are believed to be the burial grounds of the epic heroes, the spiritual giants of old.

Faith

The ethical principles of the traditional culture of the indigenous peoples of Altai have been developed over centuries. These principles presuppose the particularly careful use of natural resources. They also acknowledge the existence of specific areas which play an important role in supporting ecological balance between man and the environment. Whilst such areas may be inhabited by population groups they are also recognized as places where one may receive knowledge, strength and the stimulus for spiritual development. Just as the special relationship of the local population has secured the high levels of biological diversity one witnesses in Altai in the post-Soviet period, so the preservation of sacred lands guarantees the preservation of the traditional culture and its sustainable development.

Altai indigenous values and beliefs have been concentrated in the Karakol valley. The ideas and understanding accumulated on this sacred land have found expression in the oral culture, rituals, customs and everyday life, in 'local, sacred knowledge' which has been transmitted from one generation to another. The local population believes that their well-being depends on their direct connection to the land (the condition of their totemic animals, plants, mountains and special places) and in turn the well-being of sacred land depends on the reciprocal 'service' it is afforded by the indigenous population through preservation, protection, ritual and harmonious interaction.

People have lived here for centuries and their communication with nature has lead to the understanding of the laws of nature or as it is called today – ecological consciousness; to love and to worship not only nature but also ourselves and those close to us. We are an integral part of nature and so a person's entire inner energy and aura has to be congruent with that of nature for there to be balance in the ether. The Karakol valley itself is sacred because it creates this atmosphere of harmony. People who visit the valley immediately feel the difference, that the people here live by laws connected with nature which we call 'baily d'ang', 'taboo' or 'law'. (N. Shumarov, Tolos clan, personal communication 2008).

Rather than being quaint vestiges of a time past, the sacred local knowledge expressed in the cultural forms 'alkyshtar' (blessings), 'jangar kojhong' (sacred and ritual songs sung by women), 'kai' (the throat singing of epics) and 'bai' (sacred laws) continues to collectively support the living atmosphere in the Karakol valley. Indigenous peoples have preserved the foundation of a holistic world view which enables one to sense and consequently harmonize changes taking place in the subtle interactions within the environment. Therefore, the true value of the Altai culture lies not in its separate parts but rather in its entirety expressed within the vibrational world of this particular landscape (see Figure 23.3).

Uch Enmek – Indigenous initiative

The Uch Enmek Indigenous Park, named after Mount Uch Enmek (see Figure 23.3) is the indigenous response to threats facing the Sacred Valley and the indigenous culture that are described in detail below. The conservation of the natural, historical and cultural conditions of the Karakol valley requires that it be separated from common usage and attributed a special status. This special status has traditionally been afforded to the valley by the indigenous population. The nature park is considered an appropriate adaptation of the indigenous community's traditional role of preserving the valley in the contemporary economic, social and political climate. Hence, rather than representing a purely ecological directive, the Park offers the indigenous population a conceptual framework for their future development.

The park acknowledges the need to apply legal measures concerning the use of natural resources and protection of intellectual property, to carry out essential zoning and planning work to protect the valley from threats and develop an economic development plan, '… nature parks represent one type of special economic zone of which the ecological component is a priority principle' (Mamyev, 2008). In order to involve the local population in park-based sacred territory protection activities it is, therefore, essential to create a local economic infrastructure.

Aims of the Uch Enmek indigenous initiative

The Uch Enmek Indigenous initiative has the following aims:

Research

- Develop a scientific model for sustainable development within the valley.
- Zoning to establish landscape and recreational areas.
- Registering monuments of cultural and historical heritage where possible avoiding further invasive archaeological excavations.
- Creating thematic maps.

Figure 23.3 Mount Uch Enmek in the background and Bronze Age Stellae amongst horses

Source: J. Dobson

- Comprehensive study of the natural, social and cultural landscape.
- Social monitoring.

Nature protection

- Protecting the valley as a territory of special spiritual, ecological and scientific value.
- Ecological monitoring.
- Establishing a mechanism for the rational use of natural resources and monuments of historical and cultural heritage.

Ecological awareness campaign

- Develop a system for raising broad awareness of the indigenous knowledge of the spiritual and ecological principles of the Karakol valley through pilgrimage type of tourism.

Develop spiritual and ethical guidance in park management

- Value, love and respect nature and the indigenous culture for their own sake.
- Worship the territory of the park as sacred space.
- Revere the traditional culture advocating natural and cultural diversity.
- As far as possible observe the natural rights of wildlife, flora and fauna and the codes of the indigenous culture.
- Fulfil one's responsibilities in such a way that the spirit of the sacred land is inspired by the beauty of human emotion (Mamyev, 2008, p238).

Integrating sacred knowledge and scientific research

The 'kurgans' provide the physical loci for the central ideas and sacred knowledge encoded in the epic throat singing tradition. The kurgans and the epic heroes associated with them symbolize a time when the culture of the ancients was at its peak. The local population considers kurgans capable of having both a positive and a negative effect on a person. Highly controlled visitation is believed to minimize the effect of human emotional, mental and psychic energies on the place allowing the information fields and sacred function to exist within their own 'space'. Codes concerning how kurgans should be treated that have been passed from one generation to another are still strictly observed. Appropriate rituals were traditionally carried out often with the guidance of a shaman. Visiting a kurgan is permitted in small groups only and each individual is responsible for assuring their thoughts and intentions are pure.

In collaboration with the park, research has been carried out by Professor A.N. Dmitriev (Head of the Geophysics and Mineralogy Research Department at the Institute of Geology of the Siberian branch of the Russian Academy of Science) and Dr A.V. Shitov (Doctor of Geological and Mineralogical Science, Gorno-Altaisk State University) into the magnetic and radioactivity fields at kurgan sites (Dmitriev and Shitov, 2005). Results have shown that the magnetic and weight characteristics of a group of people in a meditative condition significantly influence the different fields at kurgan sites. It has also been established that standing in one of the series of Scythian ritual complexes affects the autonomic nervous system. In addition, a small and highly intense 'magnetic dipole' has been discovered in the immediate vicinity of a double kurgan from the Bashadar group. The magnetic field of the 'dipole' displayed variation in amplitude up to 10,000nT (nanotesla) and reacted to the presence of a human being. By means of comparison, changes in the field during magnetic storms on the earth's surface do not exceed 1000nT (see Figure 23.4 for a magnetic map of the kurgan and Figure 23.5 for a photo of an excavated kurgan) (Dmitriev et al, 2004).

The complex magnetic and radioactive fields, location and layout of kurgans in relation to the geological characteristics of the landscape partly

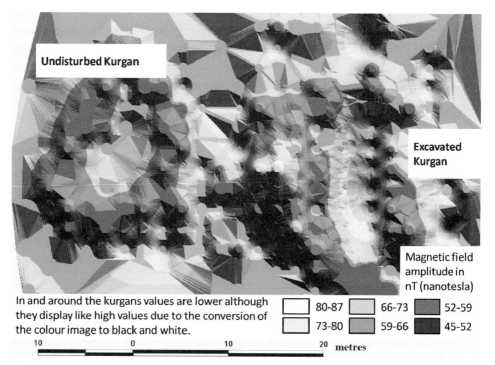

Figure 23.4 Magnetic field of the Archaeological site 'Neijhnee Soru' at the Karakol Valley

Source: Dmitriev and Shitov (2005), adapted by Danil Mamjev and Bas Verschuuren

reveal their hidden meaning (see Figure 23.2). It is possible that kurgans intentionally influence local natural magnetic and radioactivity fields and play a role in the psychological and ecological dynamics of the region. The kurgans are constructed in such a way that they represent a micro-model of the natural macrocosm. It has not yet been established exactly what information these constructions carry and how they can affect the uninitiated physically and psychologically. It is clear however, that excavation of kurgans destroys their magnetic qualities reducing the possibility of resurrecting comprehensive knowledge of this special ritual structure. Even the most preliminary scientific research carried out by the park indicates the high significance of the given territory for the modern world from an indigenous point of view.

Taking responsibility

In the Altai indigenous worldview the omnipresent energy that can be felt in the valley is also a living being and therefore responds to the human emotional, mental and psychic condition of both the individual and the ethnic group. It can be imprinted with different types of information including psychic energy, human thought, emotion and sound. Therefore, notions such as '*bai*' and '*bailu*' lie at the foundation of the indigenous relationship to the natural world. '*Bai*' means 'sacred', 'prohibition', 'modest', 'frugal', 'creating abundance' and represents the moral codes and limitations in behaviour in relationship to sacred objects in the natural world (Yaimova, 1990, p13). '*Bailu jer*' is usually translated as 'sacred land'. However, '*bailu*' also emphasizes the principle of human responsibility and action indicating that 'the sacred' demands a particular form of human behaviour.

A combination of faith, traditional knowledge and modern science is employed in park research into the true meaning of sacred sites. The enigmatic kurgan complexes are being studied to determine the principles of their layout, magnetic fields and function within the natural landscape. Altai elder N. Shodoev writes on the theme of Altai folk wisdom referred to as '*bilik*' which, he writes, is carried in the heart and memory of the Altai people. 'The content of the Bilik is constantly being re-assimilated philosophically and serves as a prism, through which solutions to contemporary problems may be found. It is the Altai people's most ancient and sacred treasure. It reveals a profound relationship to life, a deep understanding of natural energies and rhythms and a keen feeling for the dramatic contradictions of our time' (Shodoev and Kurchakov, 2005). Hence, personal responsibility is a predominant element of the indigenous relationship to the natural world that is regarded to be of significance to the modern world.

Threats and challenges

The main issues that threaten the integrity of the Karakol valley can be summarized as:

- changes in land law, land tenure and natural resource policies;
- increasing unregulated local and international tourism and infrastructure development;
- destruction of sacred sites by development, theft and archaeology.

Critical imminent changes in land tenure law

The move towards an open land market and changes in policy on the use of natural resources is starkly at odds with the Altai traditional system of land tenure and spiritual values. Russian law does not recognize the notion of sacred land. As a consequence no guidelines exist to manage natural resources of sacred lands in particular. At the same time, the social and economic condition of the indigenous population is characterized by high unemployment levels, minimal annual family income and poor social security. Moreover, the collapse of the Soviet Union and the break-up of 'kolkhoz' farms has left agricultural communities in an ideological vacuum. In the Altai worldview the homeland is not just a geographical area but an emotional and spiritual relationship to a clan's land in which a mountain represents the sacred centre. Lands were held in common by the whole clan and the territory borders clearly marked.

In Russia in the early 20th century, land, however, was declared the property of the state.

During the Soviet period traditional totemic, ancestral land rights were denied and clan rituals prohibited. In 1993 during the period of 'perestroika' by decree of the president of the Russian Federation former state and collective farm lands were subdivided among former farm workers into what are called private 'portion rights' to land plots. To assist citizens claiming their rights to private ownership regional bodies were required to issue the necessary documentation before the end of 2005. Within the Altai Republic this process was not carried out and farm workers were allocated agricultural use rights only. It is only recently, in the light of the impending open land market in Russia, that individuals eligible for land ownership have become aware of their rights. Of the 2500 people inhabiting the territory of the park approximately 1000 have the automatic right to the ownership of 'portions' (of approximately 15 hectares). However, due to the expense and convoluted nature of the privatization process these individuals have still not been able to register their legal rights. It is possible that lands not privatized by 2010 will be retrieved by the state and made available to farmers on a rental basis only. Of the 60,000 hectares of park territory (24,000 are forestry lands, 5000 represent villages and populated areas) only 15,000 hectares of land are registered by the local population as having rights to agricultural land use. Approximately 70 per cent of park land remains unregistered.

The reclaiming by the state of these lands and their potential future sale and development is currently perceived as representing the greatest threat to the survival of the traditional way of life of the native people inhabiting the park territory. Potential land sales within the park risks the loss of indigenous people's rights to visit and preserve sacred natural objects and ritual sites. There is a strong desire among the population of the Karakol valley to return to a 'totemic' system of land tenure in which certain areas of the valley are predisposed to accepted forms of behaviour and land use.

Although the 'Uch Enmek' Nature Park is a legal body and government organization, it does not have the resources to carry out surveying, zoning or land tenure activities which would enable the park territory to be registered as such within the cadastral system. The timescale involved in this situation makes indigenous land rights an emergency management issue. The situation is all the more complicated by elements of uncertainty given that no model exists for dealing with private land ownership on sacred land in a specially protected nature territory within the Republic. Park management is currently seeking resources and expertise to assist in resolving these issues.

However, presently the park stands alone in its aims and one senses neither a common commitment to the vision of the park nor a true perception of the sacredness of the land amongst the other stakeholders. Uch Enmek's current activities are limited predominantly to scientific research, tourism management and awareness raising activities with both local schools and visitors. It is hoped that support may be received from the international natural and cultural heritage community in stimulating commitment to the park's vision.

Unregulated tourism and infrastructure development

Over the past five years the Altai Republic has become a major tourist destination within Russia and is increasingly attracting tourists from abroad. Due to the absence of appropriate laws sacred lands and cultural heritage are being uncontrollably exploited by the tourist business. The lack of knowledge and respect for indigenous sacred sites can be witnessed at various mountain passes including 'Chikitiman' in the Ongudai region and the sacred spring 'Arjhan Suu'. These sites have been desecrated by tourists through the grotesque imitation of the 'Kyira' ritual tying of cloths to trees and mass graffiti on the rocks of the sacred pass. In addition to the likely ecological consequences of the planned Gazprom pipeline project and the proposed road to China the creation of the 'Altai Valley' special economic zone of tourist and recreational type threatens to rapidly increase the tourist pressure.

Although the indigenous population are still extremely cautious of visitors to their carefully structured sacred landscape, the park is becoming acknowledged for its role in regulating visitation of sacred sites, and communicating the indigenous experience of the sacred landscape. Income opportunities are provided by the Karakol guest base through the hiring of guides and horses, and the 'Kaichi' (Kai performers) who sing the epics or perform a ritual before a visiting group embarks on a pilgrimage. This type of involvement confirms the authority of highly respected 'knowledge keepers' whose role is essential in the process of making sacred land accessible to the non-indigenous community.

An excursion through approximately 20km of valley landscape constitutes the most common form of tourism on park territory. Components of the excursion include a 'kai' throat singing performance, visits to rock art sites, kurgans, places of ritual and a traditional Altai meal. Being managed by the indigenous population the excursion has organically taken on a number of interesting factors. When the indigenous people visit the valley they prepare themselves inwardly by placing negative thoughts and emotions to one side which could 'pollute' the special quality of the atmosphere. As a rule, visitors are invited to do the same, taking care that their thoughts be 'white' and 'pure'. The guide determines which specific places to visit depending on areas recognized as being 'open' or 'closed' in line with the changing energies in the valley.

Destruction of sacred sites by development, theft and archaeology

The key problems in preserving sacred areas in the recent past have been posed by the destruction of petroglyph sites due to theft, road building and the work of archaeologists who have excavated ritual burial grounds and removed monuments without carrying out complex studies of their role within the sacred landscape or the spiritual worldview of the indigenous population. This threat increases with the Russian academic community's awareness of global warming which interprets global warming as a directive to excavate all remaining permafrost burials (see Figure 23.5).

Conclusions

The relationship of the indigenous population to the Karakol valley leads us to understand that the evaluation of an area as 'sacred land' is not

Figure 23.5 Excavated kurgan

Source: Jodi Frediani Photography 2008 ©

simply dependent on the human perception of it as 'homeland'. Certain areas on the planet are 'special' due to the particular function they fulfil in regulating ecological systems. Over the course of their culture indigenous peoples have learned to live within the powerful energies of place. The result of this relationship is what is understood as 'traditional culture'. The culture itself can be considered to actually massage the land like an acupuncture point on the human body guaranteeing that the 'special area' functions to its fullest capacity. According to this worldview one may consider all the sacred natural sites across the globe as 'acupuncture points', their distinctive cultures responsible for maintaining the ecological equilibrium not only of a given area, but also of the whole.

The loss of this connection and the negation of the principles functioning at sacred lands is perceived to be the true cause of the ecological catastrophes we witness in the world today. This knowledge confirms the need to mark special areas as sacred lands at an international level. The uniqueness of the indigenous initiative Uch Enmek lies in its attempt to express its sacred knowledge via contemporary science into a language that can be accessible to contemporary societies who may have lost their special relationship to the land. Although the indigenous world view is very different from science-based environmental protection, the structure of the Uch Enmek Nature Park serves as a meeting place between nature conservation and indigenous survival. The Altai indigenous people are a reminder that people across the world are forgetting to respect the land and to communicate with it effectively. A reciprocal relationship with the land is necessary to ensure its ecological and spiritual heart.

References

Dmitriev, A.N. and Shitov, A.V. (2005) 'On the geophysical characteristics of kurgan complexes in Gorny Altai', available at www.pulse.webservis.ru/Science/Tumuli/BGeo/index.html (last accessed December 2009)

Dmitriev, A.N., Dyatlov, V.L., Gvosdarev, A.Y. and Shitov, A.V. (2004) 'The discovery of an anomolous micro-geophysical site on the territory of Gorny Altai', *The World of Science, Culture and Education*, Gorno-Altaisk, Biisk, pp63–66, available at www.pulse.webservis.ru/Science/Ether/MicroObject/index.html (last accessed December 2009)

Mamyev, D.I. (2008) *Procedure and Conditions in visiting SPNT and Sacred Areas*, Gorno-Altaisk, Barnaul, pp235–239

Roerich, N.K. (2001) *Altai-Himalaya, A Travel Diary*, Adventures Unlimited Press, New York

Shodoev, NA. and Kurchakov, R. (2005) *Altai bilik*, TAY, Kazan

Soenov, V.I. (1998) *Ancient Kurgans of Altai*, Ak Chechek, Gorno-Altaisk

Yaimova, N.A. (1990) *Euphemisms and the Vocabulary of Taboo in the Altai Language*, Gorno-altaiskii nauchnii isledovatelskii institut istorii, yazyka i literaturii, Gorno-Altaisk

24

Towards a Sustainable Management and Enhanced Protection of Sacred Marine Areas at Palawan's Coron Island Ancestral Domain, Philippines

Arlene G. Sampang

Summary

The traditional fishing grounds of the Calamian Tagbanwa, an indigenous small-scale fishing community in Coron Island, Palawan are under increasing fishing pressure. The island was once host to a diverse and ecologically intact marine ecosystem. However, modern times have brought destruction to the coral reefs. In a move to stop the illegal and destructive fishing activities over their traditional fishing grounds, the Calamian Tagbanwa asserted their rights over their ancestral waters with the intention of reinstating their traditional fishing practices. Fish sanctuaries are restricted areas, while sacred marine areas are traditionally respected and avoided because of the spirit of a giant, human-like octopus believed to live there. Interviews and group discussions were used at the two villages of the island, Banwang Daan and Cabugao to assess the current fishing practices.

Increasing numbers of Calamian Tagbanwa and immigrant fishers in the island are exposing the restricted and sacred areas to degradation. The fishing activities of the immigrants are affecting the Calamian Tagbanwa traditional fishing practices. In addition, the Council of Elders is faced with the challenge of strengthening the traditional enforcement responses to violations as well as with addressing the changing behaviour of the younger generations. Modernization and urbanization tend to influence the changing cultural and spiritual values among the youth. Sacred areas are invaluable to the Calamian Tagbanwa as these symbolize their culture. The formulation of the Ancestral Domain Sustainable Development and Protection Plan involves Calamian Tagbanwa and other management constituents. The Calamian Tagbanwa considers this plan to be a welcome step to strengthen and enhance their capacity to effectively manage their area and to intensify the protection on restricted and sacred areas within the ancestral domain. Information dissemination about their customary fishing practices should be prioritized especially within the island as well as environmental awareness activities among the younger generations. Training on legal matters pertaining to the rights of indigenous people should be organized and indigenous punishment against violators should be strictly enforced.

Introduction

Marine and coastal resources provide mankind with economic and environmental services as well as a source of animal protein among island communities. But, the rampant use of illegal and destructive fishing methods along with the increasing demand for fish and other marine animal species in the international and domestic market, have resulted to widespread degradation of marine habitats (Pauly et al, 2002; Pomeroy et al, 2005).

In the Philippines, Palawan is the largest province and designated as Man and Biosphere Reserve in 1990 which includes two World Heritage sites, the Tubbataha Reef Natural Park and the Puerto Princesa Subterranean River National Park. Marine resources in the province are bountiful and cover a remarkable biodiversity. Based on the fisheries profile of 2007, 19 per cent of the total marine catch in the municipal fisheries production came from Palawan. The Calamianes Group of Islands, which comprise the main islands of Busuanga, Culion, Coron and Linapacan, in the northern section of the province is one of the most productive fishing grounds and has relatively intact marine environments such as mangrove forests, seagrass beds and coral reefs (Werner and Allen, 2000). However, in the recent past, Calamianes marine resources have declined due to the wide-scale use of illegal, destructive fishing methods, encroachment of commercial fishing vessels into the municipal waters and resource use conflict (FISH Project, 2006). In the terrestrial realm, threats to Palawan biodiversity include illegal logging, conversion of forest to agricultural lands and other land uses. Recently, mining has also become a serious threat, not only to the loss of habitat of species but also to the lives of indigenous people. The rights of indigenous people to claim their ancestral domain are at risk because lands have been converted to mining sites even before they can apply for their ancestral domain claim.

Coron Island is declared as the ancestral domain of the Calamian Tagbanwa indigenous people. According to the Indigenous Peoples Rights Act (IPRA, 1997, Section 3a), ancestral domain refers to:

> *all areas generally belonging to the indigenous cultural communities or indigenous peoples (ICCs or IPs) comprising lands, inland waters, coastal areas and natural resources therein, held under a claim of ownership, occupied or possessed by ICCs/IPs by themselves or through their ancestors, communally or individually since time immemorial, continuously to the present except when interrupted by war, force majeure or displacement by force, deceit, stealth or as a consequence of government projects or any other voluntary dealings entered into by government and private individuals/corporations, and which are necessary to ensure their economic, social and cultural welfare. It shall include ancestral lands, forests, pasture, residential, agricultural and other lands individually owned whether alienable and disposable or otherwise, hunting grounds, burial grounds, worship areas, bodies of water, mineral and other natural resources.*

The Calamian Tagbanwa are different from the Tagbanwa found in the mainland of Palawan province. The Calamian Tagbanwa's way of life is anchored in the sea while the Tagbanwas' in the mainland spend time in the riverbanks and valleys (Wright, cited in Eder and Fernandez, 1996). The Calamian Tagbanwa established a sustainable way of life that was in harmony with nature, their avoidance of their sacred areas and existing taboos played a role in the conservation of biological diversity in the ancestral domain and helped sustain their life support system. Taboo areas around Coron Island serve as a reminder of their own culture and these sites are ecologically intact. Today, the Calamian Tagbanwa face challenges about how they can maintain the ecological balance along with the economic, social and cultural changes and the intrusion of migrant fishers around their ancestral waters. The dwindling marine resources in the *teeb ang surublien* (ancestral waters) of the Calamian Tagbanwa are attributed to the trends mentioned above resulting in the destruction of coral reef communities in their traditional fishing grounds (Luchavez, 1991; PAFID, 2000; Sampang 2005, 2007). Understanding the behavior of resource users is imperative for a successful management (Jentoft, cited in Sabetian, 2002). This chapter examines the customary fishing practices of the Calamian Tagbanwa and how they address the threats in their ancestral waters.

Coron Island Ancestral Domain: Biodiversity and legal establishment

Coron Island is a wedge-shaped limestone island located in the southeastern side of Busuanga Island at 11° 55' N and 120° 13' E. It is composed of two villages, Banwang Daan and Cabugao. The majority of the population is Calamian Tagbanwa, while immigrants coming from the Visayas region of the country are a minority.

The Calamianes Group of Islands hosts several rare fish species such as blenny (*Ecsenius kurti* and *Istiblennius colei*) and dottyback (*Labracinus atrofasciatus*) (Werner and Allen, 2000). The Coron Island ancestral domain covers 7320ha of ancestral land and 16,958ha of ancestral waters (see Figure 24.1). The island is dominated by Permian limestone of Jurassic origin, forming rugged terrains and steep cliffs. The domain has different ecosystem types such as coral reefs, seagrass, mangroves, brackish lagoons and limestone forests that support an outstanding biodiversity. There is a high rate of floral endemism and wildlife species reported are the Philippine macaque (*Macaca fascicularis*), wild pigs (*Sus barbatus*), Palawan porcupine (*Hystrix pumila*), Palawan stink badger (*Mydaus marchei*), Palawan hornbill (*Anthracoceros marchei*), various parrot species (*Tanygnathus lucionensis, Gracula religiosa*), green sea turtles (*Chelonia mydas*) and sea cow (*Dugong dugon*) (NIPAP, 2000). Coron Island is also known for Balinsasayaw (*Collocalia troglodytes*), this swiftlet produces the edible nest, made of gelatinous secretion from the salivary glands of the bird.

In 1967, Coron Island was first declared as a National Reserve, then later in 1978 as a Tourist Zone and Marine Reserve. The Tagbanwa Tribe of Coron Island Association (TTCIA) formerly known as the Tagbanwa Foundation of Coron Island (TFCI) applied for a Community Forest Stewardship Agreement (CFSA) with the Department of Environment and Natural Resources (DENR) and it was granted in 1990. The Calamian Tagbanwa realized that the CFSA is limited to land stewardship, increasing concern about how their traditional fishing grounds can be protected from illegal and destructive fishing practices; they began to search for solutions. During the passage of the National Integrated Protected Areas System (NIPAS) in 1992, Coron Island was included in the priority protected area under the National Integrated Protected Areas Programme (NIPAP) and the Strategic Environmental Plan (SEP) for Palawan also expanded the definition of ancestral domain to include the coastal zones and submerged areas. Then, in 1993, DENR passed an administrative order, which provides recognition and awarding of Certificate of Ancestral Domain Claim (CADC). The Calamian Tagbanwa started to comply with all the necessary documents with the help of Philippine Association for Intercultural Development (PAFID). With the passing of the Indigenous Peoples Rights Act in 1997, the indigenous peoples in the country now have a support system that can protect their rights over their ancestral domain. Finally, in 1998, the struggle of the Calamian Tagbanwa to be recognized was over, Coron Island was granted its ancestral domain claim by the DENR including the ancestral waters and issued a CADC. The CADC was issued pursuant to the DENR administrative order. The increasing fishing pressure around the waters of their domain has led them to assert their legal rights to control and manage the resources. The Calamian Tagbanwa was the first indigenous people to be granted of an ancestral water claim. When the IPRA law was enacted, the National Commission on Indigenous People took over as the implementing agency and passed an administrative order to convert the CADC to Certificate of Ancestral Domain Title (CADT). In 2002, there were a lot of criticisms and resolutions passed such as re-evaluation of the delineated boundaries in the claim of the Calamian Tagbanwa hindering the awarding of the title. The National

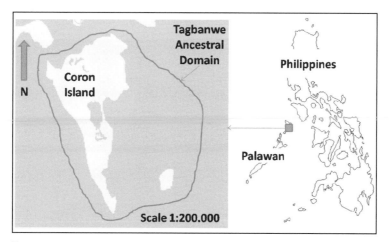

Figure 24.1 Map of the ancestral domain of the Calamian Tagbanwa in Coron Island, Palawan, Philippines

Source: PAFID. Composed by Bas Verschuuren and Arlene Sampang

Commission on Indigenous People then reviewed and revalidated the submitted documents and in 2004, Coron Island finally received their CADT.

Coron Island is an example of a community conserved area, defined as 'natural and modified ecosystems, including significant biodiversity, ecological services and cultural values, voluntarily conserved by indigenous peoples and local and mobile communities through customary laws or other effective means' (Borrini-Feyerabend et al, 2004, pxvi). The sacred or forbidden areas inside the ancestral domain such as lakes, beaches and marine areas make it equivalent to the IUCN management Category Ia, Strict nature reserve, and Category V, Protected landscape/seascape. The management of Coron Island Ancestral Domain involves three entities, the Council of Elders, Tagbanwa Tribe of Coron Island and the village officials of Banwang Daan and Cabugao.

Sacred and restricted areas inside the ancestral domain

Lakes found in the ancestral domain are considered sacred by the Calamian Tagbanwa. It is strictly prohibited to enter these areas unless for cultural purposes such as performing rituals. Cabugao Lake, the largest lake found in the island is considered to be the centre of spirits. Only two lakes were

allowed for tourism namely the Kayangan (Figure 24.2) and Luluyuwan (also known as Barracuda Lake). Both lakes have been given awards for the cleanest lake in the Philippines, but the Kayangan Lake now holds a Presidential Hall of Fame award for consistently winning from 1997 to 1999. Beaches that serve as burial grounds of their ancestors are also prohibited to visitors, only seven out of 33 beaches were open for tourism.

Sacred areas, locally known as panyaan, are areas in the sea where the Calamian Tagbanwa believes that there are spirits dwelling in the place. A panyaan is usually a big rock or coral reef formation that is separated from its main structure and in relatively deep waters. The Calamian Tagbanwa believes that a kunlalabyut or giant octopus lives in this area. This cultural knowledge is passed down from elders to the younger generation through oral tradition. Not all Calamian Tagbanwa were able to go to the sacred areas, they had to have a definite purpose if they intended to go there. Elders (mamaepet) and shaman (bawalyan) played a major role when entering sacred areas. The elders or shamans utter uliwatwat, a prayer addressing the spirits requesting to enter the sacred areas. Names of sacred areas and species found in the island show how they are interconnected with the marine environment. Some names of the sacred areas pertain to the morphological structure of the rock or reef formation and behavioural activity of

Figure 24.2 Entrance to Kayangan Lake, sacred to the Calamian Tagbanwa

Source: Arlene Sampang

the giant octopus dwelling in the area. Ten such panyaan exist on the island.

Fish sanctuaries are considered restricted areas. They are not allowed to fish, drop anchors or to culture seaweeds. There are six traditional fish sanctuaries on the island.

Methods

Initial discussions were made through the Tagbanwa Tribe of Coron Island Association regarding the assessment of the customary fishing practices. In compliance with the implementing rules and regulations of IPRA, a free and prior informed consent (FPIC) process was undertaken. As an instrument of empowerment, the FPIC process enables the indigenous people to determine whether they will accept or reject the proposed project if they see that it is not in their

priority needs. General assemblies were conducted in Banwang Daan and Cabugao to discuss the details of the purpose of the assessment (see Figure 24.3). The Calamian Tagbanwa openly accepted the research project and resolutions of consent were passed by both villages, coming from the Council of Elders, TTCIA and the Village Captain. This application then went to the municipal and provincial level for certification.

The assessment was carried out mainly by interviews and focus group discussions with the Council of Elders, officials of the village and TTCIA, and the members of the community. Customary law about the ancestral waters stated in the Calamian Tagbanwa's Ancestral Domain Management Plan (ADMP) was used as a guideline to assess the current fishing practices (TFCI, 1998). The assessment also covered the fishing activities and resource use patterns of the Calamian

Figure 24.3 General assembly in Cabugao village discussing the details of the research project

Source: Arlene Sampang

Tagbanwa. Explanations about the customary practices that were not clear to the younger generations were also expounded by the Elders.

Results

Banwang Daan and Cabugao fishers mainly fish on the three traditional fishing grounds inside their ancestral domain. They fish mainly for subsistence, although some Calamian Tagbanwa families are engaged in small-scale trading of live groupers, fresh food fish as well as marine invertebrates such as octopus, sea cucumber and seashells. Reef gleaning is mostly done by women. The fishing season for the Calamian Tagbanwa lasts from June to November (southwest monsoon or Abagat). Rough sea conditions during the months of December to May brought by strong winds associated with kamian (northeast monsoon), make

it a lean season for fishers. Fishing gear mostly used during the southwest and northeast monsoons are hook and line, spears and gill net. Fishing is carried out using small double outrigger canoes as well as rafts and motorboats. Transmission of knowledge on fishing such as making fishing gear starts as young as six years old. It is evident as well that the fishing skills of the Calamian Tagbanwa are changing. According to the elders, their ancestors used hand instruments like a trident spear for sea cucumbers and more often gathered sea shells. Nowadays, because of the demand for live groupers, the younger generations of fishers more often use hook and line. Slowly, the use of traditional fishing gear such as tridents is disappearing, also related to the dwindling stocks available for harvest. The average catch of fish has declined from 3kg per day (Luchavez, 1991) to 1.18–1.32kg per day (Sampang, 2007). Declining fish catch is attributed to degraded fishing areas because of the illegal and destructive fishing methods.

Other sources of livelihood among Calamian Tagbanwa are farming, weaving mats and harvesting luray (edible birds' nests) during the months of December to May. These nests are used to make the popular Nido soup, a delicacy in Chinese cuisine. The trade between the Chinese and the Calamian Tagbanwa dates back to the pre-Spanish colonization in the Philippines.

Based on their customary laws, fishing is prohibited in restricted and sacred areas. However, observance of the customary laws depends on the values and motivation of the fishers. Two views emerged during the course of the assessment. First, those who are still in observance of the taboo are enveloped with fear over the sea spirits inhabiting the area and they have high respect for the elders. They believe that unusual events can still happen. Second are those that are non-observers of the fishing taboo. Some fishers tend to visit or fish in these areas because of the influential activities of the migrant fishers living in the island. Others have changed their religious beliefs system and no longer consider that spirits dwelling in the sacred areas can bring them harm, although they still respect the teachings of the elders. Factors affecting the behavior of fishers especially the younger generations are also brought by modernization.

Discussion and recommendation

Achieving ancestral domain certificate

The DENR in 1996, passed the Department Administrative Order 34 (DAO 34) providing the guidelines for the management of the ancestral claim. When the Calamian Tagbanwas' struggle for recognition of their ancestral domain claim was granted in 1998, they organized a workshop to draft their initial Ancestral Domain Management Plan. The existing plan only covers regulatory framework of laws pertinent to their legal rights in the ancestral domain, indigenous punishments and customary laws to guide resource use and developments in the area and the Kayangan lake visitor management, among others. However, the management plan lacks other information that

could be a basis for monitoring and evaluation in the future. In addition, during the formulation, there was no participation of other management constituents such as the Local Government Unit (LGU) and other stakeholder groups. The status of the restricted and sacred areas helps them identify options and strengthen their management strategies in the formulation of their Ancestral Domain Sustainable Development and Protection Plan (ADSDPP). This is a long-term plan that will guide them in the sustainable management and development of their ancestral domain.

Today, very few of the customary rules are being followed. Elders have observed that these rules are ineffective nowadays. The fishing activities of the Calamian Tagbanwa and migrant fishers in the island motivated the management body of the ancestral domain to re-evaluate their role and responsibilities. Having different resource users on the island becomes a threat when there is no common vision for protecting their cultural heritage. The Council of Elders have a significant role in implementing the traditional means of discipline such as panglaw (the hands are tied and feet are placed in stocks) and burdun (12 lashes of rattan cane). Thus, the great challenge among the Elders is to revive their strict enforcement of customary rules such as respect for restricted and sacred areas and not catching juvenile species but allowing them to reach maturity and reproduce.

Fishing areas and customary fishing practices

Current activities in the restricted and sacred areas give an indication that they are not respected by migrant fishers in the island or those who occasionally visit the Calamianes Group of Islands. This calls for more dissemination of information about their customary practices. Baseline assessment of the existing restricted areas should be prioritized: knowing what area needs better protection and has the greater chance of fast recovery. The formulation of the management plan should capitalize on the traditional ecological knowledge and best fishing practices. Also, alternative livelihood options other than marine-based occupation should be identified. The managers of the ancestral domain will have to explore more options on reducing the impact of fishing.

Capacity building and strengthening of cultural and environmental awareness

The Council of Elders, Tagbanwa Tribe Association and the village officials have roles and responsibilities for the ancestral domain to be managed successfully. Providing training and knowledge enhancement on legal matters will help them in tackling issues on law enforcement against violators as well as handling conflict resolution within and outside of the community. In their traditional enforcement scheme, if a non-Calamian Tagbanwa is apprehended, the violator has the option to undergo the customary law of the Calamian Tagbanwa or national law. The management plan must contain relevant biodiversity inventories; assisting and training them in the participatory resource assessment will equip them to have their own style of monitoring in the future.

Strengthening cultural identity and integrity will require effort from the Council of Elders. Continuous transmission of cultural knowledge and practices should be in place, such as in the form of sessions among the youth. This will help the younger generations to appreciate more the uniqueness of their identity in spite of urbanization and modernization. Environmental awareness activities, such as interpretative walks along a mangrove ecosystem discussing the importance of the mangrove trees among children to encourage them to appreciate the value of natural resources on the island, will be of great value.

Conclusions

Despite the opposition of the local government units and other stakeholders in the Calamianes region on the ancestral domain claim and criticisms faced by the Calamian Tagbanwa, they were able to succeed and got hold of their domain title through perseverance. However, maintaining the balance of the economic, social and cultural changes will challenge the Calamian Tagbanwa to be resilient in the rapid changes they will encounter. The formulation of their sustainable development and

protection plan calls for more participation among them to rethink what is the best solution for them to properly manage their cultural heritage.

Lessons are to be learned about the unique relationship of the Calamian Tagbanwa with nature. It has helped them to regain control of their cultural heritage. The case of an ancestral waters claim was a precedent among indigenous peoples in the Philippines to assert their indigenous rights with the assistance of the National Commission on Indigenous People. Sacred areas are invaluable to the Calamian Tagbanwa as these symbolize their culture. The destruction of their sacred areas and loss of biodiversity is closely linked to the loss of cultural knowledge. Resurgence of customary practices and strong community effort of the Calamian Tagbanwa will ensure the sustainable management and protection of sacred areas in Coron Island.

References

Borrini-Feyerabend, G., Kothari, A. and Oviedo, G. (2004) *Indigenous and Local Communities and Protected Areas: Towards Equity and Enhanced Conservation*, IUCN, Gland, Switzerland and Cambridge, UK, ppxviii and 111

Eder, J.F. and Fernandez, J.O. (1996) 'Palawan, a last frontier', in Eder, J.F. and Eder, J.O. (eds) *Palawan at the Crossroads: Development and the environment in a Philippine Frontier*, Ateneo de Manila University Press, Quezon City, p180

FISH Project (2006) 'Coastal and fisheries profile: Calamianes Islands, Palawan', FISH, Coron, Philippines, p102

IPRA (1997) available at www.chanrobles.com/republicactno8371.htm (last accessed September 2008)

Luchavez, T. (1991) 'A brief assessment of the coastal resources of the islands of Coron and Delian', in 'Community and coastal survey report of Coron and Busuanga Islands', Philippine Association for Intercultural Development and Silliman University Marine Laboratory, Palawan, p46

NIPAP (2000) 'Coron Island Protected Area. General Management Plan', advanced draft, NIPAP, Manila, Philippines p50

Pauly, D., Christensen, V., Guénette, S., Pitcher, T.J., Sumaila, U.R., Walters, C.J., Watson, R. and Zeller, D. (2002) 'Toward sustainability in world fisheries', *Nature*, vol 418, pp689–695

PAFID (2000) 'Mapping the ancestral lands and waters of the Calamian Tagbanwa of Coron, northern Palawan', in Bennagen, P.L. and Royo, A.G. (eds) *Mapping the Earth, Mapping Life*, Legal Rights and Natural Resources Center, Inc., Kasama sa Kalikasan (LRC-KSK/Friends of the Earth–Philippines), p152

Pomeroy, R.S., Pido, M.D., Pontillas, J.F.A., Francisco, B.S., White, A.T. and Silvestre, G.T. (2005) 'Evaluation of policy options for the live reef food fish trade: Focus on Calamianes Islands and Palawan province, Philippines, with implication for national policy', Palawan Council for Sustainable Development, Fisheries Improved for Sustainable Harvest Project, and Provincial Government of Palawan, Philippines, p90

Sabetian, A. (2002) 'The importance of ethnographic knowledge to fishery research design and management in the South Pacific: A case study from Kolombangara Island, Solomon Islands', *Secretariat of the Pacific Community Traditional Marine Resource Management Knowledge Information Bulletin*, vol 14, pp22–34

Sampang, A. (2005) 'Ethnoichthyology and conservation practices of the Calamian Tagbanwa in Coron Island, Palawan, Philippines', Master's thesis, University of the Philippines Los Baños, p238

Sampang, A. (2007) 'The Calamian Tagbanwa Ancestral Domain (Coron Is., Palawan, Philippines): Evaluation of traditional fishing practices towards biodiversity conservation and sustainability', Project report submitted to the Alcoa Foundation Sustainability and Fellowship Programme and the World Conservation Union, Gland, Switzerland, p77

TFCI (1998) 'Ancestral Domain Management Plan of the Tagbanwa in Coron Island, Coron, Palawan', TFCI

Werner, T.B. and Allen, G.R. (eds) (2000) 'A rapid marine biodiversity assessment of the Calamianes Islands, Palawan province, Philippines', *Rapid Assessment Program Bulletin of Biological Assessment* 17, Conservation International, Washington DC, p128

25

Culture, Conservation and Co-management: Strengthening Soliga Stake in Biodiversity Conservation in Biligiri Rangaswamy Temple Wildlife Sanctuary, India

Sushmita Mandal, Nitin D. Rai and C. Madegowda

Summary

In India the control of forests and resources vested with the state and local communities has been marginalized either through displacement or by curtailing access to resources. Indigenous communities that have historical ties to landscapes are beginning to assert their rights over the management and use of forest landscapes. Mapping sacred natural sites within Biligiri Rangaswamy Temple Wildlife Sanctuary (BRTWS) is one such attempt to show Soliga cultural presence. This evidence is being used by Soligas to gain cultural access rights to sacred natural sites as well as forest management rights within Biligiri Rangaswamy Temple Wildlife Sanctuary under the Recognition of Forest Rights Act (RFRA, 2006, http://forestrights.nic.in/doc/Act.pdf). We highlight the ecological and cultural disengagement of the Soligas from the landscape, a phenomenon largely driven by policies and actions of the forest bureaucracy. We then show that collaborative mapping of sacred sites attempts to re-establish links and historical rights over the landscape. The mapping process is as much a cultural initiative as an ecological one.

This project has elicited interest among old and young. Sacred sites are important to Soligas because it is part of their cultural heritage and reinforce their linkages with the forest. The process of reinserting Soliga narratives to the landscape is critical to Soligas as well as to the mainstream understanding and brings to the fore human-environment interactions that have so far not been acknowledged in protected area management and governance.

Mapping is viewed by the Soligas as a political process. Mapping sacred natural sites gives them documented spatial evidence of their historic presence which can be used in governance and management processes. This way, Soligas are able to reinforce their stake in the landscape that they have lived and interacted with so keenly prior to the government take over and their political exclusion from their forests.

Documenting and mapping lead to a better understanding of traditional knowledge systems, including practices such as the Soliga fire management and prevention techniques that can be incorporated into co-management plans for managing BRTWS more effectively. For example, it reiterates the role communities can play in co-managing protected areas so that no protection and management regime can obliterate its historical use. Moreover, such protected areas are not just ecological units but part of larger, more diverse cultural-ecological mosaic including sacred sites and cultural landscapes.

Introduction

This chapter explores the meanings Soligas lend to the landscape, and how the present form and structure of the forest is a result of configuration by the Soligas. It describes how the cultural ecology of the Soligas and the historical transformations of BRTWS hold promise for a more thorough incorporation of Soligas in forest conservation and management. This chapter describes the nature of the relationships Soligas forge with their surroundings, and how such relationships have been systematically weakened and severed through state policies. Placing these human–nature relationships within the larger discourse of a 'preservationist' conservation agenda, this chapter discusses the growing understanding and need to integrate the natural with socio-cultural landscape features.

Although state control of forests is not of recent origin in the Indian subcontinent, with pre-colonial rulers controlling vast stretches of forest, the systematic negation of local cultural contexts in policy and practice has been most evident during colonial and post-colonial rule. While the initial impetus for decrying local use came from observations made by 'gentlemen environmentalists' alarmed at the degraded nature of the forest, the subsequent motivation was largely to secure forests for production of timber (Williams, 2003). This resulted in not only control of forests through systems of

reservation but also the application of scientific management and the subsequent transformation of local agrarian and forest use systems. Irreversible cultural transformations happened as a result of sedentarization of shifting cultivators, employing indigenous communities in forestry operations and more recently the displacement of forest dwellers during the establishment of protected areas for wildlife conservation. Displacement affects cultural practices that are embedded in the landscape, resulting in erosion of knowledge, practice and power. The Soligas of BRTWS are an indigenous community that have been made invisible, and their systems of knowledge unrecognized. This chapter describes the cultural linkages of the Soligas with the landscape and how the recent emergence of inclusive government policy provides scope for reaffirming Soligas' cultural linkages and practices after a long period of exclusion.

The ecological context

The Biligiri Rangaswamy Temple Wildlife Sanctuary (BRTWS) is located between 11–13' N latitude and 77–78' E longitude, covering an area of 540km², in the southeast corner of Chamarajanagara district in the state of Karnataka, India. BRTWS derives its name 'Biligiri' (white hill) either from the white rock face that constitutes the major hill crowned with the temple of Lord Rangaswamy, or from the white mist that covers the hills for a greater part of the year. Lord Rangaswamy is a resting form of Lord Vishnu, one of the foremost of Hindu Gods, well known in south India. According to legend Lord Rangaswamy was installed in Biligiri Rangan Hills by sage Vashishtha and is worshipped as the presiding deity of the forests in the Biligiri Rangan Hills. The Soligas believe that the Lord married a Soliga woman and are therefore allowed to perform some of the rituals in the temple though they are barred from entering the sanctum sanctorum.

BRTWS, located at the confluence of Western and Eastern Ghats, has high biodiversity indices. It has a diversity of vegetation types including scrub, dry and moist deciduous forests, evergreen forests, shola (a high-altitude – 1900–2200m – dwarf evergreen forest formation found in southern

India) and high-altitude grasslands, supporting a variety of fauna. BRTWS supports 776 species of higher plants (Kamathy et al, 1967), more than 36 mammals excluding bats and rodents, 245 species of birds (Aravind et al, 2001), and 145 species of butterflies (N. A. Aravind and D. Rao, 'Butterfly assemblages of Biligiri Rangaswamy Temple Wildlife Sanctuary, South India', unpublished manuscript). The forests form an important wildlife corridor between the Western Ghats and the Eastern Ghats, linking the largest populations of Asian elephant in southern India.

The Soligas in BRTWS

The Soliga are referred to in different works with different spellings: Sholaiga (Thurston, 1909; Aiyappan, 1948; Luiz, 1963); Sholiga (Nanjundayya and Iyer, 1961); Sholigars (Subbayya, 1965) and Soliga (CI, 1893; Gopal, 1965). They are an indigenous community who have been living in these forested regions for centuries. The Soligas are traditionally hunters and swidden cultivators, and collect a wide variety of Non-Timber Forest Products (NTFP) for subsistence. The declaration of the BRTWS in 1974 led to their sedentarization and a forced change in the lifestyles of these people. Post-declaration, the Forest department established podus/colonies of 10–60 households on the periphery of the forest to settle the Soligas, banned swidden agriculture and hunting. The Soligas since then have adapted to such changes although NTFP collection remained a major source of cash income but was banned in 2006 following an interpretation of a Supreme Court ruling on banning the removal of anything from wildlife sanctuaries.

The Soligas claim their descent from Karraya who was delivered through a bamboo cylinder and thus named Soliga, which literally means 'from bamboo' (Somasundaram and Kibe, 1990). Soligas are a close-knit social group who traditionally married within the group and lived in simple cave dwellings, away from contact with outsiders. Elders have pointed to the changes that occurred over time and as a consequence the community felt the need to develop a system whereby they could be regrouped into Kulas (or clans) with presiding deities, and each Kula ascribed

particular responsibilities. Six Kulas evolved: Halaru, Baleyaru, Selikiru, Suriru, Belliru and Teneyaru, and out-marriage (exogamy) between Kulas became the norm. The elders assert that there are no hierarchies between Kulas as it was only a functional mode of allocating responsibilities for better administration.

Our ethnographic mapping exercise described in this chapter reveals that Kulas operated within certain notions of bounded territories (Yelle), protected and guided by the presence of gods and demons. Yelles are Kula-specific boundaries within which they moved, lived and cultivated. Such notions of territory when mapped reveal that the entire BRTWS landscape is a composite of several such territories reflecting the configuration by Soligas of the entire landscape; the present vegetation structure is a result of such practices and will be described later.

The Soliga cosmology is an extension of the natural world and sacred sites are identified as composites of the five elements. The five elements are bounded within a Yelle. Elders identified five essential elements including 'devaru' (God, associated with sun/light) (see Figure 25.1), 'marama' (mother goddess, associated with fire), 'veeru' (demon), 'kallugudi' (burial stones, associated with wind) and 'abbi' (spring/stream, associated with water), each of these pertaining to one of the five elements of nature: earth, water, fire, wind, ether/space. They identified the role of the 'veeru' (demon) to be crucial to their existence and the 'veeru' was feared and respected. It is taboo for women to visit areas considered inhabited by veeru and these areas are generally kept out of bounds to community members and thus protected from human use or disturbance.

Mapping sacred sites

Several initiatives have been undertaken in mapping sacred sites in native forest areas across the globe: studies in Zimbabwe (Byers et al, 2009), Cameroon (Nelson and Hossack, 2003), Nicaragua, Madagascar, Indonesia and the Philippines (Geesa, 2008). The Zimbabwean study show that forest loss is less in forests which are considered sacred. It also shows that areas where traditional leaders have been disempowered by post-independence political processes the rate of loss is significantly

Figure 25.1 A Soliga paying his obeisance at a Devaru site in BRTWS

Note: Such found structures as a cluster of stones, in this case, and an unusually shaped tree are accorded sacred status and worshipped.

Source: Nitin D. Rai

high. Counter-mapping is a proven tool that leads not just to community empowerment (Alcorn, 2000; Eghenter, 2000; Geesa, 2008) but like other participatory processes, helps locate the voices of those marginalized spatially. In all such cases, the mapping process has enabled community claims to landscapes and its protection from external economic agencies.

Mapping of sacred sites engages Soligas and strengthens their stake in governance, thus redefining the engagement of communities within a protected area regime. Linking these to recent national forest policy developments, particularly the enactment of the Recognition of Forest Rights Act (RFRA), shows that such processes could go a long way towards developing inclusive approaches to conservation.

Methods of collecting information include focus group discussions and semi-structured key informant interviews with elders to ascertain the names of sacred sites, locations and oral histories.

Kulas and the sub-groups within Kulas have been documented through interactions with Soliga elders and an inventory of all such elders is also maintained.

Mapping of Soliga sacred sites in BRTWS was initiated to locate sacred natural sites using Geographic Information System (GIS) tools to record location, altitude, etc. and observations, whilst elucidating the functions of Kula and Yelle. Soliga cultural idioms, such as agriculture, forestry and ritual use, were explored to understand their practices. Based on these discussions a majority of the Soligas expressed interest in mapping sacred natural sites. However during the mapping exercise a few Soligas expressed their concern and did not want their clan sacred sites mapped; hence these

Figure 25.2 Locating yelles on the map

Topographic sheets with sacred natural sites marked on it were used to help locate the clan boundaries followed by subsequent visits to the forests to ascertain the yelle boundaries.

Source: Sushmita Mandal

sites remain unmapped. The sacred natural sites are distributed across BRTWS and in the course of a year's field work accompanied by Soliga elders most sites were spatially located using Global Positioning System (GPS) enabled devices.

The map with sacred natural sites was shared with Soligas at a workshop (see Figure 25.2). There has been overwhelming consensus on the need to circulate the map widely amongst government agencies and schools. This they feel will constitute a powerful document of their cultural heritage and of the location of places that have been left out during mainstream cartographic exercises.

The Soligas believe that with such a map they will again be able to enter and move through the forest without the restrictions imposed by government policy. They have reiterated that the forest could only be mapped because they have lived, nurtured and named all such places. Such reiteration is reflective of their sense of ownership of the forest. They claim that although forests may be renamed and classified in scientific and administrative terms, the community remains integral to the forest from which they derive their origins.

Transformations brought about as a result of policies

The cultural landscape described is emerging as a result of documenting the human history of the landscape that has until now remained in the oral tradition. Such narratives are critical to understanding protected areas in India. The mainstream discourse on protected areas for conservation in many developing countries have relied on modern mainstream values of nature, 'which deny the existence of alternative understandings of nature' (Buscher and Wolmer, 2007). This certainly holds true of the Indian context since the colonial era and again in the 1970s, when the country embarked on its grand plan of declaring a network of protected areas to protect the country's wildlife.

The declaration of BRTWS landscape as a wildlife sanctuary had far-reaching consequences for the lives of resident Soliga communities. Podus (as swidden settlements are called) were allowed to cultivate small parcels of land around these settlements and to collect NTFP under the aegis of a state-run institution called the Large-scale Adivasi Multipurpose Primary Society. This sedentarization of Soligas led to a weakening of their close links with forest resources, and an erosion of knowledge pertaining to agriculture. Before the declaration of the BRTWS, cultivation had been practiced in a forest-cultivation continuum, each complementing and optimizing the other. Their approach to settled agriculture was adapted from their knowledge of shifting cultivation. The yelles within which the Soligas moved started to blur, and Soliga cultural practice was transformed by adapting to changes that were imposed upon them by way of State policy prescriptions. Displacement resulted in the relocation of some sacred sites, especially those of presiding Kula deities, closer to the podus (colonies). Several sacred sites deep in the forest fell out of use due to access difficulties generated by administrative restrictions imposed on the movements of the Soligas. Gradually Soliga stewardship over their sacred sites changed dramatically as they were forced into changing relationships with the forest. In other cases neglect was due to the sheer physical distances and erosion of forest attachment amongst the younger generation who were born in the newly settled podus. Thus, a steady disengagement with the landscape pervaded the Soliga way of life as regulations on use and access to forest resources tightened.

At the sacred sites that were relocated closer to settlements a trend towards construction of more elaborate ritual structures, as opposed to the highly abstracted symbolic representations of deities more typical of sites located within the forest, has taken place. Many of these representations were incorporated into found structures such as prominent stones (see Figure 25.1) or unusually shaped trees. These changes can be attributed to a certain 'Sanskritisation' of Soliga culture brought about as a result of the communities' need to be accepted within existing social hierarchies. This can be linked to larger trends in the mainstreaming of Soliga culture, including a tendency to privilege the worldview of outsiders over their own, and the corresponding attempt to adopt similar ritual practices.

In 2006 a near-complete ban on NTFP collection within sanctuaries and national parks was imposed following a ruling by the country's Supreme Court. The present scenario of severely limited livelihood options, in which forest incomes are regulated due to the Protected Area regime, has further impeded efforts by Soligas to meet livelihood needs and exercise any stewardship in the forest. However, in the past despite insecure tenure over NTFP collection Soligas did practice sustainable harvest practices and as part of ATREE initiative have also been involved in resource monitoring till 2005 (Setty et al, 2008).

During our community interactions, Soligas strongly reiterated that they were wrongly labelled as destroyers of the forest:

> *Aren't we, the native dwellers of the forests who have been practicing litter-fires, managing to conserve biodiversity? What have the so-called civilized urban dwellers contributed towards it? You have prevented fires, promoted growth of weeds, increased the rate of disease and destroyed the health of the forests. The Soligas, who are the native dwellers and true children of the forest, are not responsible for today's degraded forest cover. It is only civilized folks with their law and policy who have contributed to the destruction of forests.* (Achuge Gowda, personal communication, 2007)

The Soligas believe that they have historically protected forests by preventing large fires, selectively setting fire to dried grasses and leaves. They did so in the month of January when there was still enough moisture left in the forest to prevent big fires. Soliga elders recounted how the forest understory was historically cleared by such fires and pointed out that the suppression of fire in recent decades has led directly to the spread of invasive species such as lantana (*Lantana camara*). They similarly attribute the growing incidence of hemi-parasites on gooseberry trees to the changed fire regime. Due to its extremely invasive character, lantana has strongly inhibited the regeneration of native species, medicinal plants, grasses and wild tubers. Soligas see these drastic changes as leading to severe food crises for the animals, which depend on these native species as a food source. The traditional food systems of the Soligas, based on hunting, shifting cultivation and the collection of a wide variety of NTFPs, are intrinsically linked with the forests. These traditional food systems are already being affected by reduced access to forest resources and the spread of lantana. Soligas recount a host of species (including grasses, forest fruits, climbers and tubers) that have either vanished or become rare. Despite the rich knowledge that Soligas have of the forest and the vivid descriptions of changes that have occurred, there is no acknowledgement by park managers of this knowledge. The RFRA (2006) does provide scope for such incorporation but implementation on the ground has yet to begin to assess incorporating the future success of such narratives into park management.

A framework for co-management

Much literature is available which critiques the often positively projected Joint Forest Management for its lack of institutional framework to guide the process during the 1970s and hence it met with limited success (Sarin, 1998; Sunder, 2000; Vemuri, 2008). The evolution of the current approach is seeded in the failure of this joint forest management to provide either tenure or livelihoods security to forest dwelling communities. Prescriptions for protected area management are based entirely on biophysical criteria, often ignoring human agency and its role in shaping the structure of forests. It is increasingly evident that more context-specific management tools, based on a dynamic

understanding of the history of landscape use, have to be developed within protected areas to address biodiversity loss. Mapping the landscape the way Soligas visualize it provides critical evidence of human use and access. Such history of landscape use must be taken into account when attempting to understand and manage the same.

The recent enactment of the RFRA is aimed at reversing the historical marginalization of tribal and other forest dwelling communities. The act provides rights to own and live in the forest land for habitation or cultivation, right of access and use and sale of minor forest produce. It gives the right to protect, regenerate, conserve or manage any community forest resource, right of access to biodiversity and community right to intellectual property and traditional knowledge related to biodiversity and cultural diversity and any other right customarily enjoyed by forest dwelling tribes and other traditional forest dwellers as the case may be, but excluding hunting/trapping wild animals for meat or extraction of any body parts. Critically, this Act for the first time tries to address important livelihood security issues, while also stressing the rights and responsibilities of the forest dwellers in maintaining sustainable forest use patterns and the conservation of forest biodiversity. Guaranteed under RFRA, this has immense scope to draw up plans for collaborative forest management with tenure security granted to communities. Soligas have filed claims for community rights and individual rights. While initial ground work on surveying land claimed has begun, no claims have so far been settled.

Cultural histories that closely link people with the environment provide scope for engaging with co-management systems in pursuit of better and more effective forest governance. Communities must be involved in conservation planning, in developing protocols that identify categories of both nature and people, set priorities and use varied tools to address issues of conservation along with livelihoods (Brechin et al, 2002). In such a process, local forest use practices might be incorporated and oral history narratives used to reflect on both social and environmental changes that can help assess, understand and identify causes of ecological deterioration. These can then potentially be reversed, through institutional arrangements and ecological restoration techniques.

Conclusion

Oral histories, and the spatial visualization of Soliga cultural geography, can be used to inform and provide context for better governance of the BRTWS. The mapping of sacred sites of Soligas within the protected area is an important step towards restoring their stake in a landscape that is as much a cultural construct as an ecological one. Soligas see mapping as a political process to assert their collective identity and rights over the landscape, and be recognized as an integral part of it: 'The official map makes us invisible. It recognizes forest roads, and bungalows, but does not mark our sacred sites. This is our map that has evidence of our presence in the landscape. We must circulate this map widely amongst the Government and ourselves' (Siddegowda, Buthani podu, personal communication, 2007).

There is growing recognition internationally of indigenous cultures and their sacred places and practices as repositories of knowledge of biodiversity as shown through the endorsement of the International Declaration of the Rights of Indigenous Peoples, and in particular the reference to cultural significant places in articles 11 and 12 (2007). It is time that India, a signatory to the Declaration, recognized this by effectively creating spaces for such communities to participate in governance and develop policies for the incorporation of cultural landscapes into conservation strategies. While the RFRA takes some positive steps in this direction it has not yet been implemented in BRTWS. The narratives of the Soligas provide information on their culture-environment relations. Such narratives not only inform environmental history, but also make the case for promoting a more inclusive conservation agenda for the Soligas. As has been reiterated by Soliga elders, the use, ownership and management of sacred sites can not only guarantee the sustenance of indigenous cultures, but also protect biodiversity and water resources that are part of the Soliga landscape.

References

Aiyappan, A. (1948) Report on the socio-economic conditions of the aboriginal tribes of the province of Madras, Madras Government Press, Madras, India

Alcorn, J.B. (2000) Borders, Rules and Governance: Mapping to Catalyse Changes in Policy and Management, Gatekeeper Series no. SA91, International Institute for Environment and Development, London, www.iied.org/pubs/pdfs/X180IIED.pdf

Aravind, N.A., Rao, D. and Madhusudan, P.S. (2001) 'Additions to the birds of Biligiri Rangaswamy Temple Wildlife Sanctuary, Western Ghats, India', *Zoos' Print*, vol 27, pp541–547, www.zooprint.org/ZooPrintJournal/2001/July/541-547.pdf

Brechin, S.R., Wilshusen, P.R., Fortwangler, C. and West, P.C (2002) 'Beyond the square wheel: Toward a more comprehensive understanding of biodiversity conservation as social and political process', *Society and Natural Resources*, vol 14, pp41–64

Buscher, B. and Wolmer, W. (2007) 'Introduction: The politics of engagement between biodiversity conservation and the social sciences', *Conservation and Society*, vol 5, pp1–21

Byers, B., Cunliffe, R.N. and Hudak, A.T. (2009) 'Linking the conservation of culture and nature: A case study of sacred forests in Zimbabwe', *Human Ecology*, vol 29, no 2

CI (1893) 'Census of India', 1891 Vol XXV, Part I, Mysore Report, Mysore, India

Eghenter, C. (2000) 'Mapping people's forests: The Role of mapping in community-based management of conservation areas in Indonesia', Biodiversity Support Programme, Washington DC

Geesa, S.D. (2008) 'Participatory mapping as a tool for empowerment: Experiences and lessons learned from the ILC network', International Land Coalition, Rome, www.landcoalition.org/pdf/08_ILC_Participatory_Mapping_Low.pdf

Gopal, H. (1965) 'Problems of Soligas', *Social Welfare*, vol 12, no 8, pp20–22

Kamathy, R.V., Rao, A.S. and Rao, R.S. (1967) 'A contribution to the flora of Biligirirangan Hills, Mysore State', *Bulletin of the Botanical Survey of India*, vol 9, pp206–224

Luiz, A.A.D. (1963) *Tribes of Mysore*, G.S. Viswa Publishers, Bangalore, India

Nanjundayya, H.V. and Iyer, L.K.A. (1961) *The Mysore Tribes and Castes*, The Mysore University, Myrsore, India

Nelson, J. and Hossack, L. (2003) 'Protected areas and indigenous peoples: The paradox of conservation and survival of the Baka in Moloundou region (southeast Cameroon)', United Nations Environment Programme (UNEP), Nairobi, Kenya

Sarin, M. (1998) 'From conflict to collaboration: Institutional issues in community management', in Poffenberger, M. and McGean, B. (eds) *Village Voices, Forest Choices: Joint Forest Management in India*, Oxford University Press, New Delhi, pp165–209

Setty, R.S., Bawa, K., Ticktin, T. and Gowda, C.M. (2008) 'Evaluation of a participatory resource monitoring system for non timber forest products: The case of amla (*Phyllanthus* spp.) fruit harvest by Soligas in South India', *Ecology and Society*, vol 13, no 2, p19

Somasundaram, H.N. and Kibe, R.V. (1990) *The Tribe and its Stride*, Girijana Kalyana Kendra, BR. Hills, India

Subbayya, K.M. (1965) 'Customs and life of Sholigars in Chamarajanagar', *My Forest* April, pp43–46.

Sunder, N. (2000) 'Unpacking the joint in joint forest management', *Development and Change*, vol 31, pp255–279

Thurston, E. (1909) *Castes and Tribes of Southern India*, Volume VI, Madras Government Press, Madras, India

United Nations (2007) 'Declaration on the rights of indigenous peoples', United Nations General Assembly, 61st session, Agenda item 68, Report of the Human Rights Council, Geneva, Switzerland

Vemuri, A. (2008) 'Joint forest management in India: An unavoidable and conflicting common property regime in natural resource management', *Journal of Development and Social Transformation*, Maxwell School of Syracuse University, vol 5, pp81–90

Williams, M. (2003) *Deforesting the Earth: From Prehistory to Global Crisis*, University of Chicago Press, Chicago, IL

26

The Devi as Ecofeminist Warrior: Reclaiming the Role of Sacred Natural Sites in East-Central India

Radhika Borde and Alana Jules Jackman

Summary

This chapter describes an environmental movement underway in east-central India that has resulted in the creation and regeneration of several hundred sacred natural sites. It is a grassroots-level women's movement grounded in the revivalist worship of an ancient, pre-Sanskritic earth goddess who resides in sacred groves. As a result of this movement women are restoring the biodiversity of existing sacred groves and are also designating new sites as sacred. The movement combines both feminist and environmental activism and is fuelled by instances of possession by the earth goddess. The unique features of this movement are the attempt to link the socio-economic empowerment of rural Indian women with their participation in ritual worship conducted in sacred groves, the strengthening of pre-Sanskritic religious elements among marginalized Indian women and the reclamation of an ancient spirituality and associated landscape by India's marginalized communities.

Introduction

A new religious movement is sweeping across rural east-central India. Women are rediscovering the earth goddess – in themselves, in states of divine possession and in the sacred groves that contain her power (see Figure 26.1). The consequence of this has been the birth of a feminist consciousness in women previously accustomed to patriarchal control and their spearheading of an extensive forestation programme in denuded sacred groves. Most significantly, the movement has resulted in the re-sanctifying and re-dedication of natural sites that have fallen out of the religious consciousness of the region's people. This paper will attempt to describe this movement as an example of organic ecofeminism and demonstrate the significance of sacred natural sites in relation to it.

Methodology

The research methodology was qualitative, involved a combination of participant and non-participant observation, along with loosely structured focus-group interviews. The language of communication was a combination of Hindi and Sadri, the local lingua franca. The fieldwork was conducted by Radhika Borde.

Figure 26.1 A sacred-grove worship ceremony in Arsande village, Jharkhand

Source: Radhika Borde

Ecofeminism: Theoretical background

A term coined by Francoise d'Eaubonne, ecofeminism is a form of feminism that involves a theoretical linkage between feminism and environmentalism. The mutual reinforcement of these apparently distinct spheres of activism is achieved by the positing of a 'woman–nature connection'. The terms under which this linkage is described vary. Some schools of ecofeminist thought theorize a psycho-biological connection between women and nature – Susan Griffin positing perhaps the most radical identification: 'We are Nature seeing Nature' (Griffin, 1978, p226). The criterion determining this identification is derived in large part from the cyclical aspect of womanhood and associated nurturing qualities (Braidotti et al, 1994, p70). Other strands of ecofeminist discourse posit an explanation of the 'woman–nature connection' that stems from reciprocity – stating that the instance of ecological activism having involved a significantly large proportion of women is due

to the fact that they had possibly more at stake. 'We saw that the impact on women of ecological disasters and deterioration was harder than on men.' (Mies and Shiva, 1993, p3)

In the Indian context, ecofeminist theory is coupled with an emphasis on the necessity of women's socio-economic empowerment. Ecofeminists in India also champion female ecological knowledge. Vandana Shiva, a noted Indian ecofeminist, emphasizes that rural Indian women's knowledge of ecological dependency, derived from their multi-sectored engagement with the biosphere, is the key to environmental sustainability (Mies and Shiva, 1993, p167). This expertise is understood to position them as natural environmental managers and ecofeminism in India is aimed at empowering women with the credibility that would enable them to take on this role in the public sphere.

Ecofeminism in India

When access to clean drinking water determines a woman's position on this or that side of the poverty line, it is obvious that she should speak out for the sustainable management of water resources – or so ecofeminist theory insists. Unfortunately however, in India the energy fuelling ecofeminist activism springs mostly from the pages of academic discourse rather than people's action. Some examples of grassroots-level environmental activism that have seen the participation of a significant proportion of women do however exist in this context. The well-known peasant protest movement against commercial forestry is a case in point. Known as the Chipko movement, it was spearheaded by rural Indian women who started hugging trees to prevent them being cut down by timber merchants. Chamundeyi, a Chipko activist, when asked what she felt were the most important things that she wished to conserve, stated: 'Our freedom and forests and food. Without these, we are nothing, we are impoverished. With our own food production we are prosperous – we do not need jobs from businessmen and governments – we make our own livelihood' (Mies and Shiva, 1993, p249). We must take into account however, that Chamundeyi's assertive speech is far from the norm as far as acceptable female behaviour in the Indian context is concerned – and is unlikely to be echoed by many rural Indian women with the same confidence.

Even though Indian women do in some spheres have significant ecological knowledge, they are often not allowed to articulate it publicly due to patriarchal expectations of feminine submissiveness (Jewitt, 2004, p132). Significantly, the articulation of agro-ecological knowledge by rural Indian women is often suppressed due to the fear of being accused of witchcraft (Jewitt, 2004, p133). Rural Indian women may well be closet ecofeminists but apart from a few scattered examples of the expression of this impulse in the public realm, ecofeminism in India remains a dream of the theorizing intellectual. As a theory however, it has had far-reaching influence. It has inspired the governments of various Indian states to enforce the mandatory inclusion of women in village-level forest management committees – this however, fails to be anything other than additional evidence of the necessity of feminist empowerment prior to the implementation of ecofeminist discourse (Jewitt and Kumar, 2004, p154). Empirical studies have

shown that entrenched gender expectations of the unseemliness of female participation in political decision-making result in women remaining silent at these committee's meetings (Jewitt, 2004, p132). Ecofeminism does possesses the potential to empower rural Indian women and channel their environmental knowledge into conservation initiatives – but if the ground upon which this is to occur is the stronghold of patriarchy, the cause is lost. What hope could there possibly be – except perhaps for divine intervention?

Sarna Mata: The Earth Goddess

Patriarchy's success at dulling female expression in India could perhaps only be countered by the energy deriving from the deep-rooted faith traditions of the subcontinent. As it seems to have been in east-central India – liberating voices that decades of ecofeminist rhetoric and derivative bureaucratic initiatives could not. This is the religious revival of Earth-based spirituality in the region, which has sparked off a significant environmental and socio-political movement. It is centred on the worship of Sarna Mata, or the sacred-grove goddess, who is depicted as an old crone draped in white. Parallels can be drawn between her and the 'old wise woman' aspect of the Triple-Goddess theorized by western goddess feminists – the function of which '… is to be of assistance in times of difficult passage' (Caputi, 1993, p246).

Sarna Mata is a pre-Sanskritic goddess and has long been understood to be the female compatriot of the supreme male deity worshipped by India's tribes-people also known as Adivasis (her symbolic associations with the Earth also show her to be related to several goddesses of the Sanskritic Hindu pantheon). However, the cultic phenomenon of the expression of female devotion to her is radically different from the religious contexts within which she was traditionally worshipped. The emergence of this was apparently triggered off by a series of cases of divine possession that began to be reported in the region about a decade ago. The context for this phenomenon is understood to have been provided by the religious–political awakening of the Oraon tribe, a Dravidian Adivasi tribe living in east-central India. Typically, these possession trances involved rural Indian women experiencing altered states of consciousness, during which they would believe themselves possessed by Sarna Mata. While in the grip of the possession, these women would vocalize what they believed to be the goddess's anger at the deterioration of the social scene, the environment and most specifically, her wrath at the neglect of the sacred groves where she presided. Women who experienced these possession trances in the early phases of the movement report being led to sacred natural sites that had been forgotten by their communities. The discovery of Sarna Mata in the depths of their own consciousness has provided these women and others with the energy to take up the cause of the regeneration of sacred groves – a task to which they are dedicating themselves with the greatest zeal.

Ecofeminism in Indian sacred groves?

The concept of the 'sacred grove' is shared by many cultures across the world – in almost every context harking back to an earlier, more indigenous form of religiosity. Ramakrishnan defines the 'sacred grove' as a portion of the natural eco-system type that is maintained by traditional societies for cultural/religious reasons (Ramakrishnan, 1998b, p5). Understood to be inhabited by forest deities and typically supporting high levels of biodiversity, due to the operation of prohibitions and taboos regarding utilization, (Ramakrishnan, 1998b, p17) 'sacred groves' attract the interest of conservationists for reasons of the biodiversity rich environment they constitute as well as for the replicative model they offer for the construction of forest-management systems. Sacred groves are ubiquitous in east-central India. In this region they come under the state administrative classification of 'village forests' – a common property resource. Typically consisting of a cluster of primarily Sal (*Shorea robusta*) trees along with a few examples of other tree species (Patnaik and Pandey, 1998, p315), these sacred groves are called Sarnas and as mentioned earlier, are believed to be inhabited by a Devi (female deity) generally known as Sarna Mata. Until recently, religious activity in these groves was limited to the rituals conducted during the annual fertility festival celebrated in March,

known as Sarhul. This event was chiefly concerned with the propitiation of the goddess for the purpose of ensuring a satisfactory monsoon and involved ritual sacrifices of animals, grain, etc. The religious proceedings which sought Sarna Mata's favour traditionally encouraged only the marginal participation of women and a relationship between religious practitioner and deity that was in no way devotional – a situation which in the current scenario has changed unrecognizably.

Women's involvement in Sarnas

The involvement of women in ritualistic worship in sacred groves is in violation of several taboos – the sacred-grove goddess that women have taken to worshipping in recent times is traditionally denied to them except through the mediation of a male priest or pahan. Indeed established ritual practice dictates that women are to be prohibited from entering the sacred groves where she resides – it being feared that they would pollute its sacrality (Xaxa, 1992, p106). In recent years however, as her female devotees understand, the sacred-grove goddess has become restless with this state of affairs. The waning faith of villagers in Earth-based religiosity and the consequent neglect of the sacred groves that formed the primary site of its expression has incited her to possession. As the women she possesses whirl their heads in ecstatic trances, Sarna Mata's exasperation at the social and environmental situation finds vent. After their trances, the women, feeling the touch of the divine lingering, feel empowered enough to take to religious and political assertion. Today, one can see them conducting religious services in sacred groves every week, complete with rituals of their own invention. The women often face censure from their male counterparts for these actions. In fact in one village the women were attacked as they were attempting to enter a sacred grove. Despite all this resistance, these, mostly illiterate, women have petitioned the government for money to build walls encircling the groves and have been successful in obtaining it. No one is allowed to cut trees in the sacred groves now and in fact new saplings have been planted that are flourishing under the women's devotional care. Sal (*Shorea robusta*) and Karam (*Nauclea parvifolia*) are the tree species which the women most commonly plant – both are traditionally linked to Adivasi culture through myth and ritual. Sarna Mata's devotees have come up with ingenious ways to implement their forestation program. They surround planted saplings with Ipomoea (*Ipomea carnea*) hedges. This is a perennial morning glory species and is toxic to grazing animals. They provide effective and inexpensive protection to the growing trees.

The Sarna movement, ecospirituality and new sacred sites

The Sarna movement has also resulted in the creation of several new sacred groves. The relationship of the movement to sacred natural sites is reciprocal – the strengthening of the movement results in biodiversity conservation and forestation of existing sacred groves. However, for the movement to spread across the region's villages and for the local communitarian worship that characterizes it to be conducted, sacred natural sites must exist. In this context, Sarna Mata's devotees express that the new sites that are selected for sacralization are in fact old sacred natural sites that are totally neglected and where Sarna Mata's power must be re-established. Through the movement, several such sites have been sanctified, are being planted with saplings and have become the focus of local women's spirituality.

The ecospirituality that these rural Indian women express encompasses spheres of environmental activism beyond just the upkeep of the sacred groves. The rituals enacted during the worship ceremonies held in the groves every Thursday incorporate complex levels of symbolism – the enactment of which the women believe has inculcated in them an environmental consciousness that has begun to direct their daily engagement with the ecosystem. Within the sacred groves, the ceremonial focus is typically a raised earthen platform planted with bushes of holy basil and surrounded by tall bamboo staffs mounted with red and white striped flags. The first action committed by devotees of the sacred-grove goddess upon entering the groves is a parikrama or a circumambulation of this platform. They profess that as they perform this, they imagine that they are circumambulating the entire Earth and that they pray for every living creature it

sustains. The women I interviewed claimed that after commencing regular worship in the sacred groves they had become much more conscientious about cutting trees. The reasons they gave for the change in their attitude was the influence of their devotion to Sarna Mata – their worship of the Earth translating into a reverence for nature in general. The women believe themselves influenced in many profound ways by the ceremonies they conduct in the groves. Typically, these consist of a combination of communitarian worship, individual ritual performance and personal mystic experience. The women who participate in the communitarian sacred grove rituals have formed administrative bodies to look after the upkeep of the groves, the regulation of the ceremonies and the enforcement of informal codes of conduct. Some of these bodies are formally registered and have the official status of local NGOs. Others are not registered but maintain meeting diaries which endow them with a certain level of authority in the eyes of the state. These bodies often play a part in stipulating behavioural norms that Sarna Mata's devotees are expected to follow. The consumption of alcohol is frowned upon and bodily purity is encouraged. These administrative bodies have also formed an extensive network. When a site needs to be dedicated in a distant village, women from all over the region are informed. They travel long distances to invoke Sarna Mata into themselves and into the site that needs to be sacralized. The movement has reportedly spread across the states of Jharkhand, Chattisgarh and Orissa as well as parts of Madhya Pradesh, West Bengal, Bihar and Assam. Though men do not play an active part in conducting the rituals or structuring the worship, their presence is accepted – and a few do sometimes attend. In fact the female devotees of Sarna Mata say that it is a pity more men are not attracted to the regular engaged worship of Sarna Mata that they practise. As a movement however, their communitarian worship is supported by many men – and significantly by some Adivasi politicians; it has in fact given birth to a regional political party.

Conclusions

Forest management applications

In the contemporary Indian scenario, the state is taking more and more cognisance of the value of sharing the responsibility of forest management with local people (earlier virtually the exclusive purview of the government) – allowing those who often depend on forests for their livelihood to manage and conserve them (see also Chapter 25). As a corollary to this, the potential for environmental and biodiversity preservation that the concept of forest sacredness offers is attracting much interest. Keeping the current trend in Indian forest management in mind, conservationists mourn the waning of faith and pride among forest-dwellers as to the value of their traditional knowledge and belief systems (Hughes and Chandran, 1998, p83). With this in mind, a new religious movement that combines women's empowerment with environmental activism is good news for conservation science.

The larger scope of the Sarna movement

The Sarna movement acquires greater significance (from a conservation perspective) when one considers the criticism directed at the invocation of spirituality to fuel environmentalism by one of the country's leading scholars (Guha, 1989, p71–83). Attacking the philosophical movement known as 'Deep Ecology' that celebrates an 'ethic of wilderness' and the assumedly 'biocentric' orientation of eastern philosophies and indigenous religious traditions, Ramachandra Guha asserts that the implementation of such a discourse in a setting like India would be tantamount to environmental colonialism – resulting in the disempowerment of the rural poor and the appropriation of their belief-systems (Guha, 1989, p71–74). However, the Sarna movement allows for the assertion of the belief-systems of India's rural poor – more significantly and specifically by the Adivasis who have faced perhaps millennia of marginalization at the hands of the dominant Indian religious culture. In an interesting twist to the Sanskritization process that anthropologists warn is eroding Adivasi culture due to its

interaction with the Indian mainstream, the Sarna movement has attracted non-Adivasi individuals to the worship of Sarna Mata. These non-Adivasi devotees of Sarna Mata are in no way appropriating a more marginalized culture, rather they are becoming religiously pluralized in the spirit of acceptance that is believed to characterize Indian religious thinking. Also, in response to Guha's criticism, the socio-economic empowerment of rural women can be said to be one of the foremost objectives of the Sarna movement. The groups of women who meet in the sacred groves that are located in almost each village cluster in the region are interested in forming themselves into state and NGO sponsored bodies known as self-help groups – as mentioned earlier some groups have even registered themselves as official societies. These would function as micro-financing units and would also enable women to initiate micro-enterprises involving the manufacture and sale of handmade products. In fact, one such group of Sarna Mata's devotees has reportedly achieved great success with its mushroom cultivation programme. The Sarna movement is also using the re-sanctifying and re-dedication of natural sites to reclaim land that was once used by marginalized communities.

The Sarna movement's conservation potential

Environmental scientists have expressed great enthusiasm for the Sarna movement's potential for biodiversity conservation and regeneration. Since sacred natural sites in the Adivasi religious system are chosen to represent each local ecosystem type (mountainous, aquatic, forest, grassland, etc.), the conservation of the biodiversity they contain would cover practically the whole range of the region's vegetation. Rare plant species endemic to a particular ecosystem type could also be cultivated in degraded sacred sites or even in the newly consecrated sacred sites which could be selected for the degree to which they could be made to represent the region's ecosystem diversity. The effort required to undertake such an exercise would of course be enormous, but it is argued by scientists that faith, coupled with an awareness of the value of biodiversity, would provide the required motivation (Sharat Singh, personal communication, 2009).

Sarna Mata, new sacredness

The new phenomenon of devotion to Sarna Mata is most significant when measured in terms of its discursive impact. As stated earlier, Sarna Mata's devotees understand that the symbolic ritual they practise in sacred groves influences their consciousness to include a greater ethic of care towards their natural environment. Many devotees have in fact turned to vegetarianism and all are instructed to abstain from the consumption of meat on Thursdays when the weekly communitarian ritual is conducted. Interestingly, the female devotees of Sarna Mata have criticized the traditional Adivasi practice of sacrificing fowls in sacred groves. They insist that Sarna Mata desires only the sacrifice of pure water. They also state that if it had not been for their devotion and their watering of the 'Earth', the world would have long since burnt up due to the great heat that is being generated in it in modern times. Perhaps the essence of the movement can be summed up in a myth concerning Sarna Mata's intervention in the material world at a place known as Sirasita in the district of Gumla in east-central India. On 2 February every year, thousands of Sarna Mata's devotees make their pilgrimage to this site.

In the myth, Sarna Mata appears in the avatar of the consort of Singbonga, the stern punishing tribal sky-god. Angered by the degeneration of the human race that is his creation, Singbonga rains fire on the Earth, scorching the life from it. Watching his vengeful act and taking pity on the victims of his rage, Sarna Mata hides a boy and a girl inside a water gourd in forgiving wisdom. Later she takes them to Sirasita and deposits them into a crab hole issuing forth a spring. She does not inform her consort of this subversion of his destructive passion, but waits for the regret she knows is incipient. Soon after having destroyed the whole of creation, Singbonga realizes that there is no longer anyone left to offer him sacrifices. His consort Sarna Mata can now only serve him the most meagre of repasts. She does not fail to remind him that it is all his own doing whenever he complains about this. Singbonga finally laments

his impulsive deed bitterly. When Sarna Mata sees the point has hit home, she produces the boy and girl she had hidden away – much to Singbonga's delight. From the human pair she has saved spring forth the races that now populate the Earth (Mundu, 2003, p60–62).

Ecofeminism and a sacred solution

As described earlier, ecofeminist discourse has been shown to be a malfunctioning tool in India – the logic demonstrating that women have the capacity and the interest to speak for the environment devoid of the adrenaline required in the realm of actual politics. The picture of emancipated womanhood doing battle for the ecosystem may make much sense, but holds little charm. Perhaps necessitating the Earth goddess to step in and grant the zestfulness that has for so long eluded the implementation of ecofeminist discourse? Sarna Mata's message is to learn to tread lightly upon the Earth – maybe the time has come for us to hear it. As one of her devotees states: 'Everyone worships the God of the sky, they need to remember the Goddess of the Earth.' (Phulmani Toppo, personal communication, 2008) Having made such a mess of the ground beneath its feet in its attempt to reach for the stars, what better advice could the human race heed?

References

Braidotii, R.R., Charkiewicz, E., Häusler, S. and Wieringa, S. (1994) *Women, the Environment and Sustainable Development*, Zed Books, London

Caputi, J. (1993) 'Nuclear power and the sacred', in Adams, C.J., *Ecofeminism and the Sacred*, The Continuum Publishing Company, New York

Griffin, S. (1978) *Woman and Nature: The Roaring Inside Her*, Harper & Row, San Francisco, CA

Guha, R. (1989) 'Radical American environmentalism and wilderness preservation: A third world critique', *Environmental Ethics*, vol 11, no 1, pp71–83

Hughes, J.D. and Chandran, M.D.S. (1998) 'Sacred groves around the earth: An overview', in Ramakrishnan, P.S., Saxena, K.G. and Chandrashekara, U.M., *Conserving the Sacred*, Science Publishers Inc, Enfield, pp69–86

Jewitt, S. (2004) 'Mothering earth?', in Corbridge, S., Jewitt, S. and Kumar, S., *Jharkhand: Environment,*

Development, Ethnicity, Oxford University Press, New Delhi, pp112–147

Jewitt, S. and Kumar, S. (2004) 'A political ecology of forest management', in Corbridge, S., Jewitt, S. and Kumar, S., *Jharkhand; Environment, Development, Ethnicity*, Oxford University Press, New Delhi, pp148–174

Mies, M. and Shiva, V. (1993) *Ecofeminism*, Spinifex Press, Melbourne

Mundu, J. (2003) *The Ho Christian Community*, Media House, Delhi

Patnaik, S. and Pandey, A. (1998) 'A study of indigenous community based forest management system: Sarna (sacred grove)', in Ramakrishnan, P.S, Saxena, K.G. and Chandrashekara, U.M., *Conserving the Sacred*, Science Publishers Inc, Enfield, pp315–321

Ramakrishnan, P.S, (1998a) 'Conserving the sacred for biodiversity management: Conclusions and recommendations', in Ramakrishnan, P.S, Saxena, K.G. and Chandrashekara, U.M., *Conserving the Sacred*, Science Publishers Inc, Enfield, pp13–23

Ramakrishnan, P.S. (1998b) 'Foreword', in Ramakrishnan, P.S, Saxena, K.G. and Chandrashekara, U.M., *Conserving the Sacred*, Science Publishers Inc, Enfield, pp5–7

Xaxa, V. (1992) 'Oraons: Religion, customs and environment', in Sen, G., *Indigenous Vision*, Sage Publications, New Delhi, pp101–110

27

Conclusions: Sustaining Sacred Natural Sites to Conserve Nature and Culture

Robert Wild, Bas Verschuuren and Jeffrey McNeely

This concluding chapter reviews 10 key points that have emerged out of the chapters presented. The overarching conclusion is that sacred natural sites are an important but largely unrecognized, and highly threatened, primary network of conservation sites with the power to make a significant contribution toward protecting and restoring biological and cultural diversity. The 10 conclusions discussed below establish a framework and suggest steps toward supporting sacred natural sites as an important means of conserving nature and culture. These provide the conceptual foundation for the recommendations with which the book concludes. A preliminary action plan generated to inform further steps is included in Annex 2.

10 conclusions on sacred natural sites

1. Sacred natural sites have long served as a primary conservation network for conserving nature and culture.
2. The rapid degradation and loss of sacred natural sites severely threatens critical biodiversity, ecosystem services, cultural resources and even ways of life.
3. Recognizing sacred natural sites supports community autonomy, promotes effective management and gives voice, rights and action to local people.
4. Faith, spirituality and science provide different but complementary ways of knowing and understanding human–nature relationships.
5. Mainstream, folk and indigenous religions and spiritualities have complex, sometimes conflicting relationships; enhanced mutual respect and in some cases rapprochement is required for collective care of sacred natural sites.
6. Successful co-existence of sacred natural sites and modern economic imperatives requires a better understanding of their inter-relationships, and of the broad values and benefits of sacred natural sites for human well-being and development.
7. Sacred natural sites as nodes of resilience, restoration and adaptation to climate change offer opportunities for recovering ecologically sound, local ways of life.
8. Sacred natural sites need to be consciously included as part of a coherent and coordinated response to global change.
9. Local commitment, wide public awareness, supportive national policies and laws, state protection and broad international support are essential for the survival of sacred natural sites.
10. A broad strategy for conserving sacred natural sites, defining the priority actions required and building a global coalition to carry out these actions is urgently needed.

1 Sacred natural sites have long served as a primary conservation network for conserving nature and culture

As seen from chapters in this volume, at the time of the founding of the world's first modern national park, some 150 years ago, a widespread network of what have now been termed Sacred Natural Sites (SNS) already existed. They covered almost every biome and habitat type and most parts of the globe. These sites were (and often still are) culturally paramount to the societies that had formed them but they also conserved nature. Not only were these sacred natural sites the world's earliest protected areas, it is probably not an overstatement to say that these sites have provided the backbone of the global network of modern protected areas.

The earliest cultures of our species, *Homo sapiens*, depended directly on the goods and services provided by nature, through hunting, gathering and scavenging. Archaeological evidence, art and the burial practices of Stone Age peoples indicate their strong cultural links to nature (e.g. UNESCO, 2007; Frazer, 2008). It is evident that early human societies recognized that certain sites were of particular importance and these sites – springs, seasonal breeding grounds of prey species, productive trees and so forth – were considered sacred and were protected by cultural practices, restricted hunting seasons and limited access.

Many sacred natural sites, therefore, have ancient origins and even those that do not have a current custodian community have often retained at least some strong cultural values until the present (see Figure 27.1). The cultural phenomenon of sacred natural sites therefore come down to the modern era as a universal heritage. Many of these, as described in the preceding chapters, are contained within modern protected areas, but many others remain on the lands of indigenous peoples and lands owned by major religions.

Sacred natural sites are one reminder that our species still depends on nature, not only for material needs but also for spiritual fulfilment. This dependence is, however, no longer so obvious in modern societies, especially for the 50 per cent of

Figure 27.1 Rock art in the Karakol valley in the Altai Republic, Russian Federation

Source: Joanna Dobson

people who live in cities. But as climate change, earthquakes, floods, droughts and other extreme events bring dramatic illustrations of human vulnerability, sacred natural sites prove their value as part of the natural fabric of the planet and as places central to knowledge on cultural adaptation and resilience. In the words of their custodians, they provide 'a network of planetary healing points', inspiring a more balanced relationship between people and the rest of nature (see Annex 1, Custodian Statement).

Only fairly recently, however, have conservation biologists realized that sacred natural sites are also extremely valuable in conserving biological diversity, and that this conservation is intimately linked to culture and cultural heritage (Carmichael et al, 1994; Ramakrishnan et al, 1998; Harmon and Putney, 2003; UNESCO, 2003; UN, 2007; Dudley et al, 2005; Pumarejo and Berges, 2005; Mallarach and Papayannis, 2007; Papayannis and Mallarach, 2009; see also Chapter 2). Sacred natural sites are, therefore, a primary conservation network. They often overlap with other conservation networks such as government protected areas, non-sacred indigenous and community conserved areas (e.g. grazing and other community resource use areas) and private protected areas.

Despite the wide distribution of sacred natural sites, this primary conservation network has gone unrecognized by many conservationists, developers, managers and policy-makers. Highlighting sacred natural sites as a primary conservation network will lead to a better analysis and understanding of their role in conserving biodiversity, and providing ecosystem services, such as provisioning (e.g. food and medicinal plants), regulating (e.g. water and climate), supporting (nutrient cycling and soil formation) and the more obvious cultural services (e.g. spiritual, religious and sense of place). This may also allow the economic valuation of sacred natural sites (see point 6 below) based on holistic approaches to valuation that include broad measures of human well-being (see for example Chapter 18).

2 The rapid degradation and loss of sacred natural sites severely threatens valuable biodiversity, ecosystem services, cultural resources and even ways of life

Despite their multiple values sacred natural sites are being lost in many parts of the world. Key causes include:

- destruction due to land-use change and conversion promoted by government economic policies;
- damage and deterioration from insensitive nature conservation and archaeological policies and practices;
- erosion due to cultural change, modernity and broad 'progressive' development contexts;
- damage and sometimes destruction from religious absorption, adoption, competition and impositions;
- pressures from population increase, resources shortages and material poverty.

Examples of direct land-use change include the loss of 90 per cent of sacred forest area in parts

of Yunnan, China (see Chapter 9) and 35 per cent loss of sacred groves from 1985 to 1990 in Sindhudurg District, India (see Chapter 21). In both of these cases much of the losses were due to government industrial forestry policies driven by economic imperatives. Plantation forestry, industrial agriculture, road and railway construction, urban development, mineral extraction and oil and gas pipelines are some of the causes of sacred natural site loss. These developments are also more widely disrupting natural ecosystems and the services they deliver to people (MA, 2005), as material interests have increasingly disrupted the balance between resource harvesting and spiritual values.

The progressive exclusion of local communities and indigenous peoples from their traditional lands and from access to their sacred sites due to government nature conservation policies can cause losses of biodiversity and ecological changes when traditional management ceases (see Chapter 25). In some cases the research and conservation of archaeological work damages the sites to the deep concern of traditional custodians who view this as desecration (UNESCO, 2007; Carmichael et al, 1994; see also Chapters 6 and 23; Figure 27.2).

The erosion of sacred groves in Cameroon (see Chapter 11) well illustrates how areas that have long received special attention by local people are now under pressure from changing values but within a national development context that includes population growth, resource shortages, increasing household livelihood demands, poverty, changing social beliefs, modernity and the weakening of traditional beliefs in the face of influence of mainstream faiths (Chapters 11 and 25). The relationships between faiths are further discussed under point 5.

3 Recognizing sacred natural sites supports community autonomy, promotes effective management and gives voice, rights and action to local people

Sacred natural sites need to be part of effective restoration of both ecosystems and community

Figure 27.2 Rogelio Mejia and José de los Santos are Tayrona from the Sierra Nevada de Santa Martha in Colombia

They are presenting the vision of their elders about how their sacred mountains are the 'heart of the world' and central to the Earth's well-being and that of its people.

Source: Bas Verchuuren

institutions, thus enabling sacred natural sites to support biodiversity as well as the improved well-being of growing human communities (see point 7). The wise use and protection of natural resources is best secured at the local level. Recent reports in relation to deforestation and carbon storage indicate that indigenous people and local communities are often better at conserving forests than governments are (Nelson and Chomitz, 2009; Chhatre and Agrawal, 2009). In general the greater the rule-making autonomy at the local level, the higher the amount of carbon stored and greater the benefits to local livelihoods. This is a contemporary confirmation of a growing consensus that biodiversity is often best conserved at the community level, particularly in traditional economies which receive appropriate support from the state (e.g. Berkes, 1999; Ostrom, et al, 2002; Borrini-Feyerabend et al, 2004). Mechanisms that support communities of different types are urgently needed to continue to protect and manage their sacred natural sites as well as their other territories.

In many cases the management of sacred natural sites is linked closely with indigenous and local community rights, based on the struggle for independence and control over resources. Such political issues play a key role in the policy discussions at the national level that once successfully resolved could enhance the well-being of custodians and their sacred natural sites and, at least indirectly, biodiversity as well. Development projects that aim to improve livelihood security and alleviate poverty through new economic activities may present threats to sacred sites, but this can be avoided by improved integration of cultural and spiritual values. Through such integration in development projects, sacred natural sites can become a locus where integrated conservation and development strategies can earn strong local support, especially where sacred natural sites form a focus of community cohesion.

4 Faith, spirituality and science provide different but complementary ways of knowing and understanding human-nature relationships

For communities to have greater autonomy for managing nature they may benefit from the experience of conservation biologists and other scientists in respectful mutual exchanges, regarding methods of ecosystem management. During the 4th IUCN World Conservation Congress held in Barcelona in 2008, the IUCN Specialist Group on the Cultural and Spiritual Values of Protected Areas convened a dialogue of custodians of sacred natural sites. The custodians came from eight indigenous communities from four continents and produced a statement which underscores the values that sacred natural sites have for indigenous people and local communities. This statement (Annex 1) gives voice to concerns and recommendations of custodians of sacred natural sites, and illustrates some of the different ways of knowing nature.

While recognizing the value of scientific and technical understanding of the biodiversity values of sacred natural sites, this book has also presented the complementary knowledge and wisdom from different cultural realms. This approach is in line with recent developments in the fields of nature conservation, where nature and culture are increasingly recognized as inextricably connected (Posey, 1999), especially within the unifying concept of 'biocultural diversity' (Maffi and Woodley, 2010; see also Chapter 6).

Conservationists must be engaged in the dialogue that brings sound natural science together with traditional wisdom, contributing to a holistic view of human-nature relationships (see Chapter 19). The reality is that nature conservationists are increasingly challenged to deal with social issues and beliefs, for example, when managing cultural heritage sites that are considered sacred, and this approach can bring many mutual benefits (see Chapter 5). Therefore an appropriate balance is needed between the values associated with the fields of biodiversity conservation, cultural heritage management and traditional knowledge

and wisdom (Verschuuren, 2007). In academic terms these have been conceptualized by different sciences such as anthropology, archaeology, biology, ecology, etc. The management of sacred natural sites requires knowledge from these disciplines as well as combining and adjusting planning tools from the various practitioner realms, which often include sacred knowledge. In order to effectively conserve and protect sacred natural sites, interdisciplinary approaches need to be established through negotiating mutually acceptable conservation ethics and agendas. Openness, willingness to engage in dialogue (see Chapter 7) and developing a cross cultural understanding and, where appropriate, brokering (see Chapter 10), will be important. Enhanced sensitivity to this relationship of spiritual and inter-disciplinary differences can help us find new approaches to cultural and natural conservation management (see Chapter 6).

5 Mainstream, folk and indigenous religions and spiritualities have complex, sometimes conflicting, relationships; enhanced mutual respect and in some cases rapprochement is required for collective care of sacred natural sites

Sacred natural sites exist all over the world, contrary to the assumption of some that they are confined to the non-western world. Sacred natural sites are places in which humans at different times have engaged spiritually with their topographic surroundings (see Chapter 5). Mainstream religions have historically had somewhat different interpretations of the sacred from their folk variants and animistic and indigenous traditional spiritualities. Despite these differences, many religions, faiths and spiritualities have often harmoniously shared the same sacred natural sites. This fact needs to be better understood and promoted and specific cases understood (see for example Wickramsinghe, 2003, 2005; Grainger and Gilbert, 2008). In some instances, however, these basic differences in combination with geo-political factors, primarily colonization and post-colonial power structures, have created conflict, damaged cultures and impaired the conservation of sacred natural sites. For example, Christianity, which has its own sacred natural sites (see Chapters 7 and 19), has been antithetical to sacred natural sites of other faiths. Byrne (Chapter 5) provides early examples of Christianity's strategies for the destruction or assimilation of pre-Christian sacred natural sites and Bernbaum (Chapter 3) provides an example of how Christian priests absorbed the pre-Columbian reverence of mountains in the Bolivian Andes, but are now aiming to remove this belief. While Buddhism is generally more tolerant of earlier religions, the process of Buddhism increasing its influence over previously animistic peoples in Asia is described as Buddhization by Studley (Chapter 10), Spoon (Chapter 8) and Byrne (Chapter 5) who relate the reliance of eco-Buddhist monks on earlier animistic beliefs for conservation purposes. The process of Hinduization (or Sanskritization) is also mentioned by Godbole et al (Chapter 21), Mandal et al (Chapter 25) and Dudley et al (Chapter 2). These chapters indicate a gradual adoption or absorption of sacred natural sites of indigenous groups by mainstream faiths, initially via folk variants, which are later expunged. Further, where some consider that a mainstream faith has an environmental ethic it tends to be more symbolic than the practical applications in the indigenous or folk faiths (see Chapter 10). Sacred natural sites are therefore a stronger practical ethic of care among indigenous groups and folk religions. These instances of conflict are not only restricted to the mainstream faiths mentioned but also are more widely applicable. This historically theological and ideological whirlpool of beliefs and spirituality clearly indicates differences between the established mainstream faiths and the indigenous religions and spiritualities as described in the introduction. Mainstream faiths play a major role in the conversion of traditional spiritualities and folk religions, but some of these folk religions and spiritualities show remarkable resilience and adaptability and inform and enrich the mainstream religion. Not only should indigenous and folk spiritualities be better recognized, but the mainstream religions need in general to show greater respect for other faiths and their sacred

sites. The effective common purpose and mutual respect of sacred natural sites of all religions can be an important part of a major collective effort to conserve nature.

6 Successful co-existence of sacred natural sites and modern economic imperatives require a better understanding of their inter-relationships, and of the broad values and benefits of sacred natural sites for human well-being and development

The dominant global economic system needs to be adapted to recognize and restore the values of sacred natural sites in many contexts. These include those of limited livelihoods and poverty, intensive agriculture, mass tourism and societal 'needs' for extracted minerals. This is particularly important in the light of the potential doubling of the human population over the coming century, and the additional pressures on resources that this will certainly bring. The dominant global economic system based on the premise of endless consumption and growth is 'not fit for purpose' and is seriously threatening the global ecosystem. The human economy needs to be situated in a wider context of a) broader concepts of human well-being and b) deeper meanings in relation to nature. This calls for narrow economic measures to be broadened and also for the relationship between ecology, society, economy and spirituality to be put back into proper balance (Brown and Garver, 2009).

It may well be that the alienation and social breakdown that increasingly characterizes modern industrialized and technologically developed cultures can be counteracted by helping people rediscover individual or collective spirituality, which has connections to nature. While retaining the benefits of rationality, it would seem far better to view the Earth and all its manifest and profoundly interconnected life with deep respect or in the words of faith as essentially sacred so as to ethically maintain an ecological balance (Thorley and Gunn, 2008).

However, internalizing the full value of the relationships between culture and nature remains a challenge for modern societies. As societies unnecessarily lose sacred ground to mining, forestry, infrastructure and other industries, these sectors appear largely uninformed about the values of sacred natural sites and often seem to lack incentives to engage as partners to conservation strategies. The leaders of today who are shaping these processes can induce a critical change or a 'paradigm shift' when sensitized to the multiple values in the diversity in biological and cultural systems at sacred natural sites (see Chapter 6).

7 Sacred natural sites as nodes of resilience, restoration and adaptation to climate change offer opportunities for recovering ecologically sound, local ways of life

The widespread survival of sacred natural sites amongst many cultures indicates that these sites have had significant value to humans. Those that survived were adaptable and had custodians whose cultural beliefs enabled them to adapt to the changing conditions under which they lived. Hence the traditional cultures which have survived until the present deserve our highest respect, and modern societies may have important lessons to learn from them. Sacred natural sites can be considered nodes of resilience, or even resistance, to global change. In many cases, sacred natural sites offer opportunities for building landscape connectivity networks because they form important refugia for biodiversity and maintain a dynamic cultural fabric in the face of global change. They are remnants of variety, heterogeneity and multi-functionality in increasingly simplified homogeneous landscapes, and it is increasingly recognized that diverse biological and cultural systems are more resilient and adaptable than homogeneous systems (MA, 2005).

Some communities are already taking cultural recovery into their own hands (see Chapters 23

and 26). An important message from the custodians of sacred natural sites is that these areas are not isolated but need to be thought of as a network that crosses cultural differences and brings a sense of unity of purpose and action.

The protection, restoration, management and celebration of sacred natural sites presents just one essential strategy for improved planetary care (see Chapter 23). The protection and restoration of sacred natural sites may offer a potential safeguard to critical habitats and threatened species and distinctive human cultures, but the specific approaches and technologies for this restoration are in their infancy and need research and experimentation.

8 Sacred natural sites need to be consciously included as part of a coherent and coordinated response to global change

Sacred natural sites and their associated communities have demonstrated themselves to be remarkably resilient to change, however, the scale of these changes is now taking its toll. Today, global change is a term increasingly used to describe processes in human society and the environment characterized in terms of uncertainties (UNEP, 2008). Changes such as biodiversity loss, environmental degradation, human population increase, shortages of resources, imbalances in wealth and poverty, increasing cultural homogenization and modernity all contribute to impacts on sacred natural sites. Deriving from and linked to these is global climate change, which is escalating uncertainty and is noticeable at a number of sacred natural sites. Increasing numbers of extreme droughts, floods and hurricanes and other extreme weather events constitute existential challenges to many societies. The links between human behaviour and environmental change are complex and the effects of these links on biological and cultural diversity are in many cases unpredictable.

Global trends such as increasing tourism also affect values related to sacred sites. Spoon (Chapter 8) illustrates how tourism is weakening some of these values, while reinforcing and remaking others related to place-based knowledge of Beyul sacred natural sites in the Sagarmatha (Mt Everest) region, as a result of exposure to market forces. Ormsby and Edelman (Chapter 22), on the basis of studies on the regulation of ecotourism in a sanctuary for sacred monkeys in Ghana, recognize that tourism can also help generate income and enforce cultural practices, knowledge and education, especially when developed in tandem with conservation objectives. Although sacred natural sites are most often conserved for cultural and spiritual reasons, the details of these justifications are also subject to change. Sampang (Chapter 24) discusses social changes gaining a foothold in the degradation of the traditional fishing practices of the Palawan Ancestral Domain in the Philippines. These changes are becoming more common as a result of more rapid global cultural and societal change characterized by phenomena such as language loss, acculturation, modernization and urbanization.

Valuable traditional ecological knowledge, for example on healing practices, spiritual well-being, food provisioning, seed conservation, land management and social relations are often celebrated at sacred natural sites. Ceremony, dance, song, story and arts are the intangible companions to these special places, and even while they are being strengthened in some sites, they are rapidly being lost in others.

Dudley et al (Chapter 2) confirm that the remaining sacred natural sites often contain high biodiversity values, creating opportunities for landscape connectivity and the creation of corridors between conservation areas which are much needed in the face of climate change and economic growth.

In the rapidly developing response to climate change, sacred natural sites need to be taken fully into account. They can make substantial contributions to climate change mitigation and adaptation, but there are dangers that inappropriate policies, for example in forestry, could inflict further damage. Increased research and understanding on the roles of sacred natural sites in biological and social resilience are needed and these need to be translated into effective policies.

9 Local commitment, wide public awareness, supportive national policies and laws, state protection and international support are essential for the survival of sacred natural sites

Sacred natural sites are rarely considered in national-level decision-making processes and coherent, policy, legal and management approaches are lacking (Ghosh et al, 2005). Many sacred natural sites that lie outside government protected areas are increasingly being recognized at the international level as protected areas, or Indigenous and Community Conserved Areas (ICCA) in their own right (Dudley, 2008; see also Chapter 6). In some cases this support will enable the innovative creation of conservation networks such as the extension of the protected areas network based on sacred natural sites currently under way in Benin (GEF, 2009). Such successes require the combination of wide public awareness, strong local commitment, national policies that recognize the value of both sacred sites and local knowledge and protection by the government against other competing forms of land use.

Many mechanisms are being tested to support communities to continue to protect and manage their sacred natural sites as part of their territories. At the international level increasing recognition of sacred natural sites is reflected in several policy documents, such as for example the CBD Akwé: Kon Voluntary Guidelines (CBD Secretariat, 2004); the 2007 United Nations Declaration on the Rights of Indigenous Peoples (UN, 2007) and IUCN-UNESCO Sacred Natural Sites Guidelines (Wild and McLeod, 2008). One of the major gaps in legislation is the development of national policies such as found in Guatemala (see Chapter 18) and laws that protect sacred sites in a way that does not undermine community level governance. Dobson and Mamyev (Chapter 23), Sampang, (Chapter 24) and Mandal et al (Chapter 25) indicate some useful directions.

At the national level it is particularly important that appropriate laws are developed to support traditional custodians. Care needs to be taken to avoid national government interventions that could actually jeopardize the conservation of a sacred natural site by developing inappropriate legal frameworks. Using free, prior informed consent (FPIC) can empower custodians and help reduce destructive commercial and livelihood pressures on sacred natural sites.

With some notable exceptions, recognition of sacred natural sites has continued to decline at the national level. Environmentally and culturally damaging development proposals continue to be developed in the name of 'progress and privatisation'. Some welcome exceptions include:

- the aforementioned Benin, which is currently developing a specific category of Protected Areas for Sacred Natural Sites in collaboration with UNDP and the World Bank (GEF, 2009);
- Estonia, which is completing a national inventory of over 2000 pre-Christian sacred natural sites and creating a proposal for a new law to protect these places (see Chapter 19);
- Kenya, where the Mijikenda Kayas (sacred forests) have been inscribed on the World Heritage List and protected under the National Monuments legislation;
- Australia, where the oldest contemporary piece of sacred sites legislation is from the Northern Territory, originating in 1954 but consolidated in 1983 in its present form;
- Mongolia, which has given a high emphasis on protecting sacred natural sites and designated them as Special Protection Areas (see Figure 27.3);
- Guatemala where the 'Law for Indigenous management of sacred sites' was passed by parliament (see Chapter 18).

Several countries have legislation that aids the protection and conservation of sacred sites, often as part of legislation on cultural heritage, indigenous burial places and protected areas. A systematic review of national legislation for sacred natural sites is currently lacking. This book has identified several priorities for immediate legal action. Kamga-Kamden (Chapter 11) calls for a special law recognizing sacred sites as a forest category at the national level in Cameroon; Anwana et al (Chapter

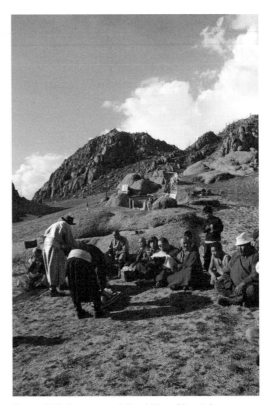

Figure 27.3 Ceremony at Bogd Khan Mountain, Mongolia

The mountain is associated with the life of Chinggis Khan and has been a nationally protected sacred natural site since 1778. Ceremonies were suppressed from 1917–1989.

Source: Robert Wild

12) uses two Ramsar Convention resolutions (Ramsar Resolution VIII.19 and IX.21) to suggest special laws enabling the recognition of traditional management practices based on sacred natural sites in the Niger Delta in Nigeria, and Delgado et al (Chapter 18) discuss the legal proposition for the recognition of indigenous custodianship over sacred natural sites at the national level in Guatemala.

The development of supportive national policies and laws probably represents the single most important gap in the conservation of sacred natural sites.

10 Developing a broad strategy for conserving sacred natural sites, defining the priority actions required and building a global coalition to carry out these actions is urgently needed

Sacred natural sites are important to humanity and collective work is required to protect them, making full use of international partnerships and networks (see Chapter 15). A growing committed international partnership could lead to a critical mass of like-minded people and agencies that will lead a major shift of consciousness which will enhance the future of sacred sites worldwide (Thorley and Gunn, 2008).

A growing group of individuals and institutions is working together to support sacred natural sites. The Christensen Fund has been taking a specific interest in this area and with its partners, specifically the Sacred Land Film Project, it is working towards facilitating a coalition. Similarly a number of conservation NGOs are taking a more strongly cultural approach to their work (e.g. Worldwide Fund for Nature, International Union for Conservation of Nature, the Gaia Foundation and Fauna and Flora International, among many others). Some parts of the commercial private sector are also getting involved, especially the resource extraction industries that often have major impacts on sacred natural sites.

Recommendations

The chapters in this book and the efforts to produce guidance for conservation action have led to the following recommendations for actions that should be initiated immediately:

- Build a global coalition among governments, United Nations agencies, non-governmental organizations, grass-roots social movements, religions and the private sector to protect sacred natural sites and publicize their values to both people and nature.
- Develop a coherent and effective strategy for the conservation of sacred natural sites.

Building on the experiences of work up to now on sacred natural sites (see Annex 2 for a preliminary strategy).

- Empower indigenous peoples to protect and manage their sacred natural sites based on the right of self determination.
- Conduct a global inventory of sacred natural sites, including issues of ownership, tenure, governance and conservation, ensuring this is consistent with free prior and informed consent (FPIC); the inventory method should strongly respect those custodians and sites whose location cannot be revealed for cultural and security reasons.
- Develop greater public awareness and incorporate in conservation and education programmes the concept of the sacred in nature that is found in all religions and indigenous spiritualities.
- Give particular attention to sacred natural sites as part of the adaptive response to global changes in climate, economics, governance, communications, education, health and human well-being.
- Encourage funding agencies of all types to support the conservation and management of sacred natural sites.
- Establish a global natural 'knowledge and wisdom' programme for carrying out multi-disciplinary research on all aspects of sacred natural sites as a primary global conservation network and identify their contributions to human well-being, biodiversity conservation, ecosystems services and poverty alleviation.
- Encourage mainstream faiths to recognize the values of sacred natural sites of folk and indigenous religions and to respect their respective spiritualities in relation to sacred natural sites.
- Develop guidance for national and local governments to take into account sacred natural sites in their policies, legal instruments and planning mechanisms.
- Develop and expand guidance and codes of conduct with the private sector, especially in tourism, agriculture, forestry and the extractive industries, to better protect sacred natural sites in their business models, social responsibility programmes, planning mechanisms and field operations.

These important broad actions need to be implemented and followed up as soon as possible. One way to ensure that sacred natural sites receive the attention they deserve would be by establishing global initiative as part of a coalition of institutions that could include sacred natural sites as well as other forms of land use that have high conservation values. To enhance the effectiveness of such conservation networks it would also be wise to indicate those forms of land use that pose potential threats to conservation, biodiversity and sacred natural sites, such as the conversion of primary forest to plantation forests and the allocation of mining concessions over areas with current high conservation value. Being able to assess the conservation potential and sacred natural sites of those lands would greatly improve planning and allocation of such activities as well as generating advice for improving the policies and market mechanisms currently guiding such practices in favour of sacred natural sites. Being able to assess what is needed to make the most effective conservation measures work for sacred natural sites would require testing these ideas through an initiative with a global scope and endorsement of a large range of institutions and organizations. Starting with demonstrations, such as those described in this book, may inspire stronger support for sacred natural sites from a far broader constituency, including governments, the mining and forestry industries, biologists and development planners.

Our planet is going through a largely human-inflicted crisis resulting in extinction of many species of animals and plants, diminution in the diversity of biological and ecosystems, loss of languages, cultures and human diversity as well as changes in the global climate. These major threats require urgent and coordinated societal action. Sacred natural sites represent places where biological and cultural diversity come together within the context of humanity's highest ethical systems. They can provide a starting point to meet humanity's greatest challenge yet. With deep respect, hard work for the diversity of life, our Earth should have ample room to sustain its wild plants, animals and ecosystems in harmony with the large variety of human cultures to which these wonderful and iconic sacred natural sites are

central. Now we need commitment to realize this vision.

References

Berkes, F. (1999) *Sacred Ecology: Traditional Ecological Knowledge and Resource Management*, Taylor & Francis, Philadelphia

Borrini-Feyerabend, G., Kothari, A. and Oviedo, G. (2004) 'Indigenous and local communities and protected areas: Towards equity and enhanced conservation, guidance on policy and practice for co-managed protected areas and community conserved areas', IUCN World Commission on Protected Areas, Best Practices Protected Areas Guidelines Series No 11, IUCN, Gland, Switzerland

Brown, P.G. and Garver, G. (2009) *Right Relationship, Building a Whole Earth Economy*, Berrett-Koehler Publishers Inc., San Francisco, CA

Carmichael, D.L., Hubert, J., Reeves, B. and Schanche, A. (1994) *Sacred Sites, Sacred Places*, Routledge, Oxford

CBD Secretariat (2004) 'Akwé: Kon voluntary guidelines for the conduct of cultural, environmental and social impact assessment regarding developments proposed to take place on, or which are likely to impact on, sacred sites and on lands and waters traditionally occupied or used by indigenous and local communities', CBD Guidelines Series, CBD, Montreal, Canada

Chhatre, A. and Agrawal, A. (2009) 'Trade-offs and synergies between carbon storage and livelihood benefits from forest commons', *Proceedings of the National Academy of Sciences of the United States of America*, vol 106, pp67–70

Dudley, N. (ed.) (2008) 'Guidelines for applying protected area management categories', IUCN, Gland

Dudley, N., Higgins-Zogib, L. and Mansourian, S. (2005) *Beyond Belief, Linking Faiths and Protected Areas to Support Biodiversity Conservation*, WWF, Equilibrium and ARC

Frazer, J.G. (2008 [1922]) *The Golden Bough: A Study in Magic and Religion*, abridged version, London

GEF (2009) 'Information document on programmatic approaches led by the World Bank in West Central Africa', World Bank, New York. Ghosh, A., Traverse, M., Bhattacharya, D.K., Brondizio, E.S., Spierenburg, M., deCastro, F., Morsello, C. and deSiqueira, A. (2005) 'Cultural services, chapter 14, policy responses', in Volume 3, 'Global and Multiscale

Assessment Report', part of the Millennium Ecosystem Assessment, Island Press, Washington DC

Grainger, J. and Gilbert, F. (2008) 'Around the sacred mountain: St Katherine protectorate in South Sinai, Egypt', in Mallarach, J.-M. (ed.) *Protected Landscapes and Cultural and Spiritual Values*, Volume 2 'Values of the Protected Landscapes and Seascapes', IUCN, GTZ and Obra Social de Caixa Catalunya, Kasparek Verlag, Heidelberg

Harmon, D. and Putney, A.D. (2003) *The Full Value of Parks: From Economics to the Intangible*, Rowman and Littlefield Publishers, Lanham, MD

Maffi, L. and Woodley, E. (2010) *Biocultural Diversity Conservation: A Global Sourcebook*, Earthscan, London

MA (2005) *Ecosystems and Human Well-being: Millennium Ecosystem Assessment Synthesis*, Island Press, Washington DC

Mallarach, J.-M. and Papayannis, T. (eds) (2007) *Protected Areas and Spirituality*, IUCN and Publicacions de l' Abadia de Montserrat, Gland, Switzerland

Nelson, A. and Chomitz, K.M. (2009) 'Protected area effectiveness in reducing tropical deforestation: A global analysis of the impact of protection status', Independent Evaluation Group Evaluation Brief 7, The World Bank, Washington DC

Ostrom, E., Dietz, T., Dolsak, N., Stern, P.C., Stonich, S. and Weber, U. (2002) *The Drama of the Commons*, National Academy Press, Washington DC

Papayannis, T. and Mallarach, J.-M. (eds) (2009) 'The sacred dimension of protected areas', Proceedings of the Second Workshop of the Delos Initiative, Ouranoupolis 2007, Gland, Switzerland, IUCN and Athens, Greece, Med-INA

Posey, D. (ed.) (1999) *Cultural and Spiritual Values of Biodiversity: A comprehensive contribution to the UNEP Global Biodiversity Assessment*, Intermediate Technology Publications, London

Pumarejo, A. and Berges, G. (2005) 'Shamanism and the forces of nature: An analysis of the cosmovision of indigenous peoples and their sacred sites', Proceedings of the Second International Nature Conference, 'Music for the World', 27–30 April 2005, WWF and IUCN, Mexico

Ramakrishnan, P.S., Saxena, K.G. and Chandrashekara, U.M. (eds) (1998) *Conserving the Sacred for Biodiversity Management*, New Delhi, India, UNESCO and Oxford and IBH Publishers

Thorley, A. and Gunn, C. (2008) 'Sacred sites an overview: A report for the Gaia Foundation' (abridged version), The Gaia Foundaion, Cape Town, South Africa

UN (2007) 'Declaration on the rights of indigenous peoples', United Nations, General Assembly, 61st Session, Agenda item 68, Report of the Human Rights Council

UNEP (2008) *One Planet, Many People: Atlas of Our Changing Environment*, United Nations Environment Programme, Nairobi.

UNESCO (2003) 'Convention for the safeguarding of the intangible cultural heritage', available at http://unesdoc.unesco.org/images/0013/001325/132540e.pdf (last accessed September 2006)

UNESCO (2007) 'Preservation of the frozen tombs of the Altai Mountains', World Heritage Centre, Paris

Verschuuren, B. (2007) 'An overview of cultural and spiritual values in ecosystem management and conservation strategies', in Haverkort, B. and Rist, S. (eds) *Endogenous Development and Bio-cultural Diversity: The Interplay of Worldviews, Globalisation and Locality*, Compas/CDE, series on Worldviews and Sciences, No 6, Leusden, The Netherlands

Wickramsinghe, A. (2003) 'Adam's peak sacred mountain forest', in Lee, C. and Schaaf, T. (eds) 'Proceedings of an international workshop on the importance of sacred natural sites for biodiversity conservation', Kunming and Xishuangbanna Biosphere Reserve, People's Republic of China, 17–20 February 2003, UNESCO, Paris

Wickramsinghe, A. (2005) 'Adam's Peak in the cultural landscape of Sri Lanka: Evidence of an eco-cultural basis for conservation', in Lee, C. and Schaaf, T. (eds) 'Proceedings of conserving cultural and biological diversity: The role of sacred natural sites and cultural landscapes', 30 May–2 June 2005, Tokyo, Japan, UNESCO-IUCN

Wild, R. and McLeod, C. (2008) 'Sacred natural sites: Guidelines for protected area managers', Best Practice Protected Area Guidelines Series No 16, IUCN, Gland, Switzerland

Annex 1

A Statement of Custodians of Sacred Natural Sites and Territories

Outcome of a dialogue between Custodians of Sacred Natural Sites and Territories 6 October 2008 at the IUCN World Conservation Congress, held in the Bibliotheca Catalunya, Barcelona.

Recognizing that the whole Earth is sacred, we the custodians and guardians of Sacred Natural Sites and Territories from four continents namely Asia, South America, Africa, Australia and the

Figure Annex 1.1 Gathering of sacred natural sites custodians, supporters and conservation biologists during a dialogue at the IUCN World Conservation Congress, Barcelona October 2008

Source: CSVPA and Sacred Land Film Project

Pacific and from the countries of Mongolia, the Altai and Buryat Republics of Russia, the Kyrgyz Republic, Colombia, Ethiopia, Australia and Papua New Guinea gathered in advance of the IUCN World Conservation Congress, held in Barcelona, Spain.

We represent indigenous religious and spiritual traditions from those regions, and we shared together the Ancestral Visions of our communities and our profoundly deep relationship between them and our Sacred Natural Sites and Territories. We examined the threats that they face and we make recommendations to IUCN and the international community for their support.

There are many and unique ways we express our relationships with our land, country and sacred sites. The following statements do not necessarily apply to all of us but give a sense of how we as diverse groups relate to our sacred country:

- Our Sacred Natural Sites and Territories, and those of other religious and faith groups, represent a great variety of natural features including mountains, rivers, springs, rocks, hills, deserts, forests, groves, individual trees, coral reefs and coastal waters. They also include works of our ancestral communities such as petroglyphs and archaeological sites.
- We also note that for many of us our whole territories are sacred and this includes our homes, communities, farms, footpaths, markets and meeting places and that these territories include layers of sacredness often with different purposes, including those that are material and functional to humans.
- We noted that conditions of some of these lands include 'pure' or original conditions such as pure water, pure air and untouched nature. We also note that many of the species of animal and plant that share our lands and territories are also sacred.
- Sacred Natural Sites and Territories are important for the transmission of stories and songs. They are the routes of pilgrimage, sites of prayer, offerings and ritual and the keeping of our laws. These activities are important work for us as custodians of our lands and our communities. They are an important part of the interrelationship between the people and the Earth.

- For many of us, we see Sacred Natural Sites and Territories as living beings. Even the rocks are alive, animated by our beliefs, and should not be disturbed. The rocks and water themselves teach important lessons to our children.
- At the deepest level we belong to the land and the sea and they give us their secrets and wisdom. They give us the laws and the rules for preserving knowledge. The land gives us unity and brings healing.
- Therefore Sacred Natural Sites and Territories can be considered on the Earth as a network of acupuncture points would be on the human body. They have a healing effect. We also consider that the relationship between them is critical and they cannot be seen in isolation from each other. The caretakers of these special places are maintaining these healing points but as our numbers become fewer our healing powers for the Earth diminish.

In considering Sacred Natural Sites and Territories we therefore:

- consider that a much higher priority has to be given to the sacred in all of human activity and all its manifestations both intangible and tangible, but especially in Sacred Natural Sites and Territories;
- reserve the right to define and describe our Sacred Natural Sites and Territories in our own ways as appropriate to our communities;
- recognize and appreciate the efforts of the international community and the IUCN in supporting the custodians of SNS, in for example producing guidance for protected area managers to improve their relationships with traditional custodians.

We request that National Governments:

- recognize the full rights of indigenous peoples to manage their territories in accordance with their traditional use and customs, to guarantee the permanence of culture and nature;
- give a high priority to Sacred Natural Sites and Territories that are now located within government or private protected areas to be recognized as Indigenous Peoples and Community Conserved Areas (ICCA).

We also request that the IUCN:

- incorporates in its concepts of nature the spiritual values and principles of traditional cultures;
- makes efforts to overcome ignorance of many conservationists in relation to the Sacred Natural Sites and Territories of indigenous and local communities;
- seeks new paradigms for the relationship between humans and the environment, based on the principles of indigenous peoples and traditional cultures;
- supports the implementation of the UN Declaration on the Rights of Indigenous Peoples;
- influence national governments to recognize or endorse sacred sites, but in a way that does not impose government management programmes upon custodians;
- increase the representation of indigenous peoples in the Task Force on Cultural and Spiritual Values of Protected Areas (CSVPA);
- give specific and respectful advice on scientific approaches to the management of Sacred Natural Sites and Territories when requested.

Considering all the above and particularly the overall degradation of the planet by modern society we therefore declare that the whole of the Earth is sacred and invite other indigenous peoples, traditional cultures, faith and religious traditions to endorse this statement.

We therefore request that communities across the Earth:

- respect nature and all the natural features;
- re-awaken and restore knowledge and practices related to the care of nature;
- give legal recognition to sacred sites, territories and landscapes and give recognition of traditional, spiritual institutions, which cannot be separated from them;
- strengthen local advocacy groups that are guided by the guardians of Sacred Natural Sites and Territories;
- re-empower the local communities to care for nature;
- strengthen the intergenerational transfer of knowledge, for example by:

- recording oral traditions, which are as much in danger as geographic sacredness, as it is the time to pass on traditional ecological knowledge in written form;
- produce children books with traditional illustrations by the guardians.

We recommend the following actions and strategies at different levels and request assistance from IUCN and other members of the conservation and development community to support these.

International level

- Develop networks of custodians and supporters of sacred natural sites reaching across cultures, technical and scientific disciplines.
- Translate international experience into national and local actions.
- Increase the awareness of sacred nature.

National level

- Inform state agencies and citizens about Sacred Natural Sites and Territories.
- Develop appropriate legislation that recognizes and endorses local ownership but does not force inappropriate regulation upon custodians.

Local level

- Local communities develop codes of conduct to guide the wider community.

Specifically it is requested that IUCN:

- make the Best Practice Guidelines 16 *Sacred Natural Sites: Guidelines for Protected Area Managers* available in other languages of both IUCN and the United Nations;
- keep the network, especially those people present at this dialogue, informed about outcomes;
- create forums at which the guardians of sacred sites may speak.

Custodians

Sheikh Chachykei Choongmurunova, Sheikh of Chynar Terek Mazar, Kök Tokoi' Village, Talas Region, Kyrgyzstan

Kadyrbek Dzhakypov, Kyrgyzstan

Yanzhinlkham Shagdar, President, Guardian of Dashbalbar ovoo Zurkhai Academy, Mongolia

Danil Mamyev, Director, Guardian of Karakol valley, Uch-Enmek ethno-natural park, Russia

Mr Djawa Yunupingu, Dhimurru Aboriginal Corporation, Australia

Mr MalangaiYunupingu, Dhimurru Aboriginal Corporation, Australia

Mr Banula Marika, Dhimurru Aboriginal Corporation, Australia

Snr Rogelio Mejia, Cabildo Gobernador Arhuaco, Organización Indigena Gonawindua Tayrona Colombia

Snr Jose de los Santos, Sauna Límaco, Mamo, Guardian of the Sierra Nevada de Santa Marta, Organización Indigena Gonawindua Tayrona, Colombia

Snr Roberto Marín, ACAIPI, Association of Traditional Indigenous Authorities and Captains of the Pirá Paraná River, Colombia

Snr Gerardo Makuna, ACIYA, Association of Indigenous Captains of the Yaigoje Apaporis

Mako Wareo, Father of Milo Mountain, Gamo Highlands, Ethiopia

Mr Jamyang Richen, Sakia Tashi Ling Buddhist Monastery, Spain

Mr Tweedy Malagian, Country Representative, CUSO-PNG, Papua New Guinea

Mr Chagat Almashev, Director, Guardian, interpreter for the Foundation for the sustainable development of Altai Russia

Translators and supporters

Jyldyz Doolbekova in-region consultant, interpreter for the The Christensen Fund, Kyrgyzstan

Petr Azhunov, Baikal Buryat Centre for Indigenous Cultures, Russia

Altantsetseg Tsedendamba, Consultant, interpreter for the Zurkhai Academy Mongolia

Ms Erjen Khamaganova, Program Officer, Central Asia and Turkey, The Christensen Fund

Mr Guillermo Rodriguez-Navarro, CSVPA, Prosierra Colombia

Mr Phil Wise, NT parks and Wildlife Service, Dhimurru Aboriginal Corporation, Australia

Dr Valerie Boll, Dhimurru Aboriginal Corporation, Australia

Dr Tadesse Wolde Gossa, Program Officer, The African Rift Valley, Ethiopia, The Christensen Fund

Ms Isabel Esono, Sakia Tashi Ling Buddhist Monastery, Spain

Facilitators

Mr Robert Wild, Chair, CSVPA, UK

Mr Bas Verschuuren Co-Chair CSVPA, Netherlands

Mr Josep Maria Mallarach, Coordinator Delos Initiative, Spain

Ms Madelon Lohbeck, CSVPA, Netherlands

Film makers

Mr Toby McLeod, Director, Sacred Land Film Project, USA

Observers/invitees

Dr Gleb Raygorodetsky, Programme Officer, The Christensen Fund, USA

Mr Jeff Campbell, The Christensen Fund, USA

Ms Liz Hosken, Director, The Gaia Foundation, UK

FionaWilton, The Gaia Foundation, Colombia

Dr Martín von Hildebrand, Fundación Gaia Amazonas and COAMA (Consolidation of the Colombian Amazon Programme) Coordinator, Colombia

Dr Sebastién Kamga Kamden, Director, Centre Africain de Recherches Forestières Appliquées et de Développement (CARFAD), Cameroon

Zakia Zouanat, Rabat University, Morocco

Gathuru Mburu, Institute for Culture and Ecology, Kenya

Ms Rhadika Borde, Davis Institute, India

Mr Rambaldi Giacomo, CTA (Technical Centre for Agricultural and Rural Cooperation), Netherlands

Annex 2

A Preliminary Strategy and Action Plan for the Conservation of Sacred Natural Sites

WCPA Specialist Group on the Cultural and Spiritual Values of Protected Areas

Overall Goal: Promote, conserve and restore sacred natural sites protecting both biological and cultural diversity

Strategic Direction 1: Support the autonomous protection and management of sacred natural sites by their custodians

Action 1.1 Recognize the rights of indigenous people and custodians from mainstream faiths to lead the management of their own sacred sites.

Action 1.2 Facilitate dialogue and mutual support between the custodians of sacred natural sites and encourage dialogue between indigenous, folk and mainstream traditions.

Action 1.3 Establish mediation processes in cases of dispute between custodians of sacred natural sites and between custodians and other stakeholders (e.g. an ombudsman or broker mechanism).

Action 1.4 Encourage government planning agencies and protected areas authorities to engage with custodians of sacred natural sites especially where those incorporated into sacred natural sites have not been properly recognized (IUCN Best Practice Guidelines 16).

Action 1.5 Encourage economic and development planning departments and other land use agencies to recognize sacred natural sites as legitimate land uses and their custodians as legitimate managers. Apply appropriate EIA procedures and other guidance (e.g. CBD Akwé: Kon Guidelines, 2004) when considering development proposals that affect SNS.

Action 1.6 Support the development, testing, dissemination and implementation of relevant international and national agreements and guidance as appropriate e.g. UNDRIP, 2007; CBD Akwé: Kon Guidelines, 2004; IUCN/ UNESCO Guidelines, 2008; IUCN policy decisions (motions).

Action 1.7 Provide specific and respectful advice on scientific approaches to the management of sacred natural sites when requested by custodians.

Access 1.8 Form multi actor networks and coalitions of organizations in support of sacred natural sites and their custodians at both national and international levels.

Figure A2.1 Custodians Chagat Almashev of Altai Republic and Kadyrbek Dzhakypov of Kyrgyzstan presenting their group's recommendations for action, Custodians Dialogue, Barcelona 2008

Source: CSVPA and Sacred Land Film Project

Strategic Direction 2: Reduce the threats and halt the loss of sacred natural sites

Action 2.1 Call upon and engage with extractive industries, plantation forestry, industrial agriculture companies and other commercial entities to respect the integrity to sacred natural sites and to support their protection.

Action 2.2 Provide livelihood support for (materially, socially and spiritually) needy communities associated with sacred natural sites when requested.

Action 2.3 Advocate for the implementation of national policies and laws that will reduce the threats to sacred natural sites and allow for bottom up action to improve the quality of sacred natural sites.

Action 2.4 Recognize the social cohesion that is promoted by well managed and maintained sacred natural sites, and promote this as part of sustainable development.

Action 2.5 Support religious and social cohesive networks of sacred natural sites custodians and communities by facilitating multi-stakeholder processes that help them face the challenges of modern change and development.

Strategic Direction 3: Support cultural revitalization and the strengthening of communities and their connections with their sacred natural sites

Action 3.1 Understand, respect and support the fundamental relationship of people to their sacred sites and lands including culture, language, prayer and ceremony.

Action 3.2 Support the revival, reawakening and rekindling of these relationships and ties to sacred land and places.

Action 3.3 Promote respectful and appropriate education that imparts to young people the language and values of custodian communities as well as the skills and the 'the laws of the land' as a crucial step to protect sacred sites.

Action 3.4 Adopt a fundamental community first (or 'bottom up') approach while creating respectful and supportive laws, policies and education processes at the district, provincial and nation state level.

Action 3.5 Develop sharing of information and experiences between and across communities, including children and youth, regarding revitalization of culture and protection of sacred natural sites.

Strategic Direction 4: Increase understanding and awareness, particularly at national level, of the importance and role of sacred natural sites and promote the formation of appropriate national policies and laws

Action 4.1 Promote mutual understanding and working relationships between sacred natural sites custodians, protected area managers, scientists, planners and decision-makers at conceptual and practical levels.

Action 4.2 Carry out a review of different national legislation and develop pilot sites and case studies.

Action 4.3 Advocate the sensitive recognition of sacred natural sites at national level, particularly through protected area and development planning authorities.

Action 4.4 Develop appropriate publicity campaigns that promote sacred natural sites using applicable forms of communication.

Action 4.5 Facilitate the exchange of experiences on traditional governance and national policy making for sacred natural sites in international fora and working groups.

Strategic Direction 5: Build up a body of increased knowledge of sacred natural sites, using different ways of knowing, including traditional knowledge, the arts and media

Action 5.1 Develop sensitive and respectful inventories of sacred natural sites at appropriate levels, documenting biological, spiritual, religious, cultural and heritage values, maintaining secrecy where required.

Action 5.2 Seek new models for the relationship between humans and the environment, based on the principles established at sacred natural sites.

Action 5.3 Promote the holistic integration of traditional knowledge, sciences, humanities and arts at sacred natural sites (e.g. traditional knowledge, ecology, anthropology, archeology, economics, media, arts, etc.).

Action 5.4 Give particular attention to understanding sacred natural sites as part of the adaptive response to global changes in climate, economics, governance, communications and so forth.

Action 5.5 Establish a global research and information programme where types of knowledge, wisdom and science can be at the basis of the improved understanding of the values of sacred natural sites for human well-being, human development and planetary care.

Strategic Direction 6: Access and generate funding for sacred natural sites identifying a diversity of resources (financial and otherwise) to support sacred natural sites

Action 6.1 Explore the possibility of establishing a dedicated fund for sacred natural sites.

Action 6.2 Understand and utilize the full range of funding options and sources that might be applicable to sacred natural sites.

Action 6.3 Increasingly advocate to funding agencies that they fund sacred natural sites as part of their portfolio of giving.

Action 6.4 Develop mechanisms for local funding and self-support of sacred natural sites to put them on a long-term sustainable footing.

UNDRIP (2007) *United Nations Declaration on the Rights of Indigenous People*, passed in 2007 and published by the United Nations in 2008 07-58681–March 2000.

Index

Page numbers in *italic* refer to Figures, Tables and Boxes. The abbreviation 'SNS' is used for sacred natural sites.

Aboriginal people (Australia) 39, 48
    land rights 60, 64, 67
acculturation 222, 222–3, 287
Adivasi 232, 274–5, 276, 277, 278
AERF (Applied Environmental Research Foundation) *159*, 160, 219, 220, 221–2, 225–6
'agency' 53
agriculture 11, 192, 220, 250, 251, 289
    shifting cultivation 268, 269
agro-pastoralism 88–9, 93, 96
Akwé Kon voluntary guidelines 5, 167, 287
Altai Republic (Russia) 245, *245*, 246, 251
    beliefs 63, 246–7, 250, 252
    see also Karakol Valley
Amerindians 140, 143, 144, 147
ancestors 4, 43, 102, 119, 142, 147, 189
ancestral domain (Coron Island) 256–61, *257–9*
ancient Egypt 182–3
Anglican Church 77, 78, 80
animal products 142
animism 3, 4, 18, 62–3, 102, 190, 284
    blended with mainstream religions 54, *54*, 56, 63, 92, 285
    Celtic pre-Christian 79–80
    sacred sites 54, *54*, 55, 56
    Tibetan 109, 110
animistic tradition 7, 92, 108
Applied Environmental Research Foundation *see* AERF
archaeological excavation 232, 244, 249–50, *249*, 252, *252*, 282
archaeological monuments 64–5, *64*, 204
Arran, Isle of (Scotland) 64, 78, 202, *204*
Assisi Declarations (1986) 43, 47
attitudes, changing 125, *125*, 126, 127
Ausangate (Peru) 35–6, *36*
Australia 4, 26, 43, 173–4, 176, 202, 288
    Aboriginal land rights 60, 64, 67
    Uluru 39
awareness 9, 225, 226, 261, 280, 287, 289

Badrinath (India) 37, 38, *48*
Bandjoun (Cameroon) 120, *120*, 123
    ancestral management system 119, 122–5
    SNS 75–6, 119–27, *121–5*, *124*

Bashadar kurgan complex (Altai Republic, Russia) 244, 246, 249–50
Benin 23, 287, 288
beyul (hidden valleys) 37, 87, 91–2, 94, 95, *95*, 110, 286–7
Bhutan 189
Biligiri Rangaswamy Temple Wildlife Sanctuary *see* BRTWS
Binsar Wildlife Sanctuary 38
bio-corridors 104, 105
biocultural conservation 18, 67–8, 217
biocultural diversity 67, 68, 189, 193, *195*, 284
biodiversity 2, 12, 60, 66, 104, 135, 280
    Altai Republic 246
    BRTWS 264–5
    conservation *see* biodiversity conservation
    Coron Island 256
    culture and 63, 168, 170
    decline 105, 127
    high levels 5, 7, 11, 19, 20, 22–3, 45–6, 67, 188, 212, 287
    Holy Hills 102–3
    hotspots 67, 68, 171–2, 220
    inventories 222, *222*, 226, 261
    losses 11, 129, 136, 168, 201, 261, 286, 290
    management 190–2, *191*, 193, 196
    mapping 47
    Mexico 209
    mountains 33, 34
    Niger Delta 76, 130, 134
    Palawan 255
    refuges of 1, 119, 280, 286
    reservoirs of 1, 119
    sacred groves 23–5, 45–6, 49, 165–6, 167, 220–2, *222*, 275
    SNS 5, 7, 11, 17–18, 19, 20, 22–3, 34, 67, 68, 190, *191*, 192, 280, 287
    South Pacific region 171–2
    and well-being 188, *191*, 192
    Yunnan 99, 101
biodiversity conservation 17, 20–7, 66–7, 105, 122, 168, 255, 283
    sacred groves 17, 45–6, 160, 219, 276, 277–8
    SNS 5, 6, 67, 161, 166, 281, 289
    South Pacific 176
    traditional 37, 270
Biosphere Reserves 66, 163–4
Blue and John Crow Mountains National Park 76, 146, 148–9, *148*, 153
    SNS *148*, 149–52, 153

Bolivia 190, *191*, *192*, 193, *195*, 285
Bon *17*, 63, 91, 92
'bonds of affection' 76, 108
BRTWS (Biligiri Rangaswamy Temple Wildlife Sanctuary, India) 232, 263, 264–9, *266*, *267*, 270
Buddhism 2, *17*, 34, 43, 55, 57–8, 63, 202
    'ecology monks' 57–8, 108, 285
    and nature 47, 57–8, 108, 182, 183
    Tibetan 109, 110–11, *111*
    see also beyul; Holy Hills; *phi*; Khumbu Sherpa
Buddhist monks 18, 45, 57–8, 108, 285
Buddhization 108, 285
Bulang people 102
burial places 4, 43, 139, 174, 257, 288
    forests *20*, 22, 166, 288
    Maroons 151, 153, 154
    see also kurgans; permafrost burials
Burkina Faso, sacred forests 22

Calamian Tagbanwa 232, 254–5, 255–61, *257–9*
Cameroon 75–6, 282, 288
    see also Bandjoun
capacity 159–60, 175–6, 242
    building 129, 136, 193, 206, 225, 226, 261
carbon sinks 144–5, 182, 283
Catholic Church 36, 59, 80, 144, 183, 200
caves 213
CBD (Convention on Biological Diversity) 5, 43, 47, 48, 136, 162, 167, 200
    Akwé Kon guidelines 5, 9, 167, 287
    community involvement 48–9, 176
CCAs (Community Conserved Areas) 105, *135*, 257
celebrations 7, 133, 184
Celtic Christianity 77, 78, 80–1, 202
Celtic pre-Christian religion 79–80
ceremonies 5, 103, *205*, 287
Chief Roi Mata's Domain (Vanuatu) *171*, 174, *174*
chiefs 166, 190–2, 234, 240
Chile *191*, 193
China 21, 25, 44, 75, 103, 104, 117
    see also Eastern Kham; Yunnan
Chipko movement 111, 274
Christensen Fund 289
Christianity 2, 58–9, 125, 144, 147
    assimilation of folk religions 54–5, *54*, 63
    Celtic 77, 78, 80–1
    missionaries 139, 140, 144
    and nature 4, 47, 79–80, 183
    Orthodox Church 183, *184*
    pilgrimages 53, 55, 59, 75, *84*
    Protestant 58–9, 200
    Reformation 17, 58–9, 81
    and sites of other faiths 54–5, *54*, 63, 125, 285
    SNS of 38, 53, 59, 200
    and traditional beliefs 36, 125, 139, 144, 152, 234, 235
    see also Catholic Church; Lindisfarne
CIPSEG (Cooperative Integrated Project on Savannah Ecosystems in Ghana) 164–7

climate change 12, 33, 186, 232, 281, 287, 290
    combating 33, 37, 40, 104
    and mountains 17, 33, 35–7, *36*, 39, 40
    and permafrost burials 244, 246, 252
    and SNS 17, 26, 168, 280, 286, 289
    and species 26
    and wetlands 182, 1136
co-management *135*, 225, 226, 232, 264, 269–70, 277
cognitive maps 111–14, *112–14*, 177
collaboration 76, 85, 185, 186, 206
Community Conserved Areas *see* CCAs
community forests 58, 126, 220
community protection (Ghana) 233–4
COMPAS network 160, 188, 189, 190, *191*, 193–6, *194–5*
conceptual framework for analysis 7–9, *8*
Confucianism 108
connectivity 46, 47, 68, 134–5, 280, 286
conservation
    biodiversity *see* biodiversity conservation
    of cultural diversity 34, 66–7
    cultural values and 47, 66–7, 105, 154, 199, 201, 206
    and culture 65–7, 101–2, 105, 154, 201, 223–6
    ecotourism and 287
    forests 46–7, 283
    and indigenous survival 252–3
    integrated approach 105
    legislation 175
    and livelihoods 46, 171, 226
    networks 287, 290
    policies 282
    and religion 20, 49, 54, 63, 164, 200–1
    and the sacred 107, 205
    and sacred forests 103, 105
    sacred groves 17, 46–7, 160, 223, 276
    sacred lakes 134–5
    of SNS 1, 8–9, 159, 168, 171, 183, 231–2, 280, 289
    SNS and 2, 5, 6, 11, 19, 20, 25–6, 26–7, 46–7, 49, 110, 277–8, 290
    spiritual values and 47, 66–7, 78, 199, 201
    strategies 19, 20, 26–7, 189, 231, 280, 289
    traditional 101–2, 217, 241
conservation movement 65, 154
conservation organizations 47, 200–1
conservation value 5, 26–7, 49, 75
conservationists 26, 58, 75, 199
Convention on Biological Diversity *see* CBD
Convention for the Protection and Promotion of the Diversity of Cultural Expressions 173, 174–5
Convention on the Safeguarding of Intangible Cultural Heritage *see* CSICH
Cooperative Integrated Project on Savannah Ecosystems in Ghana *see* CIPSEG
coral reef destruction 232, 254, 256
Coron Island (Philippines) 232, 254–5, 255, 256, *257*
    Ancestral Domain 232, 254, 254–5, 256–61, 257, *257–9*
Coronation Hill (Australia) 67
cosmologies 47, 132–3, 265
cosmopolitanism 59–60
Cotocachi, Mount (Ecuador) 35

crocodiles 76, 129, 132, 133, 134, 183
crop species, wild relatives 25, 46
CSICH (Convention for the Safeguarding of Intangible
    Cultural Heritage) 159, 163, 170, 173, 174–5, 175, 177,
    177–8, 178
    community involvement 173, 176–7
CSVPA (Specialist Group on the Cultural and Spiritual
    Values of Protected Areas) 5, 167, 168, 200
cultural change 37, 76, 282, 287
'cultural differences' 117
cultural diversity 18, 35, 67, 67–8, 99
    and biodiversity 63, 168
    conservation 34, 66–7
cultural heritage 153, 154, 170, 173, 190, 204, 263, 281
    and natural heritage 159, 176, 177
cultural homogenization 286
cultural identity 104–5, 147–8, 168, 190
cultural knowledge, transmission 152, 153, 173, 176, 232,
    257, 261
cultural landscapes 162, 168, 173, 174, 182, 264
cultural mapping 175, 176
cultural practices 65, 190, 219
cultural values 5, 7, 8, 127, 185, 254, 283
    and conservation 47, 66–7, 105, 199, 206
    and nature 65, 170
    of SNS 11, 68
culture 2, 11, 182, 186, 247, 286, 290
    and conservation 65–6, 223–6
    and nature 34, 49, 63, 66–7, 281, 284, 286
custodians 5, 6–7, 8, 24, 168, 205, 214–17, 283, 284
    Bandjoun 121, 122–3, 125
    collaboration 103, 186
    disappeared 7, 64–5, 64, 281
    empowerment 288
    influence declining 201
    local communities as 172–3
    recognition 26
    respect for 289
    secrecy 1, 11, 26, 196
    support for 175, 204
    traditional landowners 177
customary laws 132, 159, 172, 176, 177, 258, 260
customary practices 172, 176, 261
    fishing 255, 256, 258–60, 260–1

Dai people 101–2, 102, 105
Dani people 22
Daoism 2, 47, 108
decision-making 47, 84–5, 93, 96, 223, 287
'Deep Ecology' 277
deforestation 139, 144, 164, 283
degradation
    environmental 76, 146, 164, 212, 286
    fishing grounds 255, 259–60
    sacred forests 25, 103, 236, 268
    of SNS 120, 125, 127, 280, 282
deities 18, 91, 93, 107, 183, 268
    on mountains 4, 35, 75, 87, 92–3, 92, 96
    sacred groves 219, 223–4, 224, 275

in trees 44, 166
    see also fetishes; numinous sacred sites; Sarna Mata
Delos Initiative 5, 68, 160, 183, 186, 198, 199, 202–5, 203–4
desecration 33, 78, 251, 282
destruction of SNS 3, 11, 17, 63, 222
development 57, 63, 116, 116–17, 167, 168
    and SNS 280, 282, 283, 285–6, 288
displacement of indigenous peoples 264, 268
disturbance of SNS 23–5, 212
Doñana National park (Spain) 184, 201
Dravidian people 43, 274–5
dreams 132

earth care 75, 111, 115
earth goddess *see* Sarna Mata
Eastern Kham (China) 75, 107, 108–9, 108–11, 109–14,
    112–14, 117
ecofeminism 273–4, 278
'ecology monks' 57–8, 108, 285
economic development 39, 40, 103, 105, 144, 146, 171
    China 75, 104
economic growth 12, 287
economic system 285–6
ecosystem services 5, 6, 7–8, 19, 25, 46, 226, 280, 282, 289
    conservation of 63
    forests 119, 122, 148, 238
    threats to 280, 282
    wetlands 181–2
ecosystems 2, 11, 48, 76, 130, 135, 136
ecotourism 192, 226, 231, 233, 234, 235–6, 236–7
    benefits 239–40, 239, 241
    Suriname 144
    Tafi Atome 231, 233, 234, 235–6, 236–7, 238, 239–41,
        239, 241, 287
education 5, 39, 152, 153, 193, 267, 289
    environmental 109, 161, 165–6
    Khumbu Sherpa 89, 95
    sponsors 239, 239, 241
    of youth 125, 126, 259, 267
Egypt (ancient) 182–3
elders 24, 162, 223, 257, 260, 266
    enforcement role 232, 260, 261
emotional links 153–4
empowerment 190, 211, 225–6, 241, 258, 266
    women 272, 273, 275, 277
endangered species 46, 104, 219, 220
endemic species 17, 23, 46, 171, 209
endogenous development 160, 188, 189, 189–90, 192, 193–5,
    194–5, 196
energies of place 63, 190, 252
environmental activism 274, 276, 277
environmental degradation 146, 164, 212, 286
Estonia 200, 288
ethics 108, 214, 246, 278, 285, 290
Ethiopia, northern church forests 21, 22, 25
ethnic religions 160, 198
Everest, Mount (Himalaya) 4, 37, 38, 75, 90, 93
extinctions 11, 17, 35, 168, 290
extractive industries 11, 40, 67, 139, 144, 289, 290

faith 119, 280, 284
Feng Shui woods (Hong Kong) 21
festivals 133, 173, 190, *192*, 231
    in sacred groves 223, 223–4, *224*
fetish forests 233–4, 240
fetishes 233, 234
fig tree 43, 44, 121
Fiji 175, 177
fire management 264, 268–9
firewood 25, 89, 95
fish sanctuaries 254, 258
fishing *181*
    Niger Delta 76, 129, 130, 131, 133–4, *134*, 136
fishing practices 26, 131, 136, 232, 255, 256, 259–60
folk religions 2, 56–7, 59, 63, 280, 284–5
    Buddhism and 57–8
    and conservation 17, 54, 59–60
    and nature 2–3, 7, 58
    sacred sites 53–4, 60, 289
    see also indigenous religions
forest reserves 23, 47
forest spirits 139, 140, 143, 144
forestry 11, 282, 289
forests 17–18, 57, 99, 102, 115, 290
    Afromontane 21, 22, 25
    carbon storage 144–5, 283
    conservation 46–7, 283
    deforestation 57, 139, 144, 164, 283
FPIC (free, prior and informed consent) 11, 160, 214, *216*, 258, 288, 289
fuelwood 25, 89, 95
Fuji, Mount (Japan) 37

Galapagos *66*
Ganges, River 36, 183
gender 94–5, *95*, 96, 124–5, 274
George, Lake (Uganda) 181, *181*
Ghana 23, 25, 161, *191*, 233–4, 241
    see also Tafi Atome Monkey Sanctuary
glacial lakes (Nepal) 33, 36–7, 39
glacial retreat 33, 35, 35–6, *36*, 40
global changes 11–12, 168, 186, 280, 286, 289
    and cultural diversity 33, 35
    Khumbu 93, 95
    local communities and 33, 38–9
    and mountains 17, 33, 34–5, 37–9, 39–40, 40
    responses to 280, 286–7
global coalition 280, 289, 290
global warming 35–7, *36*, 40, 244, 246, 252
    see also climate change
globalization 12, 46, 170, 177, 219
    and sacred forests 103, 104, 105, 222
governance 8–9, *8*, 68, 76, 136, 177, 287
    protected areas 90, 199–200
governments 116–17, 192, 288, 289
    and indigenous cultures 75, 139, 144
grazing 25, 46, 223
greenhouse gas emissions 36, 40, 144–5
Guatemala 190, *191*, 192–3, 195, 287, 288

habitats 2, 11, 135
    remnants 19, *20*, 21–2, 25, 46, 49, 129, 212, 286
Haiti 139
Hani people 102
happiness 189
Hawaiian volcanoes 35
healing *44*, 121, 122, 162, 206, 287
    places of 63, 150–2, 154, 231–2, 281
    see also Winti
Hinduism 2, 37, 47, 108, 115
    River Ganges 36, 183
    sacred mountains *17*, 34, 63
    sacred trees 43, 45
Hinduization 202, 285
Holy Hills (Yunnan, China) 26, 44, 75, 98, 99–104, *100*, *101*, *104*
Holy Island *see* Lindisfarne
Hopi people 34, 38
house prices 77, 81, 81–2, 83
Huichol people 213, 213–14
human–nature relationships 63, 65–6, 177, 199, 280, 281–2, 284
    Karakol Valley 231–2, 247, 252–3
    Khumbu Sherpa view 87, 93–6, *95*
    SNS and 64–5, 68–9, 168, 281–2, 284
    Soligas 264, 270
    wetlands 181–2
hunting 25, 110, 111, 124, 161, 165–6
    taboos 102, 110, 124, 233, 238, 240

ICCAs (Indigenous and Community Conserved Areas) 46, 48–9, 65, 68, 119–20, 287
ICOMOS (International Council on Monuments and Sites) 162, 172, 174, 175
identities 39–40, 104–5, 147–8, 168, 270
income generation 160, 161, 167, 226, 287
India
    ecofeminism 273–4, 278
    forest management 264, 267–9, 277
    protected areas 232, 267–9
    sacred groves 4, 21–2, 22, 23, 25, 26, 44, 46, *159*, 160, 219, 275
    Sarna movement 232, 272, *273*, 274–8
    see also AERF; BRTWS; North Western Ghats; RFRA
Indigenous and Community Conserved Areas *see* ICCAs
indigenous forest values 108, 109–15, 112–15, *112–14*, 116–17
indigenous peoples 3, 8, 62, 75, 252–3, 290
    displacement 65, 90, 232
    involvement 67–8, 129, 136, 168
    land rights 60, 64, 67, 136, 139, 250–1
    rights 129–30, 185, 256, 261, 263, 290
    worldviews 188, 189, 192–3
    see also UNDRIP
indigenous religions 2, 280, 284–5, 289
    see also folk religions
individualism *125*, 126
Indonesia 22, 25, 54, 59
industrial revolution 58, 63

inequities 47, 136, 286
infrastructure development 11, 125, 192, 219, 220, 232, 251–2
inspiration 33, 34, 206
institutions 2, 43, 117, 225–6, 227
    indigenous 130, 132
    international 159–60, 161–2
    Lindisfarne 77–8, 80, 81, 81–2, 84–5
    traditional 47, 103
intangible cultural heritage 162–3, 170, 171, 172–5, 177–8, 186, 199
    Maroons 76, 148
    transmission 173, 176
intangible values 111–14, *112–14*, 117, 205
integrated approach 105, 167, 180, 185–6, 206
intellectual property rights 176
interdisciplinary approach 9, 26–7, 164, 284
international agreements 47, 159–60, 161–2, 200, 201
International Council on Monuments and Sites *see* ICOMOS
international law 170, 173–5, 176
international organizations 161–2, 162, 167, 168, 288, 289
International Union for the Conservation of Nature *see* IUCN
intrinsic values 115, 186, 205, 226
inventories
    biodiversity 221–2, *222*, 226, 261
    intangible cultural heritage 173
    SNS 160, 200, 209, 210–17, *211*, *212*, *215*, 288, 289
Ireland 43, 59
Islam 2, 10, 38, 47, 48, 182, 200
IUCN (International Union for Conservation of Nature) 5, 130, 167, 172, 199–200, 289
    and SNS 59, 183, 217, 284
    see also CSVPA; Delos Initiative; UNESCO-IUCN
        Guidelines

Jainism 2, 63
Jamaica 146–8, *148*, 149
    see also Windward Maroons
Jamaica National Heritage Trust *see* JNHT
Japan 22, 53, 59, *205*
Jinuo people 102
JNHT (Jamaica National Heritage Trust) 149, 153, 154
Judaism 34, 38, 43, 47, 140

Kailas, Mount (Tibet) *17*, 34, 63
Karakol Valley (Altai Republic, Russia) 231–2, 244–53, *245*, *246*, *248–9*, *281*
Kaya forests (Kenya) 22, 23, *24*, *45*, 46, 162, 162–3, 288
Kham (China) 107, 108–11, *109–14*, 112–14, 117
Khumbu (Nepal) 37, 87–8, *88–9*, 89, 93, 95
    sacred trees and forests 22, 93
    tourism 90, 90–1, 93, 96
    see also Khumbu Sherpa; SNPBZ
Khumbu Sherpa 87, 88, 88–9, 90, 91–6, *92*, *95*
Khumbu Yul-Lha (Khumbila) *75*, *92*, 93, 94
Kilimanjaro (South Africa) 40

knowledge-brokers 75, 116, 117, 284
kurgans 244, 245, 246, *246*, 248–50, *249*, 250, 252, *252*

land rights 60, 64, 67, 136, 139, 250–1
land tenure 136, 144, 171, 232, 244, 250–1
land use changes 105, 182, 220, 282, 290
lartse (stone mounts) 110–11, *111*
laws 9, 105, 136, 167, 192–3, 195, 280, 287–8, 289
    customary 132, 159, 172, 176, 177, 258, 260
    enforcement 260, 261
    intangible cultural heritage 176, 178
    international 170, 173–5, 176
    land tenure 244, 250–1
legal protection 162, 176, 177, 178
libations 139, 143, 235
life, sacred 66–7
lifestyles *125*, 126, 171
Lindisfarne (Holy Island, UK) 59, 75, 77–85, *79*, *82*, *84*, *203*
livelihoods 8, 11, 136, 171, 190, 226, 260–1
    forests 42, 46, 99, 226, 268, 277
    pressures on 76, 161, 164
    security 49, 268, 269
    SNS and 5, 76, 161, 188, 288
    tourism and 91
Living Human Treasures 173, 175, 177
LMMAs (Locally Managed Marine Areas) 177
local communities 8, 172–3, 214–17, 226
    autonomy 280, 282–3
    and global changes 33, 38–9
    involvement 103, 172–3, 175–6, 176–7, 206, 233
    Lindisfarne 77, 78, 81, 82, 83, 84–5
    rights 185, 283
    social ties 129, 135, *135*
    supporting 76, 283
    worldviews 188, 189
    see also endogenous development
Locally Managed Marine Areas (LMMAs) 177
Locke, John 115
logging 40, 108–9, 139, 144, 222–3
    illegal 161, 164
Lu spirits 93, 94, *95*

MA (Millennium Ecosystem Assessment) 6, 66, 186, 189–90
MAB (Man and the Biosphere) Programme 159, 161, 162, 163–7
'magic' 57, 59
magic plants 139, 140, 141, *141*, 143, 144
mainstream religions 2, 48, 282, 284–5
    and conservation 63, 200–1
    and nature 3–4, 7, 42, 47, 62, 200, 205
    and other religions 18, 36, 63, 280, 284–5, 289
    SNS 201–2, 204–5, 284
    and trees 42, 47, 48–9
    see also Buddhism; Christianity; Hinduism; Islam; Judaism
Man and the Biosphere Programme *see* MAB Programme
management of SNS 9, 68, 126, 160, 177–8, 193, 198, 283, 287
    Bandjoun 119
    Coron Island ancestral domain 257

participatory 65–6, 75, 103, 129, 233
sacred groves *159*, 223
Windward Maroons 152–4
mapping
biodiversity values 47
cognitive 111–14, *112–14*, 117
SNS 176, 232, 263–4, 265–7, *267*, *268*, 269, 270
territories 144
Maroons (Jamaica) 147–8, *148*, 149
see also Windward Maroons
Maroons (Suriname) 139, 140, 141, 143–4
see also Winti
Marx, Karl 115
mass tourism 40, 201, 234
materialism 198–9, 206
Mauritius Plan for SIDS 2005–2015 175
Maya 19, 64–5, *64*, 192, 192–3
MDS (multidimensional scaling) 112–14, *112*
medicinal plants 5, 19, 25, 46, 188, 190, 192, 269
harvesting 76, 123
Winti use 139, 140–3, *141*
Memoranda of Understanding (MoUs) 214
mental maps 111–14, *112–14*, 117
Mexico 209–17, *211*, *212*, *215*, *216*
migration to towns 139, 144, 219
Millennium Ecosystem Assessment *see* MA
missionaries 139, 140, 144
modernism, and religion 58–9, 60
modernization 11, 63, 75, 105, 282, 285, 286, 287
and folk religion 59
and sacred groves 219, 222
and sacred mountains 33, 37, 39, 40
South Pacific SIDS 170, 177
and younger generations 254, 260, 261, 287
mona monkeys 231, 233, 234–5, 238–9, *239*, 240
Mongolia 288, *288*
monitor lizards 133, 134
monks, environmental 57–8, 108, 285
Montserrat monastery (Spain) 201, *203*
Morocco 22, 23
mountains 33, 33–8, *36*, 39, 40
deities *4*, 35, 75, 87, 92–3, *92*, 93
see also sacred mountains
MoUs (Memoranda of Understanding) 214
multidimensional scaling *see* MDS
multidisciplinary approaches 6, 68, 131
multinational companies 130, *135*, 139, 144
myths 17, 34, 224–5, 278

Nanny (Nya Nya) 150, 152
Nanny Town (Jamaica) 150, 153
national identity 39–40
national parks *64*, 67, 153, 281
Jamaica 76, 146, 148–9, *149*, 153
Natural England 79, 80, 85
natural resources 5, 11, 93, 182, 255, 283, 286
beliefs and 132–3, 246–7
demand for 26, 37–8, 63
management *135*, 193

nature 42, 59, 185–6, 199, 204, 205
Christianity and 4, 47, 79–80, 183
and culture 34, 49, 63, 65, 66–7, 281, 284, 286
religions and 2–3, 4, 7, 42, 47, 62–3, 79–80, 108, 182–3, 200, 205
sacred 18, 47, 62–3, 75, 189, 199, 204, 217, 220, 289
St Cuthbert and 77, 79
spiritual value 34, 65, 77, 154, 205
and spirituality 7, 42, 49, 63, 79–80, 80–1, 285–6
women and 273
The Nature Conservancy 6, 154
nature reserves 103, 104
Lindisfarne 77, 78, *79*, 80, 81, 83–4, 85
'Nature Saints' 75, 77, 79
Navajo people 38
Nepal 33, 36–7, 39, 43, 75, 87, 90–1
see also Khumbu Sherpa; SNPBZ
The Netherlands *44*, *54*, 141, 142, 143
networks of SNS 135, 221, 232, 280
new age spirituality 65, 186
NGOs (non-governmental organizations) 6, 126, 200, 241, 242, 276, 277, 289
Nhulun (Australia) 64
Niger Delta 130, 130–1, *131*, *133–5*, *135*
sacred lakes 76, 129–36, *131*, *133–4*
Nigeria 23, 136
see also Niger Delta
Nile, River 182–3
non-timber forest products *see* NTFPs
North Western Ghats (India) 219, 220–1, *221*
northern Ethiopian church forests 21, 22, 25
NTFPs (non-timber forest products) 19, 89, 99, 123, 238
BRTWS 265, 268, 269
sacred groves (India) 223, 226
numina (deities) 18, 107
numinous sacred sites 53–60, *54*, 60, 107, 166
Nya Nya (Nanny) 150, 152

offerings 123, 139, 140, 143, 234
oil exploitation 130, *135*, 136
oral history 144, 266, 269–70
oral tradition 173, 177, 247, 257, 267–8
South Pacific 172, 174, 175, 177
Windward Maroons 150, 152
Oraon tribe 274–5
ordination of trees 45, 58
Orthodox Church 183, *184*
overharvesting 139, 140, 143
ownership 223, 267, 270

Pacific Action Plan 175–6, *176*
Pacific Islands Forum Secretariat (PIFS) 175
'pagan' religions 54
Palawan (Philippines) 255, *257*
participatory approaches 189, 190, 193, *194*, *195*, 196, 205, 266
see also mapping
participatory management 103, 233
participatory research 120, *121*, 150

permafrost burials 244, 246, 252
Peru 35–6, *36*, 190, *191*, 193
perverse economic theory 115
petroglyphs 244, 246, 252, 257, *281*
phi (spirits of place) 54, 55–6, *56*, 58
PIFS (Pacific Islands Forum Secretariat) 175
pilgrimage tourism 248, 252
pilgrimages 5, *54*, 210, 213–14, 278
    Ausangate 35–6, *36*
    Badrinath (India) 37, 38
    Christian 53, 55, 59, 75, *84*, 201
    Karakol Valley 252
planning processes 9, 115, 206, 289
plantations 282, 290
poaching 161, 164
policies 9, 68, 188, 280, 287, 288, 289, 290
    reform 105, 136
policy support 116–17
population growth 11, 37, 39, 40, 103, 105, 127, 238, 286
    China 103
    Ghana 164–5
    Jamaica 146
    South Pacific 170
possession 272, 274–5, 275
post-modern approaches to earth care 115
poverty 11, 49, 104, 189–90, 286, 289
pressures on SNS 7, 19, 25, 75, 78, 119, 232
priests 109, *110*, 140, 223, 234, 275
    see also shamans
private sector 289
profit sharing 233, 239–40, *239*, 242
Pronatura Mexico 160, 217
property values 77, 81, 81–2, 83
protected areas 18, 47, 68, 104, 126, 130, 212, 226
    co-management 264, 269–70
    and culture and spirituality 200
    governance 199–200
    India 268
    indigenous people removed from 65, 90
    Lindisfarne 80
    and livelihood needs 164
    management 40, 67, 90, 146, 168, 171, 204, 206, 248
    in mountains 34
    SNS 20, 26, 146, 154, 201, 204–5, 210, 281
Protected Areas Network 66
protection, of SNS 5, 22, 25–6, 49, 105, 175–6, 177–8, 219, 286
Protestant Churches 58, 58–9, 200
Pumpkin Hill (Jamaica) 150, *151*

Quechua people 35, 48

Ramsar Convention 77, 80, 136, 160, 180–1, 183–6, 200, 288
rare species 17, 104, 122, 219, 220
rationalism 4, 11, 59, 285
re-dedication 276, 277
re-sanctification 64, 277
Recognition of Forest Rights Act *see* RFRA

recognition of SNS 58, 188, 195, 210, 280, 282–3
    international 58, 167, 168, 177–8, 252, 287
    legal 126, 177, 256–7, 287–8
recommendations 7, 27, 47, 104, 127, 160, 176–7, 289–90
reductionism 11, 17, 18, 198, 198–9, 199
Reformation 17, 58–9, 81
refuge, places of 150, 152, 154
regeneration 212, 272, 275–6
regulations 103, 105, 223
rehabilitation 25, 49, 192, 220
reincarnation 91
'relationship' 189
religion 11, 17, 18, 43, 47, 58–60, 199
    and conservation 20, 48–9, 54, 63, 164, 200–1
    SNS and 2–4, *3–4*
    see also spirituality
religions 199, 200, 206, 222–3, 280, 281
    and nature 2, 4, 7, 42, 47, 62–3, 79–80, 108, 182–3, 200, 205
    respect between 42, 47, 280, 284–5, 289
    see also folk religions; indigenous religions; mainstream
        religions
resources *see* natural resources
respect 99, 186, 201–2, 251, 260, 289, 290
    interfaith 42, 47, 280, 284–5, 289
    for traditional culture 139, 144, 190
responsibilities 46, 161, 225, 248, 250, 269
restitution 111
restoration 49, 161, 166, 232, 270, 286
    genetic material for 46, 165
    sacred groves and forests 44, 104, 220, 226, 232
RFRA (Recognition of Forest Rights Act 2006, India) 263, 266, 269, 270
rights 46, 280
    access and management 232, 263
    to ancestral waters 254, 256–7, 261
    of custodians 205
    of indigenous peoples 60, 64, 67, 129–30, 185, 255, 269–70, 290
    land rights 60, 64, 67, 136
    of local communities 185, 269, 283
    of wildlife 248
    see also Calamian Tagbanwa; RFRA; Soligas
Rila, monastery (Bulgaria) *202*, *203*
rituals 34, 38, 40, *104*, 147, 173, 190–2, *195*
    Eastern Kham 110–11
    Karakol Valley 245, 247, 249
    Khumbu Sherpa 91, *92*, 93
    Niger Delta 130, 132
    Sarna movement 272, 275, 276, 278
    Winti 140, 141, *141*
rivers 58, 183, 210
    sacred 36, 150, 152, 182–3, 210
'robing' of sacred forests 11
rock art 244, 246, 252, 257, *281*
rocks 55, 93, 121, 166
rubber plantations 103
rules 2, 92, 132, 232, 255, 260, 261
    sacred forests 42, 123–4, 166, 223, 240, 241
Russia, land rights 250–1

sacred, the 107, 117, 146, 205, 220, 250
    in nature 18, 47, 62–3, 75, 189, 199, 204, 217, 220,
        289
sacred areas 104–5, 119, 121–2, *122*
    marine 257, 260, 260–1, 261
sacred days 133
sacred forests 17–18, 22, 23–5, 42, 235, 277
    Africa *20*, 21, 22, 119–20, 233
    Bandjoun 119–20
    China 21, 98
    community protection 233–4
    and conservation 103, 105
    Ethiopia 21, 22
    Khumbu 93
    losses of 75, 103, 105
    remnants of ecosystems *20*, 21–2
    restoration 33, 44, *48*, 104, 190–2
    'robing' 111
    Suriname 139, 143, 143–4
    Yunnan (China) 21, 23, 75, 100–5, *100–1*, *104*
    Zimbabwe 25
    see also Holy Hills; Kaya forests; sacred groves; Tafi Atome
        Monkey Sanctuary
sacred groves 42, 45–6, *45*, 49, 135, 219, 275
    biocultural importance 227
    biodiversity 23–5, 45–6, 49, 165–6, 167, 220–2, *222*,
        275
    biodiversity conservation 17, 160, 276
    Buddhism 44
    Cameroon 282
    conservation 46–7, 160, 223
    Ghana 164–7, 241
    Haiti 139
    India 4, 21–2, 22, 23, 25, 26, 44, 46, *159*, 160, 219,
        275
    losses 26, 46, 160, 222, 282
    protection 46, 223
    reviving 225, 232, 272, 275–6
    West Africa 241
    see also BRTWS; North Western Ghats; NTFPs; sacred
        forests; Sarna movement; Tafi Atome Monkey
        Sanctuary
sacred lakes 76, 129–36, *131*, *134*, 257, *258*
sacred land 246–7, 250–1, 252–3
Sacred Land Film Project 289
sacred landscapes 55, 91–2, 110, 150, 151, 210
sacred marine areas 254, 257, 260, 260–1, 261
sacred monkeys 231, 233, 234–5, 238–9, *239*, 240, 287
sacred mountains 17, *17*, 33–4, 93, 167, 213, 214, *283*
    deities *4*, 35, 75, 87, 92–3, *92*, 96
    Eastern Kham 109
    impact of global changes 35–40, *36*
    Japan 37, 53
    Karakol Valley 244, 245, 246, 247, *248*, 250
    pre-Columbian 285
    World Heritage sites 37, 38, 39, 162, *163*
    Yunnan 98
    see also mountains; Sagarmatha; yul-lha
Sacred Mountains Programme 201

sacred natural sites (SNS) 1–2, 4, 62, 107–8, 188–9, 196, 217,
    284, 290
    ancient origins 281
    as biocultural diversity indicators 68
    classification 210, 213–15
    and conservation 2, 5, 6, 11, 19, 20, 25–6, 26–7, 46–7, 49,
        110, 277–8, 290
    conservation of 168, 171, 280, 289
    dimensions of 188
    documenting 210, 232, 262–4, 267–8
    as genetic reservoirs 1, 104, 119, 212
    as healing places 63, 150–2, 154, 231–2, 281
    high biodiversity 5, 7, 11, 17–18, 19, 20, 22–3, 67, 287
    and intangible cultural heritage 172–3
    intuitively recognized 123
    as knowledge repositories 270
    locations 1, 4, 9, *10*, 21, 198, 284
    losses 7, 19, 63, 120, 280, 282
    network for conservation 68, 280, 281–2
    numbers of 1, 4, 219, 233
    and protected areas 26, 146, 154
    remnants of ecosystems 19, *20*, 21, 21–2, 22, 25, 46, 49,
        221, 286
    shared 204, 284
    threats to *see* threats to SNS
    value of 168, 206
    and well-being 160, 168, *191*, 192, 280, 281, 283, 285–6,
        289
sacred plants 139, 140, 142–3, 213, 214, 276
    see also medicinal plants
sacred rivers 36, 150, 152, 182–3
sacred rocks 55, 93, 121, 166
sacred species 37, 76, 91–2, 129, 189, 210, 213
    see also crocodiles; mona monkeys; sacred plants
sacred springs 54, 65, 251
sacred trees 17–18, 21, 22, 42–7, *44*, 102, 147, 166, 172
    deities residing in 44, 166
    mainstream religions and 42, 47, 48–9
    Winti beliefs 141, *142*, 144
    see also trees
sacred water sources 54, *54*, 65, 93, 251
    see also sacred rivers
sacred waters 21, 22–3, 213, 214, 232
sacred wells 54, *54*
sacredness 64, 107, 117, 205, 250
    of life 66–7
    of nature 18, 47, 62–3, 75, 189, 199, 204, 217, 220, 289
    of place 53–4
sacrifices 123, 133, *133*, 234, 235, 275, 278
SAEDP (Southern African Endogenous Development
    Programme) 192
Sagarmatha (Mount Everest, Nepal) *4*, 37, 38, 75, 90, 93
Sagarmatha National Park and Buffer Zone *see* SNPBZ
St Aidan 78, 81
St Catherine's Monastery (Mount Sinai) 38, *39*
St Cuthbert 77, 78, 78–80
saints 53, 54, *54*, 55, 75
    see also Lindisfarne; St Aidan; St Cuthbert
Samoa 172, 177

San Francisco Peaks (United States) 33, 34, 38, 201, *203*
Sanskritization 108, 268, 277, 285
Sarna Mata 272, 274–5, 275, 276, 278
Sarna movement 232, 272, *273*, 274–8
science 11, 58, 63, 115–16, 198–9, 280, 284
    and religion 17, 18
secrecy 11, 26, 65, 168, 176, 196, 289
    Maroon 149, 152, 153
secularization 37, 201
sedentarization 264, 265, 268
Seri territory (Mexico) 213, *213*
Sertsuo (Tibet) 65
shamanism 108, 109, 245
shamans *17*, 35, 109, *110*, 111, 249, 257
Sherpa people *4*, 36–7, 75, 111
    see also Khumbu Sherpa
shifting cultivation 268, 269
Shinto 2, 10, 22, 47, 53
shrines *3*, 55, *56*, 121, 124, 132, *133*
    fetish shrines 234, 240
SIDS (Small Island Developing States) 159–60
    Pacific 170–1, 172, 173, 175–6, 178
Sierra Nevada de Santa Marta (Colombia) 40, *283*
Sinai, Mount (Egypt) 33, 34, 38, *39*, 204
Small Island Developing States *see* SIDS
SNPBZ (Sagarmatha National Park and Buffer Zone) 87–8,
    88–9, 89–90, 286–7
    see also Khumbu Sherpa
SNS *see* sacred natural sites
social ties 129, 135, *135*
socio–economic values 7–8, *8*
Soligas *231*, 232, 263–4, 264, 265–70, *266*
South Korea, national parks 204–5
South Pacific 159–60, 170–5, *171*, *174*
    SNS 171, *171*, 172, 172–3, 173–4, 174, *174*, 175–7
Southeast Asia 55–6, 57–8
Southern African Endogenous Development Programme
    (SAEDP) 192
Spain 59, 204
Specialist Group on the Cultural and Spiritual Values of
    Protected Areas *see* CSVPA
spirit mediums 190–2
spirits 18, 56–7, 91, 110, 132, 255
    ancestors 102, 142
    animist 55–6, *56*
    forest spirits 139, 140, 143, 144
    sea spirits 257, 260
    tree spirits 43, 139
    see also numinous sacred sites
spiritual value 34, 56–7, 65, 77, 153, 154, 205
spiritual values 8, 12, 68–9, 168, 183–4, 206, 254, 283
    and conservation 47, 66–7, 78, 199, 201
    gender and 94–5, *95*, 96
    Khumbu Sherpa 90, 91–6, *92*, *95*
    South Pacific 170
    tourism and 93–6, *95*
spiritual well-being 43, 63, 161, 188, 287
spirituality 2, 43, 48–9, 68–9, 186
    and nature 7, 42–3, 47, 49, 63, 79–80, 80–1, 285–6

springs 54, 65, 251
stakeholders 38–9, 40, 116, 225, 226–7
    identification 120–1, 211
    involvement 40, 68, 126, 168, 176–7, 202–4, 206
state 121, 126, 280
stewardship 42, 48–9, *48*, 136, 256, 268
Stonehenge (UK) 65
Suriname 76, 139, 140, *142*, 143–4, 144–5
    see also Winti
sustainability 68–9, 104, 168, 171, 201, 273
sustainable development 48, 49, 168
sustainable management 126, 241, 260

taboos 124, 161, 255
    felling trees 43, 87, 92, 102
    fishing 260
    hunting 102, 110, 124, 233, 238, 240
    killing animals 87, 92, 95, *95*, 234
    overharvesting 139, 143
    planting trees 166
    polluting water sources 87, 92
    sacred groves 46, 166, 275
    on women 275
Tafi Atome (Ghana) 237–8, 238–9, 239–40, 240
Tafi Atome Monkey Sanctuary (Ghana) 231, 233–42, *235–7*,
    239
Taínos 76, 146, 147, 149, 150, *151*, 153, 154
talking trees 45
Tanzania 21, 22, 23, 25
Taoism 2, 47, 108
Tatera, Mount (Japan) 22
technologically developed countries 198, *198–9*
temples 44, *221*, 222, 223
Tengboche Monastery (Nepal) 37, *75*, 90
territories 55, 144, 265, *267*
Thailand 45, 54, 56, 59, 111
    'ecology monks' 57–8, 108, 285
    numinous sacred sites 55–6, *56*
threats to SNS 7, 19, 26, 120, 127, 170, 219, 283
    archaeological excavation 244
    cultural landscapes 162, 168
    Karakol Valley 244, 250–2
    land and tenure laws 244
    Maroon SNS 152–3
    sacred forests 46, 119, 120, 125, *125*, 234, 235, 238,
        240–1
    sacred groves 42, 220, 222–3, 226–7
    tourism 244, 251
    see also climate change; global changes
Tikal (Guatemala) 64–5, *64*, 190, 192
Togo 23, 25
Toraja people 56
totems 122, 247
tourism 5, 19, 172, 180, 257, 286–7, 289
    and conservation 65
    development model 240
    Karakol Valley 245, 251–2
    Khumbu (Nepal) 75, 87, 90, 90–1, 93–6, *95*
    Lindisfarne 75, 77, 81, 83–4, 85

and livelihoods 91
mass tourism 40, 201, 234
Niger Delta *135*
pilgrimage type 248
sacred forests 46
sacred mountains 33, 37–8
and spiritual values 65, 93–6, *95*
threat of 37, 232, 244
Uluru 39
see also ecotourism
tourists 162, 168, 239, *239*, 241
traditional beliefs 33, 37, 101–2, 132–3, 234, 277
traditional conservation 21, 217, 241
traditional culture 11, 103, 105, 144, 152, 252
traditional institutions 47, 103
traditional knowledge 105, 115–16, 144, 177, 277, 284, 287
loss of 104, 152–3, 261
transmission 152, 153, 173, 176, 232, 257, 261
understanding of 232, 264
Winti belief 139
traditional management 46, 68, 119, 120, 282, 288
traditional medicine 76, 140, 192
see also healing
traditional practices 33, 37, 38, 101–2, 105, 287
trees 17–18, 22, 42–4, 111, 139, 166
adornment 44–5, *44*, 251
Chipko movement 111, 274
felling 22, 43, 46, 55–6, 87, 92, 102, 139, 235, 236, 240, 275, 276
ordination 45, 58
planting *48*, 111, 165, 237, 240, 275–6
religions and 17–18, 42, 47
taboos on felling 43, 87, 92, 102
see also sacred trees

Uch Enmek Indigenous Nature Park (Altai Republic, Russia) 231–2, 244–5, *245*, 247–53, *248*
Uch Enmek, Mount 244, 245, 247, *248*
Uganda *191*
UK (United Kingdom) 77, 81, 81–2
Uluru (Australia) 39
UNDRIP (United Nations Declaration on the Rights of Indigenous Peoples) 3, 5–6, 136, 176, 178, 270, 287
UNESCO (United Nations Educational, Scientific and Cultural Organization) 159, 161–2, 167, 172, 175, 177, 185, 200, 217
Intangible Cultural Heritage of Humanity 76, 148
see also CSICH; MAB Programme; WHC; World Heritage sites
UNESCO-IUCN Guidelines 5, 9, 154, 161, 167–8, 172–3, 287
urban migration 139, 144, 219
urbanization 11, 105, 177, 182, 192, 219
India 220
Jamaica 146
Palawan 254, 261, 287

values, changing 234, 282
Vanatori Neamt Nature Park (Moldavia) 201, *203*

Vanuatu *171*, 173, *174*, 175, 176, 176–7, 177, 178
Virgin Mary of El Rocío (Spain) 184, 201

water 5, 17, 39, 148, 182, 270
water sources 87, 92, 122
see also rivers; springs; wells
water supplies 25, 46, 98, 148, 153–4
from mountains 33, 35, 36, 39, 101
waterfalls 21, 147, *148*, 151–2
WCPA (World Commission on Protected Areas) 167, 217
Weber, Max 59
well-being 5, 6, 7–8, *8*, 188, 196, *283*
biodiversity and 66, 188, *191*, 192
community well-being 188, 189
cultural 43
indicators 189, 193, *195*, 196
and the land 247
SNS and 160, 168, *191*, 192, 280, 281, 283, 285–6, 289
spiritual 43, 63, 161, 188, 287
wells 54, *54*
West African Guinea Forest 130
Western Ghats (India) 219, 220
sacred groves 21–2, 23, *159*, 160
wetlands 160, 180, 181–4, 185–6
Lindisfarne 77, 78, *79*, 80
Niger Delta 129–30
see also Ramsar convention; sacred lakes
WHC (World Heritage Convention, 1972) 161–2, 176, 185
and SNS 46, 159, 167, 173, 177–8, 217
see also World Heritage sites
wild relatives of crop plants 25, 46
Windward Maroons (Jamaica) 67, 76, 146, 147–8, 148–9, *148*, 149–54
Winemem Wintu 65
Winti 139, 140, 141–3, *141–2*, 144
Wirikuta (Mexico) 213–14
women 126, *159*, 165, 259, 265, 273, 275
empowerment 272, 273, 275, 277
role of 119, 121, *123*, 124–5, 274
Sarna movement 232, 272, *273*, 274–8
see also Chipko movement; ecofeminism
World Commission on Protected Areas *see* WCPA
World Heritage Convention *see* WHC
World Heritage Sites 18, 37, 66, *66*, 162, *163*, 255, 288
nominations 37, 148–9, 153, 176
sacred mountains 37, 38, 39, 162, *163*
Sagarmatha 90
South Pacific 170, *171*, 173–4, *174*, 175, 178
see also Tikal; WHC
worldviews 117, 188, 189, 195, 196
Altai 246, 250, 252
Maya 192–3
WWF (Worldwide Fund for Nature) 5, 6, 162, 289

Xishuangbanna (Yunnan, China) 75, 100–4, *100*, *101*, *104*, 105

Yelles 265, 266, *267*, 268, *268*
yew (*Taxus baccata*) 43, *45*, 64

Yi people 23, 102
Yigdrasil (sacred Ash) 43
Yolngu people 64
younger generations 125, 144, 226, 232, 268
    Calamian Tagbanwa 259, 260, 261
    Khumbu Sherpa 94, 95, 96
yul landscapes 110

yul-lha (deities) 87, 92–3, *92*, 94, *95*, 110, *111*
yul-lha (sacred mountains) 91–2
Yunnan (China) 22, 98–9, *99*, 104, 282
    sacred forests 21, 23, 75, 100–5, *100–1*, *104*

Zimbabwe 25, 190–2, *191*, 265
Zoroastrianism 2, 202